The Right to Know
A Guide to Public Access and Media Law

Authors:
James M. Chadwick, Sheppard Mullin Richter and Hampton
Roger R. Myers, Holme, Roberts & Owen

Editors:
Thomas W. Newton
Peter Scheer
James W. Ewert
Joe Wirt
Thomas R. Burke

Copyright ©2007
ISBN 978-0-9799430-0-3
California Newspaper Publishers Association and
California First Amendment Coalition

To order additional copies, contact
CNPA
708 10th Street
Sacramento, CA 95814
(916) 288-6000
www.cnpa.com
www.cfac.org

The Right to Know
A Guide to Public Access and Media Law

Introduction 1

What This Book Is About. 1
Acknowledgements. 1
And Finally, A Disclaimer. 2

Chapter 1 Access To Meetings 3

In This Chapter 3
Part I: Overview 3
    A. Introduction. 3
    B. Overview Of The Law. 4
Part II: Local Government – The Ralph M. Brown Act 5
    A. Introduction. 5
    B. What Are My Rights Under The Brown Act? 6
    C. How Do I Know If A Meeting Is Governed By The Brown Act? 9
    D. What Notice Is Required, And How Is Notice Given? 19
    E. When Can A Closed Session Be Held? 22
    F. What Information Has To Be Disclosed About Closed Sessions? 33
    G. How Is The Brown Act Enforced? 35
Part III: State Government – The Bagley-Keene Act 39
    A. Introduction To The Bagley-Keene Act. 39
    B. What Are My Rights Under The Bagley-Keene Act? 40
    C. What Meetings Are Subject To The Bagley-Keene Act? 42
    D. When Can A Closed Session Be Held? 43
    E. How Is The Bagley-Keene Act Enforced? 44
Part IV: Other State Open Meeting Laws 45
    A. The State Legislature. 45
    B. The Board Of Regents Of The University Of California. 46
    C. Student Auxiliary Organizations. 47
Part V: Federal Government Meetings 49
    A. The "Government In The Sunshine Act." 49
    B. Federal Advisory Committee Act. 50
Part VI: Private Organizations And Associations 51

Chapter 2 Access To Public Records 53

In This Chapter 53
Part I: Overview Of The Law 53
Part II: The California Public Records Act 54
    A. How Does The California Public Records Act Work? 54
    B. What Agencies Are Governed By The Act? 55
    C. What Are Public Records? 56
    D. How Do I Get Access To Records? 57

    E. What Records Are Exempt From Disclosure? 60

    F. What Can I Do If The Agency Doesn't Provide Public Records I Have Requested? 78

    G. Summary Of Rights 80

Part III: Proposition 59 80

Part IV: Legislative Open Records Act 81

    A. What Records Of The Legislature Are Covered? 81

    B. How Do I Get Access To Legislative Records? 81

    C. What Legislative Records Are Exempt From Disclosure? 82

    D. What Can I Do If The Legislature Does Not Provide Records That Are Subject To Disclosure? 83

    E. Does The Legislature Make Information Available On The Internet? 83

Part V: The Federal Freedom Of Information Act 84

    A. Introduction 84

    B. How Does The Freedom Of Information Act Work? 84

    D. What Exemptions Does The Government Most Often Assert? 90

    Chapter 3 Proposition 59: A Constitutional Right Of Access 93

In This Chapter 93

Part I: Introduction 93

Part II: Main Provisions Of The Sunshine Amendment 93

    A. A Constitutional Right Of Access 93

    B. Rules For The Interpretation And Application Of Statutes, Rules And "Other Authority" Regulating Public Access. 94

    C. Other Effects Of The Sunshine Amendment 94

Part III: Impact Of The Sunshine Amendment 95

Part IV: Conclusion 97

    Chapter 4 Government Treatment Of The Media: Discrimination And Accreditation 99

In This Chapter 99

Part I: Introduction 99

Part II: Discrimination Among News Outlets Or Reporters 100

    A. Right Of Equal Access. 100

    B. Right Of Equal Convenience 101

    C. Right Of Public Employees To Speak 102

Part II: Media Accreditation 104

    B. Press Passes Issued By Private Entities 106

    Chapter 5 Public Access To Criminal Court Proceedings 109

In This Chapter 109

Part I: Introduction 109

    A. Background On Constitutional Rights Of Access 110

    B. Importance Of Public Participation. 110

Part II: Defining The Constitutional Standard 111

    A. Legal Test For Closure Of Court Proceedings. 111

    B. Procedures Courts Must Follow Before Closing Proceedings. 112

Part III: Closure Rationales – The First And The Sixth Amendments 113

Part IV: Public Access To Bench Proceedings 114

Part V: Juvenile Court Proceedings – Limited Right Of Access.. 114
   A. Public's Right Of Access To Juvenile Delinquency Proceedings (Serious Crimes)......... 115
   B. Access At Request Of The Minor, Parent Or Guardian. 116
   C. Discretionary Public Access. 116
   D. Limitations On The Right Of Access To Juvenile Cases. 116
   E. Alternative Arguments For Media Access. 117
   F. Post-Hearing Information.. 117
   G. Obtaining Information About Juveniles Convicted Of Serious Crimes. 118
   H. Right To Publicize A Juvenile's Name. 118
   I. Public Access To Juvenile Dependency Proceedings. 118
Part VI: Access To Military Proceedings 119
Part VII: How To Protect Your Right To Access Court Proceedings 120
   A. Anticipate Closure Motions. 120
   B. Request A Hearing. 120
   C. Seek Support From The Non-Moving Party. 121

Chapter 6 Gag Orders And Prior Restraints.. 123

In This Chapter 123
Part I: Gag Orders – Limiting Discussion And Coverage Of Court Cases 123
   A. Gag Orders In Criminal Cases. 123
   B. Constitutional Requirements.. 124
   C. Alternatives To Gag Orders. 126
   D. Responding To A Proposed Gag Order. 127
   E. Some Information Generally Releasable. 127
   F. To Whom The Orders Apply. 128
   G. Rules Affecting Attorneys. 128
   H. Gag Orders In Civil Cases. 129
Part II: Prior Restraints 129
   A. Introduction. 129
   B. General Rule Of Law. 129
   C. The Criminal Defendant's Right To A Fair Trial. 130
   D. The Right To Privacy And Reputation. 133
   E. Trade Secrets. 133
   F. National Security. 134
   G. Statutes Limiting The Right To Disclose Information. 134
   H. Responding To A Restraining Order. 134

Chapter 7 Public Access To Civil Court Proceedings 137

In This Chapter 137
Part I: Introduction 137
Part II: Right Of Access 138
   A. The First Amendment Standard.. 138
   B. The California Standard. 138
Part III: Access To Particular Kinds Of Proceedings 139
   A. Domestic Or Family Proceedings. 139
   B. Mental Health Hearings. 139
   C. Trade Secrets.. 140

    D. Privacy. 140
    E. Settlement Proceedings. 141
    F. Depositions. 141
    G. Bench And Chamber Conferences 142
    H. Opposing Closure Of Civil Court Proceedings 142
Part IV: Access To Private Proceedings 143
Part V: Camera Access To Court Proceedings 143

Chapter 8 Access To Jurors And Jury Information 147

In This Chapter 147
Part I: Access To Jury Selection 147
    A. Cases Where Closure Was Held Unconstitutional. 148
    B. Cases Where Closure Was Held Constitutional. 149
Part II: Access To Juror Questionnaires 150
Part III: Access To Transcripts Of Jury Selection 151
Part IV: Access To Juror Names And Anonymous Juries 151
    A. California Law. 151
    B. Federal Law. 153
    C. Interpretive Cases. 153
Part V: Access To Jurors During Trial 154
Part VI: Photographing And Sketching Jurors During Trial 155
Part VII: Access To Jurors After Trial 155
    A. California Law. 155
    B. Interpretive Cases. 156
Part VIII: Access To Grand Juries 157
    A. Access To Grand Jurors. 158
    B. Access To Grand Jury Witnesses. 158
    C. California's Limited Right To Public Session Of The Grand Jury 159

Chapter 9 The California Shield Law And The Reporter's Privilege 161

In This Chapter 161
Part I: Introduction – Legal Protection For Journalists And Others Who Gather And Publish
Information 161
Part II: The California Shield Law. 162
    A. Persons Protected By The Shield Law. 163
    B. The Extent Of The Shield Law's Protections. 166
    C. Procedural Aspects Of Subpoenas. 168
Part III: Protection Under Federal Law – The Reporter's Privilege 170
    A. The Limited First Amendment Privilege. 170
    B. Who Can Invoke The Reporter's Privilege? 176
    C. Enforcing Gag Orders In Federal Court. 176
    D. Federal Regulations On Subpoenas To Journalists. 177
    E. Federal Legislation To Create A Reporter's Shield Law. 177
Part IV: Protection From Search Warrants 177
    A. Limited Constitutional Protection. 177
    B. Protections From Search Warrants Under California Law. 178
    C. Protections Under Federal Statute. 179

Chapter 10 Access To Judicial Records 181

In This Chapter 181
Part I: General Rules Of Access 181
    A. Basic Of Right Of Access. 181
    B. Procedure For Access To Court Records. 182
Part II: Records Of Criminal Proceedings 183
    A. Records Subject To First Amendment Right Of Access. 183
    B. Access To Evidence In Criminal Cases. 184
    C. Access To Grand Jury Transcripts And Materials. 185
    D. Access To Juror Records. 186
Part III: Civil Case Records 187
    A. Discovery Material In Civil Cases. 188
    B. Settlement Records. 190
Part IV: Statutory Confidentiality 192
    A. Juvenile Court Documents. 192
    B. Search And Arrest Warrant Documents. 193
    C. Probation Officers' Reports. 194
    B. Pre-Sentencing Diagnostic Reports. 194
    C. Adoption Records. 195
    D. Victim Statements. 195
    E. Indigent Defense Funding. 195
    F. Wiretap Records. 195
    G. Criminal History Information. 195
    H. Copies Of Court And Deposition Transcripts. 196
    I. Electronic Court Records. 196
Part V: Records Of Court Administration 197

Chapter 11   Access To Public And Private Areas And To Government Officials 199

In This Chapter 199
Part I: Introduction 199
Part II: Access To Disaster Sites, Crime Scenes And Military Areas 200
    A. Disaster Scenes 200
    B. Crime And Tactical Operations Scenes. 201
    C. Military Areas. 201
Part III: Public School Grounds 202
    A. There Is No General Right Of Access To Public Schools Under The First Amendment. . 202
    B. California Law Governing Access To Public Schools. 203
Part IV: State Prisons, Jails And Parole Board Hearings 205
    A. General Rules Of Access. 205
    B. Access To Executions. 206
Part V: Private Property 206
    A. Types Of Trespass. 206
    B. Business Establishments. 207
    C. Private Residences. 208
    D. Landlords And Rented Premises. 209
Part VI: Access To Government Officials 209

Chapter 12 Legal Perils In Newsgathering...210

In This Chapter 210
Part I: Introduction...210
Part II: Confidential Information And Documents 210
Part III: Legal Limits On Newsgathering 212
    A. Impersonation...212
    B. Trespass...214
    C. Invasion Of Privacy By Intrusion..218
Part IV: Special Considerations For Electronic Newsgathering...............................220
    A. Obtaining, Making And Using Audio And Video Recordings....................220
    B. Using Police And Emergency Scanners..226
    C. Accessing Computers And Electronic Data..227

Chapter 13 The Student Press And Student Speech...229

In This Chapter 229
Part I: Constitutional Background 229
    A. Non-Curricular Student Speech 229
    B. School-Sponsored Or Curricular Speech 232
    C. Vulgar, Lewd And Obscene Speech 234
Part II: California Laws Regarding Student Press And Speech..................................234
    A. Student Press And Speech On Public High School Campuses.....................235
    B. Student Press And Speech At Public Colleges And Universities. 237
Part III: Underground Student Newspapers And Other Materials.............................238
Part IV: Regulation Of Student Speech By Private Schools......................................239
Part V: Theft Of Student Newspapers 239

Appendix A The Brown Act 241

Appendix B The California Public Records Act..267

Appendix C Sample California Public Records Act Request Letter..........................295

Appendix D Sample Demand For Cure Or Correction; Alleged Violation Of Brown Act 297

Appendix E Sample Freedom Of Information Request Letter...................................299

Appendix F Sample Freedom Of Information Act Appeal Letter..............................301

Table Of Cases 303

INTRODUCTION

WHAT THIS BOOK IS ABOUT.

This book is basically about: (1) what information you can get; (2) how to get the information you want; and (3) what can happen once you have information.

First and foremost, this book is about finding out what is happening in your school, your community and your state. It is a guide for everyone who wants or needs information about what the government is up to, what is going on in the courts and what is happening in places such as schools and shopping malls. It will tell you what information you are and are not entitled to get.

Second, this book provides guidance for everyone engaged in gathering and publishing information – reporters, editors, bloggers, student journalists, citizens involved in publishing newsletters or fliers, lawyers, and others. It covers your rights and risks involved in gathering information for publication.

THIRD, THIS BOOK ADDRESSES CONCERNS THAT ARISE ONCE YOU HAVE INFORMATION. IT PROVIDES INFORMATION ON PROTECTING CONFIDENTIAL SOURCES AND UNPUBLISHED INFORMATION, AND IT INCLUDES A CHAPTER ON STUDENT PRESS AND FREE SPEECH RIGHTS AND LIMITATIONS.

This book will give you answers, if you know where to look. For example, a question about access to a record may cut across two, three or more statutory schemes or legal concepts. For example, you may find useful – even essential – information about your question on access to public records in Chapter 2, Access to Public Records, Chapter 3, Proposition 59: A Constitutional Right of Access and Chapter 1, Access to Meetings. We strongly recommend you initially review the entire detailed Table of Contents to understand the broad scope of the book and the interplay of various laws, rights and risks associated with obtaining and using information.

Electronic updates to this book will be available on the Internet at www.cfac.org/handbook.

ACKNOWLEDGEMENTS.

The book you are holding is the work of many hands.

First, it is the creation of the California Newspaper Publishers Association (CNPA) and the California First Amendment Coalition (CFAC), who decided to combine their resources and their dedication to informed public participation in government and in the issues of the day. In particular, this book reflects the sustained efforts of Peter Scheer, executive director of CFAC; Tom Newton, general counsel of CNPA; Jim Ewert, legal counsel and legislative advocate for CNPA; Joe Wirt, affiliate relations director for CNPA; and Thomas Burke, a partner with the San Francisco office of Davis Wright Tremaine.

Substantial contributions to the current book were made by the authors of the prior editions of two separate publications: CNPA's "Reporter's Handbook on Media Law" and CFAC's "California Journalist's Legal Notebook." Those authors deserve credit and thanks for laying the foundation on which this book is built.

The substance of this book is primarily the work of two law firms: Sheppard Mullin Richter & Hampton LLP, and Holme Roberts & Owen LLP ("HRO"). James Chadwick, a member of the board of directors of CFAC, was the lead author and editor at Sheppard Mullin. Roger Myers, who serves as general outside counsel for CFAC, was the lead author and editor at HRO. However, the book is the result of an extraordinary effort by many people.

At Sheppard Mullin, Guylyn Cummins made exceptional contributions, and chapters of the book were also written by Gary Bostwick and Jean-Paul Jassy (now of Bostwick & Jassy) and Amy Harrell Johnson (now with NBC/Universal). These attorneys not only made this book possible, but they have pursued precedent-setting litigation on behalf of CFAC.

At HRO, Myers would like to acknowledge and thank his partner Rachel Matteo-Boehm and his colleagues Katherine Keating, Isela Castaneda and Tom Kerr. Not only did they author several chapters of this book, these attorneys also work daily to answer questions on CFAC's legal hotline and litigate on CFAC's behalf to strengthen and expand the public's right of access to government information, records and meetings.

At CFAC and CNPA, we kindly thank the following for their research, technical and production assistance: Jack Bates, Nick Rahaim, Christine Caro, Kristen Lowrey and Erica Jolley-Meers.

AND FINALLY, A DISCLAIMER.

This book contains information on legal subjects, but it does not represent and cannot be relied upon as legal advice. The application of the law to any particular situation requires the consideration of the particular circumstances of the case, and you cannot assume that the information in this book will provide accurate guidance with respect to any specific situation or question. The law changes constantly, both as the result of changes in constitutions, statutes, regulations or ordinances, and because of changes in the interpretation and application of the law by the courts. In particular, you may be exposed to legal liability in circumstances in which this book states or suggests that legal liability will not or is not likely to arise. In any situation in which there is a possibility of legal liability, you should consult an attorney.

CHAPTER 1

Access to Meetings

IN THIS CHAPTER

The Brown Act and the Bagley-Keene Act are the basic laws that Californians use to access meetings of local and state governmental bodies. The Brown Act covers meetings of local legislative bodies, for example, city councils, county boards of supervisors and school districts. The Bagley-Keene Act applies to legislative bodies of state agencies, such as the Air Resources Board, the Industrial Welfare Commission and the Integrated Waste Management Board. Other open meeting laws that apply specifically to the state Legislature, the U.C. Board of Regents and federal executive agencies are discussed in more detail below.

Additionally, Article I, Section 3 of the California Constitution establishes that Californians have a constitutional right of access to information concerning the conduct of the people's business, the meetings of public bodies and the writings of public officials and agencies.

The various laws that govern open meetings have five basic tenets: (1) The public has a presumptive right to attend meetings of a legislative body, which are required to be open unless a specific exemption allows the body to meet in closed session; (2) The public is entitled to advance notice of the date, time and location of open and closed meetings, as well as an agenda describing the items the legislative body intends to discuss or act upon; (3) The public has the right to obtain copies of memos, background materials and any other writings related to matters for public discussion as soon as the materials are distributed to members of the legislative body; (4) The public has the right to speak at a meeting of a legislative body; and (5) After meeting in closed session, legislative bodies are required to publicly disclose the actions taken and any documents approved in closed session.

PART I:
OVERVIEW

A. INTRODUCTION.

Much of the business of government is conducted at meetings. In addition, meetings are one of the few – and one of the most important – ways that members of the public have to communicate with public officials about matters that affect them. This is particularly true of local governments – cities, counties, school districts, joint powers authorities and the like. Most local government activities are governed by "legislative bodies" such as city councils or school boards. They regularly make decisions involving millions of dollars and affecting millions of people. They also make decisions that may be vital to individuals, businesses, community groups and others.

California law is intended to make such meetings public, subject to certain exceptions. In addition, it generally provides that action taken in violation of the requirements of public notice and participation may be void. The purpose of California law is to ensure that not only the government's final decisions are public, but also the deliberations by which those decisions are reached. The law also is intended to ensure that the public has a meaningful opportunity to participate in government meetings.

Citizens who are interested in what the government is doing, reporters who are assigned to cover local or state government, and public officials who are involved in the work of the government need to familiarize themselves with the public's right to attend meetings of public agencies.

B. OVERVIEW OF THE LAW.

There are several different laws that regulate government meetings in California. In general, these laws operate similarly. They require that meetings of certain government bodies be conducted in public, and they establish certain limited situations in which meetings may be closed to the public. They also provide guidelines for how public meetings are to be conducted. For example, they require advance notice of meetings, describe the kind of information that must be included in agendas (including certain information about closed meetings), and provide for public comment at meetings.

There are two main sets of laws in California: (1) The Ralph M. Brown Open Meetings Act (known as the "Brown Act"), which governs local governments; and (2) the Bagley-Keene Open Meetings Act (known as the "Bagley-Keene Act"), which applies to meetings of state government agencies. However, other laws also affect the public's right to attend, participate in, or know about meetings. The following is a list of the main laws that apply to government meetings in California:

Law	Application
California Constitution, Article I, Section 3(b), known as "Proposition 59"	State executive agencies and all local government agencies. The Legislature is exempt. There is no exemption for the courts, but the application of Prop. 59 to the courts is not yet settled.
Brown Act (Government Code sections 54950-54963)	Local government agencies.
Bagley-Keene Act (Government Code sections 11120-11132)	State executive agencies. The Legislature and the courts are exempt.
Grunsky-Burton Open Meeting Act (Government Code sections 9027-9031)	State Legislature.
Local Sunshine Ordinances	Local government agencies, in places where such local ordinances have been adopted.
Government in the Sunshine Act (United States Code, Title 5, section 552b)	Federal executive agencies.

The reason this book focuses mainly on the laws governing local government meetings is because nearly all important decisions by local governments are taken in the course of meetings of legislative bodies. There are a wide variety of such bodies: county boards of supervisors, city councils, redevelopment agency boards, school boards, community hospital district boards, various commissions and committees established by local governments, and even private, nonprofit corporations that are created by the government or undertake government responsibilities. Meetings of these bodies are governed by the Brown Act.

4

PART II:
LOCAL GOVERNMENT – THE RALPH M. BROWN ACT

A. INTRODUCTION.

The Brown Act regulates the conduct of the governing bodies of all local public agencies: counties, cities, school and community college districts and other special districts, joint powers authorities (groups of public agencies from different areas working together), committees and boards created by local governments, etc. In addition to the Brown Act, several local bodies have adopted "sunshine ordinances," which provide greater access than the Brown Act. As a matter of course, always check to see if a sunshine ordinance has been adopted and what additional access rights might be available.

The Brown Act is intended to provide public access to meetings of local government agencies. Its purpose is described in the Act:

> The people of this State do not yield their sovereignty to the agencies which serve them. The people, in delegating authority, do not give their public servants the right to decide what is good for the people to know and what is not good for them to know. The people insist on remaining informed so that they may retain control over the instruments they have created.[1]

The courts have said that the Brown Act "serves to facilitate public participation in all phases of local government decision-making and to curb misuse of the democratic process by secret legislation of public bodies."[2] In order to achieve these objectives, governmental bodies subject to the requirements of the Brown Act must provide public notice of their meetings, post agendas of the subjects to be discussed at those meetings and provide public access to those meetings. *Public notice of every meeting subject to the Brown Act is required, and access is mandatory unless the meeting is held in closed session under a specific exception contained in the Act.* As the California attorney general has explained:

> Where matters are not subject to a closed meeting exception, the Act has been interpreted to mean that *all of the deliberative processes by legislative bodies, including discussion, debate and the acquisition of information, be open and available for public scrutiny*.[3]

However, the Brown Act is complex, and problems often arise in application. The following issues come up consistently: (1) What kinds of public bodies are subject to the Act? (2) What constitutes a "meeting" and what kinds of communications among members of a legislative body are permitted outside of meetings? (3) Has the public body properly given notice of the matters it intends to address in the agenda for the meeting? (4) Are the exceptions permitting closed sessions being properly applied? (5) Has the legislative body properly reported what actions were taken in closed session?

---

[1]   Government Code § 54950.

[2]   *Epstein v. Hollywood Entertainment Dist. II Business Improvement Dist.*, 87 Cal. App. 4th 862 (2001); *Bell v. Vista Unified School Dist.*, 82 Cal. App. 4th 672 (2000).

[3]   *The Brown Act: Open Meetings For Local Legislative Bodies*, Office of the Attorney General (2003), at p. 1 (emphasis added), citing *Sacramento Newspaper Guild* v. *Sacramento County Bd. of Supervisors*, 263 Cal. App. 2d 41 (1968); 42 Ops. Cal. Atty. Gen. 61, 63 (1963); 32 Ops. Cal. Atty. Gen. 240 (1958).

The full text of the Brown Act is contained in Appendix A. Many provisions of the Act have been interpreted by the courts. These cases generally control how the Brown Act is applied in certain circumstances and are important in understanding how it operates. In addition, the attorney general has issued many opinions interpreting the Act. These opinions are not binding on public agencies or the courts, but they are considered important guidance in applying the Brown Act.

B. WHAT ARE MY RIGHTS UNDER THE BROWN ACT?

When the Brown Act applies, the public has the following rights:

1. Right to Attend Most Meetings.

The main purpose of the Brown Act is to require the bodies that govern local government – such as county boards of supervisors, city councils, planning commissions and the like – to conduct their deliberations and make their decisions in public.[4] Therefore, "all meetings of the legislative body of a local agency shall be open and public, and all persons shall be permitted to attend any meeting of the legislative body of a local agency, except as otherwise provided in [the Brown Act]."[5]

2. Right to Notice of Meetings.

The public has the right to be notified in advance of all meetings, both open and in closed session. Specifically:

a. **Regular meetings** must be noticed by posting an agenda for the meeting at least 72 hours in advance.[6]

b. **Special meetings** may be called, but only upon 24 hours notice to each local newspaper of general circulation, radio station or television station that has in writing requested notice. The notice must also be posted in a location freely accessible to the public.[7]

c. **Emergency meetings** may be called under specific, drastic circumstances ("work stoppage, crippling activity, mass destruction, terrorist act, threatened terrorist activity or other activity that severely impairs public health, safety, or both, as determined by a majority of the members of the legislative body"). One-hour notification of those media that have requested notice is required, if possible.[8]

d. **Closed sessions** must be identified in an agenda posted at least 72 hours before each regular meeting and must be orally disclosed in an open session held before the closed session. The oral disclosure may be a reference to closed-session items listed in the posted agenda.[9]

---

[4]   Government Code section 54950.
[5]   Government Code section 54953(a).
[6]   Government Code section 54954.2(a).
[7]   Government Code section 54956.
[8]   Government Code section 54956.5.
[9]   Government Code sections 54954.2(a), 54957.7.

3. Right to an Agenda.

The public has the right to an agenda that contains a brief description of each item of business to be transacted.[10] The descriptions of agenda items must not be misleading.[11]

As noted, the agenda generally must be provided at least 72 hours before the meeting.

4. Right to Have No Action Taken on Matters Not on the Agenda.

Under the Brown Act, no action can be taken on items not on the agenda, except: (1) Brief responses to public testimony; (2) requests for clarification from or references of matters to staff; (3) brief reports on personal activities; (4) when there is an emergency; (5) when two-thirds of the legislative body agree there is a need to take immediate action on a matter about which the body could not have been aware earlier; or (6) when an item has been held over from a prior meeting.[12]

5. Right to Materials Provided to the Members of the Legislative Body.

The public has the right to obtain copies of the agenda, background materials and any other writings related to matters for public discussion as soon as the materials are distributed to members of the legislative body. You may be required to pay the direct cost of duplication for materials, but you may ask that the cost be waived. In any event you have the right, without fee or charge, to inspect documents as soon as they are made available.[13]

6. Right to Disclosure of Action Taken and Documents Approved in Closed Session.

The public has a right to hear oral reports of certain actions taken in closed session (and the vote on those actions) at an open session held afterwards.[14] Upon submission of a written request, the public has the right to receive copies of any contracts, settlement agreements or other documents finally approved or adopted in the closed session.[15]

7. Right Not to Sign In.

Members of the public have the right to refuse to sign any attendance sheet as a condition of attending a meeting. Attendance sheets must state that those attending have a right to attend without signing.[16]

8. Right to Speak.

The public has the right to speak on any item on the agenda, before or during the body's discussion of the item in regular and special meetings, and to address the legislative body on any

---

[10]   Government Code section 54954.2(a).

[11]   *See The Brown Act: Open Meetings For Local Legislative Bodies*, Office of the Attorney General (2003), pp. 16-17, citing *Carlson v. Paradise Unified School Dist.,* 18 Cal. App. 3d 196, 199 (1971) (construing Education Code section 966). *See also* 67 Ops. Cal. Atty. Gen. 84 (1984) (construing Bagley-Keene Act).

[12]   Government Code section 54954.2.

[13]   Government Code section 54957.5.

[14]   Government Code section 54957.1(a).

[15]   Government Code section 54957.1(b).

[16]   Government Code section 54953.3.

item of interest to the public during a regular meeting.[17] However, the Brown Act does not specify the amount of time a member of the public is allowed to speak. Instead, it allows agencies to adopt "reasonable" rules to limit the time in which a member of the public may speak or the amount of time allowed to address particular issues, depending on the circumstances giving rise to the need for the limitation (*e.g.*, the number of speakers).[18]

The attorney general has concluded that five minutes per speaker is a reasonable amount of time.[19] A court has said that it is not a violation of the Brown Act to limit public comment to two minutes per speaker on each agenda item.[20] Most agencies permit only two or three minutes.

Any limitation placed on a member of the public addressing a local body may not be based on the content of the testimony.[21] In particular, bodies cannot prevent members of the public from complaining about or criticizing the legislative body itself or employees of the public agency it represents.[22]

A court has also said that the Brown Act does not require a body to permit the public to address whether an item should be added to the agenda.[23] On the other hand, members of the public do not lose the ability to challenge actions taken by public bodies simply because they do not speak up at a meeting before the action is taken.[24]

9. Right to Insist on Public Vote.

In general, bodies subject to the Brown Act are required to make public the vote on all measures. No secret ballots, whether preliminary or final, are permitted.[25] However, votes ***not*** to take action on subjects properly addressed in closed sessions may not be required to be made public.[26]

10. Right to Record, Videotape or Broadcast Meetings.

The public has the right to make an audio, video, photographic or other recording of a meeting, and to broadcast a meeting absent a reasonable finding that continued recording or broadcast unavoidably will cause noise, illumination or obstruction of a view that constitutes a disruption of the proceedings.[27]

---

[17] Government Code section 54954.3(a).

[18] Government Code section 54954.3(b).

[19] 75 Ops. Cal. Atty. Gen. 89 (1992).

[20] *Chaffee v. San Francisco Public Library Commission*, 134 Cal. App. 4th 109 (2005).

[21] *See, e.g., Leventhal v. Vista Unified School Dist.*, 973 F. Supp. 951 (1997); *Baca v. Moreno Valley Unified School Dist.*, 936 F. Supp. 719 (1996).

[22] Government Code section 54954.3(c); *Leventhal v. Vista Unified School Dist.*, 973 F. Supp. 951 (1997); *Baca v. Moreno Valley Unified School Dist.*, 936 F. Supp. 719 (1996).

[23] *Coalition of Labor, Agriculture & Business v. County of Santa Barbara Bd. of Supervisors*, 129 Cal. App. 4th 205 (2005).

[24] *Lindelli v. Town of San Anselmo*, 111 Cal. App. 4th 1099 (2003).

[25] Government Code section 54953(c).

[26] 06 Cal. Daily Op. Serv. 4435 (2006) (finding that a local agency is not required to publicly report the votes of its members when it decides to reject a proposed dismissal of a public employee; the attorney general reasoned that the decision to not dismiss a public employee was not an "action taken to ... dismiss ... or otherwise affect the employment status of a public employee in closed session" under § 54957.1).

[27] Government Code sections 54953.5(a), 54953.6.

11. Right to View and Copy Recordings of Meetings.

To obtain a copy of any existing tape recording made by the legislative body of its public sessions and to listen to or view the body's original tape on a tape recorder or viewing device provided by the agency. [28]

12. Right to Request Greater Access.

The public has the right to request that a legislative body provide greater access to meetings than what is strictly required by the minimum standards of the Brown Act.[29]

13. Right to Remain in the Meeting.

A meeting may be closed to the public if it is seriously and intentionally disrupted. Before the public can be excluded, the body must try to restore order by removing only the individuals responsible for the disruption. If that fails, the public may be excluded. Even then, members of the media that did not participate in the disruption are allowed to remain. The body can allow those not involved in the disruption to be readmitted to the proceedings.[30]

14. Right to Non-Discriminatory Facilities.

Meetings may not be conducted in a facility that excludes people on the basis of their race, religion, color, national origin, ancestry or sex, or that is inaccessible to disabled people, or where members of the public may not be present without making a payment or purchase.[31]

15. Right to Seek Relief.

Members of the public may obtain an order from the superior court enjoining the legislative body from violating the Brown Act, mandating that the body comply with the Act, or simply declaring that the body has, in behaving in a certain manner, violated the Act.[32] In addition, the public may be able to obtain an order setting aside certain actions taken in violation of the Brown Act.[33] If a member of the public prevails in an action under the Brown Act, the courts can (and generally do) award attorneys' fees.[34]

C. HOW DO I KNOW IF A MEETING IS GOVERNED BY THE BROWN ACT?

There are two basic steps in determining whether a meeting is subject to the Brown Act: (1) Is a "legislative body" involved; and, if so, (2) is the gathering of the members of that body a "meeting?" Each of these terms is defined by the Brown Act, and each is discussed below.

---

[28]   Government Code section 54953.5(b).
[29]   Government Code section 54953.7.
[30]   Government Code section 54957.9.
[31]   Government Code section 54961(a).
[32]   Government Code section 54960.
[33]   Government Code section 54960.1.
[34]   Government Code section 54960.5.

1. Is a "Legislative Body" Involved?

The first step in determining whether the Brown Act governs a particular situation is to determine if the body in question is a "legislative body" within the meaning of the Brown Act. The Brown Act contains several definitions of the kinds of groups that are "legislative bodies."

a. Official bodies. The first and most important group of public bodies that are controlled by the Brown Act are official bodies of local agencies. These have been defined as follows:

(1) The governing body of a local agency.[35] This term includes bodies such as a board of supervisors, city council, planning commission or directors of a special district. For example, a school board that governs a local school district is a legislative body,[36] as is the board of a redevelopment agency[37] and the governing board of a county retirement system.[38]

(2) Any "local body created by state or federal law."[39] Included in this definition may be local bodies created by state or federal law for a specific purpose, such as to fight gangs or drugs.

(3) "A commission, committee, board or other body of a local agency, whether permanent or temporary, decision-making or advisory, created by charter, ordinance, resolution, or formal action of a legislative body."[40] The term "formal action" in the Act means action by the body, as opposed to action by an individual member of the body. Formal action need not be in the form of a formal motion but should indicate an agreement by a majority of the board to create the committee.[41] For example, a school board's adoption of a policy calling for the creation of an advisory committee constituted the creation of a committee subject to the Brown Act, even though the the superintendent appointed members of the committee.[42]

(4) "Standing committees of a legislative body, irrespective of their composition, which have a continuing subject matter jurisdiction, or a meeting schedule fixed by charter, ordinance, resolution, or formal action of a legislative body are legislative bodies."[43] This provision applies to committees that are a subject of a legislative body. A committee is a "standing committee," and its meetings are subject to the Brown Act if: (1) It has "continuing subject matter jurisdiction," that is, it has been created to address a particular subject over an indefinite period, not to perform a specific task within a fixed period; or (2) it has a meeting schedule established by some formal action of the legislative body of which it is part. An example of a standing committee would be a budget and finance committee of a city council.[44] However, a meeting of the members of a standing committee to address a subject that is outside the subject matter that committee was created to address may not constitute a meeting that is subject to the Brown Act.[45]

---

[35]   Government Code section 54952(a).

[36]   *Kavanaugh v. West Sonoma County Union High School Dist.*, 29 Cal. 4th 911 (2003).

[37]   *Stockton Newspapers, Inc. v. Redevelopment Agency*, 171 Cal. App. 3d 95 (1985).

[38]   *Freedom Newspapers, Inc. v. Orange County Employees Retirement System*, 6 Cal. 4th 821 (1993).

[39]   Government Code section 54952(a).

[40]   Government Code section 54952(b).

[41]   *See Joiner v. City of Sebastopol*, 125 Cal. App. 3d 799, 805 (1981) (city council's selection of two members to meet with two members of city planning commission for the purpose of screening applicants for appointment to planning commission constituted "formal action").

[42]   *Frazer v. Dixon Unified School Dist.*, 18 Cal. App. 4th 781 (1993).

[43]   Government Code section 54952(b).

[44]   *See The Brown Act: Open Meetings For Legislative Bodies*, Office of the Attorney General (2003), pp. 5-6.

[45]   *Taxpayers for Livable Communities v. City of Malibu*, 126 Cal. App. 4th 1123 (2005).

(5) Other bodies. The government may create other kinds of bodies that are subject to the Brown Act. Any governmental entity that serves as the "governing body" of a "local agency or other local body created by state or federal statute" is subject to the Brown Act.[46] The Brown Act defines a "local agency" as "a county, city, whether general law or chartered, city and county, town, school district, municipal corporation, district, political subdivision, or any board, commission or agency thereof, or other local public agency."[47] A government agency generally is a "local agency" only if it is created by statute or by the state Constitution.[48] For example, the board of directors of a multi-jurisdictional crime task force set up by various cities in Los Angeles County was subject to the Brown Act because it was a separate legal entity created pursuant to statute (the Joint Exercise of Powers Act) and governed by a board of directors and executive council.[49]

b. Meetings of less than a quorum. A "quorum" is the number of members of a group that must be present to take action. Government bodies have rules that establish how many members constitute a quorum. Generally, a majority of the members constitutes a quorum, but some bodies may have rules that require more than a majority.

In general, the requirements of the Brown Act are triggered only when at least a quorum of the legislative body in question is meeting. However, there are exceptions to this requirement.

First, a legislative body subject to the Brown Act cannot evade the requirements of the Brown Act by conducting a series of meetings, each of which involves less than a quorum. (This "serial meeting" situation is addressed in detail below.)

Second, certain committees or other groups that consist of members of a public body may have to comply with the Brown Act. As noted, standing committees are required to comply with the Brown Act. However, committees made up solely of less than a quorum of a body that do not have an indefinite or permanent period of existence or a fixed meeting schedule are *not* governed by the Act. For example, two members of a five-member council may be appointed to a committee to investigate and provide a report on downtown traffic congestion. If the committee is designed to disband after completing its task, it would probably not be a standing committee governed by the Act.[50] (Keep in mind that adding a staff person or member of the public to the committee would bring the committee under the Act as an "advisory body," since it would no longer be made up solely of members of a legislative body.)

In addition, while members representing less than a quorum of a single legislative body may be able to meet without following the requirements of the Brown Act, the same may not always be true when "subquorums" of two separate legislative bodies meet together. For example, a city council effectively created an advisory committee when it announced that two of its members would meet with two members of the planning commission to review the credentials of proposed appointees to fill a commission vacancy.[51] In addition, if two subquorums of different bodies become a "unitary body" by making collective decisions and recommendations, the group may be

---

[46] Government Code section 54952(a).

[47] Government Code section 54951.

[48] *McKee v. Los Angeles Interagency Metropolitan Police Apprehension Crime Task Force*, 134 Cal. App. 4th 354, 358-59 (2005).

[49] *McKee v. Los Angeles Interagency Metropolitan Police Apprehension Crime Task Force*, 134 Cal. App. 4th 354, 358-363 (2005). Note that the court found that the task force was also subject to the Brown Act under Government Code section 54952(c) because it was "delegated with authority possessed by city councils to exercise municipalities' police powers with public funds." *Id.*, at 363.

[50] *See The Brown Act: Open Meetings For Legislative Bodies*, Office of the Attorney General (2003), p. 6.

[51] *Joiner v. City of Sebastopol*, 125 Cal. App. 3d 799 (1981).

subject to the Brown Act.[52]   On the other hand, if the two subquorums are meeting merely to exchange information and report back to their respective bodies, they are probably not subject to the Brown Act.[53]

A Note on Committees: Consider whether local bodies are designing committees to avoid bringing them within the Act. If a less-than-a-quorum committee is initially created to investigate a single issue and then disbands, but thereafter assumes new duties, then it may become a committee with continuing subject matter jurisdiction and be subject to the Act. Furthermore, even where a less-than-a-quorum subcommittee meets infrequently or on an impromptu basis, so long as the subcommittee has the authority to hear and consider issues within the subject matter jurisdiction of the parent legislative body – and the subcommittee's authority needs no renewal – the subcommittee will be subject to the provisions of the Brown Act.[54]

c. Private bodies. There are also times when the governing body of a private entity – for example, the board of directors of a corporation – can be subject to the requirements of the Brown Act. Under Government Code Section 54952, a "legislative body" includes a private corporation or entity that either: (1) is created by the elected legislative body to exercise authority delegated to the corporation or entity by the legislative body, or (2) receives funds from the local agency and the corporation's board of directors includes a member of the governing body of the local agency appointed as a full voting member to the board of directors of the corporation.[55] The governing bodies of specially created nonprofit corporations that operate hospitals for the benefit of hospital district residents are also specifically governed by the Act.[56]

(1) Delegation of authority. One example of the delegation of authority to a private corporation subjecting it to the requirements of the Brown Act is a private, for-profit corporation created to build and operate a coal export facility on land leased by the Los Angeles Harbor Department. The Los Angeles Harbor Commission entered into an agreement with 28 Japanese companies and six U.S. firms to create the corporation. The new corporation's board of directors was held to be subject to the Brown Act. On the key issue of whether the city delegated authority to the harbor commission, the court concluded that the city council created the new corporation to develop the coal-exporting facility instead of developing the facility itself, and thus it delegated authority to the corporation.[57] Another example is an association of property owners that administered government funds raised through assessments on businesses in a certain district. The money was used to contract for such things as security patrols, maintenance, street and alley cleaning and a newsletter. Although it was not incorporated by the city council, the court said that it was required to "look at the circumstances" surrounding the creation of the body and found that it had been "formed and structured for the sole purpose of taking over [the] City's administrative

---

52   64 Ops. Cal. Atty. Gen. 856 (1981).

53   *See Taxpayers for Livable Communities v. City of Malibu*, 126 Cal. App. 4th 1123 (2005) (a closed meeting of two of five members of the city council did not violate the Brown Act because, though they were sole members of a standing committee, the subject matter discussed was outside that standing committee's jurisdiction, and the role of the two councilmembers was advisory, so they could "meet with representatives of other entities to exchange information and report back to the council without falling under the Brown Act.").

54   Ops. Cal. Atty. Gen. Opinion No. 95-614 (1996).

55   Government Code section 54952(c).

56   Government Code section 54952(d). However, specifically exempted from the Brown Act are governing boards of private corporations created to operate district hospitals before April 1, 1994.

57   *International Longshoreman's and Warehousemen's Union v. Los Angeles Export Terminal Inc.*, 69 Cal. App. 4th 287 (1999).

functions."[58] It was therefore subject to the Brown Act. Thus, a private entity may be subject to the Brown Act even though it is technically "created by" someone other than the local government that gives it authority.

A further example of a body created through the delegation of authority is the governing board of a private, nonprofit corporation established for the purpose of providing programming for a cable television channel.[59] The attorney general reasoned that the corporation was a public entity because it met both prongs of § 54953(c)(1)(A), namely "the city council of the City (an elected legislative body of a local agency) played a role in bringing the Corporation into existence" and the city council "lawfully delegated" the authority to operate the educational access channel. Moreover, the attorney general found that the corporation was a public entity under § 45953(c)(1)(B) because it received funds from the school district, a local agency, which also had the power to appoint three of the five members of the corporations board and the right to approve the final two members as well.[60]

On the other hand, the attorney general has concluded that the governing board of a jointly administered trust fund, whose members are appointed by a city and labor union representing city employees and whose purpose is to address labor-management issues, is not required to hold its meetings open to the public.[61] The attorney general reasoned that, though the city funded the governing board, whose purpose was to benefit city workers, and appointed half its members, the board did not exercise "authority that may be lawfully delegated [to it] by the elected governing body." Instead, this board only "performed limited collaborative functions as part of the collective bargaining process between the Department and the Union."

(2) Funded and with a member appointed by a local agency. If a legislative body provides financial support and appoints one of its members as a full voting representative to the governing body of a private organization, the private organization is a legislative body for purposes of the Brown Act. The financial support need not be extensive. However, a non-voting member appointed to the private organization's governing body will not subject the private organization to the Act. In addition, the Brown Act does not apply if the government body appoints someone other than one of its own members to the governing board of the private entity.[62]

d. Elected but not yet sworn individuals. The Brown Act applies to any person elected to serve as a member of a legislative body who has not yet assumed the duties of office. These individuals must conform their conduct to the requirements of the Act and are treated for purposes of enforcement of the Act as if they have already assumed office.[63]

2. Is the Gathering a "Meeting?"

Assuming that a body is subject to the requirements of the Brown Act, the next question is whether a gathering of members of that body is a "meeting" that is subject to the Brown Act. The term "meeting" is defined by the Brown Act. The Brown Act also defines specific conduct that does not constitute a "meeting" under the Act.

---

[58] *Epstein v. Hollywood Entertainment Dist. II Business Improvement Dist.*, 87 Cal. App. 4th 862, 871 (2001).
[59] 85 Ops. Cal. Atty. Gen. 55 (2002).
[60] *See also* 81 Ops. Cal. Atty. Gen. 281, 290 (1998) (community redevelopment agency created nonprofit entity and delegated authority to it).
[61] 87 Ops. Cal. Atty. Gen. 19 (2004).
[62] *See The Brown Act: Open Meetings For Legislative Bodies*, Office of the Attorney General (2003), p. 7.
[63] Government Code section 54952.1.

a. Definition of "meeting." A "meeting" includes any congregation of a majority of the members of a legislative body at the same time and place to hear, discuss or deliberate upon any item that is within the subject matter jurisdiction of the legislative body or the local agency to which it pertains.[64]

As the attorney general has explained: "***This definition makes it clear that the body need not take any action in order for a gathering to be defined as a meeting.*** A gathering is a meeting if a majority of the members of the body merely receive information or discuss their views on an issue. A meeting also covers a body's deliberations, including the consideration, analysis or debate of an issue, and any vote which may ultimately be taken."[65]

A meeting does not have to be formally announced, agendized or convened in order to be subject to the Act.[66] In fact, many violations of the Act occur during informal gatherings or through a series of communications in which the public's business is discussed.

The Act requires each legislative body of a local agency, except for advisory committees and standing committees, to provide by ordinance, resolution, bylaws or by whatever rule is required for the conduct of business by that body, the time and place for holding regular meetings.[67]

b. "Serial meetings" and other ways of deliberating through a series of communications are prohibited. Members of a legislative body do not have to meet face to face in order to have a meeting or take action within the meaning of the Brown Act. Any use of direct communication, personal intermediaries or technological devices by a majority of the members of the legislative body to develop a collective concurrence as to action to be taken on an item by the legislative body is prohibited, if used to "develop a collective concurrence as to action."[68]

For example, a series of individual telephone calls between the attorney for a redevelopment agency and the members of the agency's governing board was held to constitute a meeting. The agency attorney had individually polled the members of the body to get their approval for a real estate transaction. The court concluded that even though the members never met together, their communications constituted a meeting for the purposes of the Act. Therefore, the agency had violated the Brown Act by not complying with the requirements for meetings.[69]

Similarly, when the San Diego City Council directed staff to take certain action in an eminent domain proceeding in a letter signed by a quorum of the council, without conducting a public meeting on the subject, the court held that it had violated the Brown Act.[70]

Addressing e-mail communications, the attorney general has said: "This office [has] concluded that a majority of a body would violate the Act if they e-mailed each other regarding current issues under the body's jurisdiction, even if the e-mails were also sent to the secretary and chairperson of the agency, the e-mails were posted on the agency's Internet Web site, and a printed version of each e-mail was reported at the next public meeting of the body. The opinion concluded that these safeguards were not sufficient to satisfy either the express wording of the Act or some of its purposes. Specifically, such e-mail communications would not be available to

---

64   Government Code section 54952.2(a).

65   *The Brown Act, Open Meetings For Local Legislative Bodies*, Office of the Attorney General, 2003, at p. 8 (emphasis added). *See also Frazer v. Dixon Unified School Dist.*, 18 Cal. App. 4th 781, 794-795 (1993).

66   In *Sacramento Newspaper Guild v. Sacramento County Bd. of Supervisors*, 263 Cal. App. 2d 41 (1968), the court held that a luncheon gathering that included five county supervisors, the county counsel, a variety of county officers, and representatives of a union to discuss a strike that was underway against the county was a meeting within the meaning of the Act.

67   Government Code section 54954(a).

68   Government Code section 54952.2(b).

69   *Stockton Newspapers, Inc. v. Redevelopment Agency*, 171 Cal. App. 3d 95, 105 (1985).

70   *Common Cause v. Stirling*, 119 Cal. App. 3d 658 (1981).

persons who do not have Internet access. Even if a person had Internet access, the deliberations on a particular issue could be completed before an interested person had an opportunity to become involved."[71]

The attorney general also addressed a situation in which members of a city redevelopment agency met with subquorums of a governing body. The meetings were all held on about the same date but were broken up into groups so that there was never a quorum present at any one meeting. The meetings were held to brief members of the legislative body on upcoming agency plans and to get feedback. The attorney general concluded that the meetings were subject to the Brown Act. The attorney general noted that in some instances a particular initiative was abandoned by the redevelopment agency, demonstrating that "action" could be taken with no public knowledge or discussion.[72]

On the other hand, the California Supreme Court has said that a memo from a legislative body's attorney to the members of the body did not constitute a meeting under the Act.[73] Similarly, a court of appeal has said that the distribution of memoranda from agency staff to the legislative body of an agency does not violate the Brown Act.[74]

A Note on "Serial Meetings": It is important to be aware that *a government body need not take formal action through a serial meeting in order to have conducted a "meeting" in violation of the Act*. A court of appeal has concluded that the Act applies equally to the deliberations of a body and its decision to take action. The court reasoned that if a collective commitment were a necessary element, the body could conduct most or all of its deliberation behind closed doors as long as the body did not actually reach agreement prior to consideration in public session.[75] Thus, a court of appeal has also held that "to prevent evasion of the Brown Act, a series of private meetings (known as serial meetings) by which a majority of the members of a legislative body commit themselves to a decision concerning public business or engage in collective deliberation on public business would violate the open meeting requirement."[76] The key question to ask in all cases is whether the public is being denied the opportunity to participate in the deliberative and decision-making process of its government agencies. If the answer is yes, there may be enough to prove that a serial meeting violates the Brown Act.[77]

c. Non-legislative functions covered. If a body falls under the Brown Act, it is subject to all the provisions of the Act even when it meets to perform a non-legislative or quasi-judicial function, *e.g.,* to hear an appeal from a zoning decision of a planning commission.[78]

---

[71]   *The Brown Act, Open Meetings For Local Legislative Bodies*, Office of the Attorney General, 2003, at p. 15, *citing* 84 Ops. Cal. Atty. Gen. 30 (2001).

[72]   63 Ops. Cal. Atty. Gen. 820 (1980).

[73]   *Roberts v. City of Palmdale,* 5 Cal. 4th 363, 381 (1993).

[74]   *Frazer v. Dixon Unified School District*, 18 Cal. App. 4th 781, 797 (1993).

[75]   *Frazer v. Dixon Unified School District*, 18 Cal. App. 4th 781, 796-798 (1993).

[76]   *216 Sutter Bay Associates v. County of Sutter*, 58 Cal. App. 4th 860, 877 (1997).

[77]   Note, however, that a contrary conclusion was reached in *Wolfe v. City of Fremont*, 144 Cal. App. 4th , 533,541 WL (2006). In that case the court held that the prohibition on serial meetings is violated only if the members of the legislative body communicate with each other and reach a collective concurrence.

[78]   *See The Brown Act, Open Meetings For Local Legislative Bodies*, Office of the Attorney General, 2003, at p. 4 ("The Act's application is not limited to boards and commissions insofar as they perform "legislative" functions. Bodies that perform actions that are primarily executive or quasi-judicial in nature are also subject to the Act. (61 Ops. Cal. Atty. Gen. 220 (1978); 57 Ops. Cal. Atty. Gen. 189 (1974).)").

d. Gatherings that are not meetings. The Brown Act defines circumstances in which more than a quorum may gather, and discuss matters that may come before the body, without being governed by the Act.

(1) Individual contacts with another person. The Act allows individual contacts or conversations between a member of a legislative body and any other person.[79] This exception to the Act appears to be designed to protect the constitutional rights of citizens to petition their government.[80] A member of a body may meet with constituents or be briefed by staff without invoking the Act. Conversations between board members or staff may or may not be a meeting depending upon the context. For example, communications between two members of a body may be found to be one of a series of communications designed to develop a collective concurrence (a "serial meeting"), or simply a meeting of a less-than-a-quorum committee, which is not subject to the Brown Act.

(2) Attendance at conferences and seminars. The Act exempts attendance of a majority of a body at conferences or similar gatherings that are open to the public and that involve issues of interest to the public or to public agencies of the type represented by the legislative body, so long as a majority of members do not discuss among themselves specific issues that are within the subject matter jurisdiction of the body.[81]

For example, a majority of city council members could attend a League of California Cities conference, which is typically organized to discuss issues of concern to all cities. The conference may be other than a conference of local agencies; it may be organized by other entities, such as health care or environmental organizations, so long as the issues to be discussed are of interest to the agency or the public.

(3) Attendance at meetings organized by others to address local concerns. The Act exempts the attendance of a majority of the members of a legislative body at an open and publicized meeting to address a topic of local community concern, organized by a person or group other than the local agency, so long as members do not discuss among themselves, other than as part of the scheduled program, issues within the subject matter jurisdiction of the body.[82] This exemption is designed to allow a majority of a body to attend well-publicized community meetings. Examples include candidate nights, meetings of neighborhood organizations and meetings of local environmental groups. During the meeting, members may discuss issues directly related to the purpose of the meeting even though the issues may also be within the jurisdiction of the agency. However, members may not gather among themselves to discuss public business.

(4) Attendance at meetings of other legislative bodies. The Act exempts attendance of a majority of members of a legislative body at an open and noticed meeting of another body of the local agency or at an open and noticed meeting of another local agency, provided that a majority of the body does not discuss among themselves, other than as part of the scheduled meeting, business of a specific nature that is within the subject matter jurisdiction of the body.[83] This exemption allows, for example, a majority of members of a city council to attend a meeting of the city's planning commission.

---

[79]   Government Code section 54952.2(c)(1).

[80]   *See The Brown Act, Open Meetings For Local Legislative Bodies*, Office of the Attorney General (2003), at p. 13.

[81]   Government Code section 54952.2(c)(2).

[82]   Government Code section 54952.2(c)(3).

[83]   Government Code section 54952.2(c)(4).

(5) Attendance at social and ceremonial gatherings. The Act exempts attendance by a majority of a body at purely social and ceremonial gatherings.[84] Ribbon cutting, retirement dinners and other ceremonial occasions are embraced by this exemption. Whether a casual or incidental meeting of a quorum for ostensibly social purposes constitutes a "meeting" depends entirely on what is discussed. The Act in no way forbids members of a governmental body to socialize without inviting the general public. On the other hand, the Act does forbid a quorum of a body from discussing public business without following the requirements of the law.

In particular, habitual "social gatherings" of a quorum are suspect, since it is unlikely that members would meet consistently in a social gathering without discussing, at least on occasion, the public's business. For example, the attorney general issued an opinion saying that regularly scheduled luncheon meetings held by the members of two cities jointly with civic organizations to discuss issues such as water, airports, and school locations constituted meetings under the Brown Act, even though no decisions were made.[85]

(6) Attendance at meetings of standing committees. The Act exempts the attendance of a majority of the members of a legislative body at an open and noticed meeting of a standing committee of that body provided that the members of the legislative body who are not members of the standing committee attend only as observers.[86] However, the attorney general opinion has concluded that when the members of the legislative body attend a meeting of the standing committee as observers, they may not ask questions or make statements during the meeting.[87]

A Note on the Exemptions: For all of these exemptions, the key consideration is whether the members of the legislative body who attend discuss the business of the legislative body. An unlawful meeting can occur at any function if more than a quorum of the body discuss among themselves specific issues within the body's jurisdiction.

e. Out of town "retreats." The Brown Act requires – with limited exceptions – all regular and special meetings of a body to be held within the territory over which the local agency exercises jurisdiction.[88] A local agency cannot avoid public attendance at a meeting to discuss a controversial topic merely by packing its bags and heading to Palm Springs. Even though these retreat meetings were theoretically open and public before the 1994 changes to the Act, few, if any, constituents would follow bodies to remote locations.

Local bodies are allowed to meet outside their jurisdiction only under one of the following circumstances: (1) To comply with a state or federal law or to attend a judicial or administrative proceeding in which the body is a party; (2) to inspect real or personal property located outside the jurisdiction; (3) to participate in multi-agency meetings, so long as the meeting is held within the jurisdiction of one participating agency; (4) to meet in a nearby facility if the agency has no meeting facility within its boundaries; (5) to meet with state or federal elected and appointed officials to discuss a legislative or regulatory issue affecting the local agency; (6) to meet at a

---

[84]   Government Code section 54952.2(c)(5); *Sacramento Newspaper Guild v. Sacramento County Board* of *Supervisors*, 263 Cal. App. 2d 41 (1968); 43 Ops. Cal. Atty. Gen. 36, 38 (1964).

[85]   43 Ops. Cal. Atty. Gen. 36 (1964) ("Because of the admitted importance to the people in the area of the matters discussed by a majority of the members of the legislative body (when meeting at a regularly established time and place), we believe that the provisions of the Ralph M. Brown Act apply to such meetings and that the public is entitled to notice and the right to attend such meetings.").

[86]   Government Code section 54952.2(c)(6).

[87]   81 Ops. Cal. Atty. Gen. 156 (1998).

[88]   Government Code section 54954(b).

nearby facility owned by the local agency if the topic of the meeting is limited to the items directly related to the facility; (7) to meet with legal counsel for closed-session discussions of pending litigation if to do so would reduce legal costs.[89]

In addition to the above exceptions, governing bodies of school districts may meet outside the jurisdiction: (1) To attend conferences on non-adversarial collective bargaining techniques; (2) to interview members of the public concerning the potential employment of a superintendent; and (3) to interview a potential employee.[90]

Joint powers authorities may meet within the jurisdiction of any of their member agencies, and statewide agencies may meet anywhere in the state.[91]

Meetings that properly may be held outside an agency's jurisdiction must still comply with the notice and agenda provisions of the Act and must still be open and public unless the subject matter of the meeting allows a closed session.

f. Some electronic meetings allowed. The Brown Act allows legislative bodies to "use video teleconferencing for the benefit of the public or the legislative body."[92] The term "teleconference" means a "meeting of individuals in different locations, connected by electronic means, through either audio, video or both."[93]

A legislative body is permitted to use teleconferencing for any meeting or proceeding authorized by law. Teleconferenced meetings must comply with all Brown Act requirements – adequate notice, the right of the public to attend and speak, etc. – as well as other applicable provisions of law.[94]

Specifically, at least a quorum of the members of the legislative body must participate from locations within the boundaries of the territory over which the local agency has jurisdiction. Each teleconference location must be identified in the notice and agenda, and each location must be accessible to the public. Agencies choosing to use teleconferencing must post agendas at all teleconference locations. Each location at which a participant in the teleconference is located must be open to the public, and the public must be allowed to speak at each location. Members are prohibited from taking any action by secret ballot and must conduct all votes taken during a teleconferenced meeting by roll call.[95]

In 2005 the state legislature added new provisions relating to teleconferencing by health authorities.[96] These provisions, which are effective until January 1, 2009, are designed to make it easier for health authorities – which have large boards – to conduct teleconferences. The legislative history behind this provision suggests that the reason for the passage of this amendment is that "[t]he membership of local health initiative boards of directors is required by statute to represent a diverse group of health care professionals, and, as a result, these boards frequently are large and comprised of persons working and residing outside of the board's jurisdiction. Accordingly, these boards have a demonstrated difficulty in obtaining a quorum of members located within the board's jurisdiction as required by the teleconference provisions of the Ralph M. Brown Act."

---

[89]   Government Code section 54954(b)(1)-(7).
[90]   Government Code section 54954(c).
[91]   Government Code section 54954(d).
[92]   Government Code section 54953(b).
[93]   Government Code section 54953(b)(4).
[94]   Government Code section 54953(b).
[95]   Government Code section 54953(b)(2), (3).
[96]   Government Code section 54953(d).

D. WHAT NOTICE IS REQUIRED, AND HOW IS NOTICE GIVEN?

1. Advance Notice Is Required.

Advance notice is required for all meetings. The amount of notice that is required depends on the nature of the meeting. Under the Brown Act, there are three kinds of meetings: (1) Regular meetings; (2) special meetings; and (3) emergency meetings.

a. Regular meetings: agendas must be posted 72 hours in advance. At least 72 hours before a regular meeting, the legislative body of the local agency must post an agenda containing a "brief general description" of each item to be transacted or discussed at the meeting, including items to be discussed in closed session. The notice must be posted in a location that is freely accessible to members of the public.[97]

According to an opinion of the attorney general, weekend hours may be counted as part of the 72-hour period for posting an agenda prior to the regular meeting of the legislative body. However, if the agenda is posted in a public building that is locked during the evening or weekend hours, the statutory requirements for posting the agenda would not be satisfied.[98]

Because many standing and advisory committees of local agencies meet on an irregular basis, the Brown Act was amended in 1997 to eliminate the requirement that standing and advisory committees establish a regular meeting schedule. Subsequently, some confusion arose over whether these committees were required to comply with the 72-hour agenda-posting requirement. In 1998, the Act was amended to provide that "meetings of advisory committees or standing committees, for which an agenda is posted at least 72 hours in advance of the meeting ... shall be considered for purposes of this chapter as regular meetings of the legislative body."[99]

b. Special meetings: 24-hour notice required. Special meetings may be called, but only upon 24 hours advance notice.[100] A special meeting is a meeting of a body subject to the Brown Act that is not held at the regularly scheduled time or place and is not held to address an emergency.[101] The notice of a special meeting must be posted in a location freely accessible to the public, and notice must be given directly to all members of the legislative body and to members of the press who have asked to receive notice of special meetings. The notice must specify the time and place of the special meeting and the business to be discussed. Only the business specified for discussion at the special meeting may be addressed.[102]

c. Emergency meetings: one-hour notice required. Emergency meetings may be called under specific, drastic circumstances ("work stoppage, crippling activity, or other activity that severely impairs public health, safety, or both, as determined by a majority of the members of the legislative body"). At least one-hour notice must be given to those media that have requested notice of special meetings. In a "dire emergency" (a "crippling disaster, mass destruction, terrorist act, or threatened terrorist activity" that poses peril so immediate that even one-hour notice cannot

---

[97] Government Code section 54954.2(a).
[98] 78 Ops. Cal. Atty. Gen. 327 (1995).
[99] Government Code section 54954(a).
[100] Government Code section 54956.
[101] *See The Brown Act, Open Meetings For Local Legislative Bodies*, Office of the Attorney General (2003), at p. 16.
[102] Government Code section 54956.

safely be given), notice need only be provided to the media at or about the time it is given to members of the body.[103]

2. Agendas Must Include Descriptions of All Items to Be Discussed.

a. The agenda must contain a brief description of each item. Agendas must contain a brief description of each item of business to be discussed (generally not to exceed 20 words), and must specify the time and location of the meeting.[104]

Agendas must also include descriptions of items to be addressed in closed session.[105] The Brown Act provides a "safe harbor" for bodies that choose to describe their closed sessions in "substantial compliance" with precise formats described in the Act. The formats are contained in section 54954.5 of the Act (reprinted in Appendix A). In general, using these forms will constitute compliance with the agenda notice requirements of the Brown Act.

However, simply following the form of closed-session notice provided in the Brown Act may not be sufficient to ensure that the public receives adequate notice and that the body holding the meeting complies with the Brown Act. For example, simply following the form provided in section 54954.4(b) for closed-session discussions regarding the purchase or sale of real estate was not sufficient to give adequate notice of a complex series of transactions involving the development of a baseball stadium.[106]

b. Descriptions must not be misleading. According to the attorney general, "the purpose of the brief general description is to inform interested members of the public about the subject matter under consideration so that they can determine whether to monitor or participate in the meeting of the body."[107] Thus, the description of agenda items for both public and closed portions of meetings must be adequate and not misleading. For example, the description "continuation school site change" was insufficient to alert the public that the school board was going to discuss and take action on the closure of an elementary school and the transfer of its students.[108] The Attorney General has said that using the agenda item "flood control" to refer to a discussion on a request to Congress to exempt a certain stream from the Wild and Scenic Rivers Act was clearly inadequate.[109]

Similarly, the attorney general issued an opinion that simply listing all parcels of real property larger than 20 acres within the planning area by an open-space district (700 parcels) as potential subjects of negotiation for purchase would not satisfy disclosure requirements under the Brown Act for a closed session regarding the purchase of any one or more of such parcels. The opinion concludes that such a generic listing was inadequate because it was not sufficiently focused upon the particular parcels for which purchase was realistically an option.[110]

In addition, a city council was found to have violated the requirement that notice be given to a public employee of a closed session being held to address his or her performance, because the agenda description "provided no clue that the dismissal of a public employee would be discussed

---

[103]   Government Code section 54956.5.

[104]   Government Code section 54954.2(a).

[105]   Government Code sections 54954.2(a), 54954.5.

[106]   *Shapiro v. San Diego City Council*, 96 Cal. App. 4th 904 (2002).

[107]   *The Brown Act, Open Meetings For Local Legislative Bodies*, Office of the Attorney General (2003), at pp. 16-17.

[108]   *Carlson v. Paradise Unified School District*, 18 Cal. App. 3d 196 (1979).

[109]   *See* 67 Ops. Cal. Atty. Gen. 84 (1984) (construing Bagley-Keene Act).

[110]   73 Ops. Cal. Atty. Gen. 1, 3-5 (1990).

at the meeting," and therefore it failed to give the employee advance notice that the city council would be hearing allegations of misconduct against him at a special meeting.[111]

The Brown Act says that the length of descriptions generally does not have to exceed 20 words.[112] This was not intended to allow inadequate or misleading descriptions of items. Instead, the Legislature indicated that most topics can be adequately described in 20 words. If a 20-word description is insufficient to allow the public to understand whether it needs to attend a meeting or seek more information, then the description should be expanded to the point where it is a "brief general description of the item to be discussed."[113]

3. Action Generally Cannot Be Taken on Items That Are Not on the Agenda.

In general, a body subject to the Brown Act cannot take action on any item that is not on the agenda for a meeting.[114] This prevents bodies from avoiding the requirements of the Brown Act by simply omitting important items from the agenda.

However, there are exceptions to the rule that a legislative body may not take action on an item that is not on the agenda. Specifically:

- *Questions, responses, and references to staff:* Members of a legislative body or staff can briefly respond to statements or questions by members of the public attending the meeting. In addition, they can: (1) Ask a question for clarification, make a brief announcement or make a brief report on their own activities; (2) refer an issue to staff for factual information; (3) request staff to report back to the body at a subsequent meeting concerning any matter; or (4) take action to direct staff to place a matter of business on a future agenda.[115]

- *Emergencies:* A legislative body can take action on items not on the agenda when the body determines by a majority vote that an "emergency situation" or a "dire emergency" exists.[116] An "emergency situation" is "a work stoppage, crippling activity, or other activity that severely impairs public health [or] safety," *e.g.*, a garbage collectors' strike or an earthquake.[117] A "dire emergency" is "a crippling disaster, mass destruction, terrorist act, or threatened terrorist activity that poses peril so immediate and significant that requiring a legislative body to provide one-hour notice before holding an emergency meeting under this section may endanger the public health [or] safety."[118]

- *Need for "immediate action":* A legislative body can take action on items not on the agenda when the body finds by two-thirds vote of the members present (or by all members if less than two-thirds of the members are present) "that there is a need to take immediate

---

[111] *Moreno v. City of King*, 127 Cal. App. 4th 17 (2005).

[112] Government Code section 54952.2(a).

[113] The Legislature's purpose in limiting the length of these descriptions was merely to limit the dollar amount of reimbursement claims submitted by local agencies to the state. These claims were submitted for the cost of posting agenda descriptions under a law allowing local agencies to recover from the state any funds expended to implement a state mandated program. The Legislature has now amended section 54954.2 of the Act to state: "This section is necessary to implement and reasonably within the scope of paragraph (1) of subdivision (b) of Section 3 of Article I of the California Constitution." This amendment recognizes that Proposition 59 created a constitutional right of access to public meetings, which means that state reimbursement is no longer required.

[114] Government Code section 54954.2(a)(2).

[115] Government Code section 54954.2(a)(2).

[116] Government Code section 54954.2(b)(1).

[117] Government Code section 54956.5(a)(1).

[118] Government Code section 54956.5(a)(2).

action and that the need for action came to the attention of the local agency subsequent to the agenda being posted."[119] There must be a real "immediate need," however, and so this exception may not allow a public agency to address a topic not on the agenda even though citizens are asking it to do so. For example, a city council did not "need" to take immediate action on an unpopular decision of a planning commission simply because a large number of concerned citizens appeared at the council meeting to voice opposition to the planning commission's decision.[120]

- *Continued items:* A legislative body can take action on items not on the agenda when the item was posted as an agenda item not more than five calendar days before the date action is being contemplated and was "continued" at the prior meeting.[121]

4. Written Notice Must Be Provided Upon Request.

Anyone can request and receive by mail a copy of the agenda, or a copy of all the documents constituting the agenda packet, for any meeting of a legislative body subject to the Brown Act. The agenda or agenda packet must be mailed at the time the agenda is posted, or when they are provided to the members of the body, whichever is earlier. Note however, that because agendas only have to be provided 72 hours in advance, it is entirely possible that you will not receive the mailed materials in advance of the meeting. Furthermore, the failure of any person to receive notice by mail is not grounds for a court to invalidate any action taken by the agency at the meeting. A request for mailed copies is valid for the calendar year in which it is filed, and it must be renewed after January 1 of each year thereafter. The legislative body can establish a fee for mailing the agenda or agenda packet, but the fee cannot exceed the cost of providing the service.[122]

E. WHEN CAN A CLOSED SESSION BE HELD?

State law provides for several exceptions to the requirement that meetings be open and public. The exceptions give a legislative body authority to hold what are called "closed sessions" or "executive sessions."

A public body may hold closed sessions in the following circumstances: (1) To determine whether an applicant for a license or license renewal, who has a criminal record, is sufficiently rehabilitated to obtain the license;[123] (2) to meet with its negotiator to grant authority regarding the price and terms of payment for the purchase, sale, exchange or lease of real property ("real estate negotiations");[124] (3) to confer with, or receive advice from, its legal counsel regarding anticipated or pending litigation when discussion in open session concerning those matters would prejudice

---

[119] Government Code section 54954.2(b)(2).

[120] *Cohan v. City of Thousand Oaks*, 30 Cal. App. 4th 547 (1994) ("The appearance of a large number of interested citizens at the council meeting, many of whom had appeared at the planning commission hearing, was not a subsequently arising need to authorize an action to be taken. The Government Code does not include in its definition of 'emergency situation' a legislative body's wanting to ensure an unpopular planning commission decision is appealed.").

[121] Government Code section 54954.2(b)(3).

[122] Government Code section 54954.1. If requested, the agenda and documents in the agenda packet must be made available in appropriate alternative formats to people with disabilities, as required by the Americans with Disabilities Act.

[123] Government Code section 54956.7.

[124] Government Code section 54956.8.

the position of the local agency in the litigation ("litigation");[125] (4) to meet with the attorney general, district attorney, agency counsel, sheriff, or chief of police, or their respective deputies, or a security consultant or a security operations manager, on matters posing a threat to the security of public buildings, a threat to the security of essential public services, or a threat to the public's right of access to public services or public facilities;[126] (5) to consider the appointment, employment, evaluation of performance, discipline or dismissal of a public employee or to hear complaints or charges brought against the employee by another person or employee ("personnel");[127] (6) to meet with the local agency's designated representatives regarding the salaries, salary schedules or fringe benefits of its represented and unrepresented employees, and, for represented employees, any other matter within the statutorily provided scope of representation ("labor negotiations").[128] There are also a number of other narrow circumstances in which closed sessions may be held.[129]

By far the most frequently cited – and most controversial – closed-session provisions are those pertaining to "personnel" matters, labor negotiations, litigation and real estate deals. Each of these key provisions is discussed in detail below.

A Note on the Provisions that Allow Closed Sessions: Both the California courts and the California Constitution require that the provisions of the Brown Act that allow closed sessions must be "narrowly construed."[130] That means, in essence, that the closed-session provisions of the Brown Act should not be extended beyond the narrowest scope consistent with their terms. In addition, the Brown Act says that closed sessions may *only* be held under the limited provisions expressly allowing for closed sessions.[131] The fact that the session may address topics that are sensitive, embarrassing or controversial does not justify conducting a closed session unless it is authorized by some specific exception.[132] Rather, as the attorney general has noted, "these characteristics may be further evidence of the need for public scrutiny and participation in discussing such matters." [133] In short, if a closed session is not expressly allowed under the plain language of the Brown Act, it probably violates the Act.

If a closed session is held, only the members of the legislative body and others whose presence is required may attend; the body cannot admit others who may have an interest in the meeting without allowing the general public to attend.[134]

---

[125]   Government Code section 54956.9.

[126]   Government Code section 54957(a).

[127]   Government Code section 54957(b).

[128]   Government Code section 54957.6(a).

[129]   *See* Government Code sections 54956.86, 54956.87, 54956.95, 54957.8, and 54957.10. Because these provisions have much more limited application, they are not addressed here.

[130]   Cal. Const., Art. I, section 3(b)(2). *See also, e.g., Trancas Property Owners Assn. v. City of Malibu*, 138 Cal. App. 4th 172, 185 (2006); *Shapiro v. Board of Directors*, 134 Cal. App. 4th 170, 174 (2005); *Morrison v. Housing Authority of the City of Los Angeles Bd. of Commissioners*, 107 Cal. App. 4th 860, 873 (2003); *Shapiro v. San Diego City Council*, 96 Cal. App. 4th 904, 917 (2002); *San Gabriel Tribune v. Superior Court*, 143 Cal. App. 3d 762, 779 (1983).

[131]   Government Code section 54962 ("Except as expressly authorized by this chapter, or by Sections 1461, 1462, 32106, and 32155 of the Health and Safety Code or Sections 37606 and 37624.3 of the Government Code as they apply to hospitals, or by any provision of the Education Code pertaining to school districts and community college districts, no closed session may be held by any legislative body of any local agency.").

[132]   *Rowen v. Santa Clara Unified School District*, 121 Cal. App. 3d 231, 235 (1981).

[133]   *The Brown Act: Open Meetings For Local Legislative Bodies*, Office of the Attorney General (2003), p. 30.

[134]   46 Ops. Cal. Atty. Gen. 34, 35 (1965). *See also The Brown Act: Open Meetings For Local Legislative Bodies*, Office of the Attorney General (2003), p. 31.

1. "Personnel" Matters: Meetings About Specific Public Employees.

This exception applies only when the body considers the appointment, employment, evaluation of performance, discipline or dismissal of a specifically identified employee or candidate for employment.[135] The purpose of the exception is to prevent undue embarrassment to the public employee or candidate and to permit free and candid discussions of personnel matters by a local governmental body.[136]

"Evaluation of performance" is not restricted to formal, periodic review of the employee's job performance. It includes any review of an employee's job performance even if that review involves particular instances of job performance rather than a comprehensive review of such performance. It may also include consideration of the criteria for such evaluation, consideration of the process for conducting the evaluation, and other preliminary matters, to the extent those matters constitute an exercise of a legislative body's discretion in evaluating a particular employee.[137]

Examples of closed sessions permitted under the personnel exception include the meeting of a library commission specifically required by the city charter to participate in the selection of the city librarian, for the purposes of nominating three candidates for appointment by the mayor.[138] Another example is the evaluation of the performance of a school superintendent as part of determining whether to renew the superintendent's contract.[139]

a. Scope of closed sessions limited to discussions of specific employees. Only those aspects of a personnel discussion that involve a review of the appointment, employment, evaluation of performance, or dismissal of an employee or job applicant may be discussed in closed session. The exception does *not* apply to general discussions concerning employment classifications or general personnel problems where no employee or employees are specifically identified.[140]

b. Only "employees" can be discussed in closed session. The personnel exception applies only to discussions regarding employees or people being considered for positions as employees. Under the Act, "employee" is defined to include officers and independent contractors who function as employees.[141] Therefore, it is not limited to rank-and-file public employees.[142]

---

[135] Government Code section 54957(b).

[136] *Morrison v. Housing Authority of the City of Los Angeles Bd. of Commissioners*, 107 Cal. App. 4th 860, 873 (2003); *Bollinger v. San Diego Civil Service Commission*, 71 Cal. App. 4th 568, 574-575 (1999).

[137] *Duval v. Board of Trustees of Coalinga-Huron Join Unified School District*, 93 Cal. App. 4th 902, 908-909 (2001).

[138] *Gillespie v. San Francisco Pub. Library Comm'n*, 67 Cal. App. 4th 1165 (1998).

[139] *Duval v. Board of Trustees of Coalinga-Huron Join Unified School District*, 93 Cal. App. 4th 902, 909-910 (2001).

[140] *See, e.g., Santa Clara Federation of Teachers v. Governing Board,* 116 Cal. App. 3d 831, 846 (1981) (consideration of teacher layoff policy required to be conducted in open session); 63 Ops. Cal. Atty. Gen. 153 (1980) (creation of a new administrative position and the workload of existing positions had to be discussed in open session). *See also The Brown Act: Open Meetings For Local Legislative Bodies*, Office of the Attorney General (2003), pp. 35-36.

[141] Government Code section 54957(b)(4).

[142] For example, a decision not to rehire a district superintendent of a high school district was properly made in closed session. *Lucas* v. *Board of Trustees* (1971) 18 Cal. App. 3d 988, 990. Similarly, the California attorney general concluded that when a school board forms a committee composed of members of the community, district employees and a student, for the purpose of interviewing candidates for district superintendent and making recommendations to the board, the committee's sessions are not required to be open to the public. 80 Ops. Cal. Atty. Gen. 308 (1997).

However, the personnel exception does not apply when the individual under discussion is an elected official, a member of a local legislative body, or a candidate being considered to fill a vacancy on the legislative body itself, on one of the boards or commissions it appoints, or on one of the advisory committees it creates or supports.[143] In addition, the exception for public employee scrutiny does not apply to evaluations of independent contractors who do not function as employees. For example, the performance of an independent contractor retained to sell surplus land for a school district had to be discussed in open session.[144]

In addition, a body may not conduct a closed session if is does not have responsibility for making or participating in a personnel decision. For example, the attorney general concluded that a county board of education may not conduct a closed session on a personnel decision where that decision rested solely with the superintendent, and not with the board.[145]

c. Hearings on personnel matters must be open if requested by the employee. As a condition of holding a closed session "on specific complaints or charges brought against an employee by another person or employee," a body must give the employee or employees concerned at least 24 hours notice, and an employee may request that the hearing be open to the public.[146] In general, the courts have said that this right extends only to hearings on specific complaints or charges and does not apply to hearings on the general evaluation or consideration of appointment or discipline of an employee not based on specific complaints or charges.[147]

Some agencies have asserted the right to deliberate in closed session regarding complaints or charges brought against an employee after conducting a public session in response to an employee request. The legislative counsel, which advises the California Legislature, has concluded that they cannot.[148]

d. Individual salaries. Except for closed sessions to meet with a body's negotiator in bona fide labor relations situations concerning represented and unrepresented employees, "closed sessions may not include a discussion of or action on proposed compensation except for a reduction of compensation that results from the imposition of discipline."[149] Although the amount of a proposed increase may not be discussed in closed session, the employee's job performance may be discussed, including the threshold decision of whether the employee should receive any change in compensation. Once that decision is made, the body should discuss the amount of, and take action on, any change in compensation in open session. The issues of budget priorities, comparable salaries paid to other staff members generally or comparable jobholders in other

---

[143] Government Code section 54957(b)(4); *See also The Brown Act: Open Meetings For Local Legislative Bodies*, Office of the Attorney General (2003), p. 35.

[144] *Rowen v. Santa Clara Unified School District*, 121 Cal. App. 3d 231, 233 (1981).

[145] 85 Ops. Cal. Atty. Gen. 77 (2002).

[146] Government Code section 54957(b)(2).

[147] *See, e.g., Fischer v. Los Angeles Unified School Dist.*, 70 Cal. App. 4th 87 (1999); *Furtado v. Sierra Community College,* 68 Cal. App. 4th 876 (1998).

[148] In a May 15, 1996, letter to Sen. Quentin Kopp, the legislative counsel's office opined that the Brown Act does not allow a local agency to deliberate in closed session regarding complaints or charges brought against an employee after the employee demands a public session. Relying on *San Diego Union v. City Council*, 146 Cal. App. 3d 947 (1983), the legislative counsel reasoned that since any action taken in a closed session can be voided when notice to the employee is not given, "Section 54957 makes it clear that the right of the employee to request a public session is a significant right not to be ignored. Had the Legislature intended to authorize a local body to close a public session for subsequent deliberation, ... once complaints had been considered, ... that authorization would have been made when section 54957 was amended in 1994."

[149] Government Code section 54957(b)(4). *See also San Diego Union v. City Council,* 146 Cal. App. 3d 947, 955 (1983) ("Salaries and other terms of compensation constitute municipal budgetary matters of substantial public interest warranting open discussion and eventual electoral public ratification.").

public agencies or private enterprise can and must be discussed, if at all, in an open and public meeting.[150] In addition, the employment contract of every public employee, including pay, fringe benefits and job expectations and responsibilities, is accessible to the public under the California Public Records Act.[151]

e. Discussion of medical records of retirement applicants. The California attorney general has issued an opinion that the portion of a meeting of a county retirement board at which medical records are to be discussed in connection with an application for a disability retirement may be held in closed session.[152] The attorney general points to a provision of the Brown Act that requires reporting on action taken during a closed session: "Action taken to appoint, employ, dismiss, accept the resignation of, or otherwise affect the employment status of a public employee in closed session pursuant to Section 54957 shall be reported at the public meeting during which the closed session is held."[153] The attorney general infers that, because the information required to be reported after a closed session includes action that "otherwise affect[s] the employment status" of a public employee, a closed session to discuss any such action is permitted. Thus, the attorney general concludes that because granting a disability retirement affects the employment status of an employee, it can be discussed in closed session.

However, the Brown Act "personnel" exemption permits a closed session only to discuss "appointment, employment, evaluation of performance, discipline, or dismissal of a public employee or to hear complaints or charges brought against the employee. ..."[154] Retirement, whether pursuant to disability or otherwise, is not one of the topics that can be discussed. The requirement that an agency disclose any action taken in closed session that affects the employment status is apparently intended to prevent evasion of the reporting requirement by agencies claiming that they did something other than appoint, employ, evaluate, discipline or dismiss an employee – not to expand the scope of the closed-session provision.

2. Labor Negotiations

a. Local agencies in general. The Brown Act allows closed sessions to enable a local government body to instruct its designated representatives regarding negotiations with unions and other employee organizations, including negotiations about employee salaries, benefits and "any other matter within the statutorily provided scope of representation."[155] This provision essentially allows legislative bodies to meet in closed session with the agents who represent them in negotiating union contracts (known as "collective bargaining agreements") or other arrangements with "represented" employees. Represented employees are typically rank-and-file government employees.

A local government body can also meet in closed session with its representatives to discuss salaries and other compensation of "unrepresented employees."[156] Unrepresented employees are typically upper-level employees (such as department heads and the like). Discussions under this exception must be limited to compensation issues and do not extend to general employer-employee relations.

---

150   *San Diego Union v. City Council,* 146 Cal. App. 3d 947 (1983).
151   Government Code section 6254.8.
152   88 Ops. Cal. Atty. Gen. 16 (2005).
153   Government Code section 54957.1(a)(5).
154   Government Code section 54957(b)(1).
155   Government Code section 54957.6(a).
156   Government Code section 54957.6(a).

The closed sessions permitted by this exception must be held only for the purpose of reviewing the government's position and instructing its designated representatives.[157] For example, as the attorney general has said: "It should be emphasized that the labor negotiations exception applies only to actual bona fide labor negotiations, and a closed session may not be conducted where a legislative body merely wishes to set the salary of an employee."[158] When individual salaries are at issue, as noted in the personnel section discussed above, if the legislative body is not briefing its negotiating agent, only the discussions of the employee's performance or personnel qualifications may be discussed in closed session. Salary increases are budget issues that must be discussed in open session.[159]

Before adjourning to closed session, the agency must identify in open session its designated representatives (which may include members of the legislative body).[160] Under the Brown Act, local governments should also generally identify the organization with which it will be negotiating regarding represented employees or the job title of any unrepresented employees.[161]

Any approval of an agreement concluding labor negotiations has to be reported after the agreement is final and has been accepted or ratified by the other party. The report must "identify the item approved and the other party or parties."[162]

b. Special rules for school districts. The Rodda Act (Government Code Section 3540 et seq.) sets forth a comprehensive regulatory scheme for labor negotiations between public employees and school districts, county boards of education and county superintendents of schools.

When one of the following exemptions applies, the open meeting requirements of the Brown Act or other state open meeting laws are suspended unless the parties agree otherwise: (1) Any meeting and negotiating discussion between a public school employer and a recognized or certified employee organization; (2) any meeting of a mediator with either party or both parties; (3) any hearing, meeting or investigation conducted by a fact finder or arbitrator; or (4) any executive session of the public school employer or between the public school employer and its designated representative for the purpose of discussing its position regarding any matter within the scope of representation.[163]

To counteract the Rodda Act's suspension of the Brown Act's open meeting provisions, the Rodda Act sets forth special requirements mandating public access to information at certain stages of the negotiations. The statute specifies that all initial proposals of employee representatives falling within the Rodda Act must be presented at a public meeting of the public school employer "and thereafter shall become public records." In addition, the statute limits the right of the parties to enter into negotiations on the proposal until after the public has had sufficient time to review the proposal and make its own recommendations. The employer is then required to hold an open meeting at which it adopts its initial proposal. If new topics arise during the negotiations, they must be made public within 24 hours. The employer must also make public within 24 hours any votes taken by each member.[164]

---

[157]   Government Code section 54957.6(a).
[158]   *The Brown Act: Open Meetings For Local Legislative Bodies*, Office of the Attorney General (2003), p. 42.
[159]   *San Diego Union v. City of San Diego*, 146 Cal.App.3d 947 (1983).
[160]   Government Code section 54957.6(a).
[161]   Government Code section 54954.5(f).
[162]   Government Code section 54957.l(a)(6).
[163]   Government Code section 3549.1.
[164]   Government Code section 3547.

3. "Pending Litigation": Consulting with Attorneys.

When a legislative body's legal counsel advises it that a closed session is necessary to permit him or her to provide consultation regarding "pending litigation," the closed session is permitted if the discussion of the matter in open session would prejudice the body's position in the litigation.[165]

"Litigation" includes any "adjudicatory proceeding," meaning any proceeding in which the body's rights and obligations are to be contested and decided. Specifically included are eminent domain proceedings, court or quasi-judicial administrative hearings, trials or proceedings before a hearing officer or arbitrator.[166]

In all closed sessions for pending litigation, an attorney representing the body must be present.[167] For example, the exception would not allow a body to meet privately with an opposition party to negotiate a settlement. In addition, the pending litigation exception applies only to meetings involving the government agency that is a party to the litigation; it does not apply to meetings between the agency's attorney and another agency that is not a party to the litigation.[168]

Before conducting a closed session under the pending litigation exception, the body must include in the agenda or publicly announce the subdivision of the Act that authorizes the closed session. If the closed session is to discuss existing litigation, the case name must be disclosed unless to do so would jeopardize service of process or ongoing settlement negotiations.[169]

a. "Pending" defined. Litigation may be deemed "pending" in any of three situations: (1) Litigation has been formally commenced (*e.g.,* a lawsuit has been filed) and has not been finally adjudicated or otherwise settled; (2) based on certain existing facts and circumstances and the advice of its counsel, it is the opinion of the legislative body that a point has been reached where there exists "a significant exposure to litigation against the local agency;" or (3) based on certain existing facts and circumstances, the legislative body has decided to initiate litigation or is in the process of deciding whether to initiate litigation.[170]

b. "Facts and circumstances" limited. The Act, in an effort to limit the circumstances under which bodies may meet in closed session under the pending litigation exception, defines which "facts and circumstances" justify closed sessions. "Facts and circumstances" that create a significant exposure to litigation consist only of the following: (1) The agency believes that facts creating significant exposure to litigation are not known to potential plaintiffs (in which case the facts need not be disclosed); (2) facts creating significant exposure to litigation are known to potential plaintiffs, *e.g.*, a city vehicle causes an accident (in this case the facts must be publicly disclosed); (3) a claim or written communication threatening litigation is received by the agency (in which case the writing is available to the public); (4) a person makes a statement in an open meeting threatening litigation; or (5) a person makes a statement outside of an open and public

---

[165] Government Code section 54956.9.

[166] Government Code section 54956.9.

[167] *See The Brown Act: Open Meetings For Local Legislative Bodies*, Office of the Attorney General (2003), p. 40.

[168] *Shapiro v. Bd. of Directors*, 134 Cal. App. 4th 170 (2005).

[169] Government Code section 54956.9.

[170] Government Code section 54956.9(a)-(c). The body may hold a preliminary closed session to consider with counsel if a "significant exposure" exists to justify a closed session under the pending litigation exception.

meeting threatening litigation, and an agency official having knowledge of the threat makes a contemporaneous or other record of the statement before the meeting.[171]

c. Policy decisions required to be made in open session cannot be made in closed session. For example, a city council cannot "decide upon or adopt in closed session a settlement that accomplishes or provides for action for which a public hearing is required by law, without such a hearing."[172] Moreover, as the attorney general has stated: "The purpose of the exception is to permit the body to receive legal advice and make litigation decisions only; it is not to be used as a subterfuge to reach nonlitigation oriented policy decisions."[173]

4. Real Estate Negotiations: Price and Terms of Payment.

When a local agency governed by the Brown Act is negotiating the purchase, sale, exchange, lease or renewal of a lease of real property, the legislative body of the agency may – but is not required to – hold a closed session with its own bargaining agent. The closed session may only be held for the limited purpose of instructing the legislative body's negotiator(s) on price, payment terms or both.[174]

Before entering closed session, the body must first identify in open session its negotiator(s), the parcel(s) subject to the negotiations and the person(s) with whom it may be negotiating, *i.e.*, the prospective seller, purchaser, exchanger, lessor or lessee.[175] Failure to disclose this information in advance is a violation of the Brown Act.[176]

As with other closed-session provisions of the Brown Act, the agency's negotiator may be a member of the legislative body. However, government officials who are neither members of the legislative body nor its negotiators generally may not attend.[177]

Only price or payment terms may be discussed in closed session. Other factors affecting the transaction are not allowed to be discussed in closed session.[178] In addition, the confidentiality for such information is only temporary. The final price and payment terms must be publicly reported when the transaction is completed.[179]

---

[171]   Government Code section 54956.9(b)(3).

[172]   *Trancas Property Owners Assn. v. City of Malibu*, 138 Cal. App. 4th 172 (2006) (in closed session, city entered into a settlement in which it agreed to rescind a prior zoning decision, approve a development and exempt the development from certain zoning restrictions).

[173]   71 Ops. Cal. Atty. Gen. 96, 104-105 (1988). *Accord Trancas Property Owners Assn. v. City of Malibu*, 138 Cal. App. 4th 172 (2006).

[174]   Government Code section 54956.8.

[175]   Government Code section 54956.8.

[176]   *Shapiro v. San Diego City Council*, 96 Cal. App. 4th 904, 910 (2002) (City Council ordered to "identify its negotiators, the real property under negotiation and the persons with whom its negotiators may negotiate for each item of business, in an open and public session before each closed session").

[177]   83 Op. Cal. Atty. Gen. 221 (2000) (finding that a mayor, the designated executive head of a city pursuant to the city charter, may not attend a closed session of the city's redevelopment board because meetings "may not be semi-closed," and the mayor was not, under section 54956.8, the negotiator for the redevelopment association).

[178]   *Shapiro v. San Diego City Council*, 96 Cal. App. 4th 904, 910 (2002) (affirming injunction that required City Council to limit discussions at closed sessions to instructions to its negotiators regarding price and terms of payment for the purchase, sale, exchange or lease of specific real property by or for the city).

[179]   Government Code section 54957.1(a)(1).

5. Other Exceptions to the Open Meeting Requirement.

a. License applicants' criminal records. This exception applies when a person with a criminal record applies to a government agency for a license or a license renewal, and the legislative body determines that it is necessary to discuss whether the person is sufficiently rehabilitated to obtain a license.[180] The local body may meet with the applicant and his or her attorney in closed session for the purpose of holding the discussion and making the determination.

If the license is denied, the applicant has the opportunity to withdraw the application and nothing will be said publicly. If the applicant chooses not to withdraw, the action denying the application must be taken in open session. In any case, all matters relating to the matter discussed in closed session are confidential unless the applicant consents to disclosure or challenges the denial in court. Strangely, the Brown Act is silent with respect to what happens if the license is granted. Presumably, given that there is no authority to grant or deny a license in closed session, action to approve a license must be taken in public, but the information discussed in the closed session will not be disclosed.

b. Public facility security. The legislative body may meet in closed session with the attorney general, district attorney, law enforcement representatives or security consultants "on matters posing a threat to the security of public buildings, a threat to the security of essential public services, including water, drinking water, wastewater treatment, natural gas service, and electric service, or a threat to the public's right of access to public services or public facilities."[181] This exception could be triggered by acts of terrorism or milder disruptions.

c. Public hospitals and health plans. Many public hospitals are operated by cities or by local hospital districts. In addition, counties may oversee local health care service plans. The meetings of the governing boards of these public hospitals and health plans are subject to special requirements. The provisions governing the two categories of public hospitals (municipal hospitals and district hospitals) are nearly, but not quite, identical. In addition, there are special provisions allowing a city council involved in overseeing a municipal hospital to hold closed sessions in certain circumstances, and allowing closed sessions by the governing board of a health plan overseen by county government.

(1) Most meetings required to be open: Both district and municipal hospitals are generally required to make their meetings open to the public.[182] The board of trustees of a municipal hospital is apparently precluded by statute from using exemptions in the Brown Act to close meetings of the governing body. The statute that governs such boards requires all meetings to be open except as discussed below, and it does not incorporate the closed-session provisions of the Brown Act.[183] By comparison, the statute that governs district hospitals specifically provides that closed sessions may be held pursuant to the Brown Act.[184]

---

[180]   Government Code section 54956.7.

[181]   Government Code section 54957(a).

[182]   Government Code section 37606(a) (municipal hospitals); Health and Safety Code section 32106(a) (district hospitals).

[183]   Government Code section 37606(a) ("Except as provided in this section or Section 37624.3, all of the sessions of the board of trustees, whether regular or special, shall be open to the public, and a majority of the members of the board shall constitute a quorum for the transaction of business.").

[184]   Health and Safety Code section 32106(a) ("Except as provided in this section, Section 32155, or the Ralph M. Brown Act ... all of the sessions of the board of directors, whether regular or special, shall be open to the

(2) Special closed sessions by hospital boards: The same statutes allow governing bodies of public hospitals to close meetings to discuss certain issues. Both municipal and district hospitals may hold closed sessions

- *Quality assurance reports:* Hospital boards may hold closed-session meetings to discuss reports of the hospital medical audit or quality assurance committees. A member of the staff whose privileges are the direct subject of the report may request an open session. Deliberations of the board on these issues, however, can be held in closed session.[185]
- *Trade secrets:* Boards of directors of hospital districts and municipal hospitals may discuss reports involving trade secrets in closed session, but only "for the purposes of discussion or deliberation."[186] In other words, no action may be taken (within the meaning of the Brown Act).[187] A "trade secret" is information that is not generally known to the public or to competitors and that "derives independent economic value, actual or potential" by virtue of its restricted disclosure.[188] It also must be information that is necessary to initiate a new service or program or to add a facility, and that would, if prematurely disclosed, create a substantial probability of depriving the hospital of substantial economic benefit.[189] An example of a trade secret would be marketing information compiled by the hospital staff or a consultant showing the advantages or the demand for a certain new program or service in the community.

(3) Special closed sessions by city council: In 2006, the provisions permitting closed sessions by hospital boards were extended to city council meetings held to discuss reports of trade secrets of a hospital managed by a board of trustees that is appointed by the mayor.[190] According to the legislative history of the statute, "The bill affects only two municipal hospitals, located in El Centro and Needles. ..."[191]

(4) Specific limitations on closed sessions: The governing board of a public hospital, or a city council meeting to address the business of such a hospital, are specifically prohibited from holding a closed meeting for the purposes of discussing or deliberating issues relating to: (1) The sale, conversion, contract for management or leasing of any municipal or district hospital or its assets; (2) the conversion of any municipal or district hospital to any other form of ownership; or (3) the dissolution of any municipal hospital or hospital district.[192]

(5) Special closed sessions by governing boards of county-administered health plans. The governing board of a health care services plan that is overseen by a county board of supervisors

---

[185] public, and a majority of the members of the board shall constitute a quorum for the transaction of business.").

Government Code section 37624.3 (municipal hospitals); Health and Safety Code section 32155 (district hospitals).

[186] Government Code section 37606(b); Health and Safety Code section 32106(b).

[187] Government Code section 37606(d); Health and Safety Code section 32106(d).

[188] Government Code section 37606(c) and Health and Safety Code section 32106(c) incorporate the definition of trade secrets in Civil Code section 3426.1(d), and then add additional requirements.

[189] Government Code section 37606(c); Health and Safety Code section 32106(c).

[190] Government Code section 37606.1.

[191] S.B. 1801, Senate Floor Analysis (April 21, 2006), at p.2.

[192] Government Code section 37606(e); Government Code section 37606.1(d); Health and Safety Code section 32106(e).

can meet in closed session to discuss reports of trade secrets of the health plan.[193] It may also meet in closed session to consider and take action on contracts and contract negotiations by the health plan with providers of health care services concerning matters related to rates of payment.[194]

(6) Special closed sessions by the governing body of a local government agency that provides Medi-Cal services. The legislative body of a local government agency that provides health management services to Medi-Cal beneficiaries may hold closed sessions to address complaints by beneficiaries.[195] However, the beneficiary has the right to have the complaint heard in public.

d. Multi-jurisdictional law enforcement agencies. In California, local governments from different jurisdictions (for example, a group of cities) can join together for specified purposes to create a "joint powers agency" or "joint powers authority," known as a JPA. In various parts of California, local law enforcement agencies have established JPAs to cooperate on law enforcement.

In 2005, the California Court of Appeal held that a law-enforcement JPA was subject to the Brown Act and was required to hold its meetings in public, except to the extent that closed sessions are permitted by the Brown Act.[196] The court recognized that the Brown Act permitted JPAs created for drug law enforcement purposes to meet in closed session to address specific investigations.[197]

In response to this decision, the Brown Act was amended in 2006 to allow *all* "multi-jurisdictional law enforcement agencies" to meet in closed session to discuss the case records of any ongoing criminal investigation, to hear testimony from persons involved in the investigation and to discuss courses of action in particular cases.[198]

e. Early withdrawal of deferred compensation plan funds. In 2001, the state legislature added an exception allowing closed meetings when an employee requested an early withdrawal from deferred compensation plan funds due to "financial hardship arising from an unforeseeable emergency due to illness, accident, casualty, or other extraordinary event, as specified in the deferred compensation plan."[199]

f. Pension fund investments. In 2004, the state legislature added an exception that allows local government bodies that invest pension funds to hold closed sessions to consider "purchase or sale of particular, specific pension fund investments."[200]

g. Response to state audits. In 2004 the California Legislature added an exception permitting closed sessions to address a local government body's response to "a confidential final draft audit report from the Bureau of State Audits."[201] However, once the report has been made public, any discussion must be conducted in an open meeting.[202]

---

[193]   Government Code section 54956.87(b).
[194]   Government Code section 54956.87(c).
[195]   Government Code section 54956.86.
[196]   *McKee v. Los Angeles Interagency Metropolitan Police Apprehension Task Force*, 134 Cal. App. 4th 354 (2005).
[197]   *McKee v. Los Angeles Interagency Metropolitan Police Apprehension Task Force*, 134 Cal. App. 4th 354, 363 (2005), citing Government Code section 54957.8.
[198]   Government Code section 54957.8(b), as amended by A.B. 2945 (Sept. 22, 2006).
[199]   Government Code section 54957.10.
[200]   Government Code section 54956.81.
[201]   Government Code section 54956.75(a).
[202]   Government Code section 54956.75(b).

6. Additional Rules for Holding Closed Sessions.

a. Legislative bodies must describe the topics to be discussed in closed session. Before holding *any* closed session, the legislative body of the local agency must, in an open and public meeting, identify the item or items to be discussed in closed session. If the information required to be disclosed is contained on the posted agenda, the disclosure can take the form of a reference to the posted agenda. In the subsequent closed session, the legislative body may consider only those matters covered in this statement.[203]

b. No implied exceptions. Unless the legislative body is holding a closed session under one of the above explicitly listed categories, its proceedings must be open and public. Earlier speculation that the Act would permit implied exceptions was removed by 1987 legislation. At the urging of the California Newspaper Publishers Association, the Legislature passed Senate Bill 200, which established two points. First, there are no "implied" exceptions. Unless a closed session is expressly provided for in the Brown Act (or for hospital districts, in the Health and Safety Code rules on "hospital trade secrets"), it is not permitted.[204] Second, as a special application of this rule, there can be no closed session between a public board and its attorney other than the "pending litigation" sessions expressly provided for in the Brown Act.[205]

F. WHAT INFORMATION HAS TO BE DISCLOSED ABOUT CLOSED SESSIONS?

Before 1994, bodies governed by the Act were required to report very little information to the public concerning action taken in closed session. The Act now embraces the idea that action taken in permissible closed sessions should, in most circumstances, be reported to the public as soon as the action is taken, unless disclosure would threaten the reason for allowing the closed session in the first place (for example, if it might prejudice the agency in a lawsuit). Section 54957.1 of the Brown Act requires the body to report all actions taken in closed session and the vote or abstention of every member present.

Reports required to be made on closed-session actions can be made orally or in writing.[206] The body must provide to any person who has made a written request (either a request made with respect to a specific meeting or a standing request for all such documentation)[207] and who is present at the time the closed session ends copies of any contracts, settlement agreements or other documents that were finally approved at the closed session.[208]

The following information concerning different types of actions must be disclosed orally or in writing.

---

[203] Government Code section 54957.7(a). *Accord Shapiro v. San Diego City Council*, 96 Cal. App. 4th 904, 916-917 (2002).

[204] Government Code section 54962.

[205] Government Code section 54956.9.

[206] Government Code section 54957.1(b).

[207] *See* Government Code sections 54954.1 and 54956.

[208] Government Code section 54957.1(b). Note that if substantive amendments must be made to the documents, the documents need not be released until retyping can be accomplished during normal working hours of the agency. Documents in need of retyping must be available on the next business day following the meeting, or in the case of substantial amendments, when retyping is completed. Government Code sections 54957.1(b), (c).

1. Real Estate Transactions.

The body must report, in open session at the public meeting during which the closed session is held, its approval and the substance of any agreement approved in closed session. If final approval rests with the other party, the report must be disclosed upon inquiry, as soon as the other party has informed the agency of its approval.[209]

A Note on Real Estate Transactions: Be sure to mark your calendar to remind yourself to ask whether the other party approved the agreement and, if so, request a copy of the final agreement.

2. Litigation and Settlement.

a. Commencing a lawsuit or intervening in a pending case. When approval is given to initiate or intervene in a lawsuit, the body need not identify the action, the defendants or other particulars about the case. However, it must specify that the direction to initiate or intervene has been given, and once the lawsuit is formally commenced that information must be disclosed to any person upon inquiry, unless to do so would jeopardize service of process or existing settlement negotiations.[210]

A Note on Decisions to Commence Litigation: Although this part of the Brown Act lumps together initiating a new lawsuit and intervening in an existing lawsuit, those two situations are very different. An agency should be able to identify all of the required information about intervening as soon as the decision is made, because the lawsuit already exists. As to starting new lawsuits, once you are apprised that the decision to sue has been made, mark your calendars to remind yourself to request the information that must be released following formal commencement of the lawsuit. Once a decision is made, the lawsuit will probably be filed within a few days to a few weeks.

b. Appellate review. The body must report in open session immediately after the closed session any approval given to its legal counsel to defend an appeal, to seek appellate review or to refrain from seeking appellate review of a decision to which it is a party. It must also report any decision to participate as an amicus curiae, that is, a non-party "friend of the court" that files a brief in support of the position of one of the parties. The report must identify, if known, the adverse parties and the substance of the litigation.[211]

c. Settlement agreements. The body must report approval given to its legal counsel to settle pending litigation. If the legislative body accepts a settlement offer signed by the opposing party, the body must report its acceptance and identify the substance of the agreement in open session at the public meeting during which the closed session is held. If final approval rests with the opposing party or with the court, then as soon as the settlement becomes final, and upon inquiry by any person, the local agency must disclose the approval by the other party and the substance of the agreement.[212]

---

[209]   Government Code section 54957.1(a)(1).
[210]   Government Code section 54957.1(a)(2).
[211]   Government Code section 54957.1(a)(2).
[212]   Government Code section 54957.1(a)(3).

<u>A Note on Settlement Agreements.</u> Mark your calendar to remind yourself to ask whether the other party approved the agreement and, if so, request a copy of the final agreement. In addition, if copies of the approved settlement agreement are distributed to members of the agency at a public session, anyone in attendance at the meeting at which the approval is announced is also entitled to a copy of the agreement.[213] See Chapter 10 for a more detailed discussion of disclosure of settlement agreements.

d. Claims settled by joint powers authorities. Many local agencies governed by the Act are members of a joint powers agency (JPA) for the purpose of insurance pooling. JPAs that have local agencies as members are themselves "legislative bodies" governed by the Act.[214] The Brown Act allows JPAs to hold closed sessions to discuss claims for tort liability losses.[215] When claims discussed in closed session are resolved, JPAs are required to identify the claimant, the name of the local agency claimed against, the substance of the claim and any monetary amount approved for payment and agreed upon by the claimant.[216]

3. Public Employee Employment Status.

The body must report at a public meeting immediately following the closed session any action taken in closed session to appoint, employ, dismiss, accept the resignation of or otherwise affect the employment status of a public employee. The report of a dismissal or nonrenewal of an employment contract may be deferred until the first meeting after the completion of any administrative remedies the employee can seek, such as a civil service commission appeal or a grievance process set forth in a collective bargaining agreement.[217]

4. Labor Negotiations.

The body must report approval of an agreement concluding labor negotiations with represented employees after the agreement is final and has been accepted or ratified by the other party. The report must identify the item approved and the parties to the negotiation.[218]

G. HOW IS THE BROWN ACT ENFORCED?

Unless a local government body voluntarily agrees to reconsider action taken in violation of the Brown Act, or to modify a pattern of conduct that violates the Brown Act, the only meaningful remedy is to take the body to court. Unfortunately, although county district attorneys have the power to enforce the Brown Act, they almost never do. On the other hand, a citizen who pursues a case seeking to enforce the Brown Act and prevails may be entitled to recover attorneys' fees, which may make it possible to find an attorney who will take the case.

---

[213] Government Code section 54957.5.
[214] *McKee v. Los Angeles Interagency Metropolitan Police Apprehension Task Force*, 134 Cal. App. 4th 354 (2005).
[215] Government Code section 54956.95.
[216] Government Code section 54957.1(a)(4).
[217] Government Code section 54957.1(a)(5).
[218] Government Code section 54957.1(a)(6).

1. Any California Citizen Can Enforce the Brown Act.

Any California citizen can enforce a Brown Act violation by any local government body in the state. You do not have to be a citizen residing in the area served by that local government body.[219]

2. Nullifying Actions Taken in Violation of the Brown Act.

Any citizen or the county district attorney may seek court action to declare null and void any action that was taken in violation of the Brown Act.[220] "Action taken" means not only a formal vote but any commitment or agreement among a quorum of a legislative body to act or refrain from acting in a certain manner.[221]

A Note on Nullifying Action Taken in Violation of the Brown Act: The Brown Act imposes tight timing requirements on anyone seeking to nullify an action taken by a legislative body in violation of the Act. *You must act promptly, and you must meet all of the deadlines established by the Brown Act, or your lawsuit will probably be dismissed.* These requirements can be particularly onerous if the action you believe was improper was taken exclusively in closed session, making it nearly impossible to confirm the violation. If possible, get an attorney before you start the process.

a. **Procedure for nullifying actions taken.** As noted, the procedure for seeking to nullify action taken in violation of the Brown Act is critical. The following are the steps that must be followed in order to have an action nullified:

(1) Promptly demand that the action be cured or corrected. Before seeking a court invalidation of an illegally taken action, a party must send a written notice to the legislative body specifying the action claimed to be illegal and demanding that it be "cured or corrected."[222] If the violation arises from action taken on a topic that was not on the agenda for the meeting or based on a deficient agenda, notice to cure or correct must be given within 30 days of the action.[223] If the violation arises from action taken in closed session, the notice to cure or correct must be delivered within 90 days of the action.[224]

(2) Monitor the legislative body's response. From its receipt of the demand for correction, the legislative body has 30 days to correct the violation or to inform the person complaining that it does not intend to do so.[225] However, the time for filing a lawsuit seeking to nullify the body's action begins to run even if the legislative body does not respond.

(3)   If the action is not cured or corrected, promptly file a lawsuit. If the body responds to the notice by refusing to cure or correct, or if it takes no action to correct the action and provides no

---

[219]   *McKee v. Orange Unified School District*, 110 Cal. App. 4th 1310 (2003) (holding that "a citizen of the State of California is an 'interested person' within the meaning of sections 54960 and 54960.1 and may sue a legislative body of a local agency as provided in those sections for violations of the Brown Act.").

[220]   Government Code section 54960.1(a).

[221]   Government Code section 54952.6.

[222]   Government Code section 54960.1(b).

[223]   Government Code section 54960.1(c)(1).

[224]   Government Code section 54960.1(c)(1).

[225]   Government Code section 54960.1(c)(2).

response, a party seeking to nullify an action taken must file a lawsuit.[226] The lawsuit must be filed within 15 days of receipt of a refusal to correct. If the legislative body is silent, the lawsuit must be filed within 15 days of the end of the 30-day period for a response, that is, 45 days from the date the demand to cure or correct was sent.[227]

A Note on Curing and Correcting: The Act does not specify what a legally sufficient cure or correction might be, but presumably the legislative body should somehow reopen the process to permit public awareness of all the facts and views and give the public the opportunity to express its views on the proposal. Nothing prevents the person alleging the violation from demanding a specific form of corrective action. On the other hand, nothing prevents the legislative body, in correcting the violation, to reach a different result from that reached in violation of the Act. See Appendix D for a sample cure-and-correct letter.

b. Certain actions are immune from nullification. Actions taken in violation of the Brown Act are immune from invalidation under the following circumstances: (1) Action was taken "in substantial compliance" with the Act (this provision gives the court leeway to avoid reversing an action for a trivial or inconsequential violation); (2) action was taken in connection with the sale or issuance of bonds, notes or other revenue-raising debt instruments; (3) action was taken to award a contract, if the contractor has, "in good faith, detrimentally relied" on the validity of the contract (that is, spent a substantial amount of money or made other substantial commitments); (4) action was taken in connection with tax collection; or (5) action was taken in violation of notice or agenda provisions of the Act, if the plaintiff had actual notice of the item to be discussed at the meeting for the time period for which the notice was required to be posted.[228]

c. Effect of curing and correcting the violation. In any lawsuit to invalidate action by a body because of alleged violation of notice or agenda provisions, a court is allowed to dismiss the action with prejudice if it finds that the body has cured or corrected the error by subsequent action.[229]

2. Preventing Future Violations of the Brown Act.

Seeking to nullify a specific action taken by a legislative body is not the only way to enforce the Brown Act. Under section 54960 of the Act, a county district attorney or a citizen can sue to:

- Compel the local agency to comply with the Brown Act;
- Obtain a ruling that a particular practice of the local agency violates the Brown Act; or
- Obtain a ruling that the local agency is violating the free speech rights of one or more of its members in seeking to silence that member.[230]

In these situations, the short deadlines that must be met when seeking to set aside agency action do not apply.

---

[226]   Government Code section 54960.1(c)(4).
[227]   Government Code section 54960.1(c)(4).
[228]   Government Code section 54960.1(d).
[229]   Government Code section 54960.1(e).
[230]   Gov't Code section 54960(a).

Under section 54960 it is not necessary to demonstrate that violations of the Brown Act are ongoing or are "threatened." It is sufficient to show a pattern of past violations and that the agency has taken the position that its conduct is not a violation of the Brown Act.[231]

A Note on Enforcing the Brown Act: One court of appeal has held that a member of the public seeking to establish a violation of the Brown Act cannot use normal discovery processes available in other civil cases to compel public officials to disclose what took place in a closed session.[232] Although this decision appears to be contrary to both the purpose and the language of the Brown Act, it has not been reversed and may create a barrier to enforcement of the Act.

3. Disclosure of Closed Sessions Discussions by Participants.

The Brown Act prohibits disclosure of "confidential information" obtained at a closed session held pursuant to the Brown Act to "a person not entitled to receive it," unless the legislative body authorizes disclosure.[233] Confidential information is defined as "a communication made in a closed session that is specifically related to the basis for the legislative body of a local agency to meet lawfully in closed session under this chapter."[234] Thus, the prohibition does not apply if the closed session is not lawful, and it does not apply to statements that are not "specifically related" to the subject that justifies the closed session. The Act allows public officials who violate this restriction to be punished in a variety of ways, but it also specifically provides that the following are not a violation and cannot be punished:

> (1) Making a confidential inquiry or complaint to a district attorney or grand jury concerning a perceived violation of law, including disclosing facts to a district attorney or grand jury that are necessary to establish the illegality of an action taken by a legislative body ...
> (2) Expressing an opinion concerning the propriety or legality of actions taken by a legislative body of a local agency in closed session, including disclosure of the nature and extent of the illegal or potentially illegal action.
> (3) Disclosing information acquired by being present in a closed session under this chapter that is not confidential information.[235]

4. Criminal Enforcement of the Brown Act by the District Attorney.

A district attorney may also initiate a criminal action against a member or members of a legislative body for violations of the Act. The criminal standard creates misdemeanor liability for members of a body who attend a meeting where action is taken in violation of any provision of the Act and where "the member intends to deprive the public of information to which the member

---

[231] *Shapiro v. San Diego City Council,* 96 Cal. App. 4th 904, 913-917 (2002). *See also Duval v. Board of Trustees*, 93 Cal. App. 4th 902, 906-907 (2001); *California Alliance for Utility Etc. Education v. City of San Diego,* 56 Cal. App. 4th 1024, 1029-1031 (1997); *Common Cause v. Stirling,* 147 Cal. App. 3d 518 (1983) ("courts may presume that municipality will continue similar practices in light of city attorney's refusal to admit violation").

[232] *Kleitman v. Superior Court (Wesley)*, 74 Cal. App. 4th 324 (1999).

[233] Government Code section 54963(a).

[234] Government Code section 54963(b).

[235] Government Code section 54963(e).

knows or has reason to know the public is entitled under the Brown Act."[236] At the time of this publication, no individual has ever been convicted of a criminal violation of the Act.

5. Attorneys' Fees and Costs.

Under the Brown Act the "court may award court costs and reasonable attorney fees to the plaintiff ... where it is found that a legislative body of the local agency has violated this chapter."[237]

A decision that finds such a violation need not involve an issue of statewide impact or significance.[238] If the plaintiff prevails, fees are "presumptively appropriate" and a successful plaintiff should recover attorneys' fees unless special circumstances would make such an award unjust.[239] Courts are not obliged to award fees in every Brown Act case and must "thoughtfully exercise" their discretion by examining all the circumstances to determine whether an award of fees would be unjust. However, the burden of showing that an award of fees would be unjust rests on the government.[240]

In short, the trial court has the discretion to deny successful Brown Act plaintiffs their attorneys' fees, but only if the defendant shows that special circumstances exist that would make such an award unjust.[241]

PART III:
STATE GOVERNMENT – THE BAGLEY-KEENE ACT

A. INTRODUCTION TO THE BAGLEY-KEENE ACT.

The state body counterpart to the Ralph M. Brown Act is the Bagley-Keene Open Meetings Act. Similar to the requirements of the Brown Act, which is applicable to local government agencies, state agencies falling under the guidelines of the Bagley-Keene Act are generally required to conduct their meetings in public. Like the Brown Act, the Bagley-Keene Act specifically defines bodies covered by the Act, when closed sessions are allowed and what types of notice must be given. The provisions of the Bagley-Keene Act that permit closed sessions generally parallel those in the Brown Act.

Under Government Code section 11125, anyone wishing notice of meetings of state agencies covered by the Act can request notice in writing. Notice is required to be given to requesters within 10 days of any regularly scheduled meeting.

The Bagley-Keene Act is narrower in its application than the Brown Act. State government is dominated by executive agencies that are not required to conduct business at meetings (and hence are not subject to the Bagley-Keene Act), and by the State Legislature (which is governed by a

---

[236]   Government Code section 54959.

[237]   Government Code section 54960.5.

[238]   *Los Angeles Times Communications LLC v. Los Angeles County Bd. of Supervisors*, 112 Cal. App. 4th 1313, 1323-1324 (2003); *Common Cause v. Stirling,* 119 Cal. App. 3d 658, 664-65 (1981).

[239]   *Los Angeles Times Communications LLC v. Los Angeles County Bd. of Supervisors*, 112 Cal. App. 4th 1313, 1327 (2003); *Common Cause v. Stirling,* 119 Cal. App. 3d 658, 663 (1981).

[240]   *Los Angeles Times Communications LLC v. Los Angeles County Bd. of Supervisors*, 112 Cal. App. 4th 1313, 1323 (2003); *Common Cause v. Stirling,* 119 Cal. App. 3d 658, 665 (1981).

[241]   *Los Angeles Times Communications LLC v. Los Angeles County Bd. of Supervisors*, 112 Cal. App. 4th 1313, 1327 (2003).

separate set of rules and is not subject to the Bagley-Keene Act). However, there are many state bodies that *are* required to conduct their business at meetings, and most of those bodies are required to comply with the Bagley-Keene Act.

B. WHAT ARE MY RIGHTS UNDER THE BAGLEY-KEENE ACT?

1. Right to Attend Most Meetings of State Boards and Commissions That Do Their Business at Meetings.

The most fundamental right created by the Bagley-Keene Act is the right to attend meetings of state bodies that are subject to the Act. The Act states: "All meetings of a state body shall be open and public and all persons shall be permitted to attend any meeting of a state body except as otherwise provided in this article."[242] The act permits meetings to be held by teleconference "for the benefit of the public and state body."[243] However, special requirements apply to teleconferenced meetings.[244]

2. Right to Notice of Meetings.

The public has the right to some form of advance notice of all meetings, in both open and closed session.

a. Regular meetings must be noticed by providing notice and an agenda for the meeting at least 10 days in advance. Notice must be provided to anyone who makes a written request for notice and must also be made available on the Internet.[245]

b. Special meetings may be called, but only where "compliance with the 10-day notice provisions ... would impose a substantial hardship on the state body or where immediate action is required to protect the public interest."[246] Such meetings may be held only to address certain topics, such as litigation, proposed legislation or real estate deals. Notice must be given to each member of the state body and to all parties that have requested notice of its meetings "as soon as is practicable after the decision to call a special meeting." In addition, notice must be given to the members of the state body, provided to all national press wire services and made available on the Internet at least 48 hours before the meeting.[247]

c. Emergency meetings may be called under limited and drastic circumstances: (1) A work stoppage or other activity that "severely impairs public health or safety"; (2) a "crippling disaster that severely impairs public health or safety"; or (3) "to consider an appeal of a closure of or restriction in a fishery" or the "the disruption or threatened disruption of an established fishery."[248] One-hour notification of those media that have requested notice is required, if possible, and generally notice must also be made available on the Internet "as soon as practicable."[249]

---

[242]   Government Code section 11123(a).

[243]   Government Code section 11123(b).

[244]   Government Code section 11123(b).

[245]   Government Code section 11125(a), (b).

[246]   Government Code section 11125.4(a).

[247]   Government Code section 11125.4(b).

[248]   Government Code sections 11125.5 and 11125.6.

[249]   Government Code sections 11125.5(c) and 11125.6(c).

d. Closed sessions must be identified in an agenda posted and sent to those who have requested notice at least 10 days before each regular meeting and must be orally disclosed in open meeting held before the closed session.[250] The oral disclosure may be a reference to closed-session items listed in the posted agenda.[251]

3. Right to a Meaningful Agenda.

The public has the right to an agenda that contains a brief description of each item of business to be transacted.[252] The descriptions of agenda items must not be misleading.[253] A description of an item to be addressed in closed session must include a citation of the specific statutory authority under which a closed session is being held.[254]

4. Right to Have No Action Taken on Matters Not on the Agenda.

In general, action may not be taken on items that are not on the agenda for any regular meeting or special meeting.[255] The exceptions to this rule are: (1) When a majority of the body determines that an "emergency" exists that would justify an emergency meeting; or (2) upon a determination by a two-thirds vote of the state body, or, if less than two-thirds of the members are present, a unanimous vote of those members present, that there exists a need to take immediate action and that the need for action came to the attention of the state body after the agenda was posted.[256] In general, notice of the addition of items to the agenda for a meeting must be provided 48 hours in advance of the meeting and be posted on the Internet "as soon as practicable."[257]

5. Right to Materials Provided to the Members of the State Body.

In general, the public has the right to obtain copies of the agenda, background materials and any other writings related to matters for public discussion as soon as the materials are distributed to members of the legislative body, if they are not exempt from disclosure under the specific exemptions in the California Public Records Act (see Chapter 2).[258]

6. Right to Disclosure of Action Taken in Closed Session.

After the closed session has been completed, the body must reconvene in public.[259] However, the body is required to report only decisions to hire or fire an employee.[260]

---

[250]   Government Code sections 11125(b) and 11126.3(a).
[251]   Government Code section 11126.3(a).
[252]   Government Code section 11125(b). "A brief general description of an item generally need not exceed 20 words." *Id.*
[253]   *See The Brown Act: Open Meetings For Local Legislative Bodies*, Office of the Attorney General (2003), pp. 16-17, citing *Carlson* v. *Paradise Unified School Dist.,* 18 Cal.App.3d 196, 199 (1971) (construing Education Code section 966). *See also* 67 Ops. Cal. Atty. Gen. 84 (1984) (construing Bagley-Keene Act).
[254]   Government Code section 11125(b).
[255]   Government Code sections 11125(b) and 11125.4(b).
[256]   Government Code section 11125.3(a).
[257]   Government Code section 11125.3(b).
[258]   Government Code section 11125.1(a).
[259]   Government Code section 11126.3(f).
[260]   Government Code section 11125.2.

7. Right Not to Sign In.

Members of the public have the right to refuse to sign any attendance sheet as a condition of attending a meeting. Attendance sheets must state that those attending have a right to attend without signing.[261]

8. Right to Speak.

The public has the right to speak on any item on the agenda, before or during the body's discussion of the item in regular and special meetings, and to address the legislative body on any item of interest to the public during a regular meeting.[262] Agencies can adopt "reasonable" rules to limit the time for which a member of the public may speak or the amount of time allowed to address particular issues.[263] The state body cannot prohibit public criticism of the policies, programs or services of the state body or of the conduct of the state body.[264]

9. Right to Record, Videotape or Broadcast Meetings.

The public has the right to make an audio, video, photographic or other recording of a meeting and to broadcast a meeting absent a reasonable finding that continued recording or broadcast unavoidably will cause noise, illumination or obstruction of a view that constitutes a persistent disruption of the proceedings.[265]

10. Right to Remain in the Meeting.

A meeting may be closed to the public if it is seriously and intentionally disrupted. Before the public can be excluded, the body must try to restore order by removing only the individuals responsible for the disruption. If that fails, the public may be excluded. Even then, members of the media that did not participate in the disruption are allowed to remain. The body can allow those not involved in the disruption to be readmitted to the proceedings.[266]

11. Right to Non-Discriminatory Facilities.

Meetings may not be conducted in a facility that excludes people on the basis of their race, religion, color, national origin, ancestry or sex, or that is inaccessible to disabled people, or where members of the public may not be present without making a payment or purchase.[267]

C. WHAT MEETINGS ARE SUBJECT TO THE BAGLEY-KEENE ACT?

The Act applies only to "state bodies." Therefore, only meetings of state bodies are required to be open. The following types of state government bodies are subject to the Act:

---

[261]   Government Code section 11124.
[262]   Government Code section 11125.7(a).
[263]   Government Code section 11125.7(b).
[264]   Government Code section 11125.7(c).
[265]   Government Code section 11124.1.
[266]   Government Code section 11126.5.
[267]   Government Code section 11131.

- State boards, commissions or similar multimember bodies created by statute or required by law to conduct official meetings;

- State commissions created by executive order;

- Boards, commissions, committees or similar multimember bodies that exercise authority delegated to them by a state body;

- Advisory boards, commissions, committees and other advisory bodies of a state body, created by formal action of the state body or of any member of the state body, if the advisory body consists of three or more persons; and

- Boards, commissions, committees or similar multimember bodies on which a member of a state body serves in his or her official capacity as a representative of that state body, and that are supported, in whole or in part, by funds provided by the state body, whether the multimember body is organized and operated by the state body or by a private corporation.[268]

The Bagley-Keene Act does ***not*** apply to the courts, the Legislature, local government bodies governed by the Brown Act and certain other state government agencies.[269]

Furthermore, the Bagley-Keene Act specifically defines the type of "meetings" to which it applies. The definition closely parallels the Brown Act definition of "meetings." Like the Brown Act, it prohibits evasion of the requirement to conduct business in public meetings through the use of "serial meetings," *i.e.,* "any use of direct communication, personal intermediaries or technological devices that is employed by a majority of the members of the state body to develop a collective concurrence as to action to be taken on an item by the members of the state body. ..."[270]

According to the California attorney general: "The prohibition [on serial meetings] applies only to communications employed by a quorum to develop a collective concurrence concerning action to be taken by the body. Conversations that advance or clarify a member's understanding of an issue, or facilitate an agreement or compromise among members, or advance the ultimate resolution of an issue, are all examples of communications that contribute to the development of a concurrence as to action to be taken by the body. Accordingly, with respect to items that have been placed on an agenda or that are likely to be placed upon an agenda, members of state bodies should avoid serial communications of a substantive nature that involve a quorum of the body."[271]

D. WHEN CAN A CLOSED SESSION BE HELD?

Section 11126 of the Bagley-Keene Act includes a long list of topics that can be addressed in closed session.[272] Several of the closed-session provisions parallel similar provisions in the Brown Act. For instance, state bodies may hold closed sessions to address personnel matters,[273]

---

[268] Government Code section 11121.

[269] Government Code section 11121.1.

[270] Government Code section 11122.5.

[271] *A Handy Guide to The Bagley-Keene Open Meeting Act*, Office of the Attorney General (2004), p. 6.

[272] Government Code section 11126.

[273] Government Code section 11126(a) (state body may meet in closed session to address "appointment, employment, evaluation of performance, or dismissal of a public employee or to hear complaints or charges brought against that employee by another person or employee unless the employee requests a public hearing").

give instructions to their negotiators regarding real estate transactions,[274] confer with or receive advice from the agency's attorneys regarding pending litigation (if conducting a public session would prejudice the agency's position),[275] threats of criminal or terrorist activity[276] and the like. Presumably, these exceptions will be construed and applied in pretty much the same way as the parallel provisions of the Brown Act.[277] For example, the attorney general has stated that "although the personnel exception is appropriate for discussion of an employee's competence or qualifications for appointment or employment, we do not think that discussion of employee compensation may be conducted in closed session in light of an appellate court decision interpreting a similar exception in the Brown Act. ..."[278]

Other provisions of the Bagley-Keene Act allowing closed sessions by state bodies have no parallels in the Brown Act. For example, the Bagley-Keene Act expressly permits closed sessions for the purpose of deliberating on a decision to be reached in a proceeding required to be conducted under the state Administrative Procedure Act and similar laws.[279] Presumably, this provision exists because such proceedings are "adjudicative" hearings, conducted by administrative law judges, and the Legislature has determined that – like judges in the judicial courts – they should be able to deliberate in private.

In any event, state bodies are required to identify the provision pursuant to which a closed session is being conducted. If the closed session is not expressly permitted under the Bagley-Keene Act, it probably violates the law.[280]

E. HOW IS THE BAGLEY-KEENE ACT ENFORCED?

Like the Brown Act, the Bagley-Keene Act provides two main enforcement mechanisms. First, a lawsuit can be brought for the following purposes, without seeking to set aside any action taken by a state body at the meeting that is being challenged: (1) for the purpose of stopping or preventing violations or threatened violations of the Act; (2) to determine the application of the Act to past actions or threatened future action by members of the state body; or (3) to determine whether any rule or action by the state body to penalize or otherwise discourage the expression of one or more of its members is valid.[281] In 1999, the California Supreme Court held that an earlier version of this provision did not permit the public to obtain a determination from a court as to whether past actions of a state body violated the Act.[282] The Legislature responded almost

---

[274] Government Code section 11126(c)(7)(A) (state body may hold closed sessions "with its negotiator prior to the purchase, sale, exchange, or lease of real property by or for the state body to give instructions to its negotiator regarding the price and terms of payment for the purchase, sale, exchange, or lease").

[275] Government Code section 11126(e)(1) ("Nothing in this article shall be construed to prevent a state body, based on the advice of its legal counsel, from holding a closed session to confer with, or receive advice from, its legal counsel regarding pending litigation when discussion in open session concerning those matters would prejudice the position of the state body in the litigation.").

[276] Government Code section 11126(c)(18)(A) (state body may hold closed sessions to "consider matters posing a threat or potential threat of criminal or terrorist activity against the personnel, property, buildings, facilities, or equipment, including electronic data" of the state body, if disclosure of could compromise or impede their safety or security).

[277] *See Southern California Edison Co. v. Peevey*, 31 Cal. 4th 781, 797-801 (2003).

[278] *A Handy Guide to The Bagley-Keene Open Meeting Act*, Office of the Attorney General (2004), pp. 10-11, citing *San Diego Union v. City Council*, 146 Cal. App. 3d 947 (1983).

[279] Government Code section 11126(c)(3).

[280] Government Code section 11132.

[281] Government Code section 11130(a).

[282] *Regents of the University of California v. Superior Court*, 20 Cal. 4th 509 (1999).

immediately, adopting legislation that became effective on January 1, 2000, amending the Act to reverse the Supreme Court's decision.

Second, members of the public can bring a lawsuit seeking to have action taken in violation of the Act declared null and void.[283] As with the Brown Act, there are several categories of actions that are immune from nullification, even if taken in violation of the Act. Specifically, action cannot be declared null and void if: (1) The action taken was in connection with the sale or issuance of notes, bonds or other forms of debt; (2) the action taken gave rise to a contractual obligation upon which a party has, in good faith, relied; (3) the action taken was in substantial compliance with the Act; or (4) the action was taken in connection with the collection of any tax.[284]

A plaintiff who prevails in establishing a violation of the Bagley-Keene Act may (and should) be awarded attorneys' fees and costs.[285]

PART IV:
OTHER STATE OPEN MEETING LAWS

Several distinct regulatory schemes operate to open to the public the meetings and proceedings of some governmental bodies not covered by the Brown Act or the Bagley-Keene Act. In addition, some statutes overlap with the provisions of those acts, particularly the Bagley-Keene Act, creating a complicated relationship. A detailed discussion of each of these schemes is beyond the scope of this publication, but this section can be used to identify whether a body that does not appear to be regulated by the Brown Act or the Bagley-Keene Act may be regulated by another open meeting law. In addition, it addresses some of the additional provisions of state open meeting laws applicable to key agencies.

A. THE STATE LEGISLATURE.

1. General Open Meeting Requirement.

Open meeting laws for both houses of the California Legislature were enacted by Proposition 24 in 1984. Many of the proposition's provisions subsequently were judicially invalidated. In 1989, the Legislature repealed Proposition 24 and enacted the Grunsky-Burton Open Meeting Act.[286]

The Grunsky-Burton Act requires that meetings of either house or any committee of the Legislature be open and public.[287] Committees are defined to include a "standing committee, joint committee, conference committee, subcommittee, select committee, research committee, or any similar body."[288]

2. Notice Required for Open Sessions and Some Closed Sessions.

Section 9028 provides that whenever an open meeting is required, and also with respect to certain closed sessions, the body must provide public notice in accordance with the Joint Rules of

---

[283]   Government Code section 11130.3(a).
[284]   Government Code section 11130.3(b).
[285]   Government Code section 11130.5.
[286]   Government Code section 9027 and following.
[287]   Government Code section 9027.
[288]   Government Code section 9027.

the Assembly and Senate.[289] Although section 9028 expressly provides that even closed sessions are subject to the notice requirement, the attorney general issued an opinion in 1990 stating that no notice is required for closed sessions.

3. Permissible Closed Sessions.

Permissible reasons for a closed session include some of the same exemptions in the Brown Act applicable to local government agencies, including: (1) evaluation, hiring and dismissal of employees;[290] and (2) consultation with counsel concerning pending litigation.[291] Closed sessions also are authorized to consider matters affecting the safety and security of members of the Legislature and their staff and for party caucuses.[292]

4. Enforcement.

A violation of the Grunsky-Burton Act is a misdemeanor.[293] In addition, members of the public may bring a lawsuit to prevent future violations or to determine the application of the Act to actions or threatened future actions of the Legislature.[294] However, there is no provision for the recovery of attorneys' fees.

B. THE BOARD OF REGENTS OF THE UNIVERSITY OF CALIFORNIA.

The California Constitution provides that meetings of the Board of Regents are to be open and public, except as provided by statute.[295] In addition, the Regents are subject to the Bagley-Keene Open Meetings Act, except as otherwise provided in the California Education Code.[296] However, special statutes provide the Regents with more exceptions to the open meeting requirements than are granted to other public entities.[297]

In addition to the exemptions provided by the Bagley-Keene Act, the Education Code provides the Regents with broader (and more ambiguous) exemptions for discussions regarding "property" and "litigation."[298] Further closed sessions are permitted for discussion of national security matters (including, presumably, virtually anything dealing with the universities' involvement in national nuclear weapons laboratories), the conferring of honorary degrees, matters involving gifts, devises and bequests, and others.[299]

In 1994, the law was amended to limit the ability of Regents to hold closed sessions to address employee compensation issues. These provisions allow closed-session "consideration" of compensation, but they require actual actions on compensation issues concerning the principal officers of the Regents and the officers of the university – salary, benefits, prerequisites, severance

---

[289]   Government Code section 9028 ("Any meeting that is required to be open and public pursuant to this article, including any closed session held pursuant to subdivision (a) of Section 9029, shall be held only after full and timely notice to the public as provided by the Joint Rules of the Assembly and Senate.").

[290]   Government Code section 9029(a)(1).

[291]   Government Code sections 9029(a)(3), 9029.5.

[292]   Government Code sections 9029(a)(2), 9029(b).

[293]   Government Code section 9030.

[294]   Government Code section 9031.

[295]   California Constitution, Article IX, section 9.

[296]   Education Code section 92030.

[297]   Education Code sections 92032, 92032.5.

[298]   Education Code section 92032(b)(5), (6).

[299]   Education Code section 92032(b)-(g).

payments, retirement benefits, or any other form of compensation – to be taken in open session.[300] "Specific proposals" concerning compensation for university officers must be made available to the Regents and the public prior to the meeting on the issue.[301]

But Regents committees may meet in closed sessions to discuss Medi-Cal contract negotiations for university hospitals; to discuss nominations of individual Regents as officers of the board or as appointees to committees; and to discuss the proposal of an individual as a student Regent. A special search or selection committee may meet privately to interview candidates for university officer positions without giving notice to the media or public. The interesting result is that while its meetings are to some extent subject to the access and notice rules in the Bagley-Keene Act, the Board of Regents is not a "state body" under the Act, and neither are the governing bodies at the University of California campuses.[302]

In any event, it is clear that all discussions by the Board of Regents that are not expressly covered by the exceptions noted above are to be open and public. The notice provisions will depend on whether the meeting is regularly scheduled, in which case the Bagley-Keene Act's 10-day notice would apply, or specially called, in which case notice must be hand-delivered or mailed to each newspaper and each television or radio station that has requested notice in writing, so that the notice can be published or broadcast at least 72 hours before the time of the meeting.[303]

C. STUDENT AUXILIARY ORGANIZATIONS.

1. California State University.

a. **Student body organizations.** The Gloria Romero Open Meeting Act,[304] enacted in 2000, applies to the governing bodies and most committees of student body organizations on California State University ("CSU") campuses and stateside student body organizations representing CSU students. It requires them to comply with open meeting requirements that closely parallel the Brown Act. As with the Brown Act, 72 hours advance notice is required through the public posting of an agenda.[305] Action generally can only be taken on items on the agenda (except in emergencies, as under the Brown Act).[306] The public (including, obviously, students) is entitled to copies of agenda packets.[307] The public is entitled to address the governing body.[308] Closed sessions may be held in circumstances similar to those in which they are allowed under the Brown Act.[309] Closed sessions must be publicly announced in advance,[310] and certain actions taken in closed session must be disclosed.[311] However, the Act apparently contains no enforcement mechanism, so it is not clear how violations are established or remedied.

---

300   Education Code sections 92032(b)(7), 92032.5.
301   Education Code section 92032.5.
302   *Tafoya v. Hastings College*, 191 Cal. App. 3d 437 (1987); 66 Ops. Cal. Atty. Gen. 458 (1983).
303   Education Code section 92032(a).
304   Education Code sections 89305-89307.4.
305   Education Code section 89305.5(b)(1).
306   Education Code sections 89305.5(b)(2), 89306.5.
307   Education Code section 89305.7.
308   Education Code section 89306.
309   Education Code section 89307.
310   Education Code section 89307(b)(7).
311   Education Code section 89307(d).

b. Auxiliary organizations. The California Education Code requires open meetings for certain auxiliary organizations of the California State University system. The organizations covered and rules applicable begin with Section 89900 of the Education Code.

The following are among the auxiliary boards covered by open meeting laws:

- Any entity in which an official of the university participates as a director as part of his or her official duties;

- Any entity that operates a commercial service for the benefit of a campus of the university, on a campus or other university property; or

- Any entity whose "governing instrument" (*i.e.,* its charter, bylaws, articles of incorporation or similar set of rules) provides in substance both that (1) its purpose is to promote or assist any campus or to receive gifts, property and funds to be used for the benefit of a campus (or any person or organization having an official relationship with the campus), and (2) any of its directors, governors or trustees is appointed by, nominated by or subject to the approval of any campus of the university.[312]

Organizations such as the student council and their various boards and commissions are covered under this regulatory scheme. Note, however, that not all "student organizations" are covered.[313] Organizations expressly removed from the regulatory scheme include fraternities and sororities.

Bodies governed by these statutes must take action on issues in public meetings (in the absence of an applicable exception), and notice of meetings must be given to requesting parties. Specific guidelines relating to expenditure of funds also are spelled out in detail under the statutes, which should be referred to for specific questions.

2. University of California.

No state open meeting laws are applicable to associated bodies of University of California campuses. When access is denied to meetings of these bodies, students, members of the public and reporters should look to the bylaws or constitution from which the body derives authority. In most cases, these writings guarantee at least students (including student reporters) access to meetings. For non-students, however, access to meetings may not be possible when the body seeks to keep the public out.

3. Community Colleges.

The California attorney general has concluded that a student body association of a community college is a legislative body subject to the open meeting requirements of the Brown Act.[314]

---

[312]   Education Code section 89901.
[313]   Education Code section 89902.
[314]   75 Ops. Cal. Atty. Gen. 143 (1992).

PART V:
FEDERAL GOVERNMENT MEETINGS

As discussed above, federal government agencies are subject to an entirely different set of laws. In general, federal government agencies are executive and do not conduct the majority of their business through meetings. Nonetheless, meetings can play a significant role in the formation and implementation of government policy. For example, the meetings of the White House Energy Task Force under the direction of Vice President Cheney have been said to have been central to the formation of the United States national energy policy and to have significantly affected international relations.

A. THE "GOVERNMENT IN THE SUNSHINE ACT."

In the early 1970s, partially in response to the Watergate scandal, Congress enacted the Government in the Sunshine Act along with other anti-secrecy legislation. Congress intended the Act to open the government's deliberation processes to public scrutiny. This law, added to the Administrative Procedures Act in 1976, is considerably longer and denser than the Brown Act, chiefly due to the exceptions from the general open meeting requirement for executive branch agencies.

The Act applies to agencies "headed by a collegial body composed of two or more individual members ... and any subdivision thereof authorized to act on behalf of the agency."[315] The Act requires that "every portion of every meeting of an agency shall be open to public observation."[316] There are 10 specific exemptions allowing closed meetings for discussions of matters that are likely to result in disclosure of: (1) national defense and foreign policy; (2) internal personnel rules and practices; (3) statutory exemptions; (4) proprietary information; (5) accusation of crime or formal censure; (6) personal privacy; (7) investigatory records; (8) financial institution reports; (9)(A) financial speculation and stability; (9)(B) frustration of proposed agency action; and (10) issuance of subpoenas, participation in civil actions or proceedings, or formal agency adjudications.[317]

The Act does not require an agency to hold meetings, but it does contain procedural requirements that must be followed when an agency decides to meet for either a closed or open session. First, at least one week prior to each meeting, the agency must make a public announcement regarding the date, time and place of the meeting and whether the meeting is to be open or closed.[318] Second, to close all or a portion of a meeting, an agency must vote to do so and make publicly available a written copy of the vote and a full written explanation for the closure.[319] Also, the agency's general counsel must publicly certify that the meeting may be closed under one of the Act's exemptions.[320] Third, copies of the transcript, minutes or recording of each public meeting must be made promptly available to the public at the cost of duplication.[321]

A lawsuit may be brought in federal court to enforce the Government in the Sunshine Act, and in any such lawsuit the burden is on the government to justify its actions.[322]

---

[315] United States Code, Title 5, section 552b(a)(1) (5 U.S.C. §552b(a)(1)) (2005).
[316] United States Code, Title 5, section 552b(b) (5 U.S.C. §552b(b)) (2005).
[317] United States Code, Title 5, section 552b(c) (5 U.S.C. §552b(c)) (2005).
[318] United States Code, Title 5, section 552b(e)(1) (5 U.S.C. §552b(e)(1)) (2005).
[319] United States Code, Title 5, section 552b(d) (5 U.S.C. §552b(d)) (2005).
[320] United States Code, Title 5, section 552b(f)(1) (5 U.S.C. §552b(f)(1)) (2005).
[321] United States Code, Title 5, section 552b(f)(2) (5 U.S.C. §552b(f)(2)) (2005).
[322] United States Code, Title 5, section 552b(h)(1) (5 U.S.C. §552b(h)(1)) (2005).

To identify the agency or agencies dealing with a given subject, contact the Federal Citizen Information Center at http://www.info.gov or 1-800-333-4636. The Center also has copies of the Federal Register and is prepared to assist in searches for meeting announcements. For those needing to photocopy a meeting announcement, copies of the Federal Register are usually available in the main branches of the larger metropolitan libraries. The Federal Register can also be searched online at http://www.gpoaccess.gov/fr/index.html. For more information on how the Act operates, the Reporter's Committee on Freedom of the Press maintains a toll-free information line at (800) 336-4243. The Student Press Law Center at (703) 807-1904 provides free legal assistance to student journalists, advisers and others asking on their behalf.

B. FEDERAL ADVISORY COMMITTEE ACT.

Congress enacted the Federal Advisory Committee Act (FACA) in 1972.[323] Its purpose was to ensure that advice rendered to the executive branch by the various advisory committees, task forces, boards and commissions formed over the years by Congress and the president be both objective and accessible to the public. The Act created a process for establishing, operating, overseeing and terminating advisory bodies, and it also created the Committee Management Secretariat (MCC), which is to monitor and report on executive branch compliance with the Act. In 1976, the president delegated to the administrator of the General Services Administration (GSA) all responsibilities for implementing the Act.

FACA applies to all federal advisory committees other than those established by the CIA and Federal Reserve System unless expressly exempted by Congress.[324] All federal government agencies are required to establish guidelines and controls for advisory committees, consistent with directives of the Administrator of GSA.[325]

An "advisory committee" is any committee, board, commission, council, conference, panel, task force or other similar group that is established by statute or organization plan, established or utilized by the president, or established or utilized by one or more agencies for the purpose of providing advice or recommendations to the president or one or more agencies or offices of the federal government.[326]

Under the provisions of the Federal Advisory Committee Act, federal agencies sponsoring advisory committees must:

- Arrange meetings for reasonably accessible and convenient locations and times;
- Publish adequate advance notice of meetings in the Federal Register;
- Open advisory committee meetings to the public, as a general rule;
- Make available for public inspection, subject to the Freedom of Information Act, papers and records, including detailed minutes of each meeting; and
- Maintain records of expenditures.[327]

Advisory committee meetings may be closed or partially closed to the public based upon provisions of the Government in the Sunshine Act.[328]

---

[323]   United States Code, Title 5, Appendix 1 (5 U.S.C. App. 1), hereafter referred to as "FACA."

[324]   FACA, section 4.

[325]   FACA, section 8.

[326]   FACA, section 3.

[327]   FACA, sections 10, 11, 12; *The Federal Advisory Committee Act (FACA) Brochure*, U.S. General Services Administration, Office of Governmentwide Policy, Committee Management Secretariat (http://www.gsa.gov).

FACA has been criticized both for creating barriers to interaction between citizen groups and the government, and for being easily evaded. However, it does provide some public access to federal government meetings. Further information on the requirements of the Federal Advisory Committee Act can be obtained from the General Services Administration's Committee Management Secretariat at (202) 273-3556.

PART VI:
PRIVATE ORGANIZATIONS AND ASSOCIATIONS

By definition, the meetings of private organizations and associations are not open to the general public in the sense that an outsider has an enforceable legal right to be given notice to attend. This is the case no matter how powerful, influential or otherwise consequential the group may be.

On the other hand, as discussed above, if a legislative body of a local public agency enters into certain relationships with a private organization and its governing body, the latter may become subject to the Brown Act as a special kind of legislative body.

In addition, as the result of the enactment in 1998 of Health and Safety Code section 101860, private corporations that receive $50 million or more in public assets for the operation of a hospital are subject to many of the open meeting and open record requirements of the Bagley-Keene Act and California Public Records Act. While applicable to any entity that meets the triggering requirements, the legislation was primarily intended to apply to a merger between the University of California, San Francisco Medical Center and Stanford University Health Care.

There are other ways to gain access to meetings of private entities. One approach is to join and pay dues to local organizations that have organized bylaws providing specific participation rights to their members. Membership rights of private associations often are legally enforceable. If the organization in question is a publicly traded corporation, the purchase of shares will provide some legal right of access to meetings and corporate documents not enjoyed by the general public.

Additionally, nonprofit corporations file 1099 forms annually with the California Department of Corporations. These forms are accessible as public records through the Department of Corporations. See Chapter 2 for a more thorough discussion of accessing public records.

---

[328]   FACA, section 10(d); *The Federal Advisory Committee Act (FACA) Brochure*, U.S. General Services Administration, Office of Governmentwide Policy, Committee Management Secretariat.

CHAPTER 2

Access to Public Records

IN THIS CHAPTER

The California Public Records Act (CPRA) is the law that allows the public and journalists to access the records of government. The law covers all state and local agencies with the exception of the state Legislature, which is covered by its own law, and the courts. On the national level, the Freedom of Information Act covers records held by the federal government. The CPRA presumes that all records held by government are accessible to the public unless expressly made exempt from disclosure. It gives members of the public two main rights: the right to inspect records free of charge and the right to obtain a copy of records after paying for the direct costs of duplication or a statutory fee. Copies of records held in an electronic format must generally be provided in any form in which the agency holds the information. The law gives agencies time periods for responding to a request and provides that no provision of the law can be used to delay or obstruct access. There are hundreds of exemptions to access in the law. However, these exemptions must be narrowly applied by agencies and the courts. If a record contains exempt and public information, agencies are generally required to segregate the exempt_information and disclose the rest. Once a request is made, the agency must either produce the records in a reasonable amount of time or justify its decision to withhold the record by showing that the record is exempt under an express provision of law or that the public interest in disclosure of the record is clearly outweighed by the public interest in nondisclosure. The CPRA allows a member of the public to sue to enforce the law and provides that a prevailing plaintiff can recover attorney fees and costs of bringing the suit.

PART I:
OVERVIEW OF THE LAW

There are three branches of government: the judicial, the legislative and the executive. The judicial branch consists of the courts (Superior Court, Court of Appeal and Supreme Court), and the administrative body that runs the courts. The legislative branch consists, in California, of the State Assembly and the State Senate, along with their administrative staff. The executive branch consists of the governor and other statewide offices (such as attorney general and secretary of state), and executive agencies such as the state Department of Education.

At the state level, government is also divided into state and local government agencies. Examples of local government agencies include a city council, a county board of supervisors, city or county planning departments, and police and sheriff's departments. Local government bodies such as a city council or county board of supervisors typically act as both legislative and executive bodies.

Several different laws govern your right to obtain access to government records. For the most part, different laws apply to different parts of the government. The following is a list of the primary laws regarding access to public records in California.

Law	Application
California Constitution, Article I, Section 3(b), known as "Proposition 59"	State executive agencies and all local government agencies. Exemption for the Legislature, but its scope has not been defined. No exemption for the courts, but application to the courts is not yet settled.
California Public Records Act (Government Code sections 6250-6277)	State executive agencies and all local government agencies. The Legislature and the courts are exempt.
Legislative Open Records Act (Government Code sections 9070-9080)	State Legislature.
Local Sunshine Ordinances	Local government agencies, in places where such local ordinances have been adopted.
Freedom of Information Act (United States Code, Title 5, section 552)	Federal executive agencies.

This chapter focuses on California law, and in particular on the statewide laws: the California Public Records Act and Proposition 59. It also provides a brief summary of the Legislative Open Records Act, local Sunshine Ordinances and the Freedom of Information Act.

PART II:
THE CALIFORNIA PUBLIC RECORDS ACT

A. HOW DOES THE CALIFORNIA PUBLIC RECORDS ACT WORK?

The California Public Records Act (CPRA)[1] is the most important law providing the public in California with access to records held by state and local government agencies. The CPRA recognizes the importance of public access to information in government records:

> In enacting this chapter, the Legislature, mindful of the right of individuals to privacy, finds and declares that access to information concerning the conduct of the people's business is a fundamental and necessary right of every person in this state.[2]

The way the CPRA works is fairly simple (although applying it to particular records can be quite complicated). As the California Office of the Attorney General says: "The fundamental precept of the CPRA is that records shall be disclosed to the public, upon request, unless there is a specific reason not to do so."[3] In essence, it works as follows:

---

[1]   Government Code sections 6250-6277.
[2]   Government Code section 6250.
[3]   *Summary of the California Public Records Act, 2004*, California Office of the Attorney General, p. 2.

- All public records are subject to disclosure (i.e., a requester may inspect the records and obtain a copy) unless they fall within one of the exemptions created by the Public Records Act.[4]
- "Public records" are broadly defined. The definition of public records in the CPRA includes most documents generated or used by the government.[5]
- The CPRA is subject to numerous exemptions. There are a number of categorical exemptions in Government Code section 6254 that are often used by public agencies to deny access to records. There is a general "Catch-All" exemption created by Government Code section 6255. In addition, there are several hundred exemptions not included in the CPRA itself, but set forth in other statutes and incorporated into the CPRA under Government Code section 6254(k). Government Code sections 6275-6276.48 provide a list of many (but not all) of the statutes that may limit disclosure of information contained in public records.

The CPRA creates a presumption that all records held by government agencies are public.[6] An agency that denies access to a requested record has the burden of establishing a legal justification for its decision.[7] In addition, when a request for records is denied, the agency is required to provide the requester with the reasons it denied the request.[8]

B. WHAT AGENCIES ARE GOVERNED BY THE ACT?

1. State Agencies.

The CPRA applies to all state agencies except the Legislature and the courts.[9] Courts and court administrative bodies (such as the Judicial Council and the Administrative Office of the Courts) are not subject to the CPRA. Access to court records is governed by constitutional and common law principles established by case law, by the California Rules of Court and by separate statutes governing certain court records. State legislative records are not available under CPRA. There is a separate statute that governs records of the Legislature (the Legislative Open Records Act).[10]

2. Local Agencies.

The CPRA applies to all local agencies, including school districts and any board or commission of a city, county or other political subdivision.[11] In addition, if a legislative body is subject to the Brown Act (the law governing meetings held by local agencies – see Chapter 1) it is subject to the CPRA.[12] Thus, the CPRA also applies to certain private, nonprofit entities that perform governmental functions.

---

[4]   Government Code sections 6253, 6254.
[5]   Government Code section 6252(e).
[6]   Government Code section 6253(a).
[7]   Government Code section 6255(a).
[8]   Government Code section 6253(c).
[9]   Government Code section 6252(a), (f).
[10] Government Code sections 9070-9080.
[11] Government Code section 6252(b).
[12] Government Code section 6252(a), which incorporates Government Code section 54952, subdivisions (c) and (d), part of the definition of a "legislative body" under the Brown Act.

3. Other Agencies: Proposition 59.

The coverage of Proposition 59 (Article I, section 3(b) of the California Constitution) appears to be broader than that of the CPRA. Specifically, courts and court administrative bodies may be subject to a constitutional right of access under Proposition 59.

C. WHAT ARE PUBLIC RECORDS?

The Public Records Act creates a right to see public records. It defines "public records" as "any writing containing information relating to the conduct of the public's business prepared, owned, used, or retained by any state or local agency regardless of physical form or characteristics."[13] Here is what that definition means in practice.

1. Writing.

A "writing" includes handwritings, photographs, films, sound recordings, maps, magnetic tape, computer disks – virtually any means of recording any form of communication.[14] Computer data is included in the definition of a public record.[15]

2. Containing information relating to the conduct of the public's business.

The requirement that a record relate to the conduct of the public's business is broadly construed, and rarely contested.[16] According to the legislative history of the CPRA:

> This definition is intended to cover *every conceivable kind of record that is involved in the governmental process*. ... Only purely personal information unrelated to "the conduct of the public's business" could be considered exempt from this definition, *i.e.*, the shopping list phoned from home, the letter to a public officer from a friend which is totally void of reference to governmental activities.[17]

3. Prepared, owned, used or retained by state or local agency.

The records do not necessarily have to be in the actual custody of the public agency if they are prepared, owned or used by the agency.

4. Regardless of physical form or characteristics.

Information retained in an electronic format must be made available in any electronic form in which the agency keeps the information.[18]

---

[13] Government Code section 6252(e).

[14] Government Code section 6252(g).

[15] Government Code sections 6252(e), 6253.9.

[16] *See, e.g., California State University v. Superior Court,* 90 Cal. App. 4th 810, 824-25 (2001); *San Gabriel Tribune v. Superior Court*, 143 Cal. App. 3d 762, 774 (1983).

[17] Assembly Comm. on Statewide Information Policy, Appendix 1 to Journal of Assembly (1970 Reg. Sess.) Final Report p. 9.

[18] Government Code section 6253.9(a).

D. HOW DO I GET ACCESS TO RECORDS?

Under the CPRA, there are two ways to get access to records: You may go the office of the agency and inspect the records, or you may request copies of records. In either case, you need to make a request that identifies the records you need.

1. Making a Request

To get access to public records, you must ask for them. Your request must "reasonably describe an identifiable record or records."[19] The CPRA does not require you to make a request in writing. However, there are advantages to making a written request. First, it creates a record of your request, which may be useful in showing exactly what you requested and when you made the request. Second, if you make a request in writing, the agency is required to give you a written response.[20]

You do not have to provide your name or address when you make a request. Nothing in the CPRA requires you to provide that information, if you choose not to do so.

You are not required to state the purpose of your request. The CPRA says: "This chapter does not allow limitations on access to a public record based upon the purpose for which the record is being requested, if the record is otherwise subject to disclosure."[21]

<u>Some Notes on Requests</u>: Making a request for public records is not difficult. Many kinds of records should be routinely and readily available, for example: minutes of open meetings of government agencies, and contracts that public agencies have entered into with companies. However, you will often encounter confusion or resistance when you seek public records. The following are some tips on how to make a request:

- The way you request records may affect how likely you are to get them. If you have previously received records without making a written request, or if you know the government employee you are going to ask and get along with them, a simple, informal request may be best. A written request might create unnecessary concern. On the other hand, if you expect to meet resistance or think you may be going to court to try to force a public agency to provide information, a written request may be better.
- Remember that the Public Records Act applies to records. If possible, describe the records that the agency keeps that contain the information you want, not just the information you are seeking. If you know or suspect that the records contain information that you do not need and that the agency may be reluctant to disclose, offer to let the agency redact the unnecessary information.
- You are not required to explain the purpose of your request. However, in some circumstances the law permits a balancing of the public interest served by getting the information against the public interest in keeping it secret. In enforcing a request for records, you may be required to explain how the public will be benefited by disclosure. You may get the records you want if you can explain how disclosure will help the public generally.

---

[19] Government Code section 6253(b).
[20] Government Code section 6255(b).
[21] Government Code section 6257.5.

- If you send a formal request letter, it also may be helpful to cite a court decision that supports your position. Some of those decisions are listed in the footnotes for this chapter. The California First Amendment Coalition maintains a hotline, which you can use to ask for court decisions that have addressed certain types of records, at: http://www.cfac.org/content/index.php/cfac/legal. CNPA members can get assistance from the association's legal helpline or go to www.cnpa.com. Another source is the California attorney general's *Summary of the California Public Records Act 2004*, at: http://www.ag.ca.gov/publications/summary_public_records_act.pdf.
- A form for a written request for records pursuant to the CPRA is in Appendix C. You can also find a sample letter online at http://www.cfac.org/templates/cpraletter.html.

2. Inspection

Under the CPRA, records must be available for inspection during the regular office hours of the agency.[22] Agencies may adopt procedures to be followed, but such procedures can't limit hours during which records are available.[23] Some agencies are required to adopt written guidelines for accessibility of records and to make those guidelines available free on written request.[24]

A Note on Inspection: The CPRA allows public agencies a certain amount of time to respond to a request for *copies* of public records but says that records must be available for inspection during regular business hours. Therefore, under the CPRA, you may be able to get a quicker response if you go to the agency and ask to inspect records.

3. Copying

You are entitled to obtain a copy of public records.[25] The agency must respond to a request for a copy of a public record within 10 days. The time for responding can be extended by the agency for an additional 14 days in "unusual circumstances."[26] The CPRA defines "unusual circumstances" as:

(1) The need to search for and collect the requested records from field facilities or other establishments that are separate from the office processing the request.
(2) The need to search for, collect, and appropriately examine a voluminous amount of separate and distinct records that are demanded in a single request.
(3) The need for consultation, which shall be conducted with all practicable speed, with another agency having substantial interest in the determination of the request or among two or more components of the agency having substantial subject matter interest therein.
(4) The need to compile data, to write programming language or a computer program, or to construct a computer report to extract data.

---

[22] Government Code section 6253(a).
[23] *See Bruce v. Gregory*, 65 Cal.2d 666 (1967) (the custodian of records may "formulate reasonable regulations necessary to protect the safety of the records ... [or] to prevent inspection from interfering with the orderly function of his office and its employees").
[24] Government Code section 6253.4.
[25] Government Code section 6253(b).
[26] Government Code section 6253(c).

You are entitled to an exact copy unless it is impracticable to provide one.[27] You are entitled to obtain copies of electronic records in electronic form. Information held by an agency in any electronic format that constitutes an identifiable public record shall be made available as follows:

(1) Agencies shall make the information available in any electronic format in which it holds the information; and

(2) Agencies shall make the record available in any format requested if the format is one the agency uses to make copies for its own use or for provision to other agencies.[28]

4. Cost of Copies

Public agencies may charge a fee "covering direct costs of duplication" (or a statutory fee).[29] You are required to pay these costs in order to obtain copies. "Direct cost" generally does not include search and retrieval time.[30] "Direct cost" does include maintenance costs and the salary of the clerk for time spent copying (essentially, what a copy shop would charge – usually 10-25 cents per page, except for unusual copies, such as building plans). Counties may be allowed, by statute, to charge fees that exceed the "direct costs of duplication" for copies of certain documents, so long as the fees do not exceed the amount reasonably necessary to recover the cost of providing the copy.[31]

The fees that may be charged for obtaining an electronic copy vary. They are generally limited to the direct cost of providing a copy in an electronic format.[32] However, in certain circumstances a public agency can charge "the cost of producing a copy of the record, including the cost to construct a record, and the cost of programming and computer services necessary to produce a copy."[33] Such charges are allowed when:

(1) The public agency would be required to produce a copy of an electronic record and the record is one that is produced only at otherwise regularly scheduled intervals; or

(2) The request would require data compilation, extraction, or programming to produce the record.[34]

A Note on Charges for Copies: Unfortunately, many government agencies look at the CPRA as a burden rather than as part of their responsibility to serve the public. As a result, some agencies have tried to either deter record requests or profit from them by charging high copying costs. This has become a frequent practice with respect to requests for electronic records. There are steps you can take to address this problem. First, if you ask to *inspect* but not to receive a copy of a record, the agency cannot charge any amount to comply with the request. Second, public agencies are required to assist the public in determining what records are available.[35] You can try to use this requirement to get the agency to assist you in identifying exactly what the existing

---

[27]   Government Code section 6253(b).
[28]   Government Code section 6253.9(a).
[29]   Government Code section 6253(b).
[30]   *North County Parents Organization v. Department of Education*, 23 Cal. App. 4th 144, 146 (1994).
[31]   85 Ops. Cal. Atty. Gen. 225 (2002).
[32]   Government Code section 6253.5(a)(2). *But see* Government Code section 6253.9(b).
[33]   Government Code section 6253.9(b).
[34]   Government Code section 6253.9(b).
[35]   Government Code section 6253.1(a).

records are, and then request existing records that do not require the agency to produce a record it does not have or do any "data compilation, extraction, or programming."

5. Records Containing both Exempt and Non-exempt Information

If a public agency claims that some – but not all – of the information in a record is exempt from disclosure, you are entitled to the non-exempt portion of the record if it is "reasonably segregable."[36] Therefore, when an agency rejects a request for a record based on the fact that the record contains some exempt material, it is important to determine just how much of the information is in fact exempt. Where it would not be too onerous a task, the agency is required to segregate or redact the exempt information and provide you with the rest.

A Note on Asking for Non-exempt Information: An agency may not expressly say that only some of the information is exempt. The agency may say, for example, that the record you have requested "contains" information exempt from disclosure under the Public Records Act. It is a good idea to ask whether the agency considers any of the information you are seeking to be available to the public. When you make a written request for records, always include a request that the agency provide any reasonably segregable, non-exempt information.

6. Assistance in Obtaining Records

Government Code section 6253.1 obligates public agencies to assist the public to make focused and effective requests that reasonably describe identifiable records. Public agencies are required, to the extent reasonable, to do all of the following:

- Assist the public in identifying records and information responsive to the request or purpose of the request;
- Describe the information technology and physical location in which the records exist;
- Provide suggestions for overcoming any practical basis for denying access to the records or information sought.

A Note on Requesting Assistance: Always include in your written requests for records a request for assistance pursuant to Government Code section 6253.1. In general, ask the agency to identify the records or information responsive to your request and to describe their location. Note, however, that a public agency probably does not have an obligation to provide you with a list of all records described in your request.[37]

E. WHAT RECORDS ARE EXEMPT FROM DISCLOSURE?

1. Introduction

Although the Public Records Act applies to nearly all information held by state or local government agencies, that does not mean you will get the information you are seeking. The CPRA provides many exemptions, and it incorporates hundreds more tucked away in other laws.

---

[36]   Government Code section 6253(a).

[37]   *Haynie v. Superior Court*, 26 Cal. 4th 1061, 1072-1075 (2001). However, note that the *Haynie* case was decided before enactment of 6253.1, which imposes an obligation on public agencies to assist the public with getting information.

Under the CPRA, the public has the right to inspect and copy records held by government agencies unless an exemption applies. The burden is on the agency wishing to deny access to provide the legal basis for its position by showing that the records are covered by a specific exemption, or by showing that – based on the facts of a particular case – the public would be better served by maintaining the secrecy of the information than by making it available.[38]

Keep in mind, however, that even if there is an applicable exemption or a potential justification for non-disclosure, the exemptions created by the CPRA itself are discretionary, not mandatory. An agency may allow inspection unless disclosure is prohibited by law.[39] In addition, if an agency has disclosed the information you are requesting to someone else, it may have waived its right to claim that the information is exempt from disclosure.[40]

2. How the Exemptions Work

As noted, the CPRA contains a list of exemptions. Some of these apply to categories of records, such as drafts or personnel records. These are often called "general" exemptions.

Some of the exemptions in the CPRA apply to a very limited or specific type of records, such as records of Native American graves, cemeteries and sacred places maintained by the Native American Heritage Commission.[41] The CPRA also exempts records made confidential under federal law or other state laws. Government Code section 6254(k) incorporates literally hundreds of these specific statutory exemptions, most of which are listed at the end of the CPRA (Government Code sections 6275 and following). These are often called "specific" exemptions.

Finally, the CPRA includes a "catch-all" exemption, which the government may invoke when no specific exemption applies. Government Code section 6255(a) says:

> The agency shall justify withholding any record by demonstrating that the record in question is exempt under express provisions of this chapter *or that on the facts of the particular case the public interest served by not disclosing the record clearly outweighs the public interest served by disclosure of the record*.[42]

Not all of these exemptions can be discussed in this publication. However, the most frequently invoked general exemptions, some of the specific exemptions and the "catch-all" exemption are discussed below.

3. General Exemptions

a. Drafts and notes. Preliminary drafts, notes or memos not normally retained in the ordinary course of business are exempt, provided the public interest in withholding them outweighs the public interest in disclosure.[43]

This exemption requires an agency that wants to withhold records to show at least three things: (1) the requested records are notes, drafts, or memoranda; (2) the record is one that the agency would

---

[38] Government Code section 6255.

[39] Government Code section 6254 ("Nothing in this section prevents any agency from opening its records concerning the administration of the agency to public inspection, unless disclosure is otherwise prohibited by law.").

[40] Government Code section 6254.5. *See also Black Panther Party v. Kehoe,* 42 Cal. App. 3d 645, 656-57 (1974).

[41] Government Code section 6254(r).

[42] Government Code section 6255(a) (emphasis added).

[43] Government Code section 6254(a).

not normally retain in the ordinary course of business; and (3) the public's interest in disclosing the record clearly outweighs the public interest in making the record public.

The primary court decision addressing the "drafts" exemption is *Citizens for a Better Environment v. Department of Food and Agriculture*, 171 Cal. App. 3d 704 (1985). In this case, the California Court of Appeal established a three-step process to determine whether the exemption applies:

- First, it applies only to documents that are "pre-decisional," namely records that contribute to the reaching of some administrative or executive determination. The final report of a public agency describing its decision on a particular subject, or a follow-up report on the effectiveness of an earlier decision, would probably not meet this first requirement unless it was also prepared in the process of reaching a new decision.

- In addition, the exemption applies only to documents that are not normally kept on file. The court of appeal said that "[i]f preliminary materials are not customarily discarded or have not in fact been discarded as is customary they must be disclosed."

- Assuming a document is pre-decisional and not customarily retained "in the ordinary course of business," the exemption may apply to any portion of its contents that amounts to "recommendatory opinion." That is, statements as to what can or should be done may be withheld under the exemption, but other portions that consist of factual reporting or observations have to be disclosed. For example, suppose a city planning department conducts a survey and concludes that there are 4,000 homeless people in the city. If, in a preliminary report on the survey, the department recommends the city contribute money toward construction of a homeless shelter, the factual finding of 4,000 homeless people must be disclosed, but the recommendation for a shelter may be exempt from disclosure (at least in the preliminary report).

The attorney general has also issued opinions regarding the exemption for drafts, notes and memoranda. The attorney general has said that:

- Tape recordings of city council meetings, made for the purpose of allowing the city clerk to prepare minutes, are not exempt from disclosure, because there is no public interest in withholding them.[44]

- Interim grading documents, including geology reports, compaction reports and soils reports, submitted by a property owner to a city's building department in conjunction with an application for a building permit, are not exempt from disclosure because they are retained in the ordinary course of business, and because the public interest in disclosure outweighs the public interest in withholding them.[45]

A Note on the Drafts Exemption: If an agency denies a request for records and this section of the CPRA is cited, a good way to check on the agency's assertion is to ask for similar documents from other time periods or related to other projects. If those are produced, it may mean that the agency retains that type of record in its ordinary course of business. Remember that – as with all of the exemptions – the burden to justify withholding a record is on the agency, which must show that *all* the requirements of the exemption apply.

---

[44] 64 Ops. Cal. Atty. Gen. 317 (1981).
[45] 89 Ops. Cal. Atty. Gen. 39 (2006).

b. Pending litigation and attorney-client privilege. The CPRA contains two provisions that exempt from public disclosure certain records relating to legal matters. The first covers records that are related to "pending" litigation. The second exemption covers records that are attorney-client communications or attorney "work product" protected by the California Evidence Code.

(1) Pending litigation. Records pertaining to pending litigation, to which a public agency is a party, are exempt from disclosure if certain requirements are met.[46] The requirements that must be met in order to justify nondisclosure are:

- The records must have been prepared for use in the litigation.[47] (Note that the exemption is broader than the attorney work-product exemption; it protects any records generated by a public agency in anticipation of litigation.)[48]
- The litigation must be ongoing – the exemption no longer applies when the litigation is resolved.[49] (Note, however, that records protected by the attorney-client privilege or attorney work-product doctrine, discussed below, remain exempt from disclosure even after the litigation is resolved.)[50]

It's important to keep in mind that the only records exempted under this section are those created *after* a lawsuit has begun. In general, records that were created prior to the filing of a claim or lawsuit against a public agency are not exempt from disclosure despite their relationship to the litigation, unless the records in question are covered by the attorney-client privilege or attorney work-product doctrine.[51] For example, if a city decides to sue a contractor for poor work on a project, the original contract between the city and the contractor is still subject to public inspection, but a memorandum written by the city attorney explaining why she thought the contract was breached would not be public.

Court decisions disagree as to whether the litigation exemption applies to documents other than those created by the public agency itself. One court decision held that a claim form submitted under the California Tort Claims Act (which generally requires those who are considering suing a government official or agency to submit a claim form to the government first) is subject to disclosure under the CPRA.[52] In doing so, the court of appeal said that the exemption was intended "to protect only documents created by the public entity."[53] On the other hand, another court rejected that rule and said that the exemption applies to correspondence from an opposing

---

[46]   Government Code section 6254(b).

[47]   *County of Los Angeles v. Superior Court (Axelrad)*, 82 Cal. App. 4th 819, 830 (2000); *City of Hemet v. Superior Court*, 37 Cal. App. 4th 1411, 1420 (1995).

[48]   *Fairley v. Superior Court*, 66 Cal. App. 4th 1414, 1422, n. 5 (1998).

[49]   Government Code section 6254(b) (" ... until the pending litigation or claim has been finally adjudicated or otherwise settled.").

[50]   71 Ops. Cal. Atty. Gen. 5 (1988) ("The lawyer-client privilege and work-product rule, when relied upon by a public officer, do not automatically terminate with the settlement or adjudication of the underlying claim.").

[51]   *Fairley v. Superior Court*, 66 Cal. App. 4th 1414 (1998) (holding that the CPRA's pending litigation exemption applies only to documents or other records prepared for use in litigation); 71 Ops. Cal. Atty. Gen. 235 (1988) ("Records generated in the ordinary course of a public agency's business which may be relevant in future litigation to which the agency might be a party are not exempt from disclosure under subdivision (b) of section 6254 before a claim is filed with the agency or litigation against it commences. Nor do such records become exempt from disclosure under the subdivision once a claim is filed or litigation against the agency actually commences.").

[52]   *Poway Unified School District v. Superior Court of San Diego County*, 62 Cal. App. 4th 1498 (1998).

[53]   *Poway Unified School District v. Superior Court of San Diego County*, 62 Cal. App. 4th 1498, 1504 (1998).

counsel or party, which is in the possession of a governmental entity being sued, if it was intended that such correspondence not be disclosed outside the litigation.[54]

Because the litigation exemption applies only to records created for use in litigation, the fact that the requested record is "involved in litigation" may not be sufficient to allow the agency to withhold the record. Try to determine when and why the record was prepared and to get some idea what it contains. If the record was created prior to any legal action, it is subject to public review absent the application of another exemption.

The fact that you are in litigation with the government does not prevent you from using the CPRA to get records. The CPRA may be used to obtain documents generated in litigation in which the requester is a party.[55] The same is true if you have not yet sued the government but may have a claim against it that could result in litigation.[56] The court of appeal has said that records are available to every person in the state, and "[t]here is no exception for persons who may potentially have a claim for damages against a governmental agency."[57] Moreover, discovery in litigation is limited to records that are relevant to the issues in the litigation. Disclosure under the Public Records Act is not limited in that way. Thus, you are "entitled to the broader categories of documents available under the CPRA."[58] However, the "primary purpose" of the litigation exemption is to prevent litigants from using the CPRA "'to accomplish earlier or greater access to records pertaining to pending litigation or tort claims than would otherwise be allowed under the rules of discovery.'"[59] Therefore, it may not be possible to get records that could not be obtained through the litigation discovery process.

(2) Attorney-client privilege. Also exempt under the CPRA are records the disclosure of which would violate the California Evidence Code's provisions governing the attorney-client privilege and the work-product doctrine. The protections for such records are not expressly listed in the CPRA. Rather, they are incorporated into the CPRA by Government Code section 6254(k). That provision applies to: "Records, the disclosure of which is exempted or prohibited pursuant to federal or state law, including, but not limited to, provisions of the Evidence Code relating to privilege."

In general, California law provides that confidential communications between a lawyer and his or her client are privileged and do not have to be disclosed.[60] In addition, materials created by an attorney in the course of representing a client, known as "work product," are generally protected from disclosure.[61] (An attorney's conclusions, opinions, legal research or theories are nearly always protected. Other kinds of work product, such as factual information gathered by an attorney, is given only qualified protection and may be subject to disclosure if a sufficient need is shown.).[62]

The California Supreme Court has ruled that the attorney-client exemption covers communications that are made pursuant to pending litigation as well as those that are not: "The attorney-client privilege applies to confidential communications made within the scope of the attorney-client relationship even if the communication does not relate to pending litigation; the

---

[54]   *Board of Trustees of California State University v. Superior Court*, 132 Cal. App. 4th 889, 899-901 (2005).
[55]   *City of Los Angeles v. Superior Court*, 41 Cal. App. 4th 1083 (1996).
[56]   *Wilder v. Superior Court*, 66 Cal. App. 4th 77 (1998).
[57]   *Wilder v. Superior Court*, 66 Cal. App. 4th 77, 82-83 (1998).
[58]   *Wilder v. Superior Court*, 66 Cal. App. 4th 77, 83 (1998).
[59]   *Roberts v. City of Palmdale*, 5 Cal. 4th 363, 372 (1993).
[60]   Evidence Code sections 954, 955.
[61]   Code of Civil Procedure section 2018.030.
[62]   Code of Civil Procedure section 2018.030.

privilege applies not only to communications made in anticipation of litigation, but also to legal advice when no litigation is threatened."[63]

One particularly problematic application of the protection for attorney-client communications and attorney work product is to internal investigations of misconduct by public officials or employees.

(3) Specific records. The following describes some types of records that are often the subject of requests that may involve the litigation exemption or the attorney-client and work product protections, and whether those records are required to be made public.

- *Settlement Agreements.* Parties to litigation, including public agencies, often attempt to keep the terms of the settlement of their case confidential. When one of the parties to the case is a government agency, regardless of the type of case, the courts have said that the terms of the settlement are a matter of public record pursuant to the CPRA.[64]
- *Claims forms.* Claims forms submitted under the California Tort Claims Act must be disclosed under the CPRA.[65]
- *Depositions.* The litigation exemption does not make transcripts of depositions taken in a lawsuit exempt from disclosure.[66]
- *Correspondence from parties who have sued the government.* Correspondence from an opposing counsel or party involved in litigation with a government agency is exempt from disclosure, if it was intended that the correspondence not be disclosed outside the litigation.[67]
- *Legal bills.* One situation in which the attorney-client privilege is often asserted is when a request is made for legal bills paid by a government agency to a private law firm. Most agencies that receive requests under the CPRA for records of amounts paid to law firms take the position that the bills are exempt from disclosure under the attorney-client exemption. Many times they argue that because bills generally contain a description of the work performed, disclosure could prejudice the agency's position with respect to their legal adversary. Some agencies have argued that merely releasing the amount of monies expended could, in particular cases, prejudice their position. However, legal bills, like other records held by government agencies, are presumptively a matter of public record. While there may be portions of the bill that could prejudice the agency, the burden is on the agency to demonstrate that fact and redact those portions of the record before providing the remaining portions to the requester. Unless the information in the bill would prejudice the legal position of the agency in the case, it should be released. As a general rule, the amount of the bill always should be a matter of public record. There is no court decision allowing agencies to withhold such information.

c. Personnel, medical, and similar files.[68] This exemption, known as the "personnel exemption," is routinely invoked when the public agency believes a request seeks information pertaining to identifiable public officials or employees that is private or controversial. However,

---

[63]   *Roberts v. City of Palmdale*, 5 Cal. 4th 363 (1993).
[64]   *Register Division of Freedom Newspapers v. County of Orange*, 158 Cal. App. 3d 893 (1984); *Copley Press, Inc. v. Superior Court*, 63 Cal. App. 4th 367 (1998).
[65]   *Poway Unified School District v. Superior Court of San Diego County*, 62 Cal. App. 4th 1498 (1998).
[66]   *Board of Trustees of California State University v. Superior Court*, 132 Cal. App. 4th 889, 901 (2005).
[67]   *Board of Trustees of California State University v. Superior Court*, 132 Cal. App. 4th 889, 899-901 (2005).
[68]   Government Code section 6254(c).

this exemption was developed to protect intimate details of personal and family life, not official business judgments and relationships.[69]

The following are examples of situations in which the personnel exemption has been applied or rejected:

- *Salary information*: The California Supreme Court has held that the names and salaries of individual public employees are generally required to be made public.[70]

- *Investigations of employee misconduct*: The California courts have established a fairly liberal standard for disclosure of public records relating to complaints or investigations of misconduct by public employees. They have held that there is a public policy against disclosure of "trivial or groundless charges," but that "**where the charges are found true, or discipline is imposed**, the strong public policy against disclosure vanishes; this is true even where the sanction is a private reproval. In such cases a member of the public is entitled to information about the complaint, the discipline, and the 'information upon which it was based.'"[71] In addition, they have held that "**where there is reasonable cause to believe the complaint to be well founded, the right of public access to related public records exists**."[72] Furthermore, with respect to high-level public servants, such as a superintendent of schools, disclosure of an investigation into misconduct is required even if the charges are found not to be reliable and the official is exonerated. "In this circumstance, the public's interest in understanding why [the official] was exonerated and how the [agency] treated the accusations outweighs [the official's] interest in keeping the allegations confidential."[73]

- *Employee qualifications and applications.* The California Court of Appeal has held that "information as to the education, training, experience, awards, previous positions and publications of the (employee) ... is routinely presented in both professional and social settings, is relatively innocuous and implicates no applicable privacy or public policy exemption."[74] However, job applications may be exempt from disclosure if their disclosure would deter applicants from providing complete and accurate information.[75]

---

[69] *Bakersfield City School Dist. v. Superior Court*, 118 Cal. App. 4th 1041, 1045 (2004); *Braun v. City of Taft*, 154 Cal. App. 3d 332, 343-344 (1984).

[70] *International Federation of Professional Engineers v. Superior Court*, Case No. S134253, 2007 WL 2410093 (2007). The decision arises from a request for the names and salaries of employees earning more than $100,000 per year, but the reasoning of the Supreme Court's decision is not limited to only highly-paid employees. The decision leaves open the possibility that individual law enforcement officials might be able to justify nondisclosure of their names and salaries. Note that an opinion by the California attorney general also concluded that records showing the amounts of and reasons for performance bonuses given to city employees were not exempt from disclosure under the CPRA. *See* 68 Ops. Cal. Atty. Gen. 73 (1985).

[71] *American Federation of State, County and Municipal Employees v. Regents of the University of California*, 80 Cal. App. 3d 913, 918. (1978) (emphasis added). *Accord, Bakersfield City School Dist. v. Superior Court*, 118 Cal. App. 4th 1041, 1044, 1046 (2004).

[72] *American Federation of State, County and Municipal Employees v. Regents of the University of California*, 80 Cal. App. 3d 913, 918. (1978) (emphasis added). *Accord, Bakersfield City School Dist. v. Superior Court*, 118 Cal. App. 4th 1041, 1044, 1046 (2004).

[73] *BRV, Inc. v. Superior Court*, 143 Cal. App. 4th 742, 759 (2006).

[74] *Eskaton Monterey Hospital v. Myers*, 134 Cal. App. 3d 788, 794 (1982).

[75] *See Wilson v. Superior Court*, 51 Cal. App. 4th 1136 (1997). This case addressed only applications for appointment to a position on a county board of supervisors vacated by the death or resignation of a sitting supervisor, but may be extended to others.

- *Employee performance goals.* Employee performance goals may be exempt from disclosure, at least if individually tailored and kept confidential.[76]
- *Names of police officers involved in shootings.* A court of appeal held that the names of police officers involved in shootings were not exempt under the personnel exemption.[77] However, this rule was called into question by a recent California Supreme Court decision.[78]
- *Records of convicts employed in licensed day care centers.* The court of appeal required disclosure of the identity of every individual granted criminal conviction exemption to work in a licensed child day care facility, and the identity of each facility employing such individuals.[79]

Note that employment contracts of public employees are expressly a matter of public record pursuant to Government Code section 6254.8, which says: "Every employment contract between a state or local agency and any public official is a public record."

In order to determine whether a particular record is exempt under Section 6254(c), consider the following questions: (1) Does the record associate the person in question with an aspect of the individual's personal life rather than with the business of the public agency or the individual's performance as a government employee; and, (2) would release of the information constitute an unwarranted invasion of personal privacy? Both questions should be answered in the affirmative for the exemption to be applicable. Also remember that the burden to justify withholding a record or a portion thereof lies with the agency seeking to deny access; it is not enough merely to label the file a "personnel record."

d. Law enforcement and licensing agency records of complaints, and investigative or security files. This is a lengthy and complex exemption. Section 6254(f) of the Public Records Act says:

> Records of complaints to, or investigations conducted by, or records of intelligence information or security procedures of, the Office of the Attorney General and the Department of Justice, and any state or local police agency, or any investigatory or security files compiled by any other state or local police agency, or any investigatory or security files compiled by any other state or local agency for correctional, law enforcement, or licensing purposes ... [are exempt from disclosure].

In general, the "law enforcement" exemption provides that records that are part of the investigatory files of law enforcement agencies do not have to be made public.[80] A typical example of such records is a police report. Although available to the public in many other states, in California police reports are exempt from public disclosure.

However, law enforcement agencies are required to make certain categories of information public, even though those categories of information are generally contained in law enforcement investigatory files. The information required to be made public is discussed in more detail below.

---

[76] *Versaci v. Superior Court*, 127 Cal. App. 4th 805 (2005) (performance goals of a community college district superintendent were exempt from disclosure, based in part on the fact that the superintendent had retired, so the court found that there was no public interest in knowing what the goals were).

[77] *New York Times Co. v. Superior Court*, 52 Cal. App. 4th 97 (1997).

[78] *Copley Press, Inc. v. Superior Court*, 39 Cal. 4th 1272 (2006).

[79] *CBS Broadcasting Inc. v. Superior Court*, 91 Cal. App. 4th 892 (2001).

[80] Government Code section 6254(f).

The exemption for certain categories of records is automatic and applies from the time the records are created: complaints, records of investigations, records of intelligence information and records of security procedures.[81] The exemption for other records contained in law enforcement and licensing agency investigatory files arises "only when the prospect of enforcement proceedings becomes concrete and definite."[82] For example, a report regarding pesticide spraying contained in the files of a county agricultural commissioner were not exempt from disclosure simply because they could be used for enforcement or licensing purposes, where they had not been created for that purpose and there was no prospect of any enforcement proceeding.[83] However, once materials have become exempt, they remain permanently exempt, even after the investigation is over.[84] In addition, a court decision says that the right of access to even the limited information required to be made public applies only to "current information" that "pertain[s] to contemporaneous police activity."[85]

So, what information *do* you have a right to obtain? The answer depends, in part, on who you are and why you are making a request. Unlike other provisions of the CPRA, some law enforcement information is provided only to certain categories of people, or only if the information is requested for certain purposes. The information subject to disclosure falls into five categories:

- *Records not created as part of an investigation, if there is no definite prospect of enforcement proceedings.* As discussed above, pre-existing records that were not specifically created for or as part of an investigation or licensing proceeding are exempt only if there is a concrete and definite prospect of actual enforcement proceedings.[86] Any member of the public is entitled to such records.

- *Information regarding arrests.* With respect to arrests, Government Code section 6254(f)(1) requires the release of "[t]he full name and occupation of every individual arrested by the agency, the individual's physical description including date of birth, color of eyes and hair, sex, height and weight, the time and date of arrest, the time and date of booking, the location of the arrest, the factual circumstances surrounding the arrest, the amount of bail set, the time and manner of release or the location where the individual is currently being held, and all charges the individual is being held upon, including any outstanding warrants from other jurisdictions and parole or probation holds." All members of the public are entitled to this information. Disclosure is required *unless* the disclosure would endanger the safety of a witness or other person involved in the investigation, or unless disclosure would endanger the successful completion of the investigation or a related investigation.

- *Information regarding complaints and requests for assistance.* Government Code section 6254(f)(2) requires the release of "the time, substance, and location of all complaints or requests for assistance received by the agency and the time and nature of the response thereto, including, to the extent the information regarding crimes alleged or committed or any other incident investigated is recorded, the time, date, and location of occurrence, the time and date of the report, the name and age of the victim, the factual circumstances surrounding the crime or incident, and a general description of any injuries, property, or

---

[81]   *Haynie v. Superior Court*, 26 Cal. 4th 1061, 1069-70 (2001).

[82]   *Williams v. Superior Court*, 5 Cal. 4th 337, 356 (1993).

[83]   *Uribe v. Howie*, 19 Cal. App. 3d 194 (1971).

[84]   *Williams v. Superior Court*, 5 Cal. 4th 337, 361-62 (1993). *See also, Rivero v. Superior Court*, 54 Cal. App. 4th 1048, 1059 (1997)

[85]   *County of Los Angeles v. Superior Court*, 18 Cal. App. 4th 588, 601 (1993).

[86]   *Williams v. Superior Court*, 5 Cal. 4th 337, 356 (1993); *Uribe v. Howie*, 19 Cal. App. 3d 194 (1971).

weapons involved." All members of the public are also entitled to this information. Again, the information may be withheld if disclosure would endanger a person's safety or the successful completion of the investigation. Note that the names of victims of certain crimes (generally sex crimes) can be withheld at the request of the victim or the victim's parent or guardian. (The pertinent crimes are listed in section 6254(f).)

- *Addresses of arrestees and victims.* Government Code section 6254(f)(3) requires the disclosure of the current addresses of "every individual arrested by the agency" and "the victim of a crime." However, the disclosure of such information is limited to requesters who provide a statement, under penalty of perjury, that "the request is made for a scholarly, journalistic, political, or governmental purpose, or that the request is made for investigation purposes by a licensed private investigator..." Addresses of victims of certain crimes (again, generally sex crimes) cannot be disclosed.

A Note on Names: Law enforcement agencies often resist the disclosure of the names of arrestees and witnesses. If you can provide the statement required under Government Code section 6254(f)(3), you should get that information. Be prepared to ask specifically for it. If there is a good reason for not releasing the information – such as the fact that a witness has been threatened – be reasonable. If there is no reason for nondisclosure, be persistent. Note also, that although the CPRA itself does not limit the disclosure of the names of minors involved in crimes, courts have said that the juvenile courts have exclusive authority over the disclosure of information in juvenile court records, and that authority takes precedence over the CPRA. Therefore, the names of juvenile arrestees who are subject to the jurisdiction of the juvenile court probably are not subject to public disclosure.[87] Access to juvenile court records is addressed in Chapter 10.

- *Incident reports.* Government Code section 6254(f) also requires the disclosure of certain information to "the victims of an incident," "an insurance carrier against which a claim has been or might be made," and "any person suffering bodily injury or property damage or loss" as the result of certain categories of incidents. The information required to be disclosed to such persons are: "the names and addresses of persons involved in, or witnesses other than confidential informants to, the incident, the description of any property involved, the date, time, and location of the incident, all diagrams, statements of the parties involved in the incident, the statements of all witnesses, other than confidential informants." As with other law enforcement information, the report may be withheld if disclosure would endanger a person's safety or the successful completion of the investigation.
- *Booking photos ("mug shots").* It is not clear whether law enforcement agencies have an obligation to make mug shots (photographs of people who have recently been arrested) public. As noted above, the CPRA requires law enforcement agencies to disclose an arrestee's physical description including date of birth, color of eyes and hair, sex, height and weight.[88] However, it also exempts from disclosure records of investigations by law enforcement agencies.[89] The California attorney general has issued an opinion asserting

---

[87] *Wescott v. County of Yuba*, 104 Cal. App. 3d 103, 106 (1980); 65 Ops. Cal. Atty. Gen. 503 (1982). There is one exception to the general rule that an order of a juvenile court is required to obtain access to information about juveniles. Government Code section 6252.6 states: "Notwithstanding ... Section 827 of the Welfare and Institutions Code, after the death of a foster child who is a minor, the name, date of birth, and date of death of the child shall be subject to disclosure by the county child welfare agency pursuant to this chapter."

[88] Government Code section 6254(f)(3).

[89] Government Code section 6254(f).

that "mug shots fall within the 'records of investigations' exemption of section 6254, subdivision (f)."[90] This conclusion is based on the premise that "[a] mug shot is used by the police not only to identify the person arrested, but to determine if he or she is wanted on any other charge. Mug shots from earlier arrests may be used during subsequent investigations to identify individuals suspected of committing criminal offenses."[91] However, the mere *possibility* that a mug shot *may* be used for such a purpose does not mean that it is an investigatory record. Not all mug shots are used for such investigatory purposes. Unless the particular mug shot at issue is being used for investigatory purposes, it does not appear that it would be exempt from disclosure. The requirement for disclosure of a physical description of an arrestee indicates that mug shots are the kind of information that is required to be disclosed under section 6254(f), and that no purpose is served by depriving the public of mug shots. In any case, the attorney general also concludes that law enforcement agencies *may* disclose mug shots, and many law enforcement agencies routinely make mug shots of arrestees available.

Some other types of law enforcement information that may or may not be available are discussed below.

Of course, as with most other exemptions, agencies may release more information than is required by law.[92] In most circumstances, it is when the police want the assistance of the public in finding a suspect or solving a crime that additional information is provided to the media.

Remember that the government bears the burden of establishing a legal justification for the refusal to disclose any of the information delineated above. Each piece of information that is considered public must be considered separately. For example, if the police are justified in not disclosing the name of the victim because the crime involved is one of the listed sex crimes, that does not by itself justify a refusal to disclose other public information regarding the incident.

Despite these severe limitations on the public's right to access information about law enforcement, there may be other means to get the information in many cases. In particular, court records in criminal matters often contain police reports. The public's rights to access court records are discussed more fully in Chapter 10. Note, however, that the law has been amended to provide that district attorneys and the courts in each county must agree on a process for removing "confidential personal information" from police reports and similar law enforcement records filed with the courts.[93] For purposes of this law, "confidential personal information" means an address, telephone number, driver's license or California Identification Card number, social security number, date of birth, place of employment, employee identification number, mother's maiden name, demand deposit account number, savings or checking account number or credit card number.

e. Public interest test – the "catch all" exemption. Government Code section 6255 allows public agencies to withhold records when, "on the facts of the particular case, the public interest served by nondisclosure clearly outweighs the public interest served by disclosure of the record." As the California Supreme Court has stated: "[T]his provision contemplates a case-by-case balancing process, with the burden of proof on the proponent of nondisclosure to demonstrate a clear overbalance on the side of confidentiality."[94]

---

[90] 86 Ops. Cal. Atty. Gen. 132 (2003).
[91] 86 Ops. Cal. Atty. Gen. 132 (2003).
[92] Government Code section 6254; *see also* 86 Ops. Cal. Atty. Gen. 132 (2003).
[93] Penal Code section 964.
[94] *Michaelis, Montanari & Johnson v. Superior Court*, 38 Cal. 4th 1065, 1071 (2006).

The catch-all exemption has resulted in the creation of one broad, categorical exemption, known as the "deliberative process privilege." It has also been applied or rejected in particular cases addressing particular records.

(1) Deliberative process privilege. The "deliberative process privilege" may allow nondisclosure of records revealing the deliberations of agency officials, or information relied upon by government officials in making decisions that they would not otherwise receive if the information were routinely disclosed. This doctrine was created by the California Supreme Court in 1991 in a case involving a request for the calendars of then-Gov. George Deukmejian. In that case, the Supreme Court held that the requested records were exempt from disclosure. According to the Supreme Court, "the key question in every case is whether disclosure of the materials would expose an agency's decision-making process in such a way as to discourage candid discussion with the agency and thereby undermine the agency's ability to perform its functions." [95]

It is important to note that this "privilege" is not an absolute bar to the disclosure of records that may reveal an agency's or official's deliberative process. In the same decision in which it first recognized the deliberative process privilege, the California Supreme Court also emphasized: "Lest there be any misunderstanding, however, we caution that our holding does not render inviolate the Governor's calendars and schedules or other records of the Governor's office. There may be cases where the public interest in certain specific information contained in one or more of the Governor's calendars is more compelling, the specific request more focused, and the extent of the requested disclosure more limited; then, the court might properly conclude that the public interest in nondisclosure does not clearly outweigh the public interest in disclosure, whatever the incidental impact on the deliberative process." [96]

The deliberative process privilege has since been applied in other contexts:

- *Records of telephone calls made by city council members from city-owned cellular phones and home offices over a one-year period.* The court said the records were exempt from disclosure pursuant to the deliberative process privilege: "Disclosure of the records sought will disclose the identities of persons with whom the government official has consulted, thereby disclosing the official's mental process." [97]

- *The names and qualifications of applicants for a temporary appointment to a local board of supervisors, necessitated by the death of an elected supervisor.* The court said the records were protected by the deliberative process privilege, and also as correspondence to the governor's office (exempt under Government Code section 6254(l)): "The deliberative process privilege recognizes that the deliberative process can be impaired by exposure to public scrutiny. The disclosure of records containing only factual matters can impair the deliberative process by revealing the thought processes of the government decision maker. However, the deliberative process can be impaired in other ways as well. ... '[W]ithout the assurances of confidentiality ... flow of information to the [public agency] might be sharply curtailed, and the deliberative processes and efficiency of the agency greatly hindered.'" [98]

---

[95] *Times Mirror Co. v. Superior Court,* 53 Cal. 3d 1325, 1342 (1991).

[96] *Times Mirror Co. v. Superior Court,* 53 Cal. 3d 1325, 1346 (1991).

[97] *Rogers v. Superior Court,* 19 Cal. App. 4th 469 (1993).

[98] *California First Amendment Coalition v. Superior Court (Wilson),* 67 Cal. App. 4th 159, 171 (1998), quoting *Times Mirror Co. v. Superior Court,* 53 Cal. 3d at 1343. *See also Wilson v. Superior Court,* 51 Cal. App. 4th 1136, 1141 (1996).

A Note on Deliberative Process: Proposition 59 may have eliminated the "deliberative process privilege." It was certainly intended to do so. The Ballot Argument in favor of Proposition 59 states in part as follows: "What will Proposition 59 do? It will create a new civil right: a constitutional right to know what the government is doing, why it is doing it, and how. ... *It will allow the public to see and understand the deliberative process through which decisions are made*."[99]

(2) Other records exempt or not exempt under the catch-all exemption. Setting aside the deliberative process privilege, certain types of records have been held to be exempt or non-exempt, under the CPRA.

- *Applications to carry concealed weapons.* The California Supreme Court ruled that applications to carry concealed weapons are a matter of public record based upon the importance of the public's interest in overseeing how such permits are being dispersed.[100]
- *State law enforcement surveillance records, where the burden of redacting exempt information justified nondisclosure.* Nondisclosure of records may be justified if the information sought by a request is so voluminous it would result in inordinate time and costs to gather and segregate the information subject to disclosure.[101]
- *Names of sheriff's deputies involved in fatal shootings.* The court of appeal said that this information had to be made public. In doing so, it said: "Fear of possible opprobrium or embarrassment is insufficient to prevent disclosure. ... The perceived harm to deputies from revelation of their names as having fired their weapons in the line of duty resulting in a death does not outweigh the public interest served in disclosure of their names."[102] Note, however, that a subsequent decision of the California Supreme Court has called this decision into question.[103]
- *Names, addresses and telephone numbers of persons who have made complaints to the city about municipal airport noise.* This information was held to be exempt from disclosure under the catch-all exemption. The court of appeal held that the privacy interests of the people complaining outweighed the interest in monitoring whether the government was appropriately addressing airport noise complaints.[104]
- *A list of water district customers who had exceeded their maximum allowed usage of water under a rationing program.* Despite concerns over privacy, the California Court of Appeal ruled that the privacy interests of the customers did *not* outweigh the right of the public to review the government's conduct. In this case, the newspaper wanted to determine how well the water district was enforcing the regulations against excessive water usage in a time of drought. The court also rejected as a "mere assertion" the concern posed by the district that customers whose names were published could be subjected to physical harm.[105]
- *Manual of government audit procedures.* A group of hospitals that had been determined by the Department of Health Services to be out of compliance with Medi-Cal sought to obtain the department's fiscal audit manual. The California Court of Appeal ruled that the

---

[99] *See* http://vote2004.ss.ca.gov/voterguide/propositions/prop59-arguments.htm.

[100] *CBS v. Block,* 42 Cal App. 3d 646 (1986),

[101] *ACLU v. Deukmejian,* 32 Cal. 3d 440 (1982).

[102] *New York Times Co. v. Superior Court,* 52 Cal. App. 4th 97, 104 (1997).

[103] *Copley Press, Inc. v. Superior Court,* – Cal. 4th – , 2006 WL 2506369, 2006 Daily Journal D.A.R. 11,839 (2006).

[104] *City of San Jose v. Superior Court,* 74 Cal. App. 4th 1008 (1999).

[105] *New York Times Co. v. Superior Court,* 218 Cal. App. 3d 1579 (1990).

public's interest in disclosure of the manual was clearly outweighed by the public interest in not allowing Medi-Cal providers to circumvent governing regulations by using the audit manual as a guide for "manipulating expenditure itemizations."[106]

- *Reports of pesticide spraying.* An agricultural field worker who suffered symptoms associated with potential pesticide misuse sought access to pest control operator reports from the local county agricultural commissioner. The county refused to release the reports, claiming the public interest in withholding the record – that future reports would be unreliable if the operators knew details of their pesticide mixtures would be open to their competitors – clearly outweighed the public interest in providing the information to the sick worker. The court of appeal ordered the release of the information. It recognized a public interest in ensuring that the worker obtained adequate medical care in understanding the effects of pesticides on humans.[107]

A Note on the Catch-All Exemption: The catch-all exemption is broad and undefined. It is routinely invoked by public agencies in denying access to public records. Often, it does not justify nondisclosure. However, it's often impossible to say whether or not a court will uphold the agency's decision in a particular case. If an agency denies your request based on section 6255, press the agency to fully articulate the public interest served by nondisclosure. This may allow you to address the reasons the agency is asserting and persuade it to release information. It will also put you in a position to dispute the agency's claims if you bring an enforcement action.

4. Specific Exemptions.

The CPRA enumerates many specific types of records that are exempt from disclosure. Additionally, Section 6254(k) exempts "records the disclosure of which is exempted or prohibited pursuant to provisions of federal or state law, including, but not limited to provisions of the Evidence Code relating to privilege."

Section 6254(k) embraces hundreds of exemptions found in other California statutes and in federal statutes as well. Most of the state law exemptions are listed in the CPRA itself, in Government Code sections 6275-6276.46. These provisions contain a long list of California laws that may justify nondisclosure of public records. However, the fact that a statute is included in the list does not mean that it necessarily creates an exemption.[108] You need to look at the statute to determine if it actually prevents disclosure. Some of the more common statutory exemptions are discussed below.

a. Specific exemptions for law enforcement information. There are many specific provisions of California law limiting public access to information compiled by or about law enforcement agencies. They include the following.

(1) Peace officer personnel records and citizen complaints. California Penal Code section 832.7 exempts from disclosure personnel records of "peace officers" and "custodial officers." The statute states that: "Peace officer or custodial officer personnel records and records maintained by any state or local agency ... or information obtained from these records, are confidential and shall not be disclosed in any criminal or civil proceeding except by discovery pursuant to Sections 1043

---

[106]   *Eskaton Monterey Hospital v. Myers*, 134 Cal. App. 3d 788 (1982).
[107]   *Uribe v. Howie*, 19 Cal. App. 3d 194 (1971).
[108]   Government Code section 6275.

and 1046 of the Evidence Code."[109] This law is most often applied to police officers, but it applies to others as well, such as sheriff's deputies and prison guards. "Personnel records" is defined by the law as:

(a) Personal data, including marital status, family members, educational and employment history, home addresses, or similar information.
(b) Medical history.
(c) Election of employee benefits.
(d) Employee advancement, appraisal, or discipline.
(e) Complaints, or investigations of complaints, concerning an event or transaction in which he or she participated, or which he or she perceived, and pertaining to the manner in which he or she performed his or her duties.
(f) Any other information the disclosure of which would constitute an unwarranted invasion of personal privacy.[110]

One California Court of Appeal said that this law applies only when information was demanded in a lawsuit and that it did not preclude law enforcement agencies from releasing information contained in a peace officer's personnel file in other situations.[111] Other courts disagreed.[112] The California Supreme Court subsequently held that Penal Code section 832.7 prohibits the disclosure of information from the personal records of a peace officer requested pursuant to the CPRA and held that it is not restricted to information sought in a lawsuit.[113] The Supreme Court also said that such information was exempt from disclosure even if it was not contained in the personnel records of the agency that employs the officer, but rather was in the files of a civil service commission that hears appeals after officers have been disciplined.

Another California Court of Appeal ruled that names of law enforcement officers who fired shots at a citizen were not privileged or confidential under Section 832.7 and were required to be disclosed in response to a request under the CPRA.[114] The California Supreme Court also recently held that names, employing departments, and hiring and termination dates of California peace officers included in a statewide database were not generally exempt from disclosure.[115] The Supreme Court left open the possibility that individual officers (particularly undercover officers) could prevent the disclosure of this information by showing that it would endanger their safety or efficacy. However, in another recent case, the California Supreme Court said that even an officer's name cannot be disclosed if it comes from a disciplinary proceeding (and would thereby reveal the identity of an officer who had been disciplined).[116]

A Note on Confidential Peace Officer Information: Whenever a member of the public registers a complaint with a law enforcement agency, that agency will generally place all related records in the officer's personnel file, thereby prohibiting access to the file. Even before the Supreme

---

[109]   Penal Code section 832.7(a).
[110]   Penal Code section 832.8.
[111]   *Bradshaw v. City of Los Angeles*, 221 Cal. App. 3d 908 (1990).
[112]   *See San Diego Police Officers' Assn. v. City of San Diego Civil Service Com.,* 104 Cal. App. 4th 275, 281-288 (2002); *City of Hemet v. Superior Court*, 37 Cal. App. 4th 1411, 1425-1430 (1995); *City of Richmond v. Superior Court*, 32 Cal. App. 4th 1430, 1439-1440 (1995).
[113]   *Copley Press, Inc. v. Superior Court,* 39 Cal. 4th 1272 (2006).
[114]   *New York Times Co. v. Superior Court,* 52 Cal. App. 4th 97 (1997).
[115]   *Commission on Peace Officer Standards and Training v. Superior Court,* Case No. S134072, 2007 WL 2410091 (2007).
[116]   *Copley Press, Inc. v. Superior Court,* 39 Cal. 4th 1272 (2006).

Court's decision upholding the secrecy of information disclosed in civil service appeals, law enforcement agencies routinely refused to disclose information about misconduct by law enforcement officials. Unfortunately, the Supreme Court's decision ensures that no such information will be disclosed, no matter how egregious the misconduct.

(2) Accident reports. The California Vehicle Code provides that accident reports are confidential. Accident reports taken by the California Highway Patrol or other law enforcement agencies are not subject to access under the CPRA and are available only to drivers or other parties who have a direct interest in the accident (this would include an attorney representing one of the parties), including those who have suffered property damage or face civil liability as a result of the accident.[117] However, information may be withheld even from those directly involved if disclosure would endanger a witness or victim or jeopardize an investigation.[118] In addition, any portion of an investigative file that reflects the analysis or conclusions of the investigating officer is exempt from disclosure.[119]

The statute also classifies as confidential reports that are "supplemental" to the accident report. To the extent, for example, an arrest was made pursuant to an accident in which the driver was alleged to be driving under the influence, the arrest report would be supplemental to the accident report and might therefore be treated as confidential. Under the CPRA, however, much of the information contained in the arrest report may be a matter of public record.

(3) Campus crime reports. Education Code Section 67380 sets forth requirements for the disclosure of information regarding crimes on college campuses. It covers community colleges, California State Universities and campuses of the University of California (as well as any other postsecondary institution receiving public funds for student financial assistance). The law requires these schools to compile records of crime that involve violence, hate crimes, theft, destruction of property, illegal drugs or alcohol intoxication. Subject schools are further required to make information about all of these crimes available within two business days after a request is made by a student, an applicant for admission, school employee or member of the media, unless the information would be exempt under Government Code Section 6254(f).

Federal law now requires that schools receiving federal money make the same types of information set forth in Education Code section 67380 available to a requester within two business days after the request is made.[120] In addition, the federal Family Educational Rights and Privacy Act (FERPA) no longer prohibits the disclosure of the "final results" of disciplinary proceedings involving crimes of violence or non-forcible sex offenses.

(4) Other law enforcement information. Other records exempt from disclosure include mandated reports of suspected child abuse,[121] insurance company data provided to law enforcement agencies in vehicle theft or insurance fraud investigations[122] and certain prison records.[123]

b. Rap sheets. Under Penal Code sections 11075, 11105 and 13300 and related sections, access to state and local rap sheets is restricted to those with an official purpose for using them.

---

[117]   Vehicle Code section 20012.
[118]   Government Code section 6254(f).
[119]   Government Code section 6254(f).
[120]   20 U.S.C. section 1001.
[121]   Penal Code section 11167.5.
[122]   Vehicle Code section 10904.
[123]   Penal Code section 2081.5.

Mere unauthorized possession of rap sheets is a crime. However, the fact that you cannot get access to the official "rap sheet" does not mean that you cannot legally determine the criminal record of a subject. Since most court records are open to public inspection, you may be able to determine whether someone has been charged with or convicted of a crime by looking under his or her name in county court records. (See Chapter 10 for a full discussion of court records.)

The limitation on this type of search is that each county will have records of only those offenses for which the defendant was charged in that county. Sometimes convictions from other counties or states can be accessed by careful review of the documents, since prior convictions may be used to seek enhancement by the prosecution and may be used in probation reports to determine sentencing.

c. DMV records. Residential address records maintained by the Department of Motor Vehicles are confidential and exempt from disclosure.[124] Also exempt from disclosure: records of drug or alcohol-related driving offense convictions more than five years old;[125] abstract reports showing blood-alcohol levels of persons convicted of driving under the influence;[126] information in DMV records showing home addresses of legislators, law enforcement officers and other public officials who have requested confidentiality;[127] and records of first offenses of drivers sentenced to traffic violator schools.[128]

d. Appraisals. The contents of real estate appraisals or engineering or feasibility estimates and evaluations made for or by the state or local agency for property to be purchased or considered for purchase by the agency are exempt from disclosure prior to the purchase of the property.[129] The statute does not specifically address whether such appraisals are subject to disclosure if the agency makes a final decision not to purchase the property appraised.

A Note on Appraisals: As noted above, under the CPRA a public agency cannot selectively disclose records. Providing a record to any member of the public generally constitutes a waiver of the exemptions under the CPRA (although there are exceptions).[130] Thus, if the appraisal has been shared with the property owner or someone else involved in the transaction, you may have a basis for obtaining the appraisal.

e. Certain tax information. "Information required from any taxpayer in connection with the collection of local taxes that is received in confidence and the disclosure of which would result in unfair competitive disadvantage to the person supplying such information" is exempt from disclosure.[131] Also specifically exempted are the following: income tax returns,[132] Franchise Tax Board settlements with taxpayers providing tax reductions of less than $5,000,[133] business information acquired by the Board of Equalization[134] and real property ownership statements.[135]

---

[124] Government Code section 6254.1(b).
[125] Vehicle Code section 1807.5.
[126] Vehicle Code section 1804.
[127] Vehicle Code section 1808.4.
[128] Vehicle Code section 1808.7.
[129] Government Code section 6254(h).
[130] Government Code section 6254.5.
[131] Government Code section 6254(i).
[132] Revenue and Taxation Code section 19272.
[133] Revenue and Taxation Code section 19133.
[134] Revenue and Taxation Code section 15619.
[135] Government Code section 27280.

f. Family and welfare matters. The following categories of records (among others) are exempt: Adoption records,[136] medical and family information in birth certificates,[137] and welfare records.[138]

g. Education records. Elementary and secondary school (K-12) student records are exempt from disclosure.[139] Although Education Code section 48918(k) says that records of expulsions are disclosable public records, a California Court of Appeal has ruled that a federal law making such records confidential – the Family Educational Rights and Privacy Act (FERPA) – takes precedence over California law.[140] College and university student records are also generally exempt from disclosure.[141]

h. State investigations and audits. Exempt from disclosure are state lottery security audits;[142] information acquired in audits of lobbyists by the Franchise Tax Board;[143] information acquired in investigations of state departments; investigations of improper government activity;[144] and inspection reports and deficiency lists compiled by the Department of Health Services concerning health facilities, until verified as received by the facility.[145]

i. Medical and health information. Medical information about patients in records of hospitals, doctors and other health care providers is confidential and exempt from disclosure.[146] Also confidential are the following: information submitted to the Department of Health Services in cancer reports from health facilities,[147] blood test and other public health records identifying individuals tested for the AIDS virus,[148] patient records of drug abuse or treatment or prevention programs,[149] and mental health treatment records.[150]

A Note on Information About Patients: Note that in the absence of a written request to the contrary, a California law allows health care providers to disclose, at their discretion, the following information: "the patient's name, address, age, and sex; a general description of the reason for treatment (whether an injury, a burn, poisoning, or some unrelated condition); the general nature of the injury, burn, poisoning, or other condition; the general condition of the patient; and any information that is not medical information as defined in subdivision (c) of [Civil Code] Section 56.05."[151] Note, however, that the California Office of HIPAA Implementation has

---

[136] Civil Code section 227.
[137] Health and Safety Code section 10125.5.
[138] Welfare and Institutions Code sections 11478, 10850.
[139] Education Code sections 49073-49076.
[140] *Rim of the World Unified School Dist. v. Superior Court*, 104 Cal. App. 4th 1393 (2002).
[141] Education Code sections 67140-47.
[142] Government Code section 8880.46.
[143] Government Code section 90005.
[144] Government Code sections 8547-8547.12.
[145] Health and Safety Code section 1280.
[146] Civil Code section 56.10.
[147] Health and Safety Code section 211.3.
[148] Health and Safety Code sections 199.27-42, and 1640 and following.
[149] Health and Safety Code section 11977.
[150] Welfare and Institutions Code sections 4132, 5328.
[151] Civil Code section 56.16.

concluded that the federal Health Insurance Portability and Accountability Implementation Act (HIPAA) pre-empts this provision of California law and prohibits disclosure.[152]

A Note on Information About Hospitals: Some hospitals are owned and operated by local governments and are therefore subject to the Public Records Act. However, many publicly owned hospitals have been leased to private companies, which operate the hospitals and employ the doctors, nurses and other staff. It's important to note that these hospitals may also be subject to the CPRA. The CPRA applies to certain non-governmental entities that are governed by the Brown Act.[153] The Brown Act applies to, among others: "[T]he lessee of any hospital the whole or part of which is first leased pursuant to subdivision (p) of Section 32121 of the Health and Safety Code after January 1, 1994, where the lessee exercises any material authority of a legislative body of a local agency delegated to it by that legislative body whether the lessee is organized and operated by the local agency or by a delegated authority."

j. "Official information" – confidential submissions to the government. Under Government Code section 6254(k) and Evidence Code section 1040, the CPRA may also exempt from disclosure "official information." "Official information" means "information acquired in confidence by a public employee in the course of his or her duty and not open, or officially disclosed, to the public prior to the time the claim of privilege is made." Thus, this exemption applies only to information that is expressly acquired in confidence. In addition, this exemption applies only if "[d]isclosure of the information is against the public interest because there is a necessity for preserving the confidentiality of the information that outweighs the necessity for disclosure in the interest of justice." The California Supreme Court has held that this test is essentially the same as the test for disclosure under Government Code section 6255, the "catch-all" exemption discussed above.[154] Furthermore: (1) The exemption for official information may not be claimed under this if anyone authorized to do so has consented to disclosure; and (2) in determining whether disclosure of the information is against the public interest, the interest of the public agency may not be considered.[155]

F. WHAT CAN I DO IF THE AGENCY DOESN'T PROVIDE PUBLIC RECORDS I HAVE REQUESTED?

When an agency fails to provide requested records that you believe are subject to public disclosure, Government Code Section 6259 allows you to file a lawsuit. Lawsuits to enforce the CPRA are usually initiated by a verified petition (i.e., a request filed under oath) that asks the court to issue a "writ of mandate." A writ of mandate is a type of order directing the public agency to take specified actions. The lawsuit may be filed in the superior court of the county of the agency that is the holder of the records. Lawsuits against state agencies may be brought in Sacramento County or in any city in which the California attorney general has an office.[156]

---

[152] See *State Privacy Law HIPAA Preemption Analysis: Confidentiality of Medical Information Act*, State of California Office of HIPAA Implementation (2006), at p. 105 (http://www.calohi.ca.gov/calohi/docs/CMIA_PA_05_update.doc).
[153] Government Code section 6252(a).
[154] *CBS, Inc. v. Block*, 42 Cal. 3d 646, 656 (1986).
[155] Evidence Code section 1040(a)(2).
[156] Code of Civil Procedure section 401(1).

You may ask the judge to examine the records in private.[157] The judge will consider the briefs and evidence submitted by the parties and will determine if the agency was justified in withholding the records. If the judge determines that the records were improperly withheld, he or she must order the agency to disclose the records and to pay your court costs and reasonable attorneys' fees.[158]

Even if the records are voluntarily released before a judicial determination that the records are disclosable, you are entitled to attorneys' fees and court costs.[159] Alternatively, if the court determines that a lawsuit seeking public records is without any legal foundation, the court may – but is not required to – order the plaintiff to reimburse the agency for its costs incurred in the litigation.[160]

If a judge denies a request to make a document public, you have the right to seek an immediate rehearing on the merits by an appellate court. This is significant because public agencies could frustrate the purpose of the CPRA if they were allowed to withhold a record while a case was on appeal, a process that often can take years. The CPRA requires you to appeal by filing a petition for an "extraordinary writ" with the court of appeal *within 20 days* of the decision of the superior court. The court of appeal normally has broad discretion as to whether to hear such petitions. However, the California Supreme Court has held:

> When an extraordinary writ proceeding is the only avenue of appellate review, a reviewing court's discretion is quite restricted. ... Accordingly, when writ review is the exclusive means of appellate review of a final order or judgment, an appellate court may not deny an apparently meritorious writ petition, timely presented in a formally and procedurally sufficient manner, merely because, for example, the petition presents no important issue of law or because the court considers the case less worthy of its attention than other matters."[161]

A public agency may not sue for a declaration that records are *not* subject to disclosure. The California Supreme Court held that such actions, which can be used to pre-empt a citizen's request for records, and to force unwilling members of the pubic into litigation, are not permitted under the CPRA.[162] However, third parties interested in preventing the disclosure of information in public records, such as unions representing government employees and companies doing business with the government, are increasingly suing to prevent disclosure of public records, and generally the courts have permitted them to do so.

If you believe that you are entitled to public records that have been denied, but you do not have or believe you cannot afford an attorney, you may be able to locate an attorney by using a legal referral service. Attorneys may be willing to represent you on a pro bono basis. Most counties have local bar associations that operate legal referral services.[163] The California First Amendment Coalition also provides a legal referral service, which forwards requests to experienced lawyers: http://www.cfac.org/content/index.php/cfac/lawyers_rfp.

---

[157]   Government Code section 6259(a).
[158]   Government Code section 6259.
[159]   *Belth v. Gillespie*, 232 Cal. App. 3d 896 (1991).
[160]   Government Code section 6259(d).
[161]   *Powers v. City of Richmond*, 10 Cal. 4th 85, 113-14 (1995).
[162]   *Filarsky v. Superior Court*, 28 Cal. 4th 419 (2002).
[163]   For a list of local bar associations, with links to their websites, see, for example: http://california.resourcesforattorneys.com/barassociations.html.

G. SUMMARY OF RIGHTS

Under the CPRA, any person (natural, corporate, citizen or non-citizen) has the following rights:

1. To inspect during regular business hours any image, writing or electronically recorded or stored item containing information relating to the conduct of the public's business prepared, owned, used or retained by any state or local agency, regardless of physical form or characteristics, if not exempt from disclosure.

2. To receive a copy of any record not exempt from disclosure upon payment of fees covering direct costs of duplication, or statutory fee, if applicable. If the agency does not have legal justification to withhold the entire record, it has a duty to segregate the information that can be disclosed from the exempt portions of the record and provide the disclosable portions.

3. To be given access to the requested records or a justification for the refusal without delay; and, in the event of a denial of access, to be promptly notified of the agency's decision and the reasons for denying access.

4. To be given any statement of justification for denial of a request no later than 10 days from the date of the request or, in unusual circumstances, within an additional 14 days. Any extension must be explained to the requester in the form of a written notice setting forth the reason for the delay and the date on which a determination is expected.

5. To challenge any refusal to grant access to, or a copy of, a record by seeking a court order or a declaratory judgment from the superior court, which is required to set pleading deadlines and a hearing on the matter "at the earliest possible time."

6. To obtain, in the event the superior court determines (or the court of appeal if such review is sought) that an agency improperly withheld records, court costs and reasonable attorneys' fees, to be paid by the agency that wrongfully denied access to the records prior to litigation.

PART III:
PROPOSITION 59

Article I, section 3(b) of the California Constitution was enacted as the result of the passage of a ballot proposition in November 2004. It is generally referred to as "Proposition 59." Prop. 59 amended the California Constitution to create a new civil right of access to government records and meetings.

Prop. 59 is discussed in detail in Chapter 3. Therefore, only a brief summary of Prop. 59 will be provided here. The main provision of Prop. 59 states as follows:

The people have the right of access to information concerning the conduct of the people's business, and, therefore, the meetings of public bodies *and the writings of public officials and agencies shall be open to public scrutiny*.[164]

This constitutional provision establishes a right of access in addition to the right of access created by various California laws, such as the Public Records Act.

However, the right of access created by Prop. 59 has some limitations. Prop. 59 says that it does not affect the right of privacy also contained in the California Constitution or the laws that implement that constitutional right of privacy.[165] It also says that existing laws limiting access to public records are not repealed or nullified.[166] On the other hand, Proposition 59 says that existing laws and new laws that limit access to public records must be applied in a way that favors access. In addition, any new limitation on access must be justified by showing "the interest protected by the limitation and the need for protecting that interest."[167]

What does all this mean? To a large extent, it remains to be seen. Its impact will primarily be determined by the courts. The few public records cases decided since the enactment of Proposition 59 have not been encouraging.[168]

PART IV:
LEGISLATIVE OPEN RECORDS ACT

There are two branches of government in California whose records are not subject to the CPRA. Records of judicial proceedings held by the courts and records of the state Legislature are not covered, so the CPRA provides no right of access to such records. The rules governing access to judicial records are covered in Chapter 10. Access to records of the Legislature (the California State Senate and Assembly) are covered by the Legislative Open Records Act (Government Code Section 9070 and following). While modeled on the CPRA, the Legislative Open Records Act ("LORA") gives the Legislature more control over the release of records than agencies subject to the CPRA.

A. WHAT RECORDS OF THE LEGISLATURE ARE COVERED?

The Legislative Open Records Act covers "any writing prepared on or after December 2, 1974, which contains information relating to the conduct of the people's business prepared, owned, used or retained by the Legislature."[169] As in the CPRA, the word "record" is broadly defined to cover any form of recorded information.[170]

B. HOW DO I GET ACCESS TO LEGISLATIVE RECORDS?

As under the CPRA, any member of the public has the right to inspect records that are public under LORA during the normal office hours of the Legislature. Members of the public also are

---

[164]   Cal. Const., Article I, section (3)(b)(1).
[165]   Cal. Const., Article I, section (3)(b)(3).
[166]   Cal. Const., Article I, section (3)(b)(5).
[167]   Cal. Const., Article I, section (3)(b)(2).
[168]   *See Michaelis, Montanari & Johnson v. Superior Court*, 38 Cal. 4th 1065, 1072 (2006); *Copley Press, Inc. v. Superior Court,* 39 Cal.4th 1272 (2006).
[169]   Government Code section 9072(c).
[170]   Government Code section 9072(d).

entitled to a copy of a legislative record upon request and payment of a fee established by the Legislature to cover the costs "reasonably calculated to reimburse [the Legislature] for its actual cost in making such copies available."[171] The LORA provides that the fee cannot exceed 10 cents per page.[172]

Under the LORA, however, members of the public have no right to demand records from a particular legislator. Under Government Code Section 9074, the Rules Committee of each house of the Legislature or the Joint Rules Committee is considered to have custody of all legislative records. Any request to inspect or copy a record must, therefore, be made to one of the rules committees. Once a request is made, the committee is obligated to inform the requester "promptly" whether the record will be released, and records subject to disclosure must "be made available for inspection promptly and without unnecessary delay."

If the committee decides to deny access, the requester must be given a written justification for the committee's decision to withhold the record within four working days of the date of the request. The justification must demonstrate that "the record in question is exempt under the express provisions of this article or that on the facts of the particular case the public interest served by not making the record public clearly outweighs the public interest served by disclosure of the record." If a request is made while the Legislature is not in session, the committee is given up to 10 days to provide a written explanation of any denial.

C. WHAT LEGISLATIVE RECORDS ARE EXEMPT FROM DISCLOSURE?

The following is a list of the records that are specifically exempt from access under LORA:

1. Preliminary drafts, notes or legislative memoranda.[173]

2. Records pertaining to pending litigation to which the Legislature is a party or to claims made against the Legislature until the claim or litigation has been finally adjudicated or settled.[174]

3. Personnel, medical or similar files, the disclosure of which would constitute an unwarranted invasion of personal privacy provided that the Senate Committee on Rules, the Assembly Rules Committee or the Joint Rules Committee shall determine whether disclosure of such records constitutes an unwarranted invasion of personal privacy.[175]

4. The phone records of legislators, with the exception of the total charges incurred.[176]

5. Records of locations at which legislators purchased gasoline, with the exception of the total charges incurred.[177]

---

[171] Government Code section 9073.
[172] Government Code section 9073.
[173] Government Code section 9075(a).
[174] Government Code section 9075(b).
[175] Government Code section 9075(c).
[176] Government Code section 9075(d).
[177] Government Code section 9075(e).

6. Records in the custody of the Legislative Counsel or in the custody of or maintained by the majority and minority caucuses.[178] LORA does provide, however, that records may not be transferred to these places merely to avoid disclosure.[179]

7. Correspondence to and from members of the Legislature and their staff.[180]

8. Communications from private citizens to the Legislature.[181]

9. Records of complaints to or investigations conducted by the Legislature or relating to security procedures of the Legislature.[182]

Like the CPRA, the LORA has a "catch-all" exemption, which says that records may be withheld when, "on the facts of the particular case the public interest served by not making the record public clearly outweighs the public interest served by disclosure of the record."[183] Like the CPRA, it also exempts "[r]ecords the disclosure of which is exempted or prohibited pursuant to provisions of federal or state law, including, but not limited to, provisions of the Evidence Code relating to privilege."[184]

D. WHAT CAN I DO IF THE LEGISLATURE DOES NOT PROVIDE RECORDS THAT ARE SUBJECT TO DISCLOSURE?

A member of the public who believes that he or she has been denied access to records in violation of LORA has the right to bring an action for injunctive or declarative relief. A court will then examine the requested record privately and determine whether it must be disclosed. An individual who is successful in such a lawsuit is entitled to be reimbursed for court costs and reasonable attorneys' fees. On the other hand, the state is entitled to court costs and reasonable attorneys' fees if the judge who reviewed the record makes the determination that the lawsuit is "clearly frivolous."[185]

E. DOES THE LEGISLATURE MAKE INFORMATION AVAILABLE ON THE INTERNET?

In addition to LORA, California law requires the Legislature to make the records of all bill texts, floor and committee votes, analyses and veto messages available through the Internet.[186] This information is currently provided through two Internet websites: the California State Senate website (http://www.sen.ca.gov/), and the California State Assembly website (http://www.assembly.ca.gov/acs/defaulttext.asp). Information on contacting state legislators, legislative schedules and other kinds of information are also available on these websites.

---

[178]   Government Code section 9075(f), (g).
[179]   Government Code section 9075(g).
[180]   Government Code section 9075(h).
[181]   Government Code section 9075(j).
[182]   Government Code section 9075(k).
[183]   Government Code section 9074.
[184]   Government Code section 9075(i).
[185]   Government Code Section 9079.
[186]   Government Code section 9075(f) (in the LORA), Government Code section 6254(m) (in the CPRA), and Government Code section 10248.

PART V:
THE FEDERAL FREEDOM OF INFORMATION ACT

A. INTRODUCTION

A thorough review of the Freedom of Information Act (FOIA) is beyond the scope of this publication. However, there are many reasons why California citizens, journalists and public officials should familiarize themselves with at least the basic provisions of the FOIA. Federal government agencies and officials generally are not subject to state open government laws such as the CPRA. Nonetheless, the pervasive power of the federal government affects issues and interests that are vital to the State of California and to local communities here. For example, the creation, maintenance and treatment of parks, military installations and other government facilities; the environmental regulation of oceans, rivers, streams, and polluted properties; and the funding and operation of many programs affecting public health and welfare are all primarily, or at least substantially, governed by federal agencies. In addition, knowledge of how exemptions from FOIA have been interpreted by the federal courts may help determine how parallel exemptions under the CPRA may be construed.

B. HOW DOES THE FREEDOM OF INFORMATION ACT WORK?

The CPRA is modeled on the FOIA, and they are very similar in the way they work.[187]

1. What Agencies Are Subject to the FOIA?

The FOIA applies to all departments of the executive branch of the federal government (including the military).[188] It does not apply to Congress or to the federal courts.

2. What Information Is Covered by the FOIA?

The FOIA broadly defines the information subject to disclosure.[189] It requires government agencies to provide public access to records that are not specifically exempt from disclosure.[190] Like the CPRA, it also creates a series of exemptions for certain categories of records.[191] (These exemptions are discussed below.)

Some records are specifically required to be made public under the FOIA.[192] Federal agencies are required to publish (in the Federal Register) a description of the basic organization of the agency, including how to request information and who to ask. The agency's operating rules, procedures and opinions must also be made available for inspection and copying. Specifically, the FOIA specifically requires disclosure of the following:

---

[187] The FOIA is section 552 of Title 5 of the United States Code. It is typically referred to this way: 5 U.S.C. § 552, meaning Title 5 of the United States Code, section 552. This is the way this book will refer to particular provisions of the FOIA.

[188] 5 U.S.C. § 552(f)(1).

[189] 5 U.S.C. § 552(f)(2).

[190] 5 U.S.C § 552(a)(3)(A).

[191] 5 U.S.C. § 552(b).

[192] 5 U.S.C § 552(a)(1) and 552(a)(2).

(A) final opinions, including concurring and dissenting opinions, as well as orders, made in the adjudication of cases;

(B) those statements of policy and interpretations that have been adopted by the agency and are not published in the Federal Register;

(C) administrative staff manuals and instructions to staff that affect a member of the public;

(D) copies of all records, regardless of form or format, which have been released to any person [pursuant to a FOIA request] and which, because of the nature of their subject matter, the agency determines have become or are likely to become the subject of subsequent requests for substantially the same records; and

(E) a general index of the records referred to under subparagraph (D).[193]

The FOIA requires federal agencies to make public documents created on or after November 1, 1996, available in electronic form.[194] In general, government agencies are only required to make records available in the form they are kept by the government, or in a form that the government can readily provide.[195] If an exemption applies to a paper document requested under FOIA it will also apply to the electronic version.

3. How Do I Get Information Under the FOIA?

Like the CPRA, the FOIA allows anyone to request information from the government. In the absence of "unusual circumstances," it requires federal government agencies to respond to a request for information within 20 days.[196]

If you are uncertain about the specific kind of information that is held by a particular agency, you can begin your search with the United States Government Manual, which prints a list of all federal agencies, describes their functions and includes local or regional addresses and telephone numbers. Most main branch libraries will have a copy, or one can be obtained from the U.S. Government Printing Office in Washington, D.C. 20402. Its website is at www.access.gpo.gov. The Federal Information Center also can be of assistance.

Under the FOIA, every government agency is required to adopt regulations regarding how the public can request information and how the agency will respond to such requests. It's a good idea to read these regulations before you make a request. For example, the regulations may require that a request be in writing, or they may provide that the agency will respond to a request more quickly than the FOIA requires. They typically include information on how and to whom to submit a request, such as the address to which to direct a FOIA request. These regulations are published in the Code of Federal Regulations. (You can access and search the Code of Federal Regulations (or "C.F.R.") online at an Internet website maintained by the Government Printing Office: http://www.gpoaccess.gov/cfr/index.html.) They are also available though the Internet websites of many federal agencies. A list of federal agency FOIA websites is available on the Department of Justice Internet website: http://www.usdoj.gov/04foia/other_age.htm. (Note: These regulations cannot relieve an agency of its obligations under the FOIA. The FOIA takes precedence over any conflicting agency regulations.)

---

[193] 5 U.S.C § 552(a)(2).
[194] 5 U.S.C. § 552(a)(2).
[195] 5 U.S.C. § 552(a)(3)(B) ("In making any record available to a person under this paragraph, an agency shall provide the record in any form or format requested by the person if the record is readily reproducible by the agency in that form or format.").
[196] 5 U.S.C. § 552(a)(6).

As with the CPRA, federal agencies are required to provide any "reasonably segregable" information.[197] In other words, if a record contains some information that is disclosable and some information that is exempt, the disclosable information must be provided if it can be separated from the exempt information without too much work. Always ask for any reasonably segregable information to be provided.

In addition, if any agency denies a request for records, it must notify you of its determination "and the reasons therefor."[198] It must also "make a reasonable effort to estimate the volume of any requested matter the provision of which is denied, and shall provide any such estimate to the person making the request unless providing such estimate would harm an interest protected by the exemption ... pursuant to which the denial is made."[199] It's a good idea to remind the agency of these obligations in your request.

Appendix E contains a model FOIA request letter, which can be modified depending on the nature of your request. There are also several resources that you can use for assistance in drafting a request for information under the FOIA. One of the best is the Reporters Committee for Freedom of the Press, which has a website with a program that helps you generate a request: http://www.rcfp.org/foi_letter/generate.php.

A Note on FOIA Requests: First, as with the CPRA, it's generally a good idea to make a written request, and a written request may be required by the agency's FOIA regulations. Second, try to make your request as clear as possible. Keep in mind that you must request existing records; the government generally is not required to create a record in response to a request. You may be able to identify specific types of records maintained by the agency that have the information you want (for example, by asking for the agency's index of records). However, this is often difficult for someone outside the government. Make your request anyway, and include a request to the agency to assist you in identifying records that have the information you are seeking.

A Note on FOIA Responses: Don't expect a response within 20 days. Federal agencies routinely ignore that deadline. Unfortunately, the courts have recognized that a backlog of FOIA requests may justify an agency's delay in responding. Congress does not adequately fund FOIA compliance, so federal agencies often have long backlogs. What can you do to get a timely response? First, you can **make a request for an expedited response** under certain circumstances. Every federal agency is required to adopt regulations providing for expedited handling of requests if a "compelling need" for the information is shown.[200] Under the FOIA, a compelling need means:

> (I) that a failure to obtain requested records on an expedited basis under this paragraph could reasonably be expected to pose an imminent threat to the life or physical safety of an individual; or

---

[197] 5 U.S.C. § 552(b) ("Any reasonably segregable portion of a record shall be provided to any person requesting such record after deletion of the portions which are exempt under this subsection. The amount of information deleted shall be indicated on the released portion of the record, unless including that indication would harm an interest protected by the exemption in this subsection under which the deletion is made. If technically feasible, the amount of the information deleted shall be indicated at the place in the record where such deletion is made.")

[198] 5 U.S.C. § 552(a)(6)(A)(i).

[199] 5 U.S.C. § 552(a)(6)(F).

[200] 5 U.S.C. § 552(a)(6)(E)(i).

(II) with respect to a request made by a person primarily engaged in disseminating information, urgency to inform the public concerning actual or alleged Federal Government activity.[201]

If these circumstances exist, request expedited treatment. To properly request expedited treatment, you must certify in your request that the basis for your request is true and correct to the best of your knowledge and belief.

Second, even if you don't have a basis for making a request for expedited treatment, you can *be a squeaky wheel*. If you have difficulties getting a response, keep track of all the people you have dealt with, send a formal written request for the record(s) and follow up frequently.

4. Can the Government Charge Me for Providing Information?

One way in which the FOIA is different than the CPRA is the costs that can be charged for providing information. Under the FOIA, agencies may charge not only for the costs of making copies, but also for the time to collect the information you have requested.

However, under certain circumstances the costs that can be charged by the agency are limited. Federal agencies are required to adopt regulations regarding the fees that may be charged for responding to requests, and when fees will be waived or reduced. At a minimum, those regulations require that:

> (I) fees shall be limited to reasonable standard charges for document search, duplication, and review, when records are requested for commercial use;
>
> (II) fees shall be limited to reasonable standard charges for document duplication when records are not sought for commercial use and the request is made by an educational or noncommercial scientific institution, whose purpose is scholarly or scientific research; or a representative of the news media.[202]

In addition, you may be able to obtain a complete waiver of fees:

> Documents shall be furnished without any charge or at a charge reduced below the fees established under [the preceding] clause ... if disclosure of the information is in the public interest because it is likely to contribute significantly to public understanding of the operations or activities of the government and is not primarily in the commercial interest of the requester. [203]

Be sure to include a request for reduced fees or a waiver if you qualify under any of these provisions. Explain the circumstances justifying the reduction or waiver in your request.

Moreover, although the agency is allowed to charge a fee for collecting and copying records, it is not required to do so. Therefore, even if you are not entitled to a fee waiver under the FOIA, include a request that the agency waive the fees. Explain why you are making the request – for example, because you do not have the funds to pay more than a small amount.

---

[201]   5 U.S.C. § 552(a)(6)(E)(v).
[202]   5 U.S.C. § 552(a)(4)(A)(ii)
[203]   5 U.S.C. § 552(a)(4)(A)(iii).

5. What Can I Do If the Government Won't Provide the Information I Request?

Four things may happen when you submit a FOIA request. It may be granted, it may be rejected, it may be acknowledged and set aside or it may be ignored. Often you will receive an acknowledgement of your request, telling you that it will be addressed when the agency has dealt with earlier requests. It is safe to say that few requests are granted in full without delay.

a. If your request is denied. If the agency is denying all or part of your request, it must cite the specific basis for the denial of each record that is withheld and inform you of your appeal rights. You can sue the government to obtain the requested information. Before you do, however, there is one step that you must take, and one step to consider taking.

First, before you can sue under the FOIA, you are required to appeal the denial to the agency itself. The regulations of each agency provide an appeal process. Under the FOIA, the agency is required to respond to any appeal within 20 days. If it does not, you may proceed with a lawsuit. A sample FOIA Appeal Letter is included in Appendix F.

Second, before you appeal, consider requesting a list of the records that are responsive to your request, and which the government is refusing to provide. Such a list, referred to as a *Vaughn* index, is generally required to be provided once the case goes to court. However, you can request it at any time, and it will assist you in pursuing your appeal or your lawsuit.

If you prevail in a lawsuit under the FOIA, the court may award you attorneys' fees and certain costs. Although courts are not required to award attorneys' fees, the cases that have interpreted this provision say that fees usually should be awarded, and courts usually do award some amount of attorneys' fees.

b. If the agency does not respond in the time allowed. If the agency does not respond to your request within 20 days (or a longer period of time, in "unusual circumstances"), you are also entitled to bring a lawsuit. In this case, you do not need to appeal to the agency itself.[204] However, the FOIA provides that an agency may be allowed additional time to respond to a request if it is acting diligently, and courts are sometimes reluctant to compel federal agencies to provide records if there is a reasonable explanation for the delay.[205]

A Note on Enforcing the FOIA: Don't hesitate to make a FOIA request, but be prepared to work hard to get a response. Unfortunately, the FOIA is not a very effective mechanism for obtaining information from the government. Delay and resistance are more typical responses to FOIA requests than compliance. It often takes persistence simply to obtain a response. Delay may be allowed by the courts, the exemptions are often broadly applied, and the burden may be placed on those seeking access to justify why information should be provided, rather than on the government to show why it should not. Reforms to the FOIA are currently pending in Congress, but only strong public pressure is likely to result in their becoming law. In the meantime, enlisting the aid of a member of Congress may help expedite a meaningful response.

c. What information is exempt from disclosure under the FOIA? Unlike the CPRA, FOIA has only nine exemptions. However, like the CPRA, the FOIA has an exemption that incorporates the myriad restrictions on public access to information in government records

---

[204] 5 U.S.C. § 552(a)(6)(C)(i).
[205] 5 U.S.C. § 552(a)(6)(C)(i).

contained in other federal laws.[206] Moreover, these broad exemptions have been applied to a wide variety of records. In addition, FOIA has been extensively litigated since its inception in 1966, giving each of the nine exemptions a complex history of judicial interpretation. Each is briefly described below.

1. Exemption 1: National Security and Foreign Policy Classified Data.

Records that are (a) specifically authorized under criteria established by an Executive Order to be kept secret in the interests of national defense or foreign policy; and (b) are so classified pursuant to an Executive Order.[207]

2. Exemption 2: Internal Personnel Policies.

Records that are related solely to the internal personnel rules and practices of an agency.[208]

3. Exemption 3: Data Exempt From Disclosure Under Other Statutes.

Records that are specifically exempted from disclosure by federal statute, provided that the statute (a) requires that the matters be withheld from the public in such a manner as to leave no discretion to the agency on the issue; or (b) establishes particular types of matters to be withheld.[209]

4. Exemption 4: Confidential Proprietary Data.

Records that are trade secrets, and commercial or financial information obtained from a person that are privileged or confidential.[210] As explained by the United States attorney general, the exemption covers two categories of information in federal agency records: "(1) trade secrets; and (2) information that is (a) commercial or financial, *and* (b) obtained from a person, *and* (c) privileged or confidential."[211]

5. Exemption 5: Non-Discoverable Internal Government Communications.

Records that are inter-agency or intra-agency memoranda or letters that would not be available by law to a party other than someone in litigation with the agency.[212]

6. Exemption 6: Private Personal Data.

Records that are personnel files, medical files or similar files, the disclosure of which would constitute a clearly unwarranted invasion of personal privacy.[213]

---

[206] 5 U.S.C. § 552(b)(3).

[207] 5 U.S.C. § 552(b)(1).

[208] 5 U.S.C. § 552(b)(2).

[209] 5 U.S.C. § 552(b)(3).

[210] 5 U.S.C. § 552(b)(4).

[211] Freedom of Information Act Guide, May 2004, United States Department of Justice, available at http://www.usdoj.gov/04foia/foi-act.htm. Note that the Guide is updated every two years. Be sure to look for the most recent version.

[212] 5 U.S.C. § 552(b)(5).

[213] 5 U.S.C. § 552(b)(6).

7. Exemption 7: Investigatory/Law Enforcement Records.

Investigatory records compiled for law enforcement purposes, but only to the extent that production of such records would: (a) interfere with enforcement proceedings; (b) deprive a person of a right to a fair trial or impartial adjudication; (c) constitute an unwarranted invasion of personal privacy; (d) disclose the identity of a confidential source and, in the case of a record compiled by a criminal law enforcement authority in the course of a criminal investigation or by an agency conducting a lawful national security intelligence investigation, disclose confidential information furnished only by the confidential source; (e) disclose investigative techniques and procedures; or (f) endanger the life or physical safety of law enforcement personnel.[214]

8. Exemption 8: Financial Regulation Records.

Examination, operating or condition reports prepared by, on behalf of, or for the use of an agency responsible for the regulation or supervision of financial institutions.[215]

9. Exemption 9: Geological and Geophysical Data.

Geological and geophysical information and data, including maps concerning wells.[216]

D. WHAT EXEMPTIONS DOES THE GOVERNMENT MOST OFTEN ASSERT?

This book cannot provide a detailed description of all of the FOIA exemptions. However, certain justifications for nondisclosure are frequently relied upon by government agencies. Some of the justifications that are used most often are the following.

1. Privacy.

a. If a legitimate privacy interest is asserted, information will not be disclosed if it does not cast light on the conduct of the government. The United States Supreme Court has addressed the assertion of personal privacy as a basis for nondisclosure several times. In *United States Department of Justice, et al. v. Reporters Committee For Freedom of the Press et al.*, 489 U.S. 749 (1989), the high court denied a media request for a "rap sheet" of a reputed mobster. The court concluded that release of the information would invade the subject's privacy rights, even though all of the information was available in various public records. It said that the difficulty of gathering the information from various public sources created a "practical obscurity" for the information. It also stated that releasing the information would not shed light on the workings of government, which, the court said, was the purpose of the FOIA. Thus, the court limited the scope of the FOIA to information that can be said to cast light on the conduct of the government, at least where there is a countervailing privacy interest.

b. If a legitimate privacy interest is asserted, information will not be disclosed unless you can independently show that government impropriety may have occurred. In *National Archives and Records Administration v. Favish,* 541 U.S. 157 (2004), the Supreme Court reversed a decision that granted access to death scene photographs of Vincent Foster, a White House

---

[214]   5 U.S.C. § 552(b)(7).
[215]   5 U.S.C. § 552(b)(8).
[216]   5 U.S.C. § 552(b)(9).

attorney in the Clinton administration. The Supreme Court said that Foster's family members had a legitimate interest in preserving the privacy of the photographs, and that therefore "the requester must produce evidence that would warrant a belief by a reasonable person that the alleged Government impropriety might have occurred." The requester had not shown more than a "bare suspicion" of government misconduct, so the photographs were not subject to disclosure.

2. Proprietary Commercial Information.

A great deal of information is submitted to the government by businesses, nonprofits and individuals. The information may be submitted by those seeking to do business with the government, it may be submitted pursuant to legal requirements for disclosure of certain information or it may be provided in response to requests from the government. For example, when the merger of two large businesses creates antitrust concerns, both those businesses and other businesses in the field may be required to submit information to the government.

Exemption 4 makes much of the information submitted to the government by businesses exempt from disclosure. Although the law regarding when such information will be exempt varies somewhat around the country, in general the courts have recognized two primary interests that may justify nondisclosure:

> To summarize, commercial or financial matter is "confidential" for purposes of the exemption if disclosure of the information is likely to have either of the following effects: (1) to impair the Government's ability to obtain necessary information in the future; or (2) to cause substantial harm to the competitive position of the person from whom the information was obtained.[217]

Executive Order 12600 requires notification of an entity that submitted confidential commercial information if an agency "determines that it may be required to disclose" such information under the FOIA. They must be given a reasonable period of time within which to object to disclosure of any of the requested information.

In *Chrysler Corp. v. Brown*, 441 U.S. 281 (1979), the United States Supreme Court held that the FOIA itself does not permit a person or entity that has provided information to the government to sue to prevent disclosure. However, the court held that review of an agency's decision to disclose records under the FOIA can be brought under the Administrative Procedure Act (APA). Accordingly, a private lawsuit can be brought by a third party that has submitted information to the government in order to prevent you from obtaining that information. The lawsuits are generally referred to as "reverse FOIA" actions. According to the United States attorney general, "plaintiffs ordinarily argue that an agency's contemplated release would violate the Trade Secrets Act and thus would 'not be in accordance with law,' or would be 'arbitrary and capricious' within the meaning of the APA."[218]

3. Deliberative Process Privilege.

According to the United States attorney general, "The most commonly invoked privilege incorporated within Exemption 5 is the deliberative process privilege, the general purpose of

---

[217]   *National Parks & Conservation Ass'n v. Morton*, 498 F.2d 765, 770 (D.C. Cir. 1974).
[218]   *See* Freedom of Information Act Guide, May 2004, United States Department of Justice, http://www.usdoj.gov/oip/reverse.htm.

which is to 'prevent injury to the quality of agency decisions.'"[219] In order to be exempt from disclosure under this doctrine, two fundamental requirements must be met. First, it must be predecisional, *i.e.*, it must predate the agency decision to which it relates. Second, it must be deliberative, *i.e.*, "a direct part of the deliberative process in that it makes recommendations or expresses opinions on legal or policy matters."[220] The burden is upon the agency to show that the information in question satisfies both requirements.[221]

An important limitation on the deliberative process privilege is that it applies only to "deliberative," and generally does not apply to purely factual matters, or to the factual portions of otherwise deliberative documents.[222] However, according to the United States attorney general, courts may allow agencies to withhold factual information in two situations: "The first circumstance occurs when the author of a document selects specific facts out of a larger group of facts and this very act is deliberative in nature. ... The second such circumstance is when factual information is so inextricably connected to the deliberative material that its disclosure would expose or cause harm to the agency's deliberations."[223]

The FOIA is not the useful and effective tool for providing public access to information that it was intended to be. It has been hedged in by judicial decisions that grant broad exemptions, and that fail to rein in the frequent – indeed nearly constant – delay and evasion by federal agencies. However, for those who are patient and diligent, it remains a useful means for casting some light on the government.

---

[219] *See* Freedom of Information Act Guide, May 2004, United States Department of Justice, http://www.usdoj.gov/oip/exemption5.htm#deliberative.

[220] *See Mapother v. Dep't of Justice*, 3 F.3d 1533, 1537 (D.C. Cir. 1993) ("The deliberative process privilege protects materials that are both predecisional and deliberative."); *Vaughn v. Rosen*, 523 F.2d 1136, 1143-44 (D.C. Cir. 1975).

[221] *See, e.g., Coastal States Gas Corp. v. Dep't of Energy*, 617 F.2d 854, 866 (D.C. Cir. 1980).

[222] *See, e.g., EPA v. Mink*, 410 U.S. 73, 91 (1973) (deliberative process privilege does not apply to "factual material otherwise available on discovery merely [because] it was placed in a memorandum with matters of law, policy, or opinion").

[223] *See* Freedom of Information Act Guide, May 2004, United States Department of Justice, http://www.usdoj.gov/oip/exemption5.htm#deliberative.

CHAPTER 3

Proposition 59: A Constitutional Right of Access

IN THIS CHAPTER

Proposition 59, enacted overwhelmingly in 2004, provides a new constitutional right of access, independent of pre-existing statutory access rights, to government records and meetings. Less clear, however, is whether Prop. 59 adds anything, substantively or procedurally, to statutory rights (principally the Public Records Act and Brown Act). Published court decisions have so far avoided relying on Prop. 59, so at this point it raises more questions than it answers. Key issues: Do the Prop. 59 guidelines regarding how authorities providing or limiting access require reconsideration of older court decisions? Does Prop. 59 eliminate the "deliberative process privilege" that courts have relied upon to restrict access to a wide variety of records? Does Prop. 59 apply to the state judiciary? In the meantime, reporters and citizens should keep Prop. 59 in mind when deciding whether and how to seek access to government records and meetings.

PART I:
INTRODUCTION

A new tool has been placed in the public's open government kit. On Nov. 2, 2004, the people of California voted to amend the state constitution to create a new civil right: ***a constitutional right of access to government information***. They did so when they approved Proposition 59 with a ringing endorsement of more than 83 percent of the vote (Official title: "Public Records, Open Meetings – Legislative Constitutional Amendment"). The proposition, placed on the ballot by the Legislature after unanimous votes in both the Senate and Assembly, amended the California Constitution to add a right of public access to "information concerning the conduct of the people's business."

As a result, article I, section 3(b)(1) of the California Constitution, known as the "Sunshine Amendment" or "Prop. 59" now states: "The people have the right of access to information concerning the conduct of the people's business, and, therefore, the meetings of public bodies and the writings of public officials and agencies shall be open to public scrutiny."

PART II:
MAIN PROVISIONS OF THE SUNSHINE AMENDMENT

A. A CONSTITUTIONAL RIGHT OF ACCESS.

According to the ballot argument in favor of Prop. 59, it "create[s] a new civil right: a constitutional right to know what the government is doing, why it is doing it and how."[1] Thus, the first section of the Sunshine Amendment creates a constitutional right of access that is

---

[1]   *See* http://vote2004.ss.ca.gov/voterguide/propositions/prop59-arguments.htm.

independent of existing statutory rights, such as the California Public Records Act (*see* Chapter 2) and the Brown Act and Bagley-Keene Act (*see* Chapter 1).

B. RULES FOR THE INTERPRETATION AND APPLICATION OF STATUTES, RULES AND "OTHER AUTHORITY" REGULATING PUBLIC ACCESS.

The second section of the Sunshine Amendment sets out rules of construction that courts and public agencies are supposed to use when interpreting "a statute, court rule or other authority" that affects this new right of public access.[2] With respect to authorities in place ***before*** enactment of Prop. 59, courts are required to interpret them ***broadly*** if they ***further*** the public right of access. Authorities predating Prop. 59 that ***limit*** access, on the other hand, are to be interpreted ***narrowly***.

One reason these rules of construction are potentially important is because they can be seen as a directive to courts to take a fresh look at pre-2004 court decisions that limited or curtailed public access to government meetings or records. Ordinarily, courts are not free to reconsider legal issues that have been previously decided in published decisions issued by the California Supreme Court or courts of appeal in the same jurisdiction. This is referred to as the doctrine of *stare decisis*. But if the "other authority" in the constitution includes judicial opinions – and there is nothing in the language or history of the constitutional amendment to suggest otherwise – the new access right stands as an exception to *stare decisis*. That means it requires reconsideration of prior court decisions and overturning those that relied on a narrow interpretation of the access right or a broad interpretation of a limitation on access.

The Sunshine Amendment also prescribes rules of construction for a "statute, court rule or other authority" adopted ***after*** the constitutional amendment.[3] If those authorities *limit* public access to information, they must include findings demonstrating the specific interest or interests served by the limitation on access and the need for protecting that interest. Lawmakers contemplating new laws should be reminded of this stricture.

Thus, the thrust of the Sunshine Amendment is to require government bodies to clearly justify why information requested by the public or media should be kept from public view and to ensure that secrecy is imposed only when it is justified. The aims of the proponents of Prop. 59, including the California Newspaper Publishers Association, the California First Amendment Coalition, and both Democratic and Republican sponsors in the State Senate, were to reaffirm the principle of public access to government information and to put the burden of justifying secrecy on the relevant government entities.

Proponents believed that past administrative interpretations, subsequent legislation and court decisions – many of which are described elsewhere in this publication – had limited the thrust of the California Public Records Act, the Brown Act and other laws mandating open government to the point that important aspects of "the people's business" were being kept under wraps. Prop. 59 was intended to reverse that trend.

C. OTHER EFFECTS OF THE SUNSHINE AMENDMENT.

In what other ways does the new constitutional right of access improve on the rights of access as they existed solely on the basis of California's statutory access schemes?

One difference is that Prop. 59 may provide a public right of access to the judiciary, a branch of government that traditionally has been exempt from statutory access schemes. Prop. 59 makes

---

[2]   Cal. Const., article I, section 3(b)(2).

[3]   Cal. Const., article I, section 3(b)(2).

no exception for records of the judiciary. The Legislature that drafted Prop. 59 and submitted it to the popular vote could have excluded the courts if it chose. It did so when creating the California Public Records Act,[4] which requires disclosure of public records of local and state agencies and defines "state agency" as every state body "except those agencies provided for in Article IV ... or Article VI of the California Constitution."[5] Article IV refers to the Legislature; Article VI refers to the courts. In other words, the Public Records Act expressly exempts the judiciary. Prop. 59 does not.

Moreover, Prop. 59, expressly limits the effect of the new access right on the Legislature. It specifically says that it does not repeal or modify existing protections for legislative proceedings and records, and it refers to Article IV of the constitution. However, it contains no reference to the courts or to Article VI of the constitution. This history suggests strongly that the Legislature made a choice *not* to exclude the judiciary from the new access right.

Lawyers for the judiciary have argued that the courts are exempt under subsection 5 of Prop. 59, which states that the new access right "does not repeal or nullify, expressly or by implication, any constitutional or statutory exception to the right of access to public records or meetings of public bodies that is in effect on the effective date of this subdivision." While this clause reaffirms the courts' preexisting exemption from the Public Records Act and other statutory access rights, it says nothing about the judiciary's status under Prop. 59, which creates a constitutional right of access independent of the Public Records Act and other state laws. The better view, in our opinion, is that Prop. 59 applies to the state courts, creating a right of access to court records.

PART III:
IMPACT OF THE SUNSHINE AMENDMENT

To what extent the new constitutional amendment will achieve the aim of greater access to information is uncertain. This is so in part because the courts have not yet had many opportunities to interpret it, and in part because of the language of the amendment. For example, the amendment explicitly states that it does not modify or weaken the right of privacy guaranteed to Californians elsewhere in the state constitution.[6] Thus, the new right of access to information must still be weighed against individual privacy rights, on a case-by-case basis. Another provision, as we have seen, preserves pre-existing "exception[s] to the right of access."[7]

In addition, the new right of access remains relatively untested in the courts. A handful of cases have discussed the new right in passing. In one, a California court of appeal held that the Brown Act barred the San Diego redevelopment agency and a city-created nonprofit from holding closed sessions regarding eminent domain legislation to which they were not parties. However, the court did not rely on the new constitutional amendment in reaching its decision. In fact, it stated explicitly that because of the amendment's language about not repealing previous exceptions, the new right of access did not apply.[8]

In another case, a court held that a community college superintendent's personal performance goals were exempt from disclosure under the California Public Records Act. The court mentioned the new right of access in passing, as well as the mandate to give a narrow interpretation to laws

---

[4]   Government Code sections 6250 and following.
[5]   Government Code section 6252(f).
[6]   California Constitution, Article I, Section 3(b)(3).
[7]   California Constitution, Article I, Section 3(b)(5).
[8]   *Shapiro v. Board of Directors,* 134 Cal. App. 4th 170 (2005).

limiting access. Nonetheless, the court held that a pre-existing exemption from disclosure applied and the superintendent's privacy rights trumped the public right of access.[9]

In addition, a court held that certain police records were exempt from disclosure under the California Public Records Act. One judge partially dissented from the majority's decision, citing the new public right of access and its guidelines for interpreting the law.[10] The California Supreme Court recently overturned the appellate court's decision and allowed access to the information.

In contrast, at least one appellate decision has relied on Prop. 59 in sustaining an access claim, albeit in an unpublished opinion. In the 2005 case the court cited the new right of access in support of its decision that the meetings of a water company owned by the city of Upland and citizens of a surrounding area were meetings of a public agency and should be open to the public under the Brown Act.[11] However, courts are *not* required to follow unpublished decisions.

In early 2006, The Press-Enterprise Company and the California First Amendment Coalition petitioned for a writ against the Superior Court of California, County of Riverside, and its presiding judge seeking production of a settlement agreement between the court and one of its former commissioners.[12] The commissioner had sued the court alleging, among other things, discriminatory treatment, and a settlement had been reached. The settlement agreement contained a confidentiality clause. On that basis, the Riverside court refused to provide documents relating to the settlement to the two petitioners, and terms of the settlement remained secret. In response to the petition, the court, represented by private counsel, demurred, claiming, among other things, that Prop. 59 was not a proper vehicle for seeking the documents.

In an unpublished decision in June 2006, the demurrer was overruled. The judge (specially assigned in the matter) ruled that the court might issue a writ against the presiding judge in her official capacity, that procedures set forth in California Rule of Court 6.710[13] were not the exclusive remedy for seeking such records and that the new constitutional amendment weighed against broad interpretation of such procedural restrictions. Shortly after this decision, the Riverside court acquiesced and provided the documents requested. Thus, no published decision resulted to aid in future petitions.

Similar circumstances led to a very recent court of appeal decision. A school district's board of education hired an investigator to prepare a report analyzing allegations of misconduct by the district's superintendent. Portions of the report were released to a newspaper by people the investigator had interviewed. After receiving the full report in confidence, the board of education entered into an agreement with the superintendent accepting his resignation in exchange for terms of payment and a promise to keep the report confidential. The public and the media smelled a "sweetheart deal" and demanded the board release the report. The board refused, the trial court upheld the board's decision and the matter was appealed.

Although the appellate court referred to the Sunshine Amendment, it went on to say that it would not rely upon it in coming to its decision under the California Public Records Act.

> "By its own terms, however, the amendment has little impact on our construction of
> the Public Records Act as that statute applies to this case. The amendment requires
> the Public Records Act to 'be broadly construed if it furthers the people's right of

[9] *Versaci v. Superior Court*, 127 Cal. App. 4th 805 (2005).

[10] *California Commission on Peace Officer Standards and Training v. Superior Court*, 128 Cal. App. 4th 281 (2005), review granted July 27, 2005 (Supreme Court Case No. S134072).

[11] *California First Amendment Coalition, et al. v. San Antonio Water Co.*, Appeal No. E033804, 2005 WL 19449 (Jan. 4. 2005) [unpublished].

[12] *The Press-Enterprise Company v. Superior Court*, Case No. RIC444406 [unpublished].

[13] Rule 6.710 has been renumbered as California Rule of Court 10.803.

access, and narrowly construed if it limits the right of access.' (Cal. Const., art. I, § 3, subd. (b), para. (2).) Moreover, the amendment does not modify or further limit an individual's right of privacy as protected by the Public Records Act. Nothing in the amendment 'supersedes or modifies the right of privacy guaranteed by Section 1 [of the state constitution] or affects the construction of any statute [such as the Public Records Act], court rule, or other authority to the extent that it protects that right to privacy. ...' (Cal. Const., art. I, § 3, subd. (b), para. (3).)"[14]

The superintendent's right to privacy was implicated by the records request. The court relied on the terms of the Public Records Act and its jurisprudence to resolve the matter. Under the circumstances presented, the court concluded the Public Records Act required disclosure, subject to conditions.

Once again, a decision was made by referring to Prop. 59, but avoiding direct application or decision based upon it. Citizens, journalists and legal professionals must await further guidance from courts.

PART IV:
CONCLUSION

In sum, Prop. 59, enacted with broad public support in 2004, provides a potentially significant state constitutional right of public access to government information. It may be, and should be, cited by citizens, reporters and media organizations in disputes with government entities over access to meetings and records. Legal actions to compel access or disclosure under this right hold much promise.

However, because Prop. 59 is, at this time, largely untested, the likely outcome of litigation under this new civil right is uncertain. Also uncertain is the extent to which this new right of access will enhance access to information or meetings that were previously shielded from the public via exceptions in the California Public Records Act, the Brown Act and other sunshine laws. Only time will tell if Prop. 59, the Sunshine Amendment, will live up to its promise.

---

[14]   *BRV, Inc. v. Superior Court (Dunsmuir Joint Union High School Dist.)*, 143 Cal. App. 4th 742 (2006)

CHAPTER 4

Government Treatment of the Media: Discrimination and Accreditation

IN THIS CHAPTER

Public officials are generally not required to affirmatively communicate with media. However, state laws allow journalists to access public records and the meetings of many state and local government bodies. In addition, when public officials do speak to the media, the Constitution generally prohibits them from discriminating among news outlets. In some cases, it is unconstitutional for a public official or agency to limit the speech of other government officials and employees. A press pass is not required to access meetings of government bodies or public records, but having one issued by an employing news agency or a government agency can ease or eliminate barriers to people and places. Although no law requires a governmental agency to issue press passes, if it does so, the process is subject to constitutional principles that limit the government's ability to deny requests for press passes or revoke passes that have previously been issued.

PART I:
INTRODUCTION

As a general rule, public officials are not required to communicate with the media. This means that they are not required to return reporters' telephone calls, or hold press conferences, or grant media requests for interviews. Similarly, the media does not have an automatic right to attend all gatherings of government officials, even when those gatherings take place in government-owned buildings.

When access to public sources of information is limited or denied, a two-step analysis should be employed. The first step is to consider whether a particular law entitles the reporter to the information. The California Public Records Act provides a right to inspect and copy documents prepared, owned, used or retained by state or local agencies.[1] Similarly, the Brown Act and Bagley-Keane Act provide a right of access to the meetings of legislative bodies of local and state agencies.[2] A Sunshine Ordinance may expand the media's right of access to public records and/or meetings of public bodies in a city or county governed by such an ordinance.[3] And in 2004, California passed Proposition 59, which amended Article 1, section 3 of the California Constitution to provide a state constitutional right of access to the meetings of public bodies and the writings of public officials and agencies. If a reporter or a member of the public is denied access that is provided by law, he or she may seek redress under the particular law violated, as discussed in Chapters 1 (public meetings) and 2 (public records).

The second step is to determine if the state or federal constitution has been violated. Part II of this chapter addresses situations in which the media may have grounds for raising a constitutional challenge, even though a specific right of access does not exist, when a government agency or official grants access to some members of the media but not to others. In addition, journalists

---

[1]   Government Code sections 6250 *et seq.*
[2]   Government Code sections 54950 & 111125 *et seq.*
[3]   For a discussion of local Sunshine Ordinances, see Chapter 2.

generally do not need a press pass to attend public meetings or trials, gather information from official files open as a matter of law or perform the basic job of asking questions and gathering facts. Under the First Amendment, this activity cannot be licensed. It is everyone's right as a citizen. Sometimes, however, a government or private entity will create its own press credentials (often with restrictions attached) to distribute to journalists and photographers wishing to gain access to specific sites or events not open to the general public. As discussed in Part III, some of these restrictions can be successfully challenged.

PART II:
DISCRIMINATION AMONG NEWS OUTLETS OR REPORTERS

Once a government agency decides to release information or an official has chosen to speak to members of the media, it may be unconstitutional to exclude selected news organization or individual journalists from receiving the same information. In addition, differences in the manner in which information is provided may also be unconstitutional.

A. RIGHT OF EQUAL ACCESS.

Several cases illustrate the rule against discriminating among the media. In one wrongful death lawsuit involving contaminated drinking water, for example, the court barred the parties, counsel and others from making public statements about the suit or providing access to certain documents obtained in discovery, but it made an exception for one member of the media who wanted access for a documentary that would air after the jury was seated. After other members of the media challenged this arrangement, a federal appellate court found that it was unconstitutional:

> A court may not selectively exclude news media from access to information otherwise made available for public dissemination. ... Such a practice is unquestionably at odds with the First Amendment. Neither the courts nor any other branch of the government can be allowed to affect the content and tenor of the news by choreographing which news organizations have access to relevant information.[4]

Unconstitutional discriminatory treatment of the media can arise in many other situations. For example, courts have found violations of the First Amendment and the Equal Protection clause where a mayor excluded a particular reporter from press conferences to which the public generally was invited,[5] where a sheriff prevented department officials from releasing any information to reporters for a particular newspaper except in response to a written request,[6] and where city officials denied reporters for a particular newspaper access to police files generally available to other reporters.[7] In California, a court held that the City of Los Angeles could not constitutionally give one television station the exclusive right to film an official ceremony and celebration commemorating the Mexican War from the stage at City Hall Plaza.[8]

---

[4] *Anderson v. Cryovac, Inc.*, 805 F.3d 1, 9 (1st Cir. 1986).

[5] *Borreca v. Fasi*, 369 F. Supp. 906, 910-11 (D. Haw. 1974).

[6] *Times Picayune Publishing Corp. v. Lee*, 15 Med. L. Rep. 1713, 1716-19 (E.D. La. 1988).

[7] *Quad-City Community News Service, Inc. v. Hebens*, 334 F. Supp. 8, 15 (S.D. Iowa 1971).

[8] *Telemundo of Los Angeles v. United States District Court*, 283 F. Supp. 2d 1095, 1104 (C.D. Cal. 2003).

The rule against discriminatory access also applies to state-owned media. In a case involving a state-owned computerized database containing full text of proposed legislation, the federal Court of Appeals in New York "perceive[d] no merit in the proposition that government may accord a state organ of communication preferential access to information and deny to the private press the right to retransmit the information."[9]

The rule against discriminatory access only goes so far, however. In two recent cases – one in Ohio and another in Maryland – the media challenged policies forbidding public employees from speaking to certain reporters. In the Ohio case, the mayor of the City of Youngstown directed city officials not to speak with reporters from a publication that had been critical of the mayor and his administration.[10] In the Maryland case, Gov. Robert Ehrlich instructed employees not to speak with a reporter and columnist from a particular newspaper that the governor believed had failed to "objectively report" on issues pertaining to the administration.[11] In both instances, media challenges were unsuccessful. A court in Ohio found a "distinction between access to events and facilities open to the press and access to one-on-one interviews and off-the-record comments. ... [A] limited constitutional right of access applies only where comments by government officials are offered in a forum effectively open to all members of the press."[12]

B. RIGHT OF EQUAL CONVENIENCE.

In addition, "[a]ll representatives of news organizations must not only be given equal access, but within reasonable limits, access with equal convenience to official news sources."[13] Examples of how these so-called "convenience" issues have arisen include:

- Where a reporter for a teachers union newspaper was excluded from a school board press room reserved for "general-circulation media," the court found that it was not enough for the board to designate a separate room for "particular-profession media." The court noted that impromptu interviews with sources often occurred in the main press room, and excluding the teachers union newspaper from this press room would deprive its reporters of the same opportunity, enjoyed by others in the main press room, to seek further clarification or information from those sources.[14]

- Where a special section of the Boston City Council Chambers had been provided for TV camera operators, equipped with electrical outlets and other conveniences, a court held that the Council could not restrict another TV cameraman to the spectator's section.[15]

---

9   *Legi-Tech, Inc. v. Keiper*, 776 F.2d 728, 733 (2d Cir. 1985).

10   Youngstown Publishing Co. v. United States District Court, 2005 U.S. Dist. LEXIS 9476, *2 (N.D. Ohio 2005).

11   The Baltimore Sun Co. v. Ehrlich, 437 F.3d 410, 413 (4th Cir. 2006).

12   Youngstown Publishing Co. v. United States District Court, 2005 U.S. Dist. LEXIS 9476, *17-18 (2005).

13   Westinghouse Broadcasting Co. v. Dukakis, 409 F. Supp. 895, 896 (D. Mass. 1976); accord United Teachers of Dade v. Stierheim, 213 F. Supp. 2d 1368, 1374 (S.D. Fla. 2002) (quoting Westinghouse).

14   United Teachers of Dade v. Stierheim, 213 F. Supp. 2d 1368, 1374 (S.D. Fla. 2002).

15   Westinghouse Broadcasting Co. v. Dukakis, 409 F. Supp. 895, 896 (D. Mass. 1976).

C. RIGHT OF PUBLIC EMPLOYEES TO SPEAK.

While public officials are free to decline to comment to the media, it is unconstitutional in some cases for a government agency or official to prohibit public employees and elected officials from making public comments. This situation can arise under several circumstances.

1. Public Employees.

If a public agency forbids its employees from speaking to the media, the issue is usually whether the First Amendment rights of the employee, rather than those of the media, are being violated. When a public employee wishes to speak to the media but his or her employer forbids it, courts attempt to balance the interests of the employee as a citizen in commenting on matters of public concern and the interests of the government agency as an employer in delivering public services efficiently.

The U.S. Supreme Court has recognized that "the government has an interest in regulating the conduct and 'the speech of its employees that differ[s] significantly from those it possesses in connection with regulation of the speech of the citizenry in general.'"[16] However, this does not mean that the government may issue regulations designed to "gag" the expression of a particular political viewpoint or which govern expressions that do not jeopardize the effectiveness of the employee or the agency. In addition, if a regulation is so sweeping or vague that the employee is threatened with sanctions for statements unrelated to the perceived danger the employer relies on to justify the regulation of speech, it may be unconstitutional.

In a case involving a clerical worker who was fired after making a political remark to a co-employee during a private conversation, the U.S. Supreme Court ruled that firing the worker violated her First Amendment rights. In applying the balancing test, the court said the threshold question is whether the speech "may be fairly characterized as constituting speech on a matter of public concern." Assuming that the statements involve a matter of public concern, the next step is to balance the First Amendment interest of the employee as a citizen commenting on matters of public concern "against the interest of the State, as an employer, in promoting the efficiency of the public service it performs through its employees." This balancing process requires consideration of the specific position held by the public employee:

> [I]in weighing the State's interest in discharging an employee based on any claim
> that the content of a statement made by the employee somehow undermines the
> mission of the public employer, some attention must be paid to the responsibilities
> of the employee within the agency: The burden of caution employees bear with
> respect to the words they speak will vary with the extent of authority and public
> accountability the role entails.[17]

This test, however, may yield results inconsistent with the First Amendment policy, because the public's need to know increases with the importance of the public employees' position. For example, this test could result in a rule that a clerical employee cannot be punished for commenting to the media about how an agency is functioning (because he does not hold a policymaking position) while, on the other hand, sanctioning a city manager might be permissible,

---

[16]   *Civil Service Commission v. National Association of Letter Carriers, AFL-CIO, 75*, 413 U.S. 548, 564 (1982)
        (quoting *Pickering v. Board of Education*, 391 U.S. 563, 568 (1968)).

[17]   *Rankin v. McPherson*, 483 U.S. 378, 390 (1987).

because the city manager is charged with enforcing city policy and his or her public objection to that policy could undermine its enforcement.

However that test may work when applied to individual employees, federal courts have found that broad restrictions on the speech of all public employees in a department violates their First Amendment rights. A series of cases invalidating broad restrictions on the speech of firefighters illustrates the point. One involved a Chicago Fire Department order prohibiting departmental employees, whether on or off duty, from speaking to the media on any subject pertaining to department activities.[18] Another involved Washington, D.C., firefighters who commented about allegedly unsafe equipment and a discriminatory cadet program.[19] A third involved South Dakota firefighters whom management had required to get approval for either on-duty media interviews or comments about "internal business decisions or departmental rules and regulations."[20]

On the other hand, the courts have permitted public agencies to discipline employees who have spoken in their official capacities, as opposed to speaking as private citizens. For example, in one case, the court ruled that a city could properly discipline a recreation supervisor where she used an official interview, as a city spokeswoman, to comment on or criticize her department's policies "in a manner inconsistent with the employer's directions and misstates the employer's policy."[21] In another case, an Illinois sheriff's deputy's letter to the editor of a newspaper was not protected where the deputy identified himself and wrote as a public officer.[22]

The U.S. Supreme Court has also ruled that public employees are not protected by the First Amendment with regard to statements made in the course of their official duties. It did so in a case brought by a deputy district attorney in Los Angeles who was asked by defense counsel to review a case in which, counsel claimed, the affidavit police used to obtain a critical search warrant was inaccurate. He decided that the affidavit made serious misrepresentations, relayed his findings to his supervisors and followed up with a memo recommending dismissal. His supervisors decided to prosecute the case. He subsequently testified about his conclusions at a hearing challenging the warrant. He claimed that his superiors retaliated against him for doing so, in violation of the First Amendment. The Supreme Court rejected his claim. It held the First Amendment does not prohibit discipline based on an employee's expressions made pursuant to official responsibilities. It said that the determinative factor here was not that the employee expressed his views inside his office, rather than publicly, nor that the memo concerned the subject matter of his employment, but rather that his expressions were made pursuant to his official duties.[23]

2. Elected Officials.

Regulations restricting the speech of elected officials are often suspect, because the expressions of an elected official on matters of public concern are inherently political, and political speech enjoys the strongest protection under the First Amendment.

Thus, in a case where a sheriff made statements critical of a local judge's decision and the judge held the sheriff in contempt of court, sentenced him to jail and assessed a fine against him, the U.S. Supreme Court recognized that the sheriff "was an elected official and had the right to enter the field of political controversy, particularly where his political life was at stake. ... The

---

[18] *Grady v. Blair*, 529 F. Supp. 370 (N.D. Ill. 1981) (citing *Muller v. Conlisk*, 429 F.2d 901 (7th Cir. 1970), which struck down a similar restriction on speech by officers in the Chicago Police Department).

[19] *Fire Fighters Association v. Barry*, 742 F. Supp. 1182 (D.D.C. 1990).

[20] *Wolf v. Aberdeen*, 758 F. Supp. 551 (D.S.D. 1991).

[21] *Kotwica v. Tucson*, 801 F.2d 1182, 1184-85 (9th 1986).

[22] *Zook v. Brown*, 865 F.2d 887, 891-92 (7th 1989).

[23] *Garcetti v. Ceballos*, 547 U.S. ___, 126 S. Ct. 1951 (2006).

role that elected officials play in our society makes it all the more imperative that they be allowed freely to express themselves on matters of current public importance."[24]   Because of the importance of allowing elected officials to speak freely, the U.S. Supreme Court held that the free speech rights of an elected official can only be limited in the face of a "clear and present danger."

The "clear and present danger" standard is an exceedingly high bar and limits the ability of government agencies to restrict or punish the speech of elected officials to a few extreme situations. This issue has arisen where elected bodies enact resolutions to prohibit their members or others from revealing anything discussed in a closed meeting (*e.g.*, a closed session of a city council to discuss pending litigation). These are often self-serving gag orders used to quiet dissident members of a body. An argument can be made that they violate the First Amendment rights of the elected members of the body.

In 2002, the California Legislature added a new section to the Brown Act, Government Code section 54963, prohibiting any person from disclosing "confidential information" acquired by being present in a closed session "to a person not entitled to receive it, unless the legislative body authorizes disclosure" of the information. "Confidential information" is defined as "a communication made in a closed session that is specifically related to the basis for the legislative body of a local agency to meet lawfully in closed session under this chapter." Section 54963 goes on to state that a violation may be addressed by injunctive relief, disciplinary action or other means. As of the time this publication went to press, there have been no challenges to this statute on constitutional free speech grounds.

PART II:
MEDIA ACCREDITATION

As a general rule, journalists do not need a press pass to attend public meetings or trials, gather information from official files or perform the basic job of asking questions and gathering facts. Under the First Amendment, this activity cannot be licensed; it is everyone's right as a citizen. Nevertheless, having a press pass may make it easier for reporters and photographers to gain access to news scenes and sources not otherwise available to the general public. For example, in California, "duly authorized" representatives of the news media enjoy special access to accident and disaster scenes.[25]

This does not mean that news organizations must rely on a government agency for a press pass. As the California attorney general has concluded, "the phrase 'duly authorized' refers to the news station, newspaper, or radio or television station or network having 'duly authorized' the individual to be its representative at the site. ... Often, this is accomplished by the news media representative displaying a 'press badge.'"[26]

A press badge or pass may be created by the news organization itself and should include the staff member's name and photograph and identify the media outlet for which the journalist works. The editor or publisher should sign the pass and provide contact information should anyone need to verify or ask questions about the staff member's credentials.

A Note on Photographer's License Plates: Under California Vehicle Code section 5008, any person who is "regularly employed or engaged as a bona fide newspaper, newsreel, or television photographer or cameraman" may apply for special license plates (for an additional fee). To

---

[24]   *Wood v. Georgia*, 370 U.S. 375, 394-95 (1962).
[25]   Penal Code sections 409.05(d); 409.6(d).
[26]   67 Op. Cal. Att'y Gen. 535, 539 & n.3 (1984).

obtain plates under the statute, "the applicant shall, by satisfactory proof, show that he or she is a bona fide newspaper, newsreel, or television photographer or cameraman." The plates, like media accreditation in general, carry no special rights of access. However, because the plates provide an easy way for law enforcement and other government officials to identify members of the media, they may make it easier to obtain access to spot news events.

A. PRESS PASSES ISSUED BY GOVERNMENT ENTITIES.

Although no law requires a governmental agency to issue press passes, if it does so, the process is subject to constitutional principles that limit the government's ability to deny requests for press passes or revoke passes that have previously been issued.

1. Constitutional Requirements.

Once a governmental agency decides to issue press passes to some members of the media, its process for issuing passes becomes subject to constitutional standards and it may not refuse requests for press passes by other members of the media unless it can show a "compelling" reason for doing so, as well as clear "nexus" or logical linkage between the denial of press pass and the means used to protect that interest. To comply with the nexus requirement, the agency or entity must show that there is no less restrictive means to achieve the government's asserted goal.[27] For example, a court held that a reporter for a teachers union newspaper could not be excluded from the school board press room on the grounds that her publication did not qualify as "general circulation media." Although the school board cited an interest in controlling disruption, space constraint issues and "providing reporters with a press room unfettered from any undue influence," the court found that excluding "particular-profession" media from the press room was not the least restrictive means to reach the ends asserted by the board.[28]

Arbitrary or content-based criteria for obtaining a press pass are prohibited under the First Amendment.[29] For example, refusing to grant a press pass to one news organization based upon the perceived inaccuracy or bias of its news coverage is unconstitutional content-based discrimination. Similarly, a government entity cannot refuse to issue or recognize an individual journalist's press pass or create additional hurdles to obtaining a press pass out of personal dislike or because the journalist, in his previous reporting, has cast the government entity in an unfavorable light.[30]

Freelance reporters and photographers, and those from alternative or Internet-based publications, may find it more difficult to obtain press credentials. However, press passes may not be denied simply because the issuing agency views the publication or reporter as not "established."[31] Such distinctions have been found to constitute viewpoint discrimination.

A government agency must disclose its rationale for limiting or denying press passes. If it denies a request for a press pass, it must inform the applicant of the specific reason for denial and provide the applicant with an opportunity to respond. If the applicant takes advantage of this

---

[27]   *Sherrill v. Knight*, 569 F.2d 124, 129 (D.C. Cir. 1977); *Lewis v. Baxley*, 368 F. Supp. 768, 780-81 (M.D. Ala. 1973); *Quad-City Community News Service, Inc. v. Hebens*, 334 F. Supp. 8, 17 (S.D. Iowa 1971).

[28]   *United Teachers of Dade v. Stierheim*, 213 F. Supp. 2d 1368, 1375-76 (S.D. Fla. 2002).

[29]   *Id.*

[30]   *Borreca v. Fasi*, 369 F. Supp. 906, 910 (D. Haw. 1974); *Southwestern Newspapers Corp. v. Curtis*, 584 S.W.2d 362, 363-68 (Tex. App. 1979).

[31]   *Quad-City Community News Service v. Jebens*, 334 F. Supp. 8, 12 (S.D. Iowa 1971).

appeal opportunity but the government agency stands by its denial, the government agency must provide the applicant with a written statement of reasons.[32]

2. Legitimate Reasons for Government Denials of Press Access or Credentials.

Circumstances do exist where a government actor or entity may deny access to an individual journalist or news organization without violating the constitution, even when the event or scene is open to other members of the media or is normally open to the public generally.

a. Space/security constraints. Government entities are often faced with the task of determining which members of the press they will grant access to a scene or event. Space or security constraints may require the exclusion of some media members, and reasonable, objective criteria for rationing access must be sometimes be imposed. Press passes providing access to crowded scenes of police, fire and rescue operations may be rationed based on the applicant's demonstrated need. One legitimate and objective measure of need is whether the applicant's news organization regularly carries spot news of accidents, disasters and police operations.[33] Another legitimate measure of need is whether the applicant is regularly working as a journalist, measured in terms of time or income.[34]

b. Criminal record of a reporter. Press passes that provide access to locations of heightened security concern may be denied to convicted felons – *i.e.,* those whose offenses reasonably raise questions as to their trustworthiness.[35]

B. PRESS PASSES ISSUED BY PRIVATE ENTITIES.

In general, owners of private property – such as privately owned sports arenas and concert venues – do not have to abide by the same constitutional requirements imposed on government entities; they can exclude individual reporters arbitrarily or grant access to specific journalists as they please.

1. State Actors.

In some cases, however, the private entity qualifies as a "state actor." State actors are held to the same constitutional standards for issuing and denying press passes as government entities and must not discriminate against members of the media on the basis of content, viewpoint or for any other improper purpose.

The extent to which a private entity can be considered a "state actor" is highly fact-specific. Some of the relevant factors that a court would consider are: (1) the existence of a symbiotic relationship between the government and the private entity – *i.e.,* an interdependence between the government and private entity to the extent that the government entity is a joint participant in the private enterprise; (2) the degree of government regulation of the private entity; (3) governmental sanction of the challenged activity, either in fact or in appearance; (4) the degree of monopoly power of the private entity and its relationship to the challenged action; and (5) the governmental nature of the function performed by the private entity.[36] Examples in which a private entity was found to be a state actor include the following:

---

[32]   *Sherrill v. Knight,* 569 F.2d 124, 130-31 (D.C. Cir. 1977).

[33]   *Los Angeles Free Press v. Los Angeles,* 9 Cal. App. 3d 448, 456 (1970).

[34]   *Mintz v. Dept of Motor Vehicles,* 9 Media L. Rep. 1301, 1302-03 (9th Cir. 1982).

[35]   *Watson v. Cronin,* 384 F. Supp. 652, 658-59 (D. Colo. 1974).

[36]   *Jackson v. Metropolitan Edison Co.,* 419 U.S. 345, 349-58 (1974).

- In the 1970s, accredited female reporters were excluded from the locker room of the Yankee clubhouse in Yankee Stadium. One reporter brought suit, alleging unlawful discrimination on the basis of sex. In ruling for the reporter, the court concluded that the Yankees were a state actor, noting that the place where the discrimination occurred was owned by the City of New York and leased pursuant to a special legislative provision to the Yankees, and the facility was maintained and improved with public funds. In addition, there was a symbiotic relationship between the Yankees and the city, since the annual rentals paid to the city for the use of the stadium depended directly on the drawing power of Yankee games, and the city in turn invested substantial sums of public money to enhance that drawing power by modernizing and improving the stadium.[37]
- When a photographer was denied press credentials by a nonprofit association that owned certain thoroughbred racing tracks, the association was found to be a "state actor" because its "ability to purchase and improve its physical plants and conduct its day-to-day business activity was ... completely dependent upon state action, indeed, upon the benevolence of the Legislature," and the association was "merely a conduit" through which money passed from the betting public to state coffers.[38]

2. Special Issues for Web-Based Media.

Internet reporting can take place in real time and is not constrained by the production delays inherent in print and television news. Therefore, Internet news directly competes with both real time television broadcasts of the event and the websites of the teams, leagues and other licensed entities that display instantaneous scores and highlights.

As a result, sports leagues may try to control how and when the media disseminates scores and similar facts. For instance, in PGA golf tournaments, numerous players compete simultaneously on different holes, making it impossible for a single reporter to keep track of current scores. Thus, the PGA is the only source of compiled golf scores for all tournament players. Although the PGA provides this information to credentialed news organizations, the credential language has prohibited the media from immediately reporting the scores. One news organization challenged the PGA's requirements, arguing that the golf scores were newsworthy information that should be transmitted immediately, even if this sharing of data directly competes with the PGA's own website. A federal court of appeals disagreed. Since the PGA had made the individual effort to compile the data, it was unfair for news organizations to "free ride" on the PGA's work. Thus, the court found, it was permissible for the PGA to control the dissemination of the scores.[39]

Nevertheless, once the sports scores are publicly disseminated, sports leagues cannot prohibit the further dissemination of this information. Thus, where a pager company gathered basketball scores reported on television and electronically sent these scores to its customers, the NBA did not own this information and could not prevent it from being transmitted.[40]

---

[37]   *Ludtke v. Kuhn*, 461 F. Supp. 86, 93-95 (S.D.N.Y. 1978).

[38]   *Stevens v. New York Racing Association*, 665 F. Supp 164, 172-73 (E.D.N.Y. 1987).

[39]   *Morris Communications Corp. v. PGA Tour, Inc.*, 364 F.3d 1288, 1295-96 (11th Cir. 2004).

[40]   *NBA v. Motorola, Inc.*, 105 F.3d 841, 854 (2d Cir. 1997).

3. Other Restrictions Contained in Credentials.

Press credentials may contain additional restrictions. For example, they may require that any video footage or photographs taken be used for news purposes only or may even go so far as to mandate that the team or league have unlimited access to or sole ownership rights of video, pictures or articles arising from the events. Or the credential may require that the reporter only air footage provided by the team, league or sponsor of the event. Because the reporters are often unaware of the restrictions until credentials have been granted, it can be extremely difficult to avoid or negotiate around them.

One-sided, "take-it-or-leave-it" agreements are referred to as "adhesion contracts" and, due to the often blatant power imbalance between the party choosing the terms and the party bound by them, courts may subject these contracts to special scrutiny when determining whether or not they are enforceable. This very issue arose when the NBA sued The New York Times in July 2000 after the newspaper sold photographs taken at basketball games on its website. The NBA claimed that the credentials issued to Times reporters contained a restriction requiring that any images taken at NBA games could only be used for news purposes. According to the league, by selling the images, the paper had breached the "contract" it had entered into when the reporters accepted the NBA's media credentials. Because the case eventually settled, it remains uncertain whether The New York Times would have been able to defeat the restrictions by arguing that the credentials constituted an adhesion contract with unenforceable terms.

Surprisingly, some sports organizations have actually attempted to restrict the actual content and material contained in the news stories covering their events. For example, in 2000, the organizers of the annual Indianapolis 500 race attempted to restrict video coverage of the event to a two-minute video produced by Formula One Management. After a backlash from the media, the organizers eventually backed off this restriction.

CHAPTER 5

Public Access to Criminal Court Proceedings

"It is important that society's criminal process satisfy the appearance of justice, and the appearance of justice can best be provided by allowing people to observe it."[1]

IN THIS CHAPTER

There is a presumptive right of access to criminal court proceedings in California, which may be limited by court order only in unusual circumstances. When a court is asked to close a criminal proceeding to the public, it must follow specific procedures before doing so. Other types of proceedings involving juveniles that are charged with crimes or those that deal with allegations of abuse or neglect of a child are generally closed to the public. However, if a juvenile is charged with a serious crime (as defined by statute), these proceedings are presumed to be open to the public. The public and press may request access to other juvenile proceedings. The public also has a qualified right of access to military trials, including courts martial. At the end of the chapter, there is a discussion of some practical tips for asserting your rights if you face the potential closure of a court proceeding.

PART I:
INTRODUCTION

Two provisions of the U.S. Constitution protect public access to trials. First, the U.S. Supreme Court has held that the public has a qualified First Amendment right to attend criminal judicial proceedings. This constitutional right covers all stages of a criminal proceeding from arraignment to trial and sentencing, including but not limited to preliminary hearings, bail hearings, selection of a jury, hearings on motions to suppress evidence, and change of plea hearings. The California Constitution has been interpreted to guarantee the same public access right as the First Amendment.[2] The public and the press can assert these rights. Second, the Sixth Amendment expressly grants criminal defendants the right to a "public trial." However, generally only the defendant in a criminal trial can invoke this right.

The general rule of openness has been modified in certain situations by statute and court decisions, allowing the public to be barred from a proceeding under specified situations. For example, Sections 1061-1062 of the California Evidence Code allow a court in certain situations to block public access to trade secret information in criminal cases. These sections allow for closed hearings in certain circumstances and allow evidence containing trade secrets to be submitted under seal. The general rule, however, is that judicial proceedings are presumed to be open to the public, and judges must articulate on the record grounds for partial or total closure of a trial or other court proceeding.

---

[1]   *Richmond Newspapers, Inc. v. Commonwealth of Virginia*, 448 U.S. 555, 571-72 (1980) ("*Richmond Newspapers*").

[2]   *NBC Subsidiary (KNBC-TV), Inc. v. Superior Court*, 20 Cal. 4th 1178, 1217-1218 (1999).

A. BACKGROUND ON CONSTITUTIONAL RIGHTS OF ACCESS.

Although not specifically mentioned in the Constitution, a qualified First Amendment right to attend criminal proceedings was recognized by the U.S. Supreme Court in 1980, in a case where a newspaper was barred from a murder trial at the defendant's request. The Supreme Court reasoned that free speech carries with it a right to listen and gather the news. The Court therefore held that criminal proceedings were presumed to be open to the public unless a showing could be made that closure was needed to protect some overriding interest.[3]

In 1982, the U.S. Supreme Court again addressed the constitutionality of closing criminal trials to the public in a case involving a constitutional challenge to a Massachusetts statute closure of the courtroom during the testimony of minor victims of sexual offenses. The Supreme Court held that a law that is a *per se* ban on the public's right to attend criminal proceedings is unconstitutional. To justify closure of any individual case or portion thereof, the party seeking closure must therefore prove that closure is supported by a compelling governmental interest and that no other alternative would better protect the public's First Amendment rights. A state's general interest in protecting victims from embarrassment and humiliation, while important, does not justify mandatory closure. Rather, trial judges must determine on a case-by-case basis whether closure is necessary.[4]

B. IMPORTANCE OF PUBLIC PARTICIPATION.

The U.S. Supreme Court has spent considerable time explaining the importance of public attendance at judicial proceedings. It is crucial to understand the historical backdrop upon which this fundamental right is founded.

The American judicial system was founded using the British system as a model. Tracing the history of the American and English judicial systems, the Supreme Court said that "throughout its evolution, the trial has been open to all who cared to observe."[5] As in England, the court noted, colonial America had adopted a system of open judicial proceedings:

> [T]he historical evidence demonstrates conclusively that at the time when our
> organic laws were adopted, criminal trials both here and in England had long been
> presumptively open. This is no quirk of history; rather, it has long been recognized
> as an indispensable attribute of the Anglo-American trial.[6]

Numerous reasons support open judicial proceedings. Foremost is that openness assures the public that the judicial system is operated in conformity with the law and is fairly administered by guarding against prosecutorial misconduct and perjury: Open trials give "assurance that the proceedings [are] conducted fairly to all concerned, and it discourage[s] perjury, the misconduct of participants, and decisions based on secret bias or partiality."[7] Public involvement in the judicial process also has a therapeutic effect on the community: "When a shocking crime occurs, a community reaction of outrage and public protest often follows. Thereafter, the open processes of justice serve an important prophylactic purpose, providing an outlet for community concern,

---

[3]   *Richmond Newspapers*, 448 U.S. 555 (1980).
[4]   *Globe Newspapers v. Superior Court*, 457 U.S. 596 (1982).
[5]   *Richmond Newspapers*, 448 U.S. at 564.
[6]   *Richmond Newspapers*, 448 U.S. at 569.
[7]   *Richmond Newspapers*, 448 U.S. at 569.

hostility, and emotion." [8] Furthermore, in order for the judicial system to work effectively, "it is important that society's criminal process satisfy the appearance of justice."[9] By guaranteeing public access to judicial proceedings, public confidence in the system can better be maintained.

PART II:
DEFINING THE CONSTITUTIONAL STANDARD

A. LEGAL TEST FOR CLOSURE OF COURT PROCEEDINGS.

Two subsequent U.S. Supreme Court cases have established the standard that must be met before a proceeding can be closed to the public.[10] In 1984, the Court ruled that the presumption of open criminal proceedings applies to the jury selection process (referred to as "voir dire"). In rejecting the state's argument that voir dire should be closed to protect the privacy of jurors required to answer extremely personal questions, the court noted that jury selection, like trials themselves, historically has been public and that openness fosters public confidence in that process. Trial courts therefore must make the same specific findings on the record required to close a trial to rebut the presumption of openness to voir dire.[11]

In 1986, the Supreme Court held that preliminary hearings also are presumptively open to the public. In order to overcome the presumption, a moving party must show that, without closure, there is a "substantial probability" that the defendant's constitutional right to a fair trial would be impaired. Trial judges are required to make specific findings of fact on the record to justify closure, including a finding that no reasonable alternative to closure adequately would protect the defendant's right to a fair trial.[12]

In 1993, the United States Supreme Court also ruled unconstitutional Puerto Rico's rule allowing preliminary hearings to be closed to the public. The rule provided that preliminary hearings be privately held unless the defendant requested otherwise.[13]

The public's right to attend judicial proceedings cannot be satisfied merely by providing a transcript of the proceeding after the fact. For example, a California Court of Appeal ruled that a trial court committed reversible error when it conducted portions of juror questioning in chambers, outside of the presence of the public, even though transcripts of the proceeding were available after the fact.[14]

While requiring members of the public to leave a courtroom clearly implicates the First Amendment's public access guarantee, California's Supreme Court ruled in 1992 that a judge's decision to lock the courtroom during a lawyer's closing arguments was not unconstitutional. The case was unusual in that members of the public were present in the courtroom when the doors were locked. The court held that a judge's right to control his or her courtroom extends to the right to limit access in some circumstances.[15] The U.S. Supreme Court has more correctly stated that the First Amendment right to access judicial proceedings is subject to reasonable time, place

---

[8]   *Richmond Newspapers*, 448 U.S. at 571.
[9]   *Richmond Newspapers*, 448 U.S. at 572-73.
[10]   *Press-Enterprise Co. v. Superior Court*, 464 U.S. 501 (1984) ("*Press Enterprise I*"), and *Press-Enterprise Co. v. Superior Court*, 478 U.S. 1, 13-14 (1986) ("*Press-Enterprise II*")
[11]   *Press Enterprise I*, 464 U.S. 501.
[12]   *Press-Enterprise II*, 478 U.S. at 14.
[13]   *El Vocero de Puerto Rico v. Puerto Rico*, 508 U.S. 147 (1993).
[14]   *People v. Harris*, 10 Cal. App. 4th 672 (1992).
[15]   *People v. Woodward*, 4 Cal. 4th 376 (1992).

and manner restrictions, such as limiting the number of people who can be present in the courtroom at one time or removing people who are causing a disturbance.[16]

B. PROCEDURES COURTS MUST FOLLOW BEFORE CLOSING PROCEEDINGS.

Strict procedures must be followed before any portion of a criminal judicial proceeding can be closed to the public.[17]

1. Notice to the Public.

The public must be given notice of a motion to close a proceeding and the opportunity to challenge the motion in a public court hearing.[18] In general, the courts have limited the notice requirement to those present in the courtroom. However, to maximize the opportunity for the public to object to closed proceedings, the courts also have struck down so-called "dual-docketing" where only public proceedings are included in the court's calendar.

A United States Court of Appeals, for example, struck down as unconstitutional a dual system of calendaring, under which the schedule of private proceedings was circulated only to internal courthouse personnel and to attorneys involved in those cases. The court held that "maintenance of a dual-docketing system is inconsistent with affording the various interests of the public and the press meaningful access to criminal proceedings."[19]

2. Burden on the Party Seeking Closure.

Since court proceedings are presumed to be open, the burden is on the party attempting to close the proceeding (or on the court, if the exclusion order is to be entered by the judge on his own motion) to establish that a compelling interest exists to justify closure. Thus, anyone seeking to close a courtroom proceeding must show that there is a "substantial probability" that the interest sought be protected (such as the defendant's right to a fair trial, or the privacy of jurors) will be prejudiced, that closure would be effective in preventing that prejudice, and that alternatives to closure cannot adequately protect the interest at stake.[20]

3. Any Order Closing Proceedings Must Be Narrowly Tailored.

As the U.S. Supreme Court has stated: "proceedings cannot be closed unless ... 'closure is essential to preserve higher values and is narrowly tailored to serve that interest."[21] In other words, any proposed exclusion of the public is "narrowly tailored," *i.e.*, is no more extensive than absolutely necessary to protect an "overriding interest." For example, a finding that allowing public access to the portion of a hearing where a certain piece of highly damaging evidence is being presented would harm the defendant's right to a fair trial may, depending on the facts,

---

[16]   *Gannett Co. v. De Pasquale*, 443 U.S. 368 (1979)

[17]   *See, generally, Press-Enterprise Co. v. Superior Court*, 478 U.S. 1, 13-14 (1986) ("*Press-Enterprise II*"); *NBC Subsidiary (KNBC-TV), Inc. v. Superior Court*, 20 Cal. 4th 1178, 1217-1218 (1999).

[18]   *Gannett Co. v. De Pasquale*, 443 U.S. 368, 401 (1979) (Powell, J., concurring); *Globe Newspaper Co. v. Superior Court*, 457 U.S. 596, 609 n. 25 (1982); *NBC Subsidiary (KNBC-TV), Inc. v. Superior Court*, 20 Cal. 4th 1178, 1217 (1999).

[19]   *United States v. Valenti*, 987 F.2d 708, 715 (11th Cir. 1993).

[20]   *Press-Enterprise II*, 478 U.S. at 14. *See also NBC Subsidiary (KNBC-TV), Inc. v. Superior Court*, 20 Cal. 4th 1178, 1217-18 (1999); *United States v. Brooklier*, 685 F.2d 1162, 1169 (9th Cir. 1982).

[21]   *Press-Enterprise II*, 478 U.S. at 13-14; *People v. Cummings*, 4 Cal. 4th 1233, 1299 (1993).

justify keeping the public from that narrow portion of the hearing. However, it would not be sufficient to bar the public from the rest of the hearing.

4. Court Must Make Findings on the Record.

The court must "articulate" on the record the nature of the interest and the threats to that interest that necessitate the proposed exclusion, "with findings specific enough so that a reviewing court can determine whether the closure order was properly entered."[22]

5. Showing of Substantial Probability of Harm.

A mere conclusion that closure is justified is not sufficient to meet the strict requirements for closure.[23] The arguments and findings must be specific and compelling, not speculative: "The First Amendment right of access cannot be overcome by a conclusory assertion that publicity might deprive the defendant of [his rights]."[24] Therefore, a court may not close a proceeding based only on concern or speculation that public access might threaten the defendant's right to a fair trial. Specific facts showing a substantial likelihood that the harm would result from failing to grant the motion are required.

For example, a federal appellate court ruled that a judge violated the constitutional rights of the public when he entered an order barring public access to a change of venue hearing involving former televangelist and defendant Jim Bakker. Bakker moved for a change of venue based on the large amount of pretrial publicity. The judge ruled that the defendant's Sixth Amendment right to a fair trial would be threatened by allowing public access to the change of venue hearing because the focus of the hearing would be on the amount of publicity the case had generated. The judge felt opening the hearing to the media would cause the previously published facts about the case to be "republished." The court of appeals disagreed, holding that there was a greater likelihood of increasing media coverage by denying press access to the hearing than by permitting it. The court concluded that there was insufficient justification to close the hearing to the public.[25]

PART III:
CLOSURE RATIONALES – THE FIRST AND THE SIXTH AMENDMENTS

The typical rationale offered by the party requesting closure – almost always the defendant – is that failure to close the proceeding would threaten the defendant's Sixth Amendment right to a fair trial. That conflict between the Sixth Amendment rights of a criminal defendant and the First Amendment rights of the public and media is one of the most important and often-raised issues in media law. However, to believe these interests are diametrically opposed is wrong.

While a defendant may argue that undue publicity about his case denies his right to a fair trial, he also has a strong interest in knowing that his trial is being monitored by the press and the public. Openness of judicial proceedings checks arbitrary government action over its citizenry and assures the fairness of criminal trials guaranteed defendants by the Sixth Amendment.

---

[22]   *Press-Enterprise Co. v. Superior Court*, 464 U.S. 501, 510 (1984) ("*Press Enterprise I*"). *See also NBC Subsidiary (KNBC-TV), Inc. v. Superior Court*, 20 Cal. 4th 1178, 1217-18 (1999).

[23]   *Press-Enterprise I*, 464 U.S. at 511-12.

[24]   *Press-Enterprise II*, 478 U.S. at 15.

[25]   *United States v. Bakker*, 882 F.2d 850 (1989).

In numerous decisions, courts have faced difficult cases that forced them to choose between the competing interests of the defendant and the public. They have adopted a case-by-case approach to determine which rights ought to prevail in a particular situation. This tension will be explored in other areas of this book, including the right of a court to issue a gag order, or force a reporter to testify about confidential information, or restrain the media from publishing certain information within its possession.

PART IV:
PUBLIC ACCESS TO BENCH PROCEEDINGS

Questions arise when members of the press are denied access to private conversations between attorneys and judges. The most common examples are sidebar conferences and in-chamber conferences. In sidebar conferences, the attorneys and judge will hold a private conversation at the bench during the course of a hearing. Attorneys also may meet with the judge in his or her chambers to discuss issues relating to the case, such as the admissibility of certain evidence. Members of the public may not be granted access to these "in-chambers" or "sidebar" conferences.

The United States Supreme Court and lower federal courts have said that a trial court has authority to conduct certain conferences in chambers and bench conferences without providing the public access.[26] The California Supreme Court has held that courts must look to the type of issues being discussed to determine if closure is proper. Thus, California state courts should not conduct regular court proceedings at sidebar or in chambers to avoid public scrutiny.[27]

PART V:
JUVENILE COURT PROCEEDINGS – LIMITED RIGHT OF ACCESS

There is no First Amendment right to attend juvenile court proceedings.[28] However, a right to attend juvenile court proceedings in some circumstances is created by California law. Juvenile court proceedings are generally divided into two categories: juvenile delinquency (addressing crimes committed by minors) and juvenile dependency (addressing the protection of children that have been neglected, abused or abandoned). Welfare and Institutions Code Section 676 governs access to juvenile delinquency proceedings. Welfare and Institutions Code Section 346 governs access to juvenile dependency proceedings. This part focuses primarily on juvenile delinquency proceedings, to which access is most frequently sought.

The general rule spelled out in Welfare and Institutions Code Section 676 is that "unless requested by the minor ... and any parent or guardian present, the public shall not be admitted to a juvenile court hearing." Juveniles accused of committing a criminal offense historically have been treated differently than adults because the basic premise of the juvenile justice system has been to rehabilitate rather than to punish the youthful offender. Because of this difference, the public's right of access to a juvenile court proceeding traditionally has been substantially less than its right to attend the criminal proceedings of an adult.

---

[26]   *Globe Newspapers v. Superior Court*, 457 U.S. 596, 609 n. 25 (1982); *Richmond Newspapers*, 448 U.S. at 598 n. 23 (1980) (Brennan, J., concurring); *U.S. v. Valenti*, 987 F.2d 708, 713-714 (1993).

[27]   *NBC Subsidiary (KNBC-TV), Inc. v. Superior Court*, 20 Cal. 4th 1178, 1215-1216 (1999).

[28]   *San Bernardino County Dept. of Public Social Services v. Superior Court*, 232 Cal. App. 3d 188, 205 (1991).

As the number of juveniles committing serious crimes has increased, however, the courts and legislatures nationwide increasingly have become more willing to allow the press to attend juvenile proceedings. In California, the Legislature has enacted three exceptions to the general rule: (1) when the juvenile is charged with one of a number of specified serious crimes; (2) when the minor requests the hearing to be open; and (3) when the judge admits those people he or she determines to have a legitimate interest in the case (which could include the media). These exceptions are established by Welfare and Institutions Code section 676 ("Section 676").

A. PUBLIC'S RIGHT OF ACCESS TO JUVENILE DELINQUENCY PROCEEDINGS (SERIOUS CRIMES).

Section 676 provides that the public has the same right to attend hearings for certain enumerated serious crimes allegedly committed by juveniles as they would if the defendant were an adult. The first issue for a reporter wishing to gain access to a juvenile hearing is to determine if the charged crime is listed in Section 676. If the crime is listed, the news media may be admitted to the hearing on the same basis that it would be admitted to an adult criminal hearing. If it is not listed, the reporter needs to look for another exception to gain access.

1. Statutory Offenses.

The following are some of the offenses that trigger open hearings for juvenile defendants under Section 676:

- Murder, attempted murder or assault with intent to murder;
- Assault with a firearm or destructive device or by any means of force likely to produce great bodily injury;
- Kidnapping for ransom, for purpose of robbery or with bodily harm;
- Arson of an inhabited building;
- Discharge of a firearm into an inhabited or occupied building;
- Burglary in the nighttime, or felony burglary in the daytime of an inhabited dwelling house or trailer coach or the inhabited portion of any other building if the accused has previously been adjudged a ward of the court due to having committed any offense listed in Section 676;
- Rape with force or violence or threat of great bodily harm, or sodomy or oral copulation by force, violence, duress, menace or threat of great bodily harm;
- The use of a firearm, assault weapon or machine gun by a minor 16 years of age or older in the commission or attempted commission of a felony; and
- The commission or attempted commission against a person age 60 or older or a person who is blind, paraplegic or quadriplegic, of murder or assault with intent to commit murder, robbery, kidnapping (with or without harm), burglary of a dwelling, forcible rape, or assault with intent to commit rape, robbery or sodomy.

2. Sex Crimes Exception.

If the offense charged is of a sexual nature, the hearing will be closed to the public despite the rule specified above if (1) the victim of the crime requests the district attorney to ask that the hearing be closed; or (2) during the victim's testimony, if the victim was under 16 years old at the time of the alleged offense.

3. Fitness and Competency Hearings.

Courts have interpreted Section 676 to allow the public to attend hearings to determine if a minor is competent (competency hearings) and to determine whether the minor should be tried as an adult (fitness hearings).[29]

B. ACCESS AT REQUEST OF THE MINOR, PARENT OR GUARDIAN.

Under Section 676, the judge has the discretion to open the proceeding to the public, even if the youth is not charged with an enumerated violent crime, at the request of the juvenile and his or her parent or guardian. In the majority of cases, it is probably the desire of the minor and his family to remain anonymous. However, a defendant may seek to open the proceeding if he believes that he has been wrongly accused of criminal activity.

A Note on Access to Proceedings at the Request of a Minor or Parent: If a reporter believes the juvenile and his family would not mind having the media present, the media should consider contacting the family and request their assistance in gaining access to the proceeding. The typical way to get access in such a case is to have both the minor and parent or guardian write a letter to the judge requesting that the media be admitted.

C. DISCRETIONARY PUBLIC ACCESS.

A judge also has the discretion to admit anyone to the hearing that he deems to have "a direct and legitimate interest in the particular case." This section often has been used to grant the press access under the theory that the public has a strong interest to be informed about a particularly newsworthy case.[30]

D. LIMITATIONS ON THE RIGHT OF ACCESS TO JUVENILE CASES.

Even in cases where the offense charged requires the proceeding to be open to the public, a minor may seek to have the hearing closed on the ground that publicity would violate his Sixth Amendment right to a fair and impartial trial. In the cases that address this issue, the result has been to adopt the standard used in adult criminal proceedings to determine if a hearing should be closed.

For example, in one case a minor accused of murder sought to close a hearing to determine whether he would be tried as a minor or as an adult (known as a "fitness hearing").[31] He argued that allowing press coverage would deprive him of an impartial jury if he were forced to stand trial as an adult. The appeals court reversed the trial court's order closing the hearing on the ground that the minor failed to show a "reasonable likelihood of substantial prejudice" to his right to receive a fair and impartial trial.[32] The same standard was adopted in a subsequent case, in which the court said that when a minor is charged with a felony entitling the public to attend the proceedings, the public may attend a hearing to determine if the minor is competent to stand trial

---

[29]   *Tribune Newspapers West, Inc. v. Superior Court*, 172 Cal. App. 3d 443 (1985); *Cheyenne K. v. Superior Court*, 208 Cal. App. 3d 331, 336 (1989).

[30]   *See Brian W. v. Superior Court*, 20 Cal. 3d 618, 623 (1978).

[31]   *Tribune Newspapers West v. Superior Court*, 172 Cal. App. 3d 443 (1985).

[32]   *Tribune Newspapers West v. Superior Court*, 172 Cal. App. 3d 443, 451 (1985).

unless the minor establishes "a reasonable likelihood of substantial prejudice to the right to receive a fair and impartial trial."[33]

Note that the standard for closing a juvenile court proceeding that is subject to the right of access created by Section 676 may be lower than the standard for closing a proceeding involving an adult. The United States Supreme Court has expressly rejected the standard of "reasonable likelihood of substantial prejudice." In a criminal proceeding involving an adult, anyone seeking to close the proceeding to the public or the press must show "closure is essential to preserve higher values and is narrowly tailored to serve [an overriding] interest."[34] However, California courts continue to indicate that a "reasonable likelihood of substantial prejudice" to a minor's right to a fair trial is sufficient to justify restrictions on access to juvenile court proceedings.[35]

E. ALTERNATIVE ARGUMENTS FOR MEDIA ACCESS.

1. Purpose of Closure Has Been Removed.

One of the main purposes for keeping the public out of juvenile proceedings is to protect the defendant's identity. When the name of the minor already has been publicized, an argument can be made that the court should open the hearing even though the offense charged is not one of those statutorily open to the public. Prior publication does not give the press a *per se* right to attend a juvenile proceeding, but it does make it more likely a court will determine that there are greater interests in opening the hearing than in keeping it closed.

2. No Right to Jury Trial.

The right most often asserted as justifying the closure of courtroom proceedings or the sealing of records in criminal cases is the defendant's right to a fair trial. Typically, the argument made to support closure or sealing is that the exposure of the public to pretrial publicity will impair the defendant's ability to obtain a jury that can decide the case impartially, free from the influence of such publicity. However, a juvenile has no right to a jury trial unless tried as an adult.[36] Thus, if it has been established that the juvenile will not be tried as an adult, concern about the right to a fair trial should not justify closure or sealing.

F. POST-HEARING INFORMATION.

Generally, a district attorney may not disclose information concerning a juvenile case absent a court order permitting such disclosure. A district attorney, however, may furnish the news media with information that is revealed during the course of a proceeding open to the public under Section 676. Thus, if you do not attend the hearing, the district attorney is authorized to disclose, upon request, any information that was available to the public in the course of the proceeding.[37]

---

[33]   *Cheyenne K. v. Superior Court*, 208 Cal. App. 3d 331, 336 (1989)

[34]   *Press-Enterprise II*, 478 U.S. at 13-14; *People v. Cummings*, 4 Cal. 4th 1233, 1299 (1993).

[35]   *KGTV Channel 10 v. Superior Court*, 26 Cal. App. 4th 1673, 1684-85 (1994)

[36]   *In re Daedler*, 194 Cal. 320 (1924); *In re Clarance B.*, 37 Cal. App. 3d 676 (1974).

[37]   65 Ops. Cal. Atty. Gen. 503 (1982).

G. OBTAINING INFORMATION ABOUT JUVENILES CONVICTED OF SERIOUS CRIMES.

The public has the right to obtain, upon request to the director of the California Youth Authority, certain information about offenders who are at least 16 years old and who have been committed as wards to the Youth Authority by a court of criminal jurisdiction (*i.e.,* after being tried as adults). The information includes the ward's name, age, and current and former institution of confinement; the court of commitment; the date of commitment; actions taken by the Youthful Offender Parole Board relating to parole dates; the date that a paroled ward was placed on parole; the date on which the ward was discharged from the Youth Authority's jurisdiction and the basis for discharge; and, if the ward has escaped from an institution controlled by the Youth Authority, a physical description of the ward and the circumstances of the escape. Information need not be released that would "place an individual in personal peril" or threaten the security of the institution, or that is exempt from disclosure under the California Public Records Act.[38]

H. RIGHT TO PUBLICIZE A JUVENILE'S NAME.

Courts may impose limitations on the information that is made available to the public during juvenile court proceedings. However, if a newspaper learns the name of an accused juvenile offender – even though the proceedings are closed to the public – it has the right to publish it. The same is true with information the press lawfully obtains from juvenile proceedings. The U.S. Supreme Court has held that a state cannot impose criminal sanctions for the publication of the lawfully obtained name of an accused juvenile.[39] For a more detailed discussion of issues relating to the government's right to restrict the media's ability to publish, see the discussion on prior restraint in Chapter 6.

I. PUBLIC ACCESS TO JUVENILE DEPENDENCY PROCEEDINGS.

These proceedings usually involve removal of a child from his or her home and subsequent placement with a foster family. Like Section 676, Welfare and Institutions Code section 346 ("Section 346") states: "Unless requested by a parent or guardian and consented to or requested by the minor concerning whom the petition has been filed, the public shall not be admitted to a juvenile court hearing. The judge or referee may nevertheless admit such persons as he deems to have a direct and legitimate interest in the particular case or the work of the court." This language has been construed by the California courts to grant discretion to the juvenile court to permit members of the press and public to attend juvenile court proceedings.[40] The test adopted by the courts is that "the court should allow press access unless there is a reasonable likelihood that such access will be harmful to the child's or children's best interest in the case."[41] In addition:

> In attempting to balance these competing interests, the court should attempt to
> apply these broad principles to the unique facts of this case and may properly
> consider such factors as the age of each child, the nature of the allegations, the
> extent of the present and/or expected publicity and its effect, if any, on the children

---

[38]   Welfare and Institutions Code section 1764.1.

[39]   *Smith v. Daily Mail Publishing Co.*, 443 U.S. 97 (1979); *KGTV Channel 10 v. Superior Court*, 26 Cal. App. 4th 1673, 1679-82, 1684 (1994).

[40]   *San Bernardino County Dept. of Public Social Services v. Superior Court*, 232 Cal. App. 3d 188, 195 (1991).

[41]   *San Bernardino County Dept. of Public Social Services v. Superior Court*, 232 Cal. App. 3d 188, 208 (1991).

and on family reunification. Although not constitutionally required, the court should consider whether it would be feasible to allow press access to portions of the proceedings and excluding the press from other portions.[42]

Unlike Section 676, Section 346 does not establish an actual right to attend any juvenile dependency proceeding. However, the court always has discretion to admit the press and the public, if it can do so in a manner consistent with the best interests of the child.

A Note on Access to Juvenile Dependency Proceedings: In any case in which access is discretionary, contact the judge or the judge's clerk in advance to discuss your interest in attending, if possible. Be prepared to make accommodations, such as agreeing not to distribute information that would identify the minors – who are typically very young children. Dependency cases are often related to criminal prosecutions of parents or guardians accused of neglect or abuse. If an adult is prosecuted, you will generally have a much better chance of being able to obtain access to the criminal case than to the dependency proceeding, and much of the same information may be available in the criminal case.

PART VI:
ACCESS TO MILITARY PROCEEDINGS

A qualified First Amendment-based right of public access also applies to trials by courts-martial.[43] The Manual for Courts-Martial, Rule for Courts-Martial 806(a), also provides that "courts-martial shall be open to the public." Such openness "reduces the chance of arbitrary or capricious decision and enhances public confidence in the courts-martial process." [44]

Other military courts have held that, "absent national security concerns or other justification clearly set forth on the record," trials in the U.S. military justice system are to be open to the public.[45] Maintaining public confidence in the courts-martial and promoting accurate fact-finding require that military courts be presumptively open.[46] The highest military appellate court has affirmed that, "absent 'cause shown that outweighs the value, of openness,' there is a right to a public proceeding."[47] Further, the press enjoys the same right and has standing to complain as with other court proceedings.[48]

In November 2001, President Bush signed an executive order allowing the secretary of defense to create military tribunals to try non-citizen suspected terrorists.[49] The proceedings must be held in public pursuant to the order, but such openness is subject to substantial discretion in the appointing authority or the presiding officer. Interests such as protection of classified information, the safety of participants, law enforcement secrets or other "national security" concerns may be

---

[42] *San Bernardino County Dept. of Public Social Services v. Superior Court*, 232 Cal. App. 3d 188, 207-208 (1991).

[43] *U.S. v. Scott*, 48 M.J. 663, 665 (Army Crim. App. 1998) ("the [constitutional] right of public access to criminal trials applies with equal validity to trials of courts-martial.").

[44] *U.S. v. Anderson*, 46 MJ 728 (Army Crim. App. 1997)

[45] *U.S. v. Anderson*, 46 MJ 728.

[46] *U.S. v. Travers*, 25 M.J. 61, 62 (CMA 1987).

[47] *ABC, Inc. v. Powell*, 47 M.J. 363 (C.A.A.F. 1997).

[48] *ABC, Inc. v. Powell*, 47 M.J. 363, citing *Globe Newspaper Co. v. Superior Court*, 457 U.S. 596 (1982).

[49] *Detention Treatment and Trial of Certain Non-Citizens in the War Against Terrorism*, Federal Register, Volume 66, Number 222, pages 57831-57836 (66 Fed. Reg. 57831) (Nov. 16, 2001).

considered.[50] The constitutionality of keeping proceedings conducted pursuant to the president's order secret was challenged in a case brought by an Algerian man detained as a material witness after Sept. 11, 2001. The proceedings challenging his detention were kept secret by the federal courts. A reporter discovered the case only because a clerk of the federal court of appeals mistakenly included it on a public calendar of court arguments. The detainee challenged the secrecy of the proceedings under the First Amendment. The U.S. Supreme Court refused to hear the case.[51]

PART VII:
HOW TO PROTECT YOUR RIGHT TO ACCESS COURT PROCEEDINGS

A. ANTICIPATE CLOSURE MOTIONS.

Anticipate motions to close hearings of highly publicized cases and juvenile court hearings. In other situations, keep alert for potential closure motions by maintaining contact with attorneys for both sides. Let them know you would appreciate advance notice of any motion to close, and that letting you know early may save everyone's time by avoiding your request for a delay to summon your attorney.

B. REQUEST A HEARING.

If you are surprised by a motion for closure by a party or by the judge's own announcement of an intended closure, approach the court or the bailiff and ask for permission to address the court. If the judge allows you to give a statement, read the following protest statement or a similar statement:

> CLOSED COURTROOM PROTEST
> Your Honor, my name is _____ and I represent _____ [or: and I am a member of the public attending this proceeding]. I respectfully object to the proposed closure of this proceeding. The United States Supreme Court has established specific and substantial requirements for determining whether the public may be excluded from all or part of a criminal proceeding. I request that the court ensure that any decision to close these proceedings complies with the requirements imposed by *Richmond Newspapers v. Virginia*, 448 U.S. 555, and *Press-Enterprise v. Superior Court*, 478 U.S. 1.

If you seek not only to protest the closure but to delay it to permit your attorney to appear in opposition (decide in advance with your editor and counsel which kinds of cases merit this tactic), conclude your statement with this request:

> I believe there are some specific points and authorities that Your Honor may want to consider, and I ask for a brief pause in these proceedings to permit counsel to appear and be heard in our behalf.

---

[50] *Detention Treatment and Trial of Certain Non-Citizens in the War Against Terrorism*, 66 Fed. Reg. 57831 (Nov. 16, 2001).

[51] *M.K.B. v. Warden*, 540 U.S. 1213, 124 S. Ct. 1405 (2004).

C. SEEK SUPPORT FROM THE NON-MOVING PARTY.

Your position opposing closure will be stronger if it is joined by the moving party's adversary in the case. As a practical matter, it is almost always the defendant who makes a request for closure. Also as a practical matter, in certain cases prosecutors may wish to have hearings conducted in public and in the eye of the media. Prosecutors often can be enlisted to bolster your argument that the hearing should remain open. If the court grants a delay for your attorney to appear, ask the non-moving lawyer if he or she plans to express opposition as well. If the attorney says no, ask why. The answer may alert your attorney to potential problems with your position.

CHAPTER 6

Gag Orders and Prior Restraints

"[P]rior restraints on speech and publication are the most serious and the least tolerable infringement on First Amendment rights."[1]

IN THIS CHAPTER

In general, laws or court orders that prohibit private citizens or the media from publishing or disseminating information are "prior restraints," which violate the First Amendment. Orders limiting the ability of participants in court proceedings – known as "gag orders" – are often issued, but often they impose a prior restraint that violates the right of free speech. However, not every limitation on speech is a prior restraint. For example, an injunction prohibiting copyright infringement is not considered a prior restraint, even though it prevents a form of speech[2]. In addition, a prior restraint may be permissible in very limited circumstances. This chapter discusses the conditions that must exist for the court to lawfully impose a gag order. It also addresses the extraordinary circumstances in which a court may be able to prevent the news media and others from publishing information. It covers the factors a court must weigh and the constitutional requirements it must follow before ordering someone not to speak or to publish.

PART I:
GAG ORDERS – LIMITING DISCUSSION
AND COVERAGE OF COURT CASES

A. GAG ORDERS IN CRIMINAL CASES.

The First Amendment protects the public's right of access to the courts and the public's right to speak about what it knows. However, there are other constitutional rights that sometimes conflict with the public's First Amendment rights.

In court proceedings, perhaps the most important countervailing interest is a criminal defendant's Sixth Amendment right to a fair and impartial jury. The right of parties in a civil case to have a fair trial, the protection of trade secrets, privacy and other rights may also come into conflict with First Amendment rights. Even when the public is not barred from attending a court proceeding, a judge – in very

---

[1]   *Nebraska Press Association v. Stuart,* 427 U.S. 539 (1976).

[2]   *Religious Technology Center v. Netcom On-Line*, 923 F.Supp. 1231, 1257-58 (N.D. Cal. 1995).

limited circumstances – has authority to prohibit parties to, or people involved in, a case from speaking to the media or the public. Orders limiting the disclosure of information from court proceedings are referred to as "gag orders."

The United States Supreme Court has ruled that courts have the power to control publicity generated by criminal trials. This power, the court said, means a trial judge must take steps to protect court proceedings from prejudicial outside interference, including trying the case in a "carnival atmosphere," with prejudicial publicity.[3]

Gag orders – sometimes referred to as "protective orders" – usually limit attorneys, witnesses and parties to the action from discussing the case with anyone not directly involved in the trial. Jurors *always* are under admonition not to discuss a case while it is pending, whether or not a judge has issued a gag order.

The idea behind a gag order is to keep the parties from "trying the case in the media" in order to protect the defendant's constitutional right to a fair trial. When a gag order is issued, the media and the public generally are limited to attending the open court proceedings of the trial and to reviewing the court records used in the case. Violation of a gag order can lead to criminal contempt charges against anyone subject to the gag order.

Even though the U.S. Supreme Court has ruled that gag orders may sometimes be allowed, it also has said that judges should be reluctant "to place any direct limitations on the freedom traditionally exercised by the news media because '[w]hat transpires in the courtroom is public property.'" The court recognized the vital role that the media plays in the administration of justice: The media "does not simply publish information about trials but guards against the miscarriage of justice by subjecting the police, prosecutors, and judicial processes to extensive public scrutiny and criticism."[4]

Because of the strong constitutional interest the media and the public have in monitoring trials and other judicial proceedings, the courts have established rules that limit the situations in which a judge is allowed to impose a gag order.

B. CONSTITUTIONAL REQUIREMENTS.

Gag orders are considered ***prior restraints*** on speech (a full discussion of prior restraints follows). Therefore, they should be issued only in extreme situations. The Supreme Court has established the following requirements for issuing a gag order:

- The order must be necessary to prevent a "clear and present danger" of a serious and imminent threat to the administration of justice," or with respect to attorneys, there must be at least a substantial likelihood of material prejudice from prejudicial publicity that will prevent a fair trial;
- There must not be less restrictive alternatives available, like changing the trial to another county or sequestering the jury;

---

[3]   *Sheppard v. Maxwell*, 384 U.S. 333 (1966).
[4]   *Craig v. Harney,* 331 U.S. 367, 374 (1947).

- The order cannot be entered unless it is likely to be effective; and
- The order must be narrowly drawn to avoid unnecessary infringement of First Amendment rights. [5]

Interpretive Cases and Examples.

The U.S. Supreme Court indicated in a 1991 decision that it was reluctant to approve gag orders. In a case involving a criminal defense attorney disciplined for holding a press conference six months before the trial of his client, in violation of Nevada's rules of professional responsibility that prohibit attorneys from making statements that they know or reasonably should know will have a "substantial likelihood of materially prejudicing" a judicial proceeding, the court said that while the rule itself is constitutional, its application to the case was not:

Only the most occasional case presents a danger of prejudice from pretrial publicity. Empirical research suggests that in the few instances when jurors have been exposed to extensive pretrial publicity, they are able to disregard it and base their verdict upon the evidence presented in court. [6]

The attorney told the Nevada State Bar's disciplinary committee that he made the statement in part to counter information about the state's case that had already been made public by the prosecution. "Public awareness and criticism have even greater importance where, as here, they concern allegations of police corruption," the Supreme Court wrote. The Supreme Court also pointed out that the statements in this case were made six months before jury selection and in a county with a population in excess of 600,000. [7]

A California court of appeal has ruled that an order prohibiting the parties to a civil lawsuit from discussing information they had (which was obtained independent of the discovery conducted after the case was filed) constitute an unconstitutional prior restraint. [8] On the other hand, an admonition that witnesses before a grand jury may be held in contempt for revealing anything they learned as a result of appearing before the grand jury has been held not to constitute a prior restraint – at least when challenged by the press. [9] However, witnesses may **not** properly be admonished not to talk about information they obtained independent of their appearance before the grand jury. [10]

The mere existence of extensive pretrial publicity is not sufficient to establish an imminent and serious threat to the fair trial rights of a defendant. For example, a Florida trial court denied a criminal defendant's motion to prohibit public disclosure of any information related to the case by counsel, law enforcement officials or potential witnesses. The case was a highly publicized one involving the murder of five co-eds at the University of Florida: "No case known to this

---

[5]   *Nebraska Press Association v. Stuart*, 427 U.S. 539, 561-566 (1976).

[6]   *Gentile v. State Bar of Nevada*, 501 U.S. 1030, 1054-1055 (1991).

[7]   *Gentile v. State Bar of Nevada*, 501 U.S. 1030 (1991).

[8]   *Hurvitz v. Hoefflin*, 84 Cal. App. 4th 1232 (2000).

[9]   *San Jose Mercury News, Inc. v. Criminal Grand Jury of Santa Clara County*, 122 Cal. App. 4th 410, 418 (2004).

[10]   *San Jose Mercury News, Inc. v. Criminal Grand Jury of Santa Clara County*, 122 Cal. App. 4th 410, 418 (2004).

jurist has ever so captured the attention of the citizens of this circuit or generated the volume of media coverage experienced with these five homicides," the Florida court wrote in its opinion. Despite the intensive publicity, the court refused to enter the order sought by the defendant, instead admonishing the parties to conform their behavior to the state's ethical code for lawyers.[11]

In deciding whether an impartial jury can be impaneled, courts should consider a number of factors, including the nature of the publicity, the time between the publicity and the trial and the behavior of the trial participants. Even if there are grounds for the issuance of a gag order, the scope of the order that may be issued is limited. The Supreme Court has ruled that trial courts are not permitted to preclude the media from publicizing events, including testimony, that occur in open court.[12]

The parties to a case who are directly subject to a gag order obviously can challenge the order. The courts have generally held that the press also has standing to challenge gag orders.[13]

C. ALTERNATIVES TO GAG ORDERS.

Trial courts must consider alternatives before entering a gag order. It is important to be familiar with those alternatives when you are faced with having to oppose a proposed gag order. The courts have outlined some of the alternatives to a gag order:

1. Change of Venue. A trial normally is held in the county in which the alleged crime was committed. Courts will sometimes move the "venue" – the location of the trial – in an effort to reduce the potential prejudicial impact of publicity on jurors.

2. Postponement of Trial. This often will result in a reduction in publicity and the public's loss of interest in a case. It is not always possible to postpone a trial, however, because of a defendant's constitutional right to a speedy trial, nor is a postponement likely to be effective in a truly high-profile case.

3. Voir Dire. "Voir Dire" is the technical term for the questioning of prospective jurors by the judge and attorneys in the case. This is an important way for attorneys to eliminate prospective jurors whose opinion about the case may have been influenced by media coverage of the events.

4. Jury Instructions. Judges always instruct jurors to avoid discussing the case with anyone and from reading or listening to any media accounts of the trial

---

[11] *State of Florida v. Rolling*, 20 Media L. Rptr. 1127 (1992).
[12] *Smith v. Daily Mail Publishing Co.*, 442 U.S. 97 (1979).
[13] *See, e.g., Radio & Television News Ass'n v. U.S. District Court*, 781 F.2d 1443 (9th Cir. 1986); *Journal Pub. Co. v. Mecham*, 801 F.2d 1233 (10th Cir. 1986).

or underlying events.

5. Sequestering the Jury. Judges sometimes will order members of a jury to remain confined to a particular location, often a hotel, for the duration of the proceeding to ensure they do not receive information about the trial before its completion.

D. RESPONDING TO A PROPOSED GAG ORDER.

Members of the media have standing to challenge the imposition of a proposed gag order. This means that media representatives must be given notice before a proposed gag order is imposed and an opportunity to be heard by the judge on the issue.

<u>A Note on Responding to Gag Orders</u>: Whenever a party or a judge proposes issuing a gag order, it is important to immediately request a hearing and possibly consult with counsel. When a gag order is imposed, get a copy of the proposed order and have it reviewed by counsel to determine whether it should be challenged constitutionally. Remember that a judge is required to state on the record the factual premises relied on in determining that unrestricted coverage of the case would interfere with a fair trial.[14] If the justification offered in the order does not relate to any truly unusual circumstances about the case or how the media has covered it, a newspaper should consider challenging the gag order. When opposing a gag order, it is useful to supply the court with examples of prior cases – even more highly publicized – in which no order was issued and the trial was held in the local court. A newspaper challenging a proposed order also should point to the amount of coverage the case received, including the placement of the story in the newspaper (*e.g.*, was it on the front page on top of the fold or was it buried in the back of the paper), and other factors such as whether photographs were included as part of the coverage.

E. SOME INFORMATION GENERALLY RELEASABLE.

Even if issued, a gag order cannot prevent the media from covering trial proceedings. Courts have said that even the most comprehensive gag order must make allowance for the dissemination of some information by some of the people involved in the case. Many orders will limit discussion of things such as the strength of the evidence but will allow the parties to provide basic information about the crime, such as information that normally could be released from police reports.

Other limits also have been placed on protective orders. For example, in the period shortly before jury selection in the Los Angeles federal trial of two Russian émigrés charged with conspiring with an FBI agent to spy for the Soviet Union, the defendants' attorneys gave an exclusive interview, published in the *Los*

---

[14]   *Radio and Television News Association v. U.S. District Court*, 781 F.2d 1443 (9th Cir. 1986).

127

Angeles Times, critical of the government's case. The interview took place after the trial judge had admonished both sides several times to stop trying the case in the media. The court then issued an order, ultimately directed at counsel only, prohibiting out-of-court comments to the media "concerning any aspect of this case that bears upon the merits to be resolved by the jury." The court of appeals found the order overbroad. The threat to the fair administration of justice could be said to be "serious and imminent," it agreed, and alternative measures to check it probably would be less effective. However, not all statements by counsel on the merits of the case would be prejudicial or should be silenced.[15]

F. TO WHOM THE ORDERS APPLY.

The protective order will name those people whose free speech in the case is being restricted. An order may include those directly involved: prosecution and defense attorneys, other judicial officers and personnel, law enforcement officers and witnesses. In an even broader approach, a federal court of appeals upheld a federal district court's order, issued before the trial, prohibiting comment by any "potential" witness notified by the government or the defense that he or she might be called as a witness in a highly inflammatory murder trial stemming from a confrontation between the Ku Klux Klan and members of the Communist Party.[16]

G. RULES AFFECTING ATTORNEYS.

Regardless of whether a gag order has been issued in a case, it is important for journalists to understand the rules to which all attorneys are subject when dealing with the media. Rules of professional conduct limit the kinds of information attorneys are allowed to disclose to the media about pending litigation. Among the types of information attorneys are prohibited from disclosing to the media are the existence of a confession, statements about the credibility of a witness, and the lawyer's opinion on the guilt or innocence of a criminal defendant. The rule relating to trial publicity is just one of the many issues covered in the American Bar Association Model Rules of Professional Conduct.

California Rule of Professional Conduct 5-120, which applies in both civil and criminal cases, prohibits an attorney participating in a matter from making a statement for public dissemination if the attorney "knows or reasonably should know that it will have a substantial likelihood of materially prejudicing an adjudicative proceeding in the matter." This standard is generally consistent with the standard adopted by the Supreme Court.[17] The California rule further provides that certain pieces of information may be disclosed about the claims and defenses, and that statements may be made to counter prejudicial statements made by others.

---

[15]   *Levine v. District Court*, 775 F.2d 1054 (1985).
[16]   *In re Russell*, 726 F.2d 1007 (1984).
[17]   *Gentile v. State Bar of Nevada*, 501 U.S. 1030 (1991).

H. GAG ORDERS IN CIVIL CASES.

While gag orders most often arise in the context of a criminal prosecution, the issue also occasionally arises in a civil trial. Courts have recognized the rights of the litigants to a fair jury trial under the constitutional amendment that affords litigants the right to a jury trial in specified types of cases. In general, courts faced with the issue of a gag order in a civil case have required a showing similar to that required in a criminal case, namely evidence that, in the absence of the order, causes a serious threat to the rights of the litigants to a fair trial.[18]

PART II:
PRIOR RESTRAINTS

When a judge issues a gag order, he is preventing certain people from giving information to the media or the public. When a judge issues a prior restraint order, he is telling the media or members of the public that they are prohibited from disclosing certain information already in their possession.

A. INTRODUCTION.

As discussed above, courts can sometimes limit access to newsworthy people and facts by issuing a gag order, by limiting the right to speak to jurors and grand jurors, or by preventing a party to a case from publishing information gained only through the discovery process before the information is introduced as evidence. All of these actions are, in a sense, examples of "prior restraint." That is, they are instances where the government is acting to prevent the media from gathering or publishing information that is likely to come into its possession.

When the government acts to regulate the content of the media by restricting its right to publish information in its possession, however, a serious issue arises as to whether the action violates the media's First Amendment rights. As a result, the U.S. Supreme Court has issued numerous rulings over the last several decades that make it extraordinarily difficult for courts to issue orders or for government agencies to pass laws restraining the media from publishing information.

B. GENERAL RULE OF LAW.

The general rule is that a court order or law that acts to restrain the media from publishing information in its possession is ***presumptively unconstitutional***.[19]

---

[18]   *Hurvitz v. Hoefflin*, 84 Cal. App. 4th 1232 (2000); *Quinn v. Aetna Life & Casualty Co.*, 482 F.Supp. 22 (1979).

[19]   *Nebraska Press Association v. Stuart*, 427 U.S. 539, 558-59 (1976) (emphasis added); *Vance v. Universal Amusement Co., Inc.*, 445 U.S. 308, 317 (1980) ("'[a]ny system of prior restraints of expression comes to this Court bearing a heavy presumption against its constitutional validity'") (emphasis in original; quoting *Bantam Books, Inc. v. Sullivan*, 372 U.S. 58, 70 (1963)).

The burden is on the party seeking to impose the prior restraint to prove that the order is necessary despite its interference with the media's First Amendment rights. Because the courts have classified freedom of speech as a fundamental right, due process requires a judicial determination of extreme necessity before the government can interfere with the media's First Amendment rights.[20]

Only the most extreme cases of injury to a vital governmental interest that cannot be remedied adequately by subsequent legal process are likely to qualify for prior restraint. These are cases that are unquestionably and immediately imperiled and that cannot be mitigated by other means. Prior restraints on speech and publication are the most serious and "the least tolerable infringement on First Amendment rights."[21] The types of burdens that must be met to uphold any prior restraint are discussed below.

California courts are further guided by the free speech and free press provision found in Article I, Section 2(a) of the California Constitution. The protections found in that provision are "more definitive and inclusive than the First Amendment," and the burden on a party seeking a prior restraint in California is even greater.[22]

C. THE CRIMINAL DEFENDANT'S RIGHT TO A FAIR TRIAL.

The most likely place for an issue of prior restraint to arise is in coverage of a criminal prosecution. These cases generally involve a conflict between the First Amendment, which guarantees freedom of the press, and the Sixth Amendment, which guarantees criminal defendants a trial by a fair and impartial jury. Some courts have attempted to go beyond the issuance of a gag order and prevent the media from publishing accounts of the proceedings or information about the case obtained from other sources (for example, a police report stating that the defendant confessed upon his arrest).

The justification offered to support a proposed prior restraint generally is that failure to prevent the media from publishing the information or accounts of the proceeding will make it impossible for the defendant to get a fair trial because of the threat that jurors will be exposed to prejudicial information in the media.

1. The Right to a Fair Trial Generally Does Not Justify a Prior Restraint.

As a general rule, concerns about potential prejudice to a defendant's right to a fair trial do not justify prior restraints.[23] The test to be applied to determine if a

---

[20]   *Organization for a Better Austin v. Keefe*, 402 U.S. 415 (1971) and *New York Times Co. v. United States*, 403 U.S. 713 (1971).

[21]   *Nebraska Press Ass'n v. Stuart*, 427 U.S. 539, 558-59 (1976).

[22]   *In re Marriage of Candiotti*, 34 Cal. App. 4th 718, 724 (1995). *See also Gilbert v. National Enquirer, Inc.*, 43 Cal. App. 4th 1135, 1144 (1996) ("the California Constitution provides an even broader guarantee of the right of free speech and the press than does the First Amendment").

[23]   *Procter & Gamble Co. v. Bankers Trust Co.*, 78 F.3d 219, 226-27 (6th Cir. 1996) ("[t]he Supreme Court has never upheld a prior restraint, even when faced with the competing interest of national security or the Sixth Amendment right to a fair trial.")

restraint is constitutional was stated by the Supreme Court in *Nebraska Press Association v. Stuart*.[24] The trial court issued an order prohibiting the media from publishing accounts of a preliminary hearing in the case of a defendant charged with six murders. The media also was prevented from publishing information relating to confessions or admissions of the defendant or other information that was strongly probative of the defendant's guilt. The ban was to remain in effect until a jury was seated and the jurors could be advised not to pay attention to media reports of the case. The preliminary hearing was open to the public, but the media was prohibited from reporting on the proceedings.

The U.S. Supreme Court struck down the prohibition as an unconstitutional prior restraint on free speech. The fact that the order only delayed and did not forever prevent publication did not matter to the Supreme Court: "[T]he burden on the government is not reduced by the temporary nature of the restraint," the court wrote. "To the extent that this order prohibited the reporting of evidence adduced at the open preliminary hearing, it plainly violated settled principles," the court said.[25]

The Supreme Court also made it clear that preventing publication of information gained outside of the judicial proceedings, such as police reports indicating the evidence available to implicate the defendant, will not be tolerated except in extreme situations. The court suggested that it could imagine few situations where a fair and impartial trial could not be achieved in the absence of prior restraint, even in a trial that involved extensive and sensational media coverage.

The Supreme Court held that before imposing an order, a court must make specific findings as to: (1) the nature and extent of actual pretrial news coverage; (2) whether other measures, including a thorough voir dire of potential jurors or a change of venue, would be likely to mitigate the effects of unrestrained pretrial publicity; and (3) whether a restraining order against a publication would in fact prevent the threatened danger of prejudicing the jury pool against the defendant.[26]

When evaluating a criminal defendant's rights against the First Amendment, it is important to keep in mind that pre-trial publicity does not create a presumption a defendant cannot get a fair trial: "Pretrial publicity, *even if pervasive and concentrated*, cannot be regarded as leading automatically and in every kind of criminal case to an unfair trial."[27]

2. Interpretive Cases and Examples.

The standard for obtaining a prior restraint is an extraordinarily exacting one. A federal court vacated a restraining order issued by the trial judge in the cocaine smuggling conspiracy trial of automotive executive John DeLorean. The vacated

---

[24]   *Nebraska Press Association v. Stuart,* 427 U.S. 539 (1976).
[25]   *Nebraska Press Association v. Stuart,* 427 U.S. 539, 568 (1976).
[26]   *Nebraska Press Association v. Stuart,* 427 U.S. 539, 562 (1976).
[27]   *Nebraska Press Association v. Stuart,* 427 U.S. 539, 565 (1976) (emphasis added). *See also People v. Jennings,* 53 Cal. 3d 334, 362 (1991) ("[t]he fact that a case received enormous publicity does not by itself establish error nor does conceded 'massive' publicity automatically translate into prejudice").

order would have prohibited the broadcast by CBS news of a secretly recorded videotape purporting to show the defendant conferring with co-conspirators in a hotel room.[28]

A California court of appeal ruled unconstitutional an order of a municipal court prohibiting a television station in San Diego from broadcasting a facial sketch of a sexual assault defendant. The rendering had been done by an artist for the station who viewed the subject in open court during his arraignment. The court of appeal noted that restraints on photo or film coverage authorized under the California Rules of Court do not cover artists' sketches and, therefore, no permission was needed to create the drawings. "On this record, once the drawing was lawfully obtained, its dissemination in normal media publication could not be constitutionally restrained."[29]

California courts have also recognized as prior restraints (and reversed) orders prohibiting the press from publishing photographs of the facial features of the defendants in a highly publicized trial,[30] or prohibiting the press from publishing the name of a juvenile accused of murder.[31]

In 1990, a federal court upheld a temporary restraining order. The case arose after ousted Panamanian dictator Manual Noriega won an order from the federal trial court in Florida preventing CNN from broadcasting a tape-recorded conversation between Noriega and his attorneys. The network apparently received the recording from an unknown third party. The trial court and the court of appeals both noted that this case went beyond the typical criminal case where the only issue was the right of the defendant to be assured a fair and impartial jury. Because Noriega had not waived his attorney-client privilege (he did not know the conversation was being recorded), publication of the tapes would not only violate his Sixth Amendment right to counsel, but it would also divulge to the prosecution the defense's strategy in the case, thereby depriving him of his constitutional right to a fair trial. The U.S. Supreme Court denied the network's request for a stay of the order without comment. While on its face the case proved disturbing to many media proponents, it should be noted that the unique facts of the case suggest that it probably does not represent a retreat from the strict standards needed to justify a prior restraint as set forth by the courts over the years.[32]

A federal district court in Ohio issued an order prohibiting *Business Week* from publishing an article based in part on documents filed with the court under seal in a securities case. The magazine had lawfully obtained the documents. The Court of Appeals for the Sixth Circuit reversed, finding that the district court had erred in restraining publication because the case did not fall "into that 'single, extremely narrow class of cases' where publication would be so dangerous to fundamental government interests as to justify a prior restraint." Indeed, the court

---

[28]   *CBS v. District Court*, 729 F. 2d 1174 (1984).

[29]   *KCST-TV Channel 39 v. Municipal Court*, 201 Cal. App. 3d 143 (1988).

[30]   *South Coast Newspapers, Inc. v. Superior Court*, 85 Cal. App. 4th 866 (2000).

[31]   *KGTV Channel 10 v. Superior Court*, 26 Cal. App. 4th 1673, 1684 (1994).

[32]   *U.S. v. Noriega*, 917 F.2d 1543 (1990).

even criticized the district court for issuing such a broad protective order that allowed discovery and court proceedings to be conducted largely in secret.[33]

D. THE RIGHT TO PRIVACY AND REPUTATION.

Judges are highly unlikely to issue a prior restraint to bar publication of information likely to injure a person's or company's reputation. Courts that have addressed these situations consistently have refused to restrain publication of information based on allegations that publication will defame an individual or otherwise invade some protected right. Instead, the courts have limited such individuals to post-publication remedies – such as a lawsuit – for any injuries or damages.

A federal court of appeals suggested the improbability of valid prior restraints by federal courts in California to protect individuals' rights to privacy and reputation. The court upheld the district court's refusal to restrain a magazine's publication of a story about a prison inmate who charged that the article placed him in a false light and endangered his chances for parole.[34] These rulings, although based primarily in constitutional doctrine, echo the traditional common law principle that courts will not restrain the publication of allegedly libelous statements but will leave it to the subject of the statements to seek damages resulting from publication.

However, the California Supreme Court recently held that once a statement has been determined by a court, at trial, to be defamatory, the court might issue an order prohibiting the defendant who made that statement from repeating it.[35] A violation of such an order is punishable as contempt, which may result in incarceration and fines.

E. TRADE SECRETS.

The publication or dissemination of information that truly constitutes a trade secret is prohibited by law and can be prevented by court order.[36] However, the fact that someone claims that information constitutes a trade secret does not mean that a prior restraint is justified. For example, obtaining and publishing information obtained from court records sealed by court order because the parties assert that they contain trade secrets may not justify a prior restraint.[37]

---

[33] *Procter & Gamble v. Bankers Trust*, 23 Med. L. Rptr. 2505 (1995).

[34] *Rifkin v. Esquire*, 7 Med. L. Rptr. 1231 (1981).

[35] *Balboa Island Village Inn, Inc. v. Lemen*, 156 P.3d 339, 57 Cal.Rptr.3d 320, 07 Cal. Daily Op. Serv. 4553, 2007 Daily Journal D.A.R. 5805 (2007).

[36] *See, e.g., DVD Copy Control Assn., Inc. v. Bunner* 31 Cal. 4th 864, 880-885 (2003) (First Amendment does not preclude injunction to prevent disclosure of trade secrets); Civil Code section 3426 and following (Uniform Trade Secrets Act).

[37] *See, e.g., Procter & Gamble Co. v. Bankers Trust Co.*, 78 F.3d 219, 225 (6th Cir. 1996) (refusing to enjoin publication of trade secrets improperly obtained in violation of a protective order, noting, " [t]he private litigants' interest in protecting their vanity or their commercial self-interest simply does not qualify as grounds for imposing a prior restraint.").

F. NATIONAL SECURITY.

Another area where the issue of prior restraint may arise is national security. The U.S. Supreme Court held in the "Pentagon Papers" case that the threat must not be just one of serious harm but one of "grave damage," which is "direct, immediate and irreparable."[38] In the Pentagon Papers case, the Supreme Court refused to grant a prior restraint to prohibit the publication of information from a 47-volume history of decision-making leading up to and during the United States' involvement in the Vietnam War. It did so even though the war was still going on, the information at issue was classified, and it had apparently been provided to the press in violation of the law. Pragmatically, however, if prior restraint is to be upheld it is likely to involve a case of national security. As the Supreme Court noted in the Pentagon Papers case: "No one would question that a government might prevent actual obstruction to its recruiting service or the publication of the sailing dates of transports or the number and location of the troops."[39]

G. STATUTES LIMITING THE RIGHT TO DISCLOSE INFORMATION.

In addition to gag orders, statutes or local ordinances may limit individuals' rights to disclose information to the media or the public in general. These statutes often are the target of challenges based on unconstitutional prior restraint.

A Rhode Island district court struck down as unconstitutional a state statute and regulations that prohibited all public discussion of the existence or contents of complaints lodged with the Rhode Island Ethics Commission before the final adjudication of the complaint unless the party subject to the complaint formally consented to the disclosure: "This court has no hesitation in first finding that the speech at issue in this case, namely public discussion of the existence and substance of an ethics complaint formally filed under oath by a public official, is speech protected by the First Amendment of the Constitution."[40]

H. RESPONDING TO A RESTRAINING ORDER.

A newspaper's options under an order restraining publication may vary depending on many factors. Publishers are well advised to consult legal counsel before violating a restraining order or statute.

1. California Law.

Under California law, violation of a court order will not be punishable as contempt if the order or the law upon which it is based is later determined to be

---

[38] *New York Times Co. v. United States*, 403 U.S. 713 (1971).
[39] *New York Times Co. v. United States*, 403 U.S. 713, 726 (1971).
[40] *Providence Journal Co. v. Newton*, 17 Med. L. Rptr. 1033 (1990).

unconstitutional.[41]   In certain rare circumstances, a newspaper might seriously consider publishing the information in violation of the order if it is confident that the order is unconstitutional and if time does not permit seeking appellate relief. This risky action should be taken only upon advice of counsel and after weighing the urgency of the public's need for the information against the inevitable perception of the newspaper's disrespect of the law.

2. Federal Courts.

Federal courts may operate under a "collateral bar" rule, which provides that disobedience of an order or violation of a law cannot subsequently be defended on the ground that the order or law is unconstitutional.[42]   The only option is to comply with the order until a writ of mandamus can be obtained from a higher court overturning the invalid order.

3. Transparently Invalid Orders.

Despite the "collateral bar" rule, some courts find it gives way when the restraining order is "transparently invalid." These orders may, in other words, be violated and challenged as a defense to a criminal contempt citation, providing certain conditions are met. Always consult with legal counsel before considering disregarding any court order.[43]

---

[41]   *People v. Gonzales*, 12 Cal. 4th 804, 818 (1996) (California citizens may elect to challenge the constitutional validity of a speech injunction when it is issued or reserve such a challenge until a violation of the injunction is found).

[42]   Compare *In re Providence Journal Company*, 820 F.2d 1342, 1347 (1986) (finding that an order entered by a court clearly without jurisdiction or transparently invalid may be disobeyed and is not protected by the collateral bar rule); *Walker v. City of Birmingham*, 388 U.S. 307, 316-317 (1967) ("Equally well-established is the requirement of any civilized government that a party subject to a court order must abide by its terms or face criminal contempt. Even if the order is later declared improper or unconstitutional, it must be followed until vacated or modified.")

[43]   *In re Providence Journal*, 820 F.2d 1342 (1986).

CHAPTER 7

Public Access to Civil Court Proceedings

IN THIS CHAPTER

There is a presumptive right of physical access to civil court proceedings in California. That right of access may be limited by court order in some circumstances. This chapter discusses the types of cases that are heard in civil courts and the circumstances in which physical access to specific proceedings may be limited or in some instances prohibited. Also discussed are the procedures a court must use before it can lawfully limit access to a proceeding and how long that limitation may last.

PART I:
INTRODUCTION

Court proceedings not classified as criminal are known as civil proceedings. Examples include actions for personal injuries, defamation claims, contract disputes, actions involving real or personal property, and family law matters such as divorce proceedings and custody disputes between divorced parents. Government prosecutors, who normally enforce criminal laws, will sometimes pursue civil proceedings, including actions brought against violators of certain business regulations.

Neither the United States Supreme Court or the Ninth Circuit Court of Appeals – the federal appellate court that serves California – has specifically addressed the issue of whether the First Amendment guarantees the public's right of access to civil cases. In 1999, however, the California Supreme Court ruled that the First Amendment, as well as article I, section 2(a) of the California Constitution, provide a right of access to civil trials and proceedings, just like criminal proceedings. Civil trials are presumptively open, and closure is permitted only in the rarest of circumstances under the same test applied to close criminal proceedings.[1] The California Supreme Court's opinion indicates that the constitutional right of access applies to records as well as hearings or trials.[2] This right of access to civil court records has now been incorporated into the California Rules of Court.[3]

Federal courts that have addressed the question generally have held that the First Amendment provides a right of access to federal civil proceedings. The reasons for this conclusion are simple: "[T]he [same] policy reasons for granting public access to criminal proceedings apply to civil cases. These policies relate to the public's right to monitor the functioning of our courts, thereby insuring quality, honesty and respect for our legal system."[4]

Finally, the Ninth Circuit Court of Appeals has held that federal common law and the Federal Rules of Civil Procedure give the press and the public a right of access to civil proceedings and

---

[1]   *NBC Subsidiary (KNBC-TV), Inc. v. Superior Court,* 20 Cal. 4th 1178 (1999).
[2]   *NBC Subsidiary (KNBC-TV), Inc. v. Superior Court,* 20 Cal. 4th 1178, 1217-1218 (1999)
[3]   Cal. Rules of Court 2.550 and 2.551.
[4]   *In re Continental Illinois Securities Litigation*, 732 F.2d 1302, 1308-1309 (7th Cir. 1984).

civil court records.[5] This right of access is similar in its application to the constitutional standard, although the common law right of access may not be as strong.

In California, journalists can reasonably expect the same right of access that governs criminal proceedings to apply to civil proceedings. However, as with criminal cases, the right of access is not absolute, and there are some situations when the public and the press may constitutionally be denied access to a civil proceeding.

PART II:
RIGHT OF ACCESS

A. THE FIRST AMENDMENT STANDARD.

Under the First Amendment test adopted in criminal cases, and also applied by many courts in civil cases, a party seeking to deny access to a civil proceeding must justify the request by demonstrating that the closure of the courtroom or the sealing of documents is *strictly and inescapably necessary* to protect a compelling government interest.[6] In other words, under the First Amendment, denial of access must be necessitated by an overriding government interest and must be narrowly tailored to serve that interest.[7]

B. THE CALIFORNIA STANDARD.

Under the test adopted by California's Supreme Court – after notice is given and before proceedings are closed or records are sealed – a hearing must be held. In order to justify denying access, the court must, based on the facts presented, make the following findings:

- There exists an overriding interest supporting closure or sealing;
- There is a substantial probability that the interest will be prejudiced absent closure or sealing;
- The proposed closure or sealing is narrowly tailored to serve the overriding interest; and
- There is no less restrictive means of achieving the overriding interest.[8]

Presently, California Rules of Court set forth this test and narrowly circumscribe the situations in which court records of any description may be sealed. Under these rules, court records are presumed to be open.[9] A record "must not be filed under seal without a court order."[10] A party, member of the public or the court on its own motion may move to unseal a record.[11] The court may order that a record be filed under seal only if it expressly finds that: (1) There exists an overriding interest that overcomes the right of public access to the record; (2) The overriding interest supports sealing the record; (3) A substantial probability exists that the

---

[5]   *San Jose Mercury News, Inc. v. U.S. Dist. Ct.,* 187 F.3d 1096 (9th Cir. 1999).

[6]   *Gannett Co. v. DePasquale,* 443 U.S. 368, 440 (1979) (Blackmun, J., concurring); *Associated Press v. U.S. District Court,* 705 F.2d 1143, 1145 (9th Cir. 1983).

[7]   *Press-Enterprise Co. v. Superior Court,* 464 U.S. 501, 510 (1984)

[8]   *NBC Subsidiary (KNBC-TV), Inc. v. Superior Court,* 20 Cal. 4th 1178, 1217-1218 (1999).

[9]   California Rule of Court 2.550(c).

[10] California Rule of Court 2.550(a).

[11] California Rule of Court 2.550(h).

overriding interest will be prejudiced if the record is not sealed; (4) The proposed sealing is narrowly tailored; and (5) No less restrictive means exist to achieve the overriding interest.[12]

Access to civil proceedings also typically includes access to documents filed with the court in connection with those proceedings. The rule that governs access to filed documents thus is the same as access to the courtroom.

PART III:
ACCESS TO PARTICULAR KINDS OF PROCEEDINGS

Certain types of civil proceedings historically have been considered confidential, and the California Legislature has adopted a number of rules allowing certain courts to close particular types of proceedings to the public.

A. DOMESTIC OR FAMILY PROCEEDINGS.

The First Amendment presumption of public proceedings applies equally to proceedings held in family law courts. A court of appeal recently reaffirmed that the public has an interest "in all civil cases, in observing and assessing the performance of its public judicial system, and that interest strongly supports a general right of access in ordinary civil cases, including family law cases."[13] Other California courts have also noted that neither article I, section 1 of California's Constitution (California's privacy provisions) nor California Family Code section 214 allow any court files or records to be automatically sealed.[14]

California's Supreme Court affirmed that Family Code section 214 permits closure of only court proceedings involving narrow, triable issues of fact "when … necessary in the interests of justice" and based upon a "showing of particularized need by the moving party." The First Amendment compelling interest test must be satisfied, as "no California case holds or even hints" that the principles with respect to sealing family law files are different; rather, those files should be treated as any other case files are treated, *i.e.,* subject to the compelling interest test.[15]

Section 214 notwithstanding, certain types of domestic proceedings *must* be closed, e.g., adoptions (Family Code section 8611), paternity hearings (Family Code section 7643), mediation of custody and visitation rights (Family Code section 3177), conciliations (Family Code section 1818), and waiver of premarital examinations (Family Code section 591(e)). Other proceedings may be closed at the discretion of the court, e.g., custody hearings (Family Code section 3041). Due to the public policy behind these closure statutes and the sensitive topics with which they deal, they probably will satisfy closure requirements.

B. MENTAL HEALTH HEARINGS.

Proceedings under the Lanterman-Petris-Short Act to establish a conservatorship or force an involuntary commitment may be closed, unless a public hearing is requested by a party to the proceedings.[16]

---

[12]   California Rule of Court 2.550(d).
[13]   *Burkle v. Burkle,* 135 Cal. App. 4th 1045, 1052-1063 (2006).
[14]   See *In re Marriage of Lechowick,* 65 Cal. App. 4th 1406 (1998).
[15]   *NBC Subsidiary (KNBC-TV), Inc. v. Superior Court,* 20 Cal. 4th 1178, 1195 (1999), citing *In re Marriage of Lechowick, supra,* 65 Cal. App. 4th 1406 (1998).
[16]   Welfare & Institutions Code section 5118.

C. TRADE SECRETS.

Trade secret protection is an important consideration under California law. A trade secret is information that has economic value because it is not generally known.[17] Public disclosure of information is fatal to a claim that the information is a trade secret. For example, telemarketing scripts used to sell credit card services were not trade secrets, because their contents were disclosed in sales calls to the public.[18]

Courts have authority to adopt measures necessary to protect a trade secret. In a civil case involving a claim that a trade secret has been stolen, courts have authority to adopt protective orders and conduct "in camera" proceedings, from which the public may be excluded[19] A similar process has been adopted by courts applying the First Amendment right of access to civil cases involving information claimed to constitute trade secrets.[20] California law gives courts the authority to issue protective orders in all civil cases to prevent the disclosure of trade secrets.[21]

The problem faced by journalists and others seeking access to court records is that litigants frequently designate materials produced in discovery or used in court as trade secrets, whether or not they actually are. Courts have a responsibility to make a determination that a claim of trade secret protection is, in fact, a legitimate one. In criminal cases, California law expressly permits the closure of criminal court proceedings while trade secrets are being discussed, and it sets out the procedure for demonstrating that information that may be used in the case is actually a trade secret.[22] A California Court of Appeal has held that these rules should also be followed in civil cases, where a party seeks an order limiting access to documents claimed to contain trade secrets.[23] If trade secrets are actually at issue, closure of court proceedings may be justified. However, the court should also determine whether the trade secrets are relevant to public health, and if they are it is required to balance the interests of the public and the parties, then decide whether access should nonetheless be allowed.[24]

D. PRIVACY.

Personal privacy has been recognized as an interest that may justify closure of court proceedings.[25] In California, the right of privacy is included in the state constitution.[26] However, "state constitutional privacy rights do not automatically 'trump' the First Amendment right of

---

[17]   Civil Code section 3426.1(d) defines trade secrets as follows: "'Trade secret' means information, including a formula, pattern, compilation, program, device, method, technique, or process, that: (1) Derives independent economic value, actual or potential, from not being generally known to the public or to other persons who can obtain economic value from its disclosure or use; and (2) Is the subject of efforts that are reasonable under the circumstances to maintain its secrecy."

[18]   *In re Providian Credit Card Cases*, 96 Cal. App. 4th 292, 304-306 (2002).

[19]   Civil Code section 3426.5.

[20]   *See, e.g., In re Iowa Freedom of Information Council*, 724 F.2d 658, 662 (8th Cir. 1983).

[21]   *See, e.g.*, Code of Civil Procedure section 2031.060(b).

[22]   Evidence Code sections 1060-1063.

[23]   *Stadish v. Superior Court*, 71 Cal. App. 4th 1130, 1144 (1999).

[24]   *Stadish v. Superior Court*, 71 Cal. App. 4th 1130, 1146 (1999).

[25]   *Burkle v. Burkle,* 135 Cal. App. 4th 1045, 1053, 1063 (2006) ("We entertain no doubt that, in appropriate circumstances, the right to privacy may be properly described as a compelling or overriding interest."). Note that this case addresses the sealing of court records in divorce proceedings. However, it notes that "[n]o meaningful distinction may be drawn between the right of access to courtroom proceedings and the right of access to court records that are the foundation of and form the adjudicatory basis for those proceedings." *Id.*, at 1052.

[26]   Cal. Const., article I, section 1.

access under the United States Constitution."[27] In practice, privacy rights are rarely found to justify closure of civil court proceedings.

Nonetheless, California's constitutional right of privacy complicates the question of whether a claim of privacy will justify closure. Courts generally balance the factors unique to the particular situation to determine whether the privacy interest sufficiently outweighs the qualified right of access. Although embarrassment alone should not justify closure, the circumstances – for example, how private the matter is, the age of the individual involved, and the public interest in the information – may determine whether closure satisfies First Amendment requirements.

In any case, however, any closure of court proceedings based on privacy concerns must be "narrowly tailored," and it must be the "least restrictive means available" to protect the asserted privacy interest.[28]

E. SETTLEMENT PROCEEDINGS.

Settlement proceedings are an important part of every civil case. Public access to these proceedings is routinely denied because the presence of individuals other than the litigants in the process is believed to be a barrier to settlement efforts. The strong public policy in favor of settlement does not bode well for attempts to gain access to proceedings that further the public policy objective. For example, "summary" or mock jury trials have been used as a method to facilitate settlement. The right of access has been held not to apply to these types of proceedings.[29]

F. DEPOSITIONS.

There is no public access right to attend depositions. However, in California journalists are not automatically excluded from depositions. A party seeking to exclude a reporter from a deposition must demonstrate good cause.[30] Unfortunately, good cause is routinely found.

In the federal courts, the Federal Rules of Civil Procedure provide that discovery proceedings are presumptively open, and that good cause must be shown to close or seal discovery matters such as depositions.[31] However, it is unusual for journalists to actually attend depositions. On the other hand, it is often possible to obtain transcripts of depositions, and the sealing of such transcripts has been successfully challenged.

---

[27] *Burkle v. Burkle,* 135 Cal. App. 4th 1045, 1059 (2006).

[28] *Burkle v. Burkle,* 135 Cal. App. 4th 1045, 1052-1053, 1065-1067 (2006).

[29] *Cincinnati Gas & Electric Co. v. General Elec. Co.,* 854 F.2d 900 (1988).

[30] *See* Code of Civil Procedure section 2025.420(b), which allows the following orders, but only upon a showing of good cause: "(5) That the deposition be taken only on certain specified terms and conditions;" and "(12) That designated persons, other than the parties to the action and their officers and counsel, be excluded from attending the deposition." This statute indicates that a protective order is necessary to limit a deposition to parties/counsel or to exclude anyone else. In *Condit v. Dunne,* 225 F.R.D. 113 (2004), the court addressed the very similar federal rule (Federal Rule of Civil Procedure 26(c)) and found that there was no good cause showing to seal the videotape transcript of Dominick Dunne's deposition.

[31] *Public Citizen v. Liggett Group, Inc.,* 858 F.2d 775, 789-90 (1st Cir. 1988) (citation omitted), cert. denied, 488 U.S. 1030 (1989) ("'as a general proposition, pretrial discovery must take place in the public unless compelling reasons exist for denying the public access to the proceedings.'"); *Welsh v. City and County of San Francisco,* 887 F. Supp. 1293, 1297 (N.D. Cal. 1995); *Condit v. Dunne,* 225 F.R.D. 113 (S.D.N.Y. 2004).

G. BENCH AND CHAMBER CONFERENCES

These types of conferences have historically occurred outside of public view. The California Supreme Court has, however, stressed that "a proceeding that would be subject to a right of access if held in open court does not lose that character simply because the trial court chooses to hold the proceeding in chambers."[32] Thus, the public and the press have a right of access to such proceedings if they involve substantive matters that would otherwise be heard in the courtroom itself.

Administrative or technical legal matters that do not involve fact-finding historically have been discussed at the bench or in chambers; access to these proceedings will probably be denied for practical or logistical reasons. However, reporters or members of the public attending court proceedings should try to obtain assurance that substantive matters are not relegated to the secrecy of bench or chambers conferences, absent compliance with the constitutional standards described above.

H. OPPOSING CLOSURE OF CIVIL COURT PROCEEDINGS

Try to anticipate when a court proceeding may be closed. If you are surprised by a motion for closure by a party or by the judge's own announcement of an intended closure, approach the court or the bailiff and ask for permission to address the court. If the judge allows you to, read the following statement or a similar statement:

CLOSED COURTROOM PROTEST

Your Honor, my name is _____ and I represent _____ [or: and I am a member of the public attending this proceeding]. I respectfully object to the proposed closure of this proceeding. The California Supreme Court has established specific and substantial requirements for determining whether the public may be excluded from all or part of a criminal proceeding. Federal courts have also ruled that the First Amendment and common law protect the public's right of access to civil proceedings. I request that the court ensure that any decision to close these proceedings complies with the requirements imposed by *NBC Subsidiary (KNBC-TV), Inc. v. Superior Court*, 20 Cal. 4th 1178.

If you seek not only to protest the closure but also to delay it to permit your attorney to appear in opposition (decide in advance with your editor and counsel which kinds of cases merit this tactic), conclude your statement with this request:

I believe there are some specific points and authorities that Your Honor may want to consider, and I ask for a brief pause in these proceedings to permit counsel to appear and be heard in our behalf.

---

[32]   *NBC Subsidiary (KNBC-TV), Inc. v. Superior Court*, 20 Cal. 4th 1178, 1215 (1999).

PART IV:
ACCESS TO PRIVATE PROCEEDINGS

Many litigants are using private judges and mediators to resolve their disputes. Private judges are used in two capacities: (1) as "adjuncts" to the courts; and (2) as mediators or decision-makers completely independent of the official judicial process. An example of the first proceeding is where a judge – generally at the request of one or both of the litigants – appoints a private judge to play some official role in the case; the private judge may handle only one part of the case, act as a special master with respect to certain matters, or even try the whole case. The second type of proceeding occurs when the public judicial system is not used to resolve the dispute. Instead, the parties select and pay for a private judge and agree to be bound by the private judge's decision.

The first type of proceeding is part of the official civil process. Accordingly, the same rules that govern access to court proceedings – particularly the First Amendment right of access – apply. If the private judge holds a hearing to determine an issue that otherwise would be before the court, that hearing is open to the public. Indeed, if appointed as a referee or special master by the court, the private judge must make the facility in which any hearings are held open to the public.[33] If, however, the private judge acts as a mediator at the request of the court, the proceeding would not be open because such a settlement activity is generally not open to the public even when conducted by the court. Access to the second type of proceeding – because it is outside of the court system – may not be compelled. There exist no statutory or constitutional provisions that would permit public access to such proceedings.

PART V:
CAMERA ACCESS TO COURT PROCEEDINGS

Camera access to court proceedings is governed in California by California Rules of Court. The rules governing cameras in the courtroom are the same for civil and criminal proceedings. California courts treat camera access as discretionary. California Rule of Court 1.150 ("Rule 1.150," formerly Rule 980) states:

> Rule 1.150. Photographing, Recording, and Broadcasting in Court.
> * * *
> (c) Photographic, recording, and broadcasting prohibited. Except as provided in this rule, court proceedings may not be photographed, recorded, or broadcast. This rule does not prohibit courts from photographing or videotaping sessions for judicial education or publications and is not intended to apply to closed-circuit television broadcasts solely within the courthouse or between court facilities if the broadcasts are controlled by the court and court personnel.
> * * *
> (e) Media coverage. Media coverage may be permitted only on written order of the judge as provided in this subdivision. The judge in his or her discretion may permit, refuse, limit, or terminate media coverage. This rule does not otherwise limit or restrict the right of the media to cover and report court proceedings.
>
> (1) *Request for order.* The media may request an order on Media Request to Photograph, Record or Broadcast (form MC-500). The form must be filed at least five court days before the portion of the proceeding to be covered unless good

---

[33]   California Rule of Court 3.926.

cause is shown. A completed, proposed order on *Order on Media Request to Permit Coverage* (form MC-510) must be filed with the request. The judge assigned to the proceeding must rule upon the request. If no judge has been assigned, the request will be submitted to the judge supervising the calendar department, and thereafter be ruled upon by the judge assigned to the proceeding. The clerk must promptly notify the parties that a request has been filed.

(2) *Hearing*. The judge may hold a hearing on the request or rule on the request without a hearing.

(3) *Factors to be considered by the judge*. In ruling on the request, the judge is to consider the following factors:

(A) Importance of maintaining public trust and confidence in the judicial system;

(B) Importance of promoting public access to the judicial system;

(C) Parties' support of or opposition to the request;

(D) Nature of the case;

(E) Privacy rights of all participants in the proceeding, including witnesses, jurors and victims;

(F) Effect on any minor who is a party, prospective witness, victim or other participant in the proceeding;

(G) Effect on the parties' ability to select a fair and unbiased jury;

(H) Effect on any ongoing law enforcement activity in the case;

(I) Effect on any unresolved identification issues;

(J) Effect on any subsequent proceedings in the case;

(K) Effect of coverage on the willingness of witnesses to cooperate, including the risk that coverage will engender threats to the health or safety of any witness;

(L) Effect on excluded witnesses who would have access to the televised testimony of prior witnesses;

(M) Scope of the coverage and whether partial coverage might unfairly influence or distract the jury;

(N) Difficulty of jury selection if a mistrial is declared;

(O) Security and dignity of the court;

(P) Undue administrative or financial burden on the court or participants;

(Q) Interference with neighboring courtrooms;

(R) Maintaining orderly conduct of the proceeding; and

(S) Any other factor the judge deems relevant.

These factors are to be weighed by trial courts in determining whether to admit cameras. The judge ruling on the request to permit media coverage is not required to make findings or a statement of decision.[34] In addition, an order may incorporate any local rule or order of the presiding or supervising judge regulating media activity outside of the courtroom.[35]

The judge may condition the order permitting media coverage on the media agency's agreement to pay any increased court-incurred costs resulting from the permitted media coverage (for example, for additional court security or utility service).[36] Another condition a court may

---

[34]   California Rule of Court 1.150(e)(4).
[35]   California Rule of Court 1.150(e)(4).
[36]   California Rule of Court 1.150(e)(4).

impose is a pooling arrangement, requiring media to share a single camera, for instance, or permitting only a limited number of reporters into the courtroom and requiring them to share their reports with other media. Such arrangements are not unusual in high-profile cases.

Each media agency is responsible for ensuring that all of its media personnel who cover the court proceeding know and follow the provisions of the court order and this rule. [37]

While the judges may have discretion in determining whether to allow cameras in a courtroom, in applying Rule 1.150 to determine whether to permit cameras in the courtroom, the courts should "fairly balance the respective interests of the parties and the public and the effect of electronic coverage on the fair administration of justice," and they "cannot ignore the important role the electronic media play in disseminating public information."[38] The U.S. Supreme Court has recognized that "[i]nstead of acquiring information about trials by first hand observation or by word of mouth from those who attended, people now acquire it chiefly though the print and electronic media."[39] Therefore, requests by the press for permission to use cameras in the courtroom should be given serious consideration.

A Note on Cameras in the Courtroom: There is a special form for seeking permission to use a camera in the courtroom. (You are not required to use the form, but it is a convenient method for making a request.) As noted above, Rule 1.150 requires you to file your request "at least five court days before the portion of the proceeding to be covered unless good cause is shown." If you have an interest in using a camera in a particular case, track the case carefully. In some California counties, case dockets and scheduled hearings are available online. In any event, try to file your request as soon as you can. However, you often will not know that a particular event is scheduled until less than five days before the event. In that case, explain to the court in your request why you did not (and often could not) get notice earlier.

---

[37]   California Rule of Court 1.150(e)(4).

[38]   *KFMB-TV Channel 8 v. Municipal Ct.*, 221 Cal. App. 3d 1362, 1367-68 (1990) (construing an earlier but substantially similar version of Rule 980).

[39]   *Richmond Newspapers, Inc. v. Virginia*, 448 U.S. 555, 572-573 (1980).

CHAPTER 8

Access to Jurors and Jury Information

"In a democracy, criminal trials should not, as a rule, be decided by anonymous persons."[1]

IN THIS CHAPTER

There is a presumptive right of public access to judicial proceedings involving jury selection for criminal and civil trials. The presumptive right of access may be overcome only after the court makes specific findings on the record that there is an overriding need to close the proceedings. Similarly, the public has a right of access to certain juror information. However, California law limits public access to names and other personal information about jurors. In addition, the public and the press are legally prohibited from contacting a juror at any time while a trial is underway, and the law limits the circumstances under which jurors can be contacted once the trial concludes.

Access to those serving on grand juries is much more limited than to individuals who serve on trial juries. Generally, grand jury information is made readily available only when a public report is issued or an indictment has been handed down. However, materials produced as a result of a grand jury's civil watchdog function may be more accessible. This chapter also discusses when it may be appropriate for a witness who has appeared before a grand jury to talk to a journalist.

PART I:
ACCESS TO JURY SELECTION

In most California counties, prospective jurors are selected at random from lists of residents compiled from licensed drivers, registered voters or other sources. Those selected for jury duty are sent a summons, which is an order to appear at the courthouse on a specified date and time for jury duty.

The process of selecting a jury generally involves the oral questioning of prospective jurors by attorneys who are involved with the case (prosecutors and defense counsel in a criminal prosecution and plaintiff and defense counsel in a civil suit). This process is known as "voir dire." The recent trend in California, however, is to have the judge perform most of the questioning to save time.[2]

In a landmark decision, the U.S. Supreme Court ruled that the public has a presumptive First Amendment right to attend jury selection proceedings, just as the public has a presumptive right to attend other portions of judicial proceedings.[3] Public voir dire is critical not only to ensure the

---

[1]   *In re Globe Newspapers Co.*, 920 F.2d 88, 91 (1st Cir. 1990).
[2]   California Code of Civil Procedure sections 222.5 and 223.
[3]   *Press Enterprise I*, 464 U.S. 501 (1984).

fairness of trials, but to create assurances for those not in attendance that the trial is being conducted fairly, which is essential to maintaining public confidence in the judicial system.[4]

At times, especially in highly publicized cases, a judge may allow some or all of the questioning of prospective jurors to be done outside of the presence of the public and the media. But such a decision must satisfy strict requirements, as judges have very limited discretion to bar the public from the jury selection process.

The Supreme Court has ruled that "the presumption of openness" to voir dire "may be overcome only by an overriding interest based on findings that closure is essential to preserve higher values and is narrowly tailored to serve that interest." Therefore, before a judge can close voir dire, the judge must find that: (1) there is a substantial probability that the defendant's right to a fair trial would be prejudiced by publicity; (2) there is a substantial probability that closure would prevent that prejudice; and (3) reasonable alternatives to closure cannot adequately protect the defendant's fair trial rights.[5] A judge is also required to give the public notice of the proposed closure of *any* court proceeding, including voir dire, and an opportunity to challenge it before any closure occurs.[6]

A Note on Opposing Closure: Anyone faced with a proposal to close voir dire should ask the judge to hold a public hearing and make all of the required factual findings **on the record**. If the judge makes findings, the adequacy of those findings can be challenged. In addition, consider asking the court for a delay to permit counsel to appear on your behalf.

A. CASES WHERE CLOSURE WAS HELD UNCONSTITUTIONAL.

In *Press-Enterprise I*, the U.S. Supreme Court held unconstitutional a trial court's closure of six weeks of voir dire and his refusal to release any portion of the transcript in a rape and murder trial of a teenage girl. The Supreme Court stated that, even if the trial court had made adequate findings to support closure, the order closing voir dire still would have been unconstitutional because the trial court failed to consider whether any adequate alternatives existed, such as a change of the trial venue, delay of the trial or emphatic jury instructions that the case be decided only on the evidence introduced at trial.[7]

Following *Press Enterprise I,* in a federal criminal trial in the District of Columbia, the media was successful in overturning a trial court's order closing voir dire on the ground that several of the responses to the juror questionnaire might involve matters of personal privacy. The court of appeals held that (1) the trial court had no evidence and made no findings that open hearings would touch on personal matters of the jurors; (2) the jurors did not make an affirmative request for a closed hearing; and (3) the trial court did not consider alternatives, such as closing only portions of the questioning that actually raised sensitive matters to individual jurors.[8]

The Second Circuit Court of Appeals similarly concluded, in the criminal case against Martha Stewart in New York federal court, that intense public interest and extensive media coverage of her trial was insufficient to warrant a closed voir dire proceeding. The voir dire transcripts failed to show that the questions asked were aimed at a discussion of gender bias or any other "socially polarizing issues," and therefore the media had a right to attend. In fact, the court said that such

---

[4]   *Press Enterprise I*, 464 U.S. at 508.
[5]   *Press-Enterprise I,* 464 U.S. at 510.
[6]   *Globe Newspapers v. Superior Court*, 457 U.S. 596 (1982); *Press-Enterprise I.* 464 U.S. 501; *United States v. Brooklier*, 685 F.2d 1162 (9th Cir. 1982).
[7]   *Press Enterprise I*, 464 U.S. at 511.
[8]   *Cable News Network v. U.S. (Deaver)*, 824 F.2d 1046 (D.C. Cir. 1987) (per curiam).

media presence might help discourage fabrication and promote honesty on the part of potential jurors.[9]

California courts apply the same standard as the federal courts. For example, a California appellate court concluded that voir dire proceedings where the jury was "death qualified" did not constitute an exceptional circumstance warranting automatic closure of voir dire proceedings. The court rejected the argument that prospective jurors would be intimidated by the media or would hold back responses because of the public's presence.[10]

B. CASES WHERE CLOSURE WAS HELD CONSTITUTIONAL.

Under limited circumstances, courts have upheld closed voir dire proceedings, but generally only when particularly sensitive or controversial issues were explored.

The Fourth Circuit Court of Appeals concluded that a trial judge acted constitutionally when he barred the public from voir dire of prospective jurors in the trials of three South Carolina legislators charged with vote selling, narcotics and other criminal offenses. The trial court reasoned that "frank and forthright responses from potential jurors would be chilled if they felt their remarks would be published in the media and that requiring jurors to demand private hearings did not alleviate that problem." The court of appeals upheld the private questioning as constitutional, agreeing with the trial court that prospective jurors would not be as candid as necessary to impanel an impartial jury if the questioning were conducted in public due to the unusual circumstances of these cases.[11]

The Fifth Circuit Court of Appeals has also held that, "for First Amendment purposes, no presumption of openness attaches to proceedings involving the midtrial questioning of jurors for alleged jury tampering." The court acknowledged that an accusation of juror misconduct goes to the very heart of public confidence in judicial proceedings, but at the same time recognized the need of the trial court to control jury proceedings. The court determined that, "[i]f the questioning of impaneled jurors were held in open court, there [would be] a substantial probability that what may have begun as a 'tempest in a teapot' [would] end up in a mistrial, a hung jury, or a reversal on appeal." In the end, "the interest in preserving the jury as an impartial, functioning, deliberative body" had a higher value than openness.[12]

A federal trial court in New York relied on the Fifth Circuit's opinion to conclude that closed midtrial juror questioning in the case of alleged crime boss John Gotti was constitutional.[13]

Closure was also upheld in the trial of boxing promoter Don King. A federal court of appeals concluded that, in light of the widespread and largely negative publicity concerning King, and the racial tensions heightened by some aspects of the publicity shown by the record, the trial court was entitled to question jurors in private. The trial court had rejected the alternative of assigning jurors numbers and redacting their names from questionnaires because even the "indicia of anonymity might well convey a sense of danger entirely inappropriate to the present case." While the private voir dire proceedings were upheld on appeal, the Second Circuit Court of Appeals noted that such closure was only for a limited time and for the sole purpose of impaneling the jury.[14]

Fortunately, these decisions are not the norm. There are very few cases in which the facts have been held to justify closing voir dire to the public.

---

9   *ABC, Inc. v. Stewart*, 360 F.3d 90, 101-02 (2d Cir. 2004) (distinguishing this case from *U.S. v. King*, 140 F.3d 76 (2d Cir. 1998), mentioned below.

10   *Ukiah Daily Journal v. Superior Court*, 165 Cal. App. 3d 788 (1985).

11   *In re South Carolina Press Ass'n*, 946 F.2d 1037, 1039 (4th Cir. 1991).

12   *United States v. Edwards*, 823 F.2d 111, 117 (5th Cir. 1987).

13   *United States v. Gotti*, 787 F. Supp. 319 (E.D.N.Y. 1992).

14   *United States v. King*, 140 F.3d 76 (2d Cir. 1998).

A Note on Opposing Closure: When confronted with a motion for closure, review the facts – if possible with counsel – to determine whether a challenge to the closure should be made. Be prepared to discuss alternatives to closure with the court.

PART II:
ACCESS TO JUROR QUESTIONNAIRES

Under California Code of Civil Procedure section 205, a jury commissioner may require prospective jurors to complete a questionnaire for the purposes of *qualifying* the individual for jury duty. The preliminary questionnaire may only ask questions related to juror identification, qualification and ability to serve, and may not be used to assist voir dire.

A California Court of Appeal has upheld a jury commissioner's refusal to release such prospective jurors' preliminary questionnaires pursuant to a public records act request where the questionnaire expressly stated that it was confidential and for the exclusive use of the court. The court reasoned that disclosure would add little to the extensive and probing voir dire process and would "undercut efforts to encourage citizen participation in the justice system."[15]

Section 205 also authorizes the courts to expedite the voir dire process by asking prospective jurors to answer certain prepared questions in writing. Using this process, attorneys and judges can eliminate prospective jurors without having to take the time to question them orally.

A California Court of Appeal has ruled that the constitutional right of the public to attend oral voir dire extends to such written juror questionnaires. The court stated, "[t]he questionnaire is part of the voir dire itself. The fact that a lawyer does not orally question a juror about a certain answer does not mean that the answer was not considered in accepting or rejecting the juror." The right of access, however, applies only to those prospective jurors who are also subjected to verbal questioning.[16]

Another California Court of Appeal agreed that questionnaires distributed to more than 300 people, instructing prospective jurors that their answers were part of the court record but would not be distributed to the general public, was unconstitutional. The court held that access to questionnaires should be permitted in all future criminal proceedings, excluding telephone numbers, social security numbers and driver's license numbers. The court reminded trial courts that the jury should not be promised confidentiality regarding questionnaire responses.[17]

Under the federal Jury Selection and Service Act of 1968, juror information must be made available to the public. Each federal district court has its own plan for handling juror information. Interested media should ask the court to see the plan. The media can challenge these plans if they are inconsistent with United States Supreme Court decisions.[18]

A Note on Juror Privacy: Jurors who are concerned about public access to certain highly embarrassing information can request to answer those questions privately in the judge's chambers. If the judge later determines that the potential juror has a legitimate overriding privacy concern, the judge can also order the transcript of that questioning be sealed.

---

[15]   *Pantos v. San Francisco*, 151 Cal. App. 3d 258, 265 (1984).

[16]   *Lesher Communications, Inc. v. Contra Costa Superior Court*, 224 Cal. App. 3d 774 (1990).

[17]   *Copley Press, Inc. v. Superior Court*, 228 Cal. App. 3d 774 (1991).

[18]   28 U.S.C. section 1861 et seq.

PART III:
ACCESS TO TRANSCRIPTS OF JURY SELECTION

Even where the court has applied the *Press Enterprise I* standard to close voir dire, the media may still be entitled to redacted versions of the transcripts of jury selection. In *Press Enterprise I*, the Supreme Court concluded that a trial judge should only seal the parts of the transcript that would reveal identities or personal information entitled to be protected. Trial judges must explain why the material in the transcript is entitled to privacy. Judges must also consider whether it is possible to disclose the substance of sensitive answers while preserving the anonymity of the jurors involved. Transcripts of closed proceedings must be released when the danger of prejudice passes.

In a criminal racketeering trial, the trial court decided not to release transcripts of voir dire until after the completion of the trial, reasoning that the rights of the defendants might be compromised if the transcript was released during trial. The trial court also feared the possibility that jurors might feel pressure from family and friends based upon news accounts of the jurors' responses during voir dire. The Ninth Circuit Court of Appeals disapproved of the trial court's decision for (1) not making specific findings of a "substantial probability" that defendant's right to a fair trial might be prejudiced, and (2) not considering alternatives such as admonitory instructions to the jurors or a voluntary agreement by the media as to the scope and timing of coverage.[19]

Agreements by the media with the court can become problematic. A New Jersey federal district court requested that the media voluntarily leave the courtroom during voir dire of a criminal securities fraud trial to permit more prospective jurors to sit in the courtroom. The media politely agreed and left the courtroom. Consequently, the media did not have the names and addresses of the jurors that had been publicly announced during voir dire. The media requested a copy of the transcript to prepare for post-trial juror interviews. The court immediately sealed it without a hearing and without making findings of necessity. The court did not unseal the transcripts until after the trial had concluded and only upon several conditions. The Third Circuit Court of Appeals reversed and firmly stated that the media must be notified and specific on-the-record findings regarding a compelling interest (*e.g.* immediacy of juror harassment) made *before* the voir dire transcript may be sealed.[20]

PART IV:
ACCESS TO JUROR NAMES AND ANONYMOUS JURIES

A.   CALIFORNIA LAW.

California controls access to juror information by statute. California Code of Civil Procedure section 237 currently provides, in part, as follows:

> (a)(1) The names of qualified jurors drawn from the qualified juror list for the superior court shall be made available to the public upon request unless the court

---

[19]   *United States v. Brooklier*, 658 F.2d 1165 (9th Cir. 1982).
[20]   *United States v. Antar*, 38 F.3d 1348 (3d Cir. 1994).

determines that a compelling interest, as defined in subdivision (b), requires that this information should be kept confidential or its use limited in whole or in part.

(2) Upon the recording of a jury's verdict in a criminal jury proceeding, the court's record of personal juror identifying information of trial jurors, as defined in Section 194, consisting of names, addresses, and telephone numbers, shall be sealed until further order of the court as provided by this section.

. . .

(b) Any person may petition the court for access to these records. The petition shall be supported by a declaration that includes facts sufficient to establish good cause for the release of the juror's personal identifying information. The court shall set the matter for hearing if the petition and supporting declaration establish a prima facie showing of good cause for the release of the personal juror identifying information, but shall not set the matter for hearing if there is a showing on the record of facts that establish a compelling interest against disclosure. A compelling interest includes, but is not limited to, protecting jurors from threats or danger of physical harm. If the court does not set the matter for hearing, the court shall by minute order set forth the reasons and make express findings either of a lack of a prima facie showing of good cause or the presence of a compelling interest against disclosure.

A Note on Obtaining Information About Jurors: Although any person may petition the court to access these records, the petitioner now has the burden of proving good cause to release personal juror identifying information. If the court finds that good cause has not been shown, the court is not required to set the matter for a hearing. If the court finds there is a showing on the record that establishes a compelling interest against disclosure, even if the petitioner demonstrates that good cause exists for the information's release, the court is *prohibited* from conducting a hearing on the matter. Jurors also have the right to challenge the petition. Additionally, even if a petitioner succeeds in persuading the court that good cause exists to release juror information, Code of Civil Procedure section 237(d) provides that "the court may require the person to whom disclosure is made, or his or her agent or employee, to agree not to divulge jurors' identities or identifying information to others [and] may otherwise limit disclosure in any matter it deems appropriate."

The procedure for implementing these rules is found in Rules 8.332 and 8.610(c) of the California Rules of Court. According to Rule 8.332, the names of trial jurors will be redacted from all documents and substituted with identifying identification numbers, the key of names and juror IDs will be kept under seal in the court's file. Rule 8.332 also requires addresses and telephone numbers of trial jurors to be deleted from all documents. Any information about people who were called but not selected as jurors will be sealed unless an order is issued pursuant to section 237. To the extent that local court rules conflict, Code of Civil Procedure section 237 pre-empts the local rule.

At least one court of appeal has found a local rule providing for juror anonymity in all civil and criminal proceedings to be invalid.[21] However, another appellate court has upheld a trial court's misinterpretation of section 237 to withhold juror identities *even from counsel*, finding the error to be harmless beyond a reasonable doubt. The court reasoned that counsel had access to substantial information about the prospective jurors and knowing their names would not have

---

[21]   *Erickson v. Superior Court*, 55 Cal.App.4th 755 (1997).

added anything more. The court also found that using IDs would help facilitate the clerk's later redacting of names and as such the rule was merely for efficiency.[22]

A Note on Working with the Court: Reporters should consider working with their court's media liaison to better understand each court's local rules.

B.   FEDERAL LAW.

The federal scheme for providing juror names and identification information is set forth in the Jury Selection and Service Act of 1968.[23] Under this section, juror's names must be available to the public after jurors have either appeared or failed to appear in response to a summons. A court has discretion to withhold jurors' names only if the court specifically determines that the "interests of justice so require." This term has been defined strictly, so that the desire of the juror to remain anonymous is not a sufficient basis to deny public access.

C.   INTERPRETIVE CASES.

A federal district court judge denied the media the names and addresses of jurors at the completion of a Mafia-related criminal trial. On appeal, the circuit court held that absent particularized findings reasonably justifying non-disclosure, juror names and addresses must be made public. The court explained that "[k]nowledge of juror identities allows the public to verify the impartiality of key participants in the administration of justice, and thereby ensures fairness and public confidence in the system." While acknowledging the privacy interest of jurors, the court elaborated on a juror's public duty, "[j]urors may be citizen soldiers, but they are soldiers nonetheless, and ... [t]heir participation in publicized trials may sometimes force them into the limelight against their wishes."[24]

In other federal cases, secrecy has been justified based on a threat of harm to an individual juror or a threat of jury tampering. In the trial of the surviving Branch Davidians after the gun battle with federal agents in Waco, Texas, the federal district court ordered an anonymous jury on its own. The defendants objected, arguing that they or their associates did not pose any threat to the jurors as other courts had found in organized crime cases. The court of appeals upheld the trial court's order on the ground that anonymity did not prejudice the defendants' right to a fair trial, while the worldwide attention and deep passions about the trial raised legitimate concerns about potential disruption of jurors. As evidence, the jurors had presented the court with letters they had received about the trial.[25]

A federal district court in California also ordered that jurors in the high-profile trial of the Unabomber, Theodore Kaczynski, sit anonymously during the trial (but their names would be released at its conclusion). The judge based his order on extensive publicity rather than a threat to juror safety. The media challenged the order stating that the court did not provide sufficient evidence to support the closure orders. Upon review, the Ninth Circuit Court of Appeals found the point to be moot since the names and addresses of the jurors were released after the guilty plea was entered. The court avoided ruling on the constitutionality of an anonymous jury.[26]

---

22   *People v. Phillips*, 56 Cal. App. 4th 1307 (1997); see also *People v. Goodwin*, 59 Cal. App. 4th 1084 (1998).

23   United States Code, Title 28, section 1861 (28 U.S.C. § 1861) and following sections.

24   *In re Globe Newspaper*, 920 F.2d 88, 94, 98 (1st Cir. 1990); see also *In re the Baltimore Sun*, 841 F.2d 74 (4th Cir.1988) (relying on the history of juries in the United States to hold that juror names and addresses should be made available to the public).

25   *United States v. Branch*, 91 F.3d 699 (5th Cir. 1996).

26   *Unabom Trial Media Coal. v. District Court*, 183 F.3d 949 (9th Cir. 1999) (per curiam).

Most federal courts confronting the issue have found anonymity constitutionally permissible in certain circumstances.[27] Generally, federal courts will not impanel an anonymous jury without (a) concluding that there is a strong reason to believe the jury needs protection, and (b) taking reasonable precautions to minimize any prejudicial effects on the defendant and to ensure that his fundamental rights are protected.[28] In determining whether a jury needs protection, a number of these circuits have relied on a five-factor analysis: (1) the defendant's involvement in organized crime; (2) the defendant's participation in a group with the capacity to harm jurors; (3) the defendant's or his cohorts' past attempts to interfere with the judicial process; (4) the potential that, if convicted, the defendant would suffer lengthy incarceration and substantial monetary penalties; (5) extensive publicity that could enhance the possibility that juror's names would become public and expose them to intimidation or harassment.[29]

While the mere desire for anonymity on the part of an individual juror or agreement of the parties should not be sufficient to overcome the presumption of access, some courts have found otherwise. The Fifth Circuit Court of Appeals upheld a decision to impanel an anonymous jury, and to keep jurors' names and addresses secret even after the verdict had been announced, based on the court's polling of the sitting jurors, who wanted anonymity.[30]

PART V:
ACCESS TO JURORS DURING TRIAL

Reporters' access to jurors is limited during the course of a criminal or civil trial. In the case of a grand jury (discussed in Part VIII below), the limitations are even more severe. Because jurors must be free from outside influence, reporters are barred from speaking to them during the trial and deliberation process. In addition to refraining from reading or viewing media accounts, jurors are routinely instructed not to speak to anyone about the case until they are discharged.

Jurors are permitted to speak to the media at their own discretion after a verdict is entered or a mistrial is declared. As discussed below, a court's discretion to prohibit jurors from discussing a case subsequent to their discharge is limited by constitutional principles.

A Note on Contact with Jurors: During the course of a trial, reporters and members of the public who are attending the trial should avoid even the appearance of contact with jurors. That means they should stand in a different part of the courtroom while jurors are assembled and wait to enter the courtroom. Anyone who speaks to a juror knowing they are serving on a jury could be held in contempt of court or compelled to testify as to the nature of the discussion to determine whether a mistrial should be declared or the juror dismissed. If a reporter talks to a juror, the

---

[27] *See U.S. v. Collazo-Aponte*, 216 F.3d 163 (1st Cir. 2000); *U.S. v. Marrerro-Ortiz*, 160 F.3d 768 (1st Cir. 1998); *United States. v. Paccoine*, 949 F.2d 1183 (2d Cir. 1991); *United States v. Barnes*, 604 F.2d 121 (2d. Cir. 1979 (first case in United States to allow fully anonymous jury); *United States. v. Thornton*, 1 F.3d 149 (3d Cir. 1993); *U.S. v. Salvatore*, 110 F.3d 1131 (5th Cir. 1997); *United States v. Talley*, 164 F.3d 989 (6th Cir. 1999); *United States v. Crockett*, 979 F.2d 1204 (7th Cir. 1992); *United States v. Darden*, 70 F.3d 1507 (8th Cir. 1995); *U.S. v. Ross*, 33 F.3d 1507 (11th Cir. 1994); *United States v. Wilson*, 160 F.3d 732 (D.C. Cir. 1998).

[28] *U.S. v. Edmond* 52 F.3d 1080, 1090-1091 (D.C. Cir. 1995); *United States v. Paccione*, 949 F.2d 1183, 1192 (2d Cir.1991), *cert. denied*, 505 U.S. 1220 (1992); *United States v. Ross*, 33 F.3d 1507, 1519-22 (11th Cir.1994); *United States v. Crockett*, 979 F.2d 1204, 1215-17 (7th Cir.1992), *cert. denied*, 507 U.S. 998 (1993).

[29] *U.S. v. Edmond* 52 F.3d 1080, 1091 (D.C. Cir. 1995); *United States v. Ross*, 33 F.3d 1507, 1520 (11th Cir.1994).

[30] *United States v. Brown*, 250 F.3d 907, 920 (5th Cir. 2001).

media leaves its role of observer and becomes a participant in the proceedings. This conduct harms not only the proceedings but also the reputation and credibility of the media.

PART VI:
PHOTOGRAPHING AND SKETCHING JURORS DURING TRIAL

The U.S. Supreme Court has not extended the public's First Amendment right to attend judicial proceedings to the right to photograph the proceedings. (See the discussion of cameras in the courts in Chapter 7, part IV). Lower courts addressing the issue have held that the media can be constitutionally prohibited from photographing jurors.

In California, the media should review California Rules of Court Rule 1.150 for guidance on the court's authority over the use of cameras or other electronic recording devices inside the courtroom. Rule 1.150(e)(6) provides that the judge shall not permit cameras or electronic coverage during jury selection or photographing jurors (or spectators). The judge may limit coverage not just in the courtroom but throughout the courthouse, including its entrances and exits. This rule cannot prevent the media from photographing jurors outside those defined areas or obtaining pictures of jurors through lawful means. Such a restriction would be an unlawful prior restraint.

The media often use sketch artists in court to draw jurors. In the third trial of conspirators involving organized crime where the jurors feared for their personal safety in Arizona, the trial court required sketches to be reviewed by the court before publication. The media petitioned for a stay in the United States Supreme Court. In reviewing the media's petition, then-U.S. Supreme Court Chief Justice Rehnquist suggested that the trial court's order appeared in the abstract to constitute a prior restraint and would have been more defensible if it had been a total ban on sketching. Nevertheless, Rehnquist denied the petition because he believed that the issue should be heard first by the Arizona State Supreme Court. Rehnquist also downplayed the importance of juror sketches in covering a trial:

> "I would think that of all conceivable reportorial messages that could be conveyed by reporters or artists watching ... trials, one of the least necessary to appreciate the significance of the trial would be individual juror sketches."[31]

PART VII:
ACCESS TO JURORS AFTER TRIAL

A. CALIFORNIA LAW.

Jurors cannot be prohibited from speaking with anyone, including the media, about the case on which they served, after the jury has been discharged.

Section 206 of California's Code of Civil Procedure ("Section 206") provides that, prior to discharging the jury from the case, the judge in a criminal action shall inform the jurors that they have an absolute right to discuss or not to discuss the deliberation or verdict with anyone. A court order that restricts the media's contact with former jurors that is not based on a compelling government interest and is not narrowly tailored to serve that interest is invalid.

Arguments have been made that these types of orders are needed to protect the privacy of jurors and to protect the independence of the jury. These arguments carry little weight, however,

---

[31]   *KPNX Broad. Co. v. Arizona Supreme Court*, 459 U.S. 1302, 1308 (1982).

because individual jurors have their own First Amendment rights, including the right to turn down media requests for interviews.

Courts do have authority to punish reporters who continue to request an interview after one already has been denied. A court of appeals upheld a trial court order forbidding anyone from making repeated requests for an interview once a juror had made their refusal known. The court noted that a juror who refuses an interview is unlikely to change his or her mind, but in the event that it happens, the juror is always free to contact the reporter. The court also upheld the portion of the trial judge's order that prohibited interviewers from inquiring into the votes of other jurors.[32]

The level of restriction that can be constitutionally imposed also depends to some degree on the circumstances under which the jury is discharged. In general, there are three ways that a criminal trial can end: a guilty verdict, a not-guilty verdict and a mistrial.

When a jury returns a not-guilty verdict, the rule of double jeopardy means that the case can never be retried, and therefore the prosecution cannot appeal. When a guilty verdict is returned, the defendant has the right to appeal the verdict. Depending on the disposition of the appeal, a new trial may be necessary. A mistrial can be declared for any number of reasons, including that the jury is unable to reach a unanimous verdict. When a mistrial is declared, the jury is dismissed and a new jury must be impaneled if the case is to be retried.

Higher courts have recognized that the legitimate needs of individual jurors and the jury system can be protected with less drastic measures than prohibition of all contact with former jurors in the wake of a new trial. Courts generally allow more restrictions to be placed on access to jurors who have been discharged in the case of a mistrial. The least amount of restriction may be applied in the case of a not-guilty verdict, since there is no danger that a subsequent jury in the same case could be prejudiced by comments of the previous jury.

B. INTERPRETIVE CASES.

The Ninth Circuit Court of Appeals found little weight in a trial judge's oral remarks ordering the media to stay away from jurors once the verdict was entered. The justifications provided for this order were the need to protect jurors from harassment, and the fear that if jurors spoke to the media they would no longer be able to sit on future juries.[33]

A California appellate court in applying Section 206, ruled that the trial court's order in a criminal trial that the media not contact the jurors was impermissibly broad. Despite the defendant's motion, there was no compelling state interest to restrict the media, and the jurors were free to discuss the case.[34]

A federal court struck down a local rule prohibiting anyone from interviewing jurors about the jury's deliberations or verdict without the prior permission of the court. The Court of Appeals held that the order was too broad, calling it:

> "unlimited in time and in scope, applying equally to jurors willing and anxious to speak and jurors desiring privacy, forbidding ... courteous as well as uncivil communications, and foreclosing questions about a juror's general reactions as well as specific questions about other jurors' votes that might, at least under some circumstances, be inappropriate."[35]

---

[32] *United States v. Harrelson (El Paso Times)*, 713 F.3d 1114 (5th Cir. 1983).

[33] *United States v. Sherman*, 581 F.2d 1358 (9th Cir. 1978).

[34] *Contra Costa Newspapers, Inc. v. Superior Court (Bishop)*, 61 Cal. App. 4th 862 (1998).

[35] *In re Express News Corp.*, 695 F.2d 807, 810 (5th Cir. 1982).

The court distinguished an order preventing all communications from an order prohibiting repeated requests once a juror has expressed a desire not to talk about the case. It is constitutional to prohibit "nagging inquiries."[36]

PART VIII:
ACCESS TO GRAND JURIES

Grand juries are special bodies of citizens who have either been elected or appointed to serve for a yearlong term. They are broadly empowered to investigate alleged government wrongs, issue reports and recommendations on their findings, and issue criminal indictments when necessary. Unlike court proceedings, which operate best under public scrutiny, grand juries generally are conducted under the shroud of secrecy.[37]

Grand jury proceedings are conducted in private, with often the nature of such proceedings kept hidden from the public. Grand jury information is made readily available only when a public report is issued or an indictment has been handed down. Once an indictment has been reached, the transcript is presumptively a matter of public record. Once the grand jury votes to indict a defendant, the court reporter who prepares the transcript is required to deliver a copy of the transcript to the defendant and file the original transcript with the court clerk. The transcript filed with the court clerk is required to be open for public inspection ten days after the defendant or his attorney have received a copy of the transcript unless all or a portion of the transcript is sealed by the court. The transcript may only be withheld upon a finding that making all or part of it public "may prejudice the defendant's right to a fair and impartial trial."[38] Before a transcript may be sealed, the trial court must find, based on the record, that the publicity will so prejudice the entire community that twelve unbiased jurors cannot be found and no adequate alternatives exist.[39]

In California, a court's authority to disclose grand jury materials to the public is defined by statute. And as such, the California Supreme Court has determined that the state legislature did not intend for a court to have general authority over the disclosure of grand jury materials. The media therefore does not have the presumptive right to grand jury transcripts nor does a trial judge have the discretion to release a transcript when a case reaches settlement after testimony has been given but before the grand jury deliberates because such a scenario is not outlined by statute.[40]

In 1998, the state Legislature did expand the public's ability to gain access to grand jury materials. In civil investigations, the grand jury is now allowed to make public part or all of the evidentiary material, findings and other information relied upon by, or presented to, the grand jury.[41] Several requirements must be met, however. The release must be approved by the presiding judge of the superior court or his or her designee, and "the name of any person, or facts leading to the identity of any person, who provided information to the grand jury shall not be released." A judge also may require the redaction or masking of any part of the materials determined to contain information that is of "a defamatory or libelous nature." At this time, there is no similar provision for criminal grand jury investigations.

---

[36] *In re Express News Corp.*, 695 F.2d 807, 810 (5th Cir. 1982).
[37] California Penal Code section 939.
[38] California Penal Code section 938.1.
[39] *Press Enterprise v. Superior Court* (Scott), 22 Cal. App. 4th 498, 504 (1994).
[40] *Daily Journal Corp v. Superior Court*, 20 Cal. 4th 1117 (1999).
[41] California Penal Code section 929.

A. ACCESS TO GRAND JURORS.

Except pursuant to a court order, the disclosure by a grand juror of evidence, statements or votes of which he or she has become aware during the jury proceedings is punishable as a misdemeanor.[42] In California, each grand juror is required to take an oath not to disclose any evidence before it. The oath is as follows: "I will not disclose any evidence brought before the grand jury, nor anything which I or any other grand juror may say, nor the manner in which I or any other grand juror may have voted on any matter before the grand jury."[43]

B. ACCESS TO GRAND JURY WITNESSES.

In 1983, California's attorney general issued an opinion declaring that the grand jury, in its criminal indictment role, has the authority to admonish a witness not to reveal questions asked, answers given, or other matters he or she learns during examination by the jury. A violation of such warning may result in contempt of court. The attorney general further stated that the admonition could not prevent a witness from revealing what he or she already knew before the examination, or what had been learned subsequently, independent of the grand jury proceeding.

In June 2003, a similar opinion was again handed down by the attorney general, but this time it provides authority to the grand jury in its civil "watchdog" capacity.[44]

These declarations by California's attorney general are consistent with U.S. Supreme Court decisions. The court has held a witness has the "right to divulge information of which he was in possession before he testified [in front of] the grand jury, and not information which he may have obtained as a result of his participation in the proceedings of the grand jury."[45] A California court of appeal has also made this distinction.[46]

Similarly, the Eleventh Circuit Court of Appeals has ruled that the Federal Rules of Criminal Procedure do not require witnesses before a federal grand jury to preserve secrecy after their testimony. A federal district court may order a witness not to disclose materials prepared for, or testimony given in, the proceedings based on a finding of "compelling necessity" to preserve the integrity of a criminal investigation. The court noted, however, that an order would be unconstitutional as "too broad" if it attempted to prevent "disclosure of documents prepared and assembled independent of the grand jury proceedings such as ... records compiled in the ordinary course of business."[47]

More recently, the Tenth Circuit Court of Appeals upheld a Colorado state statute that prohibits witnesses from disclosing their grand jury testimony. The court determined the state statute did not prohibit a witness from disclosing information known prior to a grand jury appearance and therefore does not violate the First Amendment.[48]

In California, the pending felony child molestation case against Michael Jackson may reflect the growing trend of limited access the media has to grand jury witnesses. In March 2004, a Santa Barbara Superior Court issued a Decorum Order forbidding grand jury witnesses from talking to anyone about anything connected to the grand jury deliberations, including the existence of

---

[42]   California Penal Code section 924.1.
[43]   California Penal Code section 911.
[44]   66 Ops. Cal. Atty. Gen 85.
[45]   *Butterworth v. Smith*, 494 U.S. 624, 632-626 (1990).
[46]   *San Jose Mercury News, Inc. v. Criminal Grand Jury of Santa Clara County*, 122 Cal. App. 4th 410 (2004).
[47]   *In re Subpoena to Testify Before Grand Jury*, 864 F.2d 1559 (11th Cir. 1989).
[48]   *Hoffman-Pugh v. Keenan*, 338 F.3d 1136 (10th Cir. 2003), cert. denied, 540 U.S. 1107 (2004).

possible documents, exhibits, etc. The order even went so far as to forbid media personnel from photographing grand jury witnesses entering or leaving the courtroom.[49]

C. CALIFORNIA'S LIMITED RIGHT TO PUBLIC SESSION OF THE GRAND JURY.

The main exception to the general rule that all sessions of a grand jury be private is codified in California Penal Code section 939.1, which provides that the grand jury and the attorney general or a district attorney can make a joint written request to the superior court to hold a public session. The judge has the discretion to order the public session if the judge:

> "finds that the subject matter of the investigation affects the general public welfare, involving the alleged corruption, misfeasance, or malfeasance in office or dereliction of duty of public officials or employees or of any person allegedly acting in conjunction or conspiracy with such officials or employees in such alleged acts. In this case, the court or judge may make an order directing the grand jury to conduct its investigation in a session or sessions open to the public."

Despite this exception, the deliberation and voting of the grand jury must still be conducted in private.

---

[49] Grand Jury Decorum Order, In re Santa Barbara Criminal Grand Jury, No. 04-00 (Cal. Super. Ct. Mar. 24, 2004).

CHAPTER 9

The California Shield Law and the Reporter's Privilege

IN THIS CHAPTER

Journalists in California have a limited "privilege" to protect confidential sources and unpublished information from compelled disclosure in a judicial proceeding. Protection is provided by both the state's shield law (article I, section 2(b) of the California Constitution, and Evidence Code section 1070) and federal law (the First Amendment to the United States Constitution, as interpreted by the courts). The degree of protection depends on the circumstances. In civil cases in California state courts, the privilege is absolute – disclosure cannot be compelled. In criminal cases, a defendant may be able to overcome the protection, but the prosecution generally cannot. In civil cases in federal court, the protection provided by the California shield law may not apply. First Amendment protection applies but can be overcome. The biggest loophole: The privilege may not help in federal criminal proceedings (particularly grand jury investigations), because the California shield law does not apply, and First Amendment protections, which previously seemed substantial, today are routinely held by the courts to be inapplicable or readily overcome.

PART I:
INTRODUCTION – LEGAL PROTECTION FOR JOURNALISTS AND OTHERS WHO GATHER AND PUBLISH INFORMATION

This chapter primarily addresses special protections for journalists. Although it is not always clear who qualifies for the designation of "journalist," because of the role that journalists play in society and the fact that they are often the subject of efforts to force them to provide unpublished information, they have been given certain legal protections under state law and the First Amendment. In the case of the First Amendment, these protections are extended not just to journalists, but also to others who gather and publish information, such as book authors.

The job of journalists is to gather and publish information of interest to their community. During this process, journalists learn facts and witness events that are significant in other people's lives. Because journalists not only gather information, but publicly identify themselves as possessing it, parties to civil and criminal litigation will sometimes attempt to obtain information gathered by journalists. For example, a journalist may be asked to testify in a trial about things he or she observed, or to turn over notes of interviews conducted while gathering the news, or to turn over video outtakes that the journalist has chosen not to make public.

The more time journalists must spend testifying and acting as de facto private investigators for litigants in civil and criminal cases, the more difficult it is to do their jobs. Sources become more reluctant to speak to the media if journalists can be called into court to divulge their identities or the contents of their communications with reporters. By testifying in response to one party's subpoena, there is a danger that the journalist will be viewed as being something other than an objective observer – for example, if a journalist testifies for the prosecution in a criminal case, sources may view journalists as an arm of the prosecution and therefore refuse to provide information. Because of these significant ramifications, most journalists oppose attempts to compel production of their source material or testimony. This chapter deals with the laws that allow journalists to refuse to divulge information in civil and criminal cases in which they are not a party.

Whether a reporter or news organization will be able to resist testifying or producing documents without sanction may depend on whether the underlying case is pending in state or federal court, and whether it is civil or criminal in nature.

In most state court cases, journalists may assert California's constitutional "shield law," which provides strong protection for both confidential sources and unpublished information. The California Supreme Court has held that the shield law is absolute in civil cases, meaning it cannot be pierced even if one of the parties demonstrates a need for the journalist's testimony. The only exception is in civil cases in which the journalist or news organization is a party, in which case the shield law does not apply and testimony or records have to be provided unless the court determines they are protected by the reporter's privilege provided by the First Amendment and California court decisions. In criminal cases, the California Supreme Court has held that the shield law generally bars prosecutors from compelling journalists to reveal unpublished information or confidential sources, but that, in certain cases, the shield law must give way when the testimony or records sought are necessary for a criminal defendant to obtain a fair trial under the United States Constitution. The California shield law applies only to journalists.

In federal court cases the California shield law may not apply, and journalists generally must rely on the "reporter's privilege" that courts have recognized as being established by the First Amendment. This protection is called "qualified" because even where it applies a court will order the journalist to testify if the judge determines that various factors warrant piercing the privilege. Federal courts have held the First Amendment reporter's privilege does not apply to federal grand jury subpoenas. Thus, for example, in 2006 federal courts ordered three California journalists imprisoned for refusing to provide testimony to a grand jury. However, in some ways the First Amendment privilege is broader than the California shield law, because it is not restricted exclusively to journalists. It may also extend to others who gather and disseminate information, such as book authors and the like.

The qualified constitutional reporter's privilege has also been recognized by the California Supreme Court and is applicable in California state court cases. It may provide protection in cases in which the shield law does not apply.

PART II:
THE CALIFORNIA SHIELD LAW

When a party to a civil or criminal action in California state court wishes to compel a journalist (or any other witness who is not a party to the case) to testify or turn over evidence, they serve the potential witness with a subpoena. A subpoena is an order that is enforced by the court in which the case has been filed. Ordinarily, a person who refuses to comply with a subpoena – for example, a witness who refuses to show up in court or at a deposition to testify – can be held in contempt of court by the judge. The judge has the power to jail and fine someone who has been cited for contempt. Judges can put witnesses in jail until they agree to comply with a subpoena.

Under California Evidence Code Section 1070 and Article I, Section 2 of the California Constitution – commonly known as the California "reporter's shield law" – journalists are immune from contempt for failing to comply with a subpoena under specific circumstances detailed below. California is one of many states that have enacted "shield laws" designed to protect journalists' confidential sources and other unpublished information. It is important to remember that the procedures and protections explained in this section only apply when a California state court has issued the subpoena. As noted above, for the most part the California shield law does not apply to subpoenas issued by other states' courts or by federal courts (even those in California). Issues pertaining to federal court subpoenas are discussed in Part III.

A. PERSONS PROTECTED BY THE SHIELD LAW.

When a journalist is subpoenaed to testify or to turn over notes or other physical evidence and wishes to invoke the protections of the California shield law, the journalist has the burden of establishing the following elements: 1) that he or she is among those entitled to protection under the shield law; 2) that the information was obtained in the course of gathering information "for communication to the public"; and 3) that the information requested is unpublished or confidential. These requirements are explained further in the sections that follow.

1. Who is Protected?

To invoke the protections of the shield law, the person must be a "publisher, editor, reporter or other person connected with or employed upon a newspaper, magazine or other periodical publication, or by a press association or wire service, or any person who has been so connected or employed." The privilege also extends to "a radio or television news reporter or other person connected with or employed by a radio or television station, or any person who has been so connected or employed." Thus, by its terms, the shield law covers most newsroom employees, including photographers and copy editors.[1]

There is rarely any dispute over the shield law's applicability when the person is a regular employee of a recognized newsgathering agency. Questions do arise from time to time when the person attempting to invoke the protections of the shield law is a freelancer or stringer, or some other person not "regularly employed" by a newsgathering agency. Most courts that have addressed the issue have held that so long as the person obtained the information in question while gathering news intended for publication, the protections of the shield law apply.

For example, in one case, a freelancer entered into a contract to write an article on a sensational crime for a magazine.[2] One of the defendants charged with the crime, Von Villas, served the freelancer with a subpoena asking the freelancer to turn over notes and tapes of interviews conducted before and after he contracted to write the story for the magazine. The court ruled that the reporter was entitled to protections of the shield law for the notes and tapes made both before and after he entered into the contract.

The key to finding protection under the shield law, in light of this and other recent cases, is to show that the person was gathering information for the purpose of publishing it. The fact that the person has already made arrangements for publication with a particular publisher at the time the information is gathered may be relevant evidence in determining whether the information was gathered for the purpose of publication, but such an agreement is not necessary for the shield law to apply.

The ability of any person to become a publisher by virtue of the Internet has raised questions as to whether bloggers and other web publishers come within the scope of the reporter's shield law. In a 2006 case, the California Court of Appeal held that two bloggers who had posted

---

[1]   Cal. Const., article I, section 2(b); Evid. Code section 1070(a); *see also Delaney v. Superior Court*, 50 Cal. 3d 785, 793 (1990).

[2]   *People v. Von Villas*, 10 Cal. App. 4th 201 (1992).

information on the Internet about a rumored new Apple computer product were among the people entitled to protection under the shield law. The court explained that "the language of the law ... extends to every 'publisher, editor, reporter, or other person connected with or employed upon a newspaper, magazine, or other periodical publication.' (Cal. Const., art. I § 2, subd. (b)). We can think of no reason to doubt that the operator of a public Web site is a 'publisher' for purposes of this language. ... Moreover, even if [the bloggers'] status as 'publishers' is debatable, [the bloggers] have flatly declared that they are also editors and reporters, and Apple offers no basis to question that characterization."[3]

2. Was the Information Obtained While Gathering Information "For Communication to the Public"?

The person asserting the shield law must show that the information in question was obtained in the process of "gathering, preparing or processing of information for communication to the public."[4] The mere fact that a person is a journalist does not automatically mean he or she can invoke the shield law. For example, a reporter who happens to witness a traffic accident while driving to the grocery store on the weekend cannot invoke the protections of the shield law to avoid testifying about the accident simply by virtue of his or her employment as a reporter. On the other hand, if the reporter were to stop at the scene and take photographs or prepare a story for the newspaper, his actions would fall within the protection of the shield law.[5]

The shield law does not necessarily extend to paid advertisements or "advertorials" – advertisements formatted in the same style as a news article or editorial. In a 1999 case, a weekly newspaper received a subpoena demanding unpublished documents relating to a series of published paid advertorials. Although the court of appeal left open the possibility that the shield law could apply to a variety of editorial functions and might even extend to paid advertorials under certain circumstances, it found that the circumstances of that particular case did not warrant application of the shield law. The court explained that "[a]t a minimum the phrase 'information for communication to the public' requires that the person or entity invoking the shield law be engaged in legitimate journalistic purposes, or have exercised judgmental discretion in such activities. ... [T]here remains a fundamental distinction between the reporting and editorial functions of a newspaper and the buying, selling and placing of commercial advertisements." Although the court hastened to add that the shield law is not limited to "news" or "newsgathering" activities, it found that the newspaper had not made a sufficient showing that its employees obtained the advertorials for the purpose of communicating information to the public, as there was nothing to establish that it was the newspaper's intent to publish the advertorials as part of the editorial process or to transmit news or commentary on matters of public interest.[6]

3. Is the Information Unpublished or Confidential?

Before 1990, the California courts were split over whether the shield law's definition of "unpublished information" applied only to confidential information, or whether it also extended to information gathered without any expectation of privacy – for example, eyewitness observations, unaided video outtakes or unpublished photographs. Some courts had determined that only confidential information was protected. The dispute was laid to rest in 1990 with the California

---

[3]   *O'Grady v. Superior Court*, 139 Cal. App. 4th 1423, 1459-60 (2006).

[4]   Cal. Const., article I, section 2(b); Evidence Code section 1070(a).

[5]   *See Delaney v. Superior Court*, 50 Cal. 3d 785, 798 n.8 (1990).

[6]   *Rancho Publications v. Superior Court*, 68 Cal. App. 4th 1538, 1544-47 (1999).

Supreme Court's decision in *Delaney v. Superior Court*.[7] The court said that the shield law protects two classes of information: 1) unpublished information, whether confidential or not; and 2) confidential sources. The court interpreted "unpublished information" to include all "factual information" obtained in the course of newsgathering "that is within the newsperson's knowledge, whether contained in source material or in memory."[8]

The facts of the *Delaney* case help to illustrate what type of information constitutes "unpublished" information. A newspaper reporter and photographer were accompanying members of the Long Beach Police Department when they saw the defendant sitting on a bench in a shopping mall. The officers stopped to talk to the man when they noticed a plastic bag protruding from his pocket. Their suspicions aroused, the officers asked the man for identification. When the man reached for his jacket, the officers reportedly asked if they could check the garment for weapons. The officer found brass knuckles, possession of which is a misdemeanor under California law. The newspaper published an account of the incident but did not include in the story whether the defendant had consented to the search of his jacket, as the police contended. At a suppression hearing, the defendant subpoenaed the reporter and photographer to help prove he had not consented to the search.

The reporter and photographer refused to testify about their observations and asserted that the shield law prevented the court from finding them in contempt for refusing to testify about their unpublished observations. The trial court held that the shield law did not apply to "eyewitness observations" by members of the media. The California Supreme Court disagreed, finding that the shield law's definition of "unpublished information" includes a journalist's unpublished, nonconfidential eyewitness observations of an event or incident.[9]

One source of common confusion among civil and criminal litigants is the extent to which questions about a published article or report seek unpublished information. While a reporter might, in certain cases, be required to verify direct quotations published in an article, the same is not true for paraphrases because they do not "publish" exactly what was said. Rather, paraphrases represent a compilation of various statements made by an interviewee, the reporter's interpretation of the interviewee's statements and inferences the reporter draws from them. To verify a paraphrase, a reporter must reveal unpublished quotations, the circumstances of the interview and the reporter's mental observations, all of which are protected by the shield law. In light of this, some trial courts have recognized a distinction between quotes and paraphrases for the purposes of the reporter's shield law.[10] But the court of appeal has not addressed this issue yet, which means that some trial courts may not recognize the distinction between quotations and paraphrases. With respect to a statement in quotation marks, one court of appeal has said a reporter need only verify the quotation where it can be determined from the article itself that the quoted source made the statement directly to the reporter. In that case, the court said that it could not determine from the article itself that the reporter had interviewed the supposed source of a quoted statement, and therefore it held that the state shield law was properly invoked.[11]

---

[7]   *Delaney v. Superior Court,* 50 Cal. 3d 785 (1990).

[8]   *Delaney v. Superior Court,* 50 Cal. 3d 785, 798-800 (1990). *See also Playboy Enterprises v. Superior Court,* 154 Cal. App. 3d 14 (1984).

[9]   *Delaney v. Superior Court,* 50 Cal. 3d 785, 805 (1990).

[10]   *See Cooke v. Connolly*, 21 Media L. Rptr. 1575, 1576 (Cal. Super. Ct. 1993).

[11]   *In re Howard*, 136 Cal. App. 2d 816, 819 (1955); *accord People v. Swanson*, 30 Media L. Rptr. 2396, 2401 (Cal. Super. Ct. 2000) (citing and following *Howard*).

B. THE EXTENT OF THE SHIELD LAW'S PROTECTIONS.

The protection provided by the shield law depends on whether a journalist is being asked to provide evidence in a civil or criminal case. In criminal cases, protection also depends on whether the prosecution or defendant is requesting the information.

1. Civil Cases: Absolute Immunity.

In *New York Times Co. v. Superior Court*, the California Supreme Court held that the state's shield law provides an absolute immunity from contempt for a journalist who refuses to comply with a subpoena for unpublished or confidential information in a civil case. In that case, a husband and wife were injured in an accident in Santa Barbara while driving their Volkswagen. After the couple sued Volkswagen for personal injuries, the automaker subpoenaed the newspaper to deliver possession of all photographs and negatives related to the accident, including photographs that were never published. The newspaper refused. The Supreme Court concluded that the newspaper reporter could not be held in contempt for refusing to turn over the requested photographs because the immunity from contempt in a civil case is absolute. Unlike a criminal defendant who can, on some occasions, overcome the protection of the shield law (see discussion below), in civil cases the shield law "cannot be overcome by showing a need for unpublished information."[12]

2. Criminal Cases: Qualified Immunity.

In criminal cases, the type of immunity offered by the shield law depends upon which party is seeking the information. The shield law offers absolute immunity where the information is sought by the prosecution (subject to the court of appeal's decision in *Fost v. Superior Court,* discussed below). However, where the information is sought by a criminal defendant, the immunity is only qualified. Because a criminal defendant's right to a fair trial is guaranteed by the United States Constitution (which takes precedence over state law), a defendant may be able to overcome the shield law and compel a reporter to provide unpublished information or documents. In order to do so, the defendant must show that his or her interest in obtaining the testimony outweighs the interests protected by the shield law.

A criminal defendant seeking to overcome the reporter's shield law must satisfy the test established by the California Supreme Court in the *Delaney* case. As an initial matter, the defendant must show "a reasonable probability the information will materially assist his defense."[13] Once the defendant makes this showing, a court must determine, on the basis of a four-part balancing test, whether the defendant's need for the information at issue outweighs the interests underlying the shield law. The factors to be considered are as follows:

- **The nature of the unpublished material:** There is a greater interest in protecting confidential or sensitive information, since its publication has a greater chance of restricting a newsperson's future access to the news by dissuading sources from cooperating with the press.
- **The interests sought to be protected by the shield law:** The court will consider whether the policies behind the shield law discussed above will, in fact, be thwarted by disclosure. For example, there may be circumstances that may, as a practical

---

[12]   *New York Times Co. v. Superior Court*, 51 Cal. 3d 453 (1990).
[13]   *Delaney v. Superior Court,* 50 Cal. 3d 785, 808 (1990).

matter, mitigate or eliminate the adverse consequences of disclosure. Alternatively, there may be circumstances that would make disclosure particularly damaging to a journalist's ability to perform his or her job.

- **The importance of the information to the criminal defendant:** Stated simply, the more important the evidence is to the defendant's case, the more likely the court will require its disclosure.
- **Whether there is an alternative source for the information:** A court will be less likely to force a reporter to disclose the information when the defendant has an alternative means of discovering the same evidence.[14]

Although a criminal defendant may in certain circumstances pierce the shield law by virtue of his or her federal constitutional right to a fair trial, the California Supreme Court left open in *Delaney* the question of whether the prosecution in a criminal proceeding can have a constitutional interest sufficient to overcome the shield law. In 1999, the court answered that question with its decision in *Miller v. Superior Court*, concluding that the prosecution did not enjoy any such conflicting right and that in the case of a prosecutor's subpoena, the immunity offered by the shield law is absolute.[15]

Unfortunately, the prosecution may still be able to obtain unpublished information through a complicated, back door route. In *Fost v. Superior Court*, a California court of appeal held that where a reporter subpoenaed by a criminal defendant to testify as to published information is asked by the prosecution to testify about unpublished information on cross-examination but refuses to do so under the shield law, the remedy is to strike the reporter's testimony altogether – **unless** the defendant can show that his need for the published information he seeks on direct examination satisfies the *Delaney* test. If the defendant is able to do so, the reporter cannot refuse to respond to cross-examination by the prosecution, even as to unpublished information, without being held in contempt. In reaching this conclusion, the court appears to have accepted the prosecution's argument that its right to conduct cross-examination derived from the defendant's Sixth Amendment right to a fair trial, which seems inconsistent with the California Supreme Court's decision in *Miller*.[16]

But what about the opposite situation: when the prosecution seeks testimony as to only published information, but the defendant wants to conduct a cross-examination that would elicit unpublished information protected by the reporter's shield law? Unless the defendant can show that the unpublished information he seeks in cross-examination satisfies *Delaney*, the proper remedy would seem to be to strike the reporter's testimony about published information on direct examination – or, preferably, to allow the journalist to avoid having to give any testimony in the first place. But a court of appeal has concluded that although the defendant failed to satisfy the *Delaney* test and was not allowed to cross-examine the reporter as to unpublished information, the trial court acted properly in allowing the journalist to testify as to published information in response to the prosecution's questions on direct examination.[17]

Until the California Supreme Court provides further direction, these decisions may make it difficult for journalists to avoid prosecution subpoenas in criminal cases.

---

[14]   *Delaney v. Superior Court,* 50 Cal. 3d 785, 807-13 (1990).
[15]   *Miller v. Superior Court,* 21 Cal. 4th 883, 887, 896-902 (1999).
[16]   *Fost v. Superior Court,* 80 Cal. App. 4th 724 (2000).
[17]   *People v. Vasco,* 131 Cal. App. 4th 137, 158-60 (2005).

3. Immunity from Contempt, Not Privilege.

The reporter's shield law does not provide a privilege for the media. Instead, article I, section 2 of the California Constitution and section 1070 of the California Evidence Code are worded as an immunity from contempt of court for refusing to disclose confidential sources or unpublished information. There is a significant difference between a privilege and an immunity. When someone has a "privilege" to take certain action, they are protected from ***any*** kind of punishment by the privilege. The shield law, however, offers only an "immunity" from a particular type of punishment, namely, contempt. This means that reporters who properly invoke the shield law to protect themselves from a contempt charge still may face other sanctions.

In the *New York Times* case, the California Supreme Court addressed the issue of whether the shield law allows a trial court to impose sanctions other than contempt, including monetary sanctions, for failure to comply with a subpoena. The court concluded in the affirmative, saying that monetary sanctions are allowed because "the unambiguous language of the shield law refers only to an immunity from contempt."[18] However, in most cases, contempt is the only truly meaningful sanction. Code of Civil Procedure section 1992 provides that a witness who disobeys a subpoena must pay the "aggrieved party" the sum of $500 together with monetary damages, if any, attributable to the witnesses' refusal to testify. Since the aggrieved party must file a separate civil lawsuit to obtain such damages – which is unlikely to happen – there is little monetary exposure where the court finds that a reporter has properly invoked the shield law.

A Note on an Alternative to the Shield Law in State Court Cases: In cases in which a reporter is a party to the case – for example, if a journalist or news organization has been sued for libel or invasion of privacy – the availability of sanctions other than contempt renders the shield law largely inapplicable. For example, if the reporter refuses to disclose a confidential source, the court may not hold the reporter in contempt, but it ***may*** instruct the jury that the source did not exist. Such an instruction can be tantamount to holding the reporter or news organization liable for damages. However, in this case – and in other cases in which the shield law does not apply – the information may be protected by the reporter's privilege (discussed in Part III). The California Supreme Court has recognized the reporter's privilege and has applied it to preclude the disclosure of confidential sources and information provided by confidential sources in a case in which a small newspaper was sued for libel.[19]

C. PROCEDURAL ASPECTS OF SUBPOENAS.

The shield law protects a reporter from a contempt charge for refusing to testify only to the extent the reporter is asked to testify about unpublished information or produce documents that would reveal such information. This means that a journalist who is subpoenaed to testify in a deposition or other court proceeding, or is ordered to produce documents, cannot simply ignore the subpoena. Unless the subpoena is withdrawn, the journalist must obey a subpoena that commands his or her appearance in court or at a deposition, and the journalist generally has no protection against a contempt charge if he or she is asked to testify only about matters already published. For example, a reporter cannot refuse to verify that he or she wrote a particular published article. Similarly, if any portion of a subpoena demanding the production of documents requests published information (for example, published articles or photographs) the journalist must produce those documents as directed in the subpoena. As to any unpublished documents (for

---

[18]   *New York Times Co. v. Superior Court*, 51 Cal. 3d 453, 463 (1990).
[19]   *See Mitchell v. Superior Court*, 37 Cal. 3d 268 (1984).

example, notes or unpublished video outtakes), the journalist must take appropriate procedures to object, which vary depending on whether the reporter has been subpoenaed in a civil or criminal case.[20]

However, Code of Civil Procedure section 1986.1, enacted in 2000, and the California Supreme Court's decision in the *New York Times* case provide several important procedural protections for a journalist who is subpoenaed to testify or produce documents.

1. No Waiver.

Section 1986.1 makes it clear that a journalist does not waive his or her ability to assert the protections of the shield law by giving testimony or other evidence pursuant to a subpoena in a civil or criminal case. In other words, a journalist who provides testimony as part of a deposition may nevertheless refuse to testify about unpublished information at the trial of the case. Similarly, a reporter may agree to testify about certain unpublished information but refuse to testify about other unpublished information.[21]

If a journalist has revealed the information at issue not pursuant to a prior subpoena but by disclosing it in conversations with one of the parties or another news source, the party seeking the information may argue that the journalist "waived" his or her protection under the shield law. In an unpublished opinion, the California Court of Appeal rejected such an argument.[22] In that case, a journalist working on an article disclosed to a terminated employee what her ex-employer had said in a prior conversation with the journalist. The terminated employee sued her former employer, based on the statements made to the journalist. Even though the correspondent had initially signed a written statement attesting to what the employer had said, the court of appeal held that the journalist did not waive the shield law. It found that the shield law can only be waived by publishing the information through a medium of communication to the public.

2. Five Days Notice.

Section 1986.1 states that absent "exigent circumstances," a journalist who is subpoenaed in any civil or criminal proceeding "shall be given at least five days' notice by the party issuing the subpoena that his or her appearance will be required," thus allowing a journalist a minimal period of time to challenge subpoenas seeking unpublished information protected by the shield law.[23]

3. Judicial Findings Supporting Judgment of Contempt.

Section 1986.1 provides that if a trial judge holds a journalist who has invoked the shield law in contempt, the court must set forth findings on the record stating "at a minimum, why the information will be of material assistance to the party seeking the evidence, and why alternate sources of the information are not sufficient to satisfy the defendant's right to a fair trial."[24]

---

[20] In a civil case, a journalist may simply serve the subpoenaing party with written objections based on the shield law. *See Monarch Healthcare v. Superior Court*, 78 Cal. App. 4th 1282, 1287-90 (2000). However, in a criminal case, a journalist must seek relief directly from the court.

[21] Code of Civil Procedure section 1986.1(a).

[22] *Littlefield v. Superior Court*, Appeal No. A049935 (Cal. Court of Appeal 1991).

[23] Code of Civil Procedure section 1986.1(b).

[24] Code of Civil Procedure section 1986.1(c).

4. Appeal and Stay.

In the *New York Times* case, the California Supreme Court made two important rulings concerning appeals of trial court orders requiring journalists to testify or provide documents despite their invocation of the California shield law. First, the journalist cannot ask the court of appeal to overturn the trial court's order until the journalist has refused to testify or provide documents and has been held in contempt.[25] Second, the court attempted to ameliorate the potential harshness of that rule by also holding that, "[t]o avoid confinement under a judgment of contempt that may subsequently be set aside, a trial court should stay its judgment of contempt to allow the ... newsperson sufficient time" to ask the court of appeal to overturn the contempt citation – at least "if the trial court believes there is any colorable argument the newsperson can make."[26] If the trial court nevertheless declines to stay its contempt order, the court of appeal "should do so" pending its decision.[27]

PART III:
PROTECTION UNDER FEDERAL LAW –
THE REPORTER'S PRIVILEGE

As noted in the introduction to this chapter, the California shield law may not apply in federal cases in the federal courts. There is no federal statute that provides protection comparable to California's shield law. The First Amendment provides some protection to journalists from whom information or materials gathered in the newsgathering process are sought. However, several recent cases have demonstrated the serious limitations of this protection, as journalists were ordered to jail for refusing to identify sources or turn over unpublished materials. In the wake of these incarcerations, federal lawmakers have renewed efforts to create a federal shield law, but that effort had not borne fruit as this book went to press.

A. THE LIMITED FIRST AMENDMENT PRIVILEGE.

In the seminal case *Branzburg v. Hayes*, the U.S. Supreme Court declined to recognize a broad testimonial privilege for journalists, leaving it to Congress to create a shield law for reporters if one is necessary.[28] Although the court observed that newsgathering does qualify for First Amendment protection – because "without some protection for seeking out the news, freedom of the press could be eviscerated" – it held that the First Amendment did not shield a reporter from testifying about illegal activity before a grand jury.[29] The decision left room, however, for a limited First Amendment-based privilege, at least in other situations.[30]

In a 1975 case, the federal Court of Appeals for the Ninth Circuit, which covers California and the western United States, interpreted *Branzburg* as recognizing "some First Amendment protection of news sources" and requiring "the claimed First Amendment privilege and the opposing need for disclosure be judicially weighed in light of the surrounding facts and a balance

---

[25]   *New York Times Co. v. Superior Court*, 51 Cal. 3d 453, 460 (1990).
[26]   *New York Times Co. v. Superior Court*, 51 Cal. 3d 453, 460 (1990).
[27]   *New York Times Co. v. Superior Court*, 51 Cal. 3d 453, 460 (1990).
[28]   *Branzburg v. Hayes*, 408 U.S. 665 (1972).
[29]   *Branzburg v. Hayes*, 408 U.S. 665, 681 (1972).
[30]   *Branzburg v. Hayes*, 408 U.S. 665, 710 (1972) (Powell, J., concurring).

struck to determine where lies the paramount interest."[31]   Since then, the federal courts in California and elsewhere have recognized a qualified First Amendment privilege for reporters to withhold the names of confidential sources and unpublished information in civil and some criminal cases, but not in response to a grand jury subpoena.

1. Grand Jury Subpoenas.

The ramifications of the *Branzburg* case drew national attention in 2005 when *New York Times* reporter Judith Miller was jailed for contempt after refusing to provide the name of a confidential government source in response to a grand jury subpoena. Affirming the trial court's order holding Miller in contempt, the Court of Appeals for the District of Columbia Circuit said there was "no material factual distinction" between Miller's appeal and the *Branzburg* case and that its decision was therefore compelled by precedent.[32]   Miller eventually identified the source, explaining that she had by then received permission from him to do so.

In 2006, a federal trial court in California refused to quash a grand jury subpoena to two San Francisco Chronicle reporters, Lance Williams and Mark Fainaru-Wada, who used leaked grand jury transcripts in reporting on use of steroids by prominent athletes. Finding that the reporters had failed to distinguish their case from *Branzburg*, the court held that the First Amendment did not provide a basis for refusing to appear before a grand jury to answer questions and produce documents related to the leaked transcripts.[33]   The court also thought *Branzburg* prevented it from recognizing a federal common law reporter's privilege, but that, even if it did apply the test articulated by federal courts for the reporter's privilege in other contexts, it would still refuse to quash the subpoenas because the government had exhausted all reasonable alternatives, the evidence would be noncumulative, and it would be relevant to an important issue in the investigation (*i.e.*, who leaked the transcripts in violation of law and a court order).[34]   The reporters were sentenced to imprisonment until they agreed to testify or the grand jury term expired (the confinement not to exceed 18 months).[35]   They remained free, pending the outcome of their appeal. Shortly before their appeal hearing in March 2007, the Justice Department voluntarily withdrew the subpoenas because the FBI, by means independent of the reporters, had identified their source for the grand jury transcripts (a lawyer for one of the people indicted by the grand jury). The appeal was dismissed as moot.

Josh Wolf, a freelance videographer and blogger in California, was sent to federal prison for refusing to comply with a grand jury subpoena. Wolf had videotaped a street protest in San Francisco that turned violent. He sold some of his footage to a local television station (which broadcast it) and he posted the same footage on his website. Wolf was jailed for refusing to turn over to the federal grand jury unaired outtakes from his taping (although, through his lawyers, he subsequently altered this position, offering to release the outtakes but declining to testify about their contents). After initially ordering Wolf released on bail pending the outcome of his appeal, the federal court of appeals affirmed the contempt citation and ordered him back to jail.[36]   As of

---

[31]   *Farr v. Pitchess*, 522 F.2d 464, 467-68 (9th Cir. 1975).

[32]   *In re Grand Jury Subpoena, Judith Miller*, 370 U.S. App. D.C. 4 (D.C. Cir. 2005).

[33]   *In re Grand Jury Subpoenas to Mark Fainaru-Wada and Lance Williams*, 438 F. Supp. 2d 1111, 1118 (N.D. Cal. 2006).

[34]   *In re Grand Jury Subpoenas to Mark Fainaru-Wada and Lance Williams*, 438 F. Supp. 2d 1111, 1119-1120 (N.D. Cal. 2006).

[35]   *In re Grand Jury Subpoenas to Mark Fainaru-Wada and Lance Williams*, 2006 U.S. Dist. LEXIS 73134 * 9-10 (N.D. Cal. 2006).

[36]   *In re Grand Jury Subpoena, Joshua Wolf*, 2006 U.S. App. LEXIS 23315 (9th Cir. 2006).

this writing he had been in jail for approximately eight months before being released after agreeing to provide the outtakes to the grand jury, after posting them on his website.

In another nationally publicized attempt to identify reporters' confidential sources, federal prosecutors in a grand jury investigation sought telephone records of two *New York Times* reporters to determine who informed them of government plans to seize assets of certain Islamic charities that were suspected of funding terrorists. After receiving information about the plans but before any government action was taken, the reporters contacted the charities for comment – effectively tipping them off to the imminence of government enforcement action. Federal prosecutors claimed that the reporters' conduct endangered federal agents and undermined the government's actions against the charities.

The reporters sought a court order prohibiting telephone companies from releasing their records to federal prosecutors. The district court found that the federal courts covering New York had recognized a qualified reporter's privilege under both the First Amendment and federal common law, and that the government had failed to make the necessary showing to defeat the privilege in this case.[37] Specifically, the district court found that the government failed to make "'a clear and specific showing that the sought information is" [1] highly material and relevant, [2] necessary or critical to the maintenance of the claim, and [3] not obtainable from other available sources.'"[38] The appellate court reversed, holding that the Supreme Court's *Branzburg* decision precluded First Amendment protection under the circumstances.[39] The court further held that even if a reporter's privilege were applicable under either the First Amendment or federal common law, the privilege had been overcome because the government had a compelling interest in maintaining the secrecy of imminent asset freezes and searches, the reporters were the only source of the information sought, and any overbreadth in the phone records could be cured by the reporters' cooperation in redacting the records.[40] The Supreme Court refused to relieve the reporters of the requirement to comply with the order while they sought to have the Supreme Court review the decision.[41]

As these cases illustrate, federal courts in California and elsewhere appear unwilling to allow reporters to assert a First Amendment privilege in response to a grand jury subpoena requesting confidential sources or unpublished information. This leaves journalists and their sources in a bind. Although California's shield law provides at least some protection in state court, sources have no way of knowing, in advance, whether a potential subpoena demanding the source's identity will issue from a federal or state investigation.

2. Criminal Cases.

Outside the grand jury context, federal courts have been more willing to recognize a First Amendment reporter's privilege. Generally speaking, the qualified First Amendment privilege allows a journalist to withhold the identities of confidential sources or other unpublished information unless the party seeking disclosure meets several requirements.

In the 1974 case *Farr v. Pitchess*, the Ninth Circuit Court of Appeals observed that it was "clear that *Branzburg* recognizes some First Amendment protection of news sources" and that "[t]he application of the *Branzburg* holding to non-grand jury cases seems to require that the

---

[37] *New York Times Co. v. Gonzales*, 382 F. Supp. 2d 457 (S.D.N.Y. 2005), *rev'd*, 459 F.3d 160 (2d Cir. 2006).

[38] *New York Times Co. v. Gonzales*, 382 F. Supp. 2d 457, 510 (S.D.N.Y. 2005), *rev'd*, 459 F.3d 160 (2d Cir. 2006) (quoting *United States v. Burke,* 700 F.2d 70, 77 (2d Cir. 1983)).

[39] *New York Times Co. v. Gonzales*, 459 F.3d 160, 173-74 (2d Cir. 2006).

[40] *New York Times Co. v. Gonzales*, 459 F.3d 160, 169-174 (2d Cir. 2006).

[41] *New York Times Co. v. Gonzales*, 549 U.S. --, 127 S. Ct. 721 (Nov. 27, 2006) (denying application for stay of mandate pending filing of petition for writ of certiorari).

claimed First Amendment privilege and the opposing need for disclosure be judicially weighed in light of the surrounding facts and a balance struck to determine where lies the paramount interest."[42] However, as discussed in more detail below, *Farr* ultimately held that the court's interest in enforcing its gag order outweighed a journalist's interest in protecting the identity of confidential sources who had violated the gag order.

Almost 20 years later, the Ninth Circuit reiterated its holding in *Farr* that "the journalist's privilege recognized in *Branzburg* was a 'partial First Amendment shield' that protects journalists against compelled disclosure in all judicial proceedings, civil and criminal alike" and that the privilege must be balanced against other considerations to determine the "paramount interest" in the particular situation.[43]

In an unpublished 2003 decision, a federal trial court in California considered whether to quash a subpoena issued by the government to a television network for materials gathered during its undercover investigation of the defendant's offshore banking schemes. Although acknowledging in a footnote the Ninth Circuit's determination in *Farr* that applying *Branzburg* to non-grand jury cases required judicial balancing of the interests at stake, the court nevertheless characterized the qualified privilege in the criminal setting as "exceptionally thin" and held that "the reporter must demonstrate that the criminal investigation is proceeding in bad faith, or that the government has otherwise exhibited 'harassment of newsmen.'"[44]

Despite finding that the qualified reporter's privilege did not apply in the case, the court quashed the subpoena on the grounds that it was "oppressive and unreasonable" under Rule 17(c) of the Federal Rules of Criminal Procedure, which governs the issuance of subpoenas for documents and objects.[45] Applying a test articulated by the U.S. Supreme Court for Rule 17(c) subpoenas, the court found that the government had failed to show:

> (1) [T]hat the [materials] are evidentiary and relevant; (2) that they are not otherwise procurable reasonably in advance of trial by exercise of due diligence; (3) that the party cannot properly prepare for trial without such production ...; and (4) that the application is made in good faith and is not intended as a general "fishing expedition."[46]

Outside the Ninth Circuit, courts that have considered the qualified reporter's privilege in non-grand jury criminal proceedings have tended to require a balancing of the need for the information or material against the interests underlying the reporter's privilege, considering factors such as the exhaustion of alternative sources and importance of evidence to the underlying case.[47]

---

[42]   *Farr v. Pitchess*, 522 F.2d 464, 467-68 (9th Cir. 1975).

[43]   *Shoen v. Shoen*, 5 F.3d 1289, 1292-93 (9th Cir. 1993) ("*Shoen I*") (the proceeding at issue in *Shoen* was civil, however, and the particular test articulated in that case was explicitly limited to civil litigation).

[44]   *United States v. Schneider*, 2003 U.S. Dist. LEXIS 27324 at ¶. *6 & n.1, *10 (N.D. Cal. 2003).

[45]   *United States v. Schneider*, 2003 U.S. Dist. LEXIS 27324 at ¶. *16-21 (N.D. Cal. 2003).

[46]   *United States v. Schneider*, 2003 U.S. Dist. LEXIS 27324 at ¶. *16-17 (N.D. Cal. 2003) (*quoting United States v. Nixon*, 418 U.S. 683, 699-700 (1974)).

[47]   *See, e.g., United States v. LaRouche Campaign*, 841 F.2d 1176, 1180-1182 (1st Cir. 1988) (First Amendment interests of reporter must be weighed against criminal defendant's interests in production of subpoenaed materials); *United States v. Burke,* 700 F.2d 70, 76-77 (2d Cir. 1983) ("We see no legally principled reason for drawing a distinction between civil and criminal cases when considering whether the reporter's interest in confidentiality should yield to the moving party's need for probative evidence."); *In re: Coordinated Pretrial Proceedings in Petroleum Products Antitrust Litigation*, 680 F.2d 5, 8 (2d Cir. 1982) ("The law in this Circuit is clear that to protect the important interests of reporters and the public in preserving the confidentiality of journalists' sources, disclosure may be ordered only upon a clear and specific showing that the information is: highly material and relevant, necessary or critical to the maintenance of the claim, and not

3. Civil Litigation.

In overturning a contempt judgment against an investigative journalist who refused to turn over materials gathered while researching a book, the Ninth Circuit held that the reporter's privilege applies regardless of whether the journalist promised confidentiality to his sources.[48] The court subsequently adopted a three-part test to be applied in the context of civil litigation where non-confidential information is sought from a nonparty journalist: The material must be shown to be (1) unavailable despite exhaustion of all reasonable alternative sources; (2) noncumulative; and (3) clearly relevant to an important issue in the case.[49]

Applying this test, a federal trial court refused to quash a subpoena issued to a television network for a complete interview tape of a defendant in a defamation action. The defendant sought the tape in order to establish that her statements were not defamatory in the context of the overall interview (and were distorted in the three-minute excerpted version that aired publicly). Because the evidence to be supplied by the interview footage was relevant to her defenses, not cumulative of other evidence, and not available from any other source, the qualified federal reporter's privilege did not shield the network from having to produce the tape.[50]

In a case involving disclosure of a confidential source, a federal trial court refused to order a tabloid newspaper to provide the name of a justice department source in Carolyn Condit's libel suit against the paper, finding that Condit had failed to exhaust alternative sources for the information she sought.[51]

Another federal trial court refused to order a non-party journalist to submit to deposition and produce documents in an action against the FBI and DOJ based on alleged privacy violations. Although the plaintiff established the exhaustion of alternative sources and the non-cumulative nature of the evidence sought, his motion to compel the journalist's testimony failed because the information that had been disclosed to the journalist was already in the public domain, and therefore his testimony would not be relevant to the plaintiff's privacy claims.[52]

In 2005, the federal court of appeals in Washington, D.C., addressed a civil lawsuit brought against scientist Wen Ho Lee, who had been employed at Los Alamos nuclear laboratory until he was accused of mishandling classified information. Lee claimed that prior to and during his criminal prosecution, the government had leaked information to the press about him and his family members, in violation of federal law. After taking the depositions of 20 government officials, Lee sought to force several reporters to identify their sources and the information they had been

---

obtainable from other available sources."); *United States v. Cuthbertson*, 630 F.2d 139, 147-48 (3d Cir. 1980) ("[J]ournalists possess a qualified privilege not to divulge confidential sources and not to disclose unpublished information in their possession in criminal cases" and the court "must balance the defendant's need for the material against the interests underlying the privilege."); *United States v. Criden*, 633 F.2d 346, 357 (3d Cir. 1980) ("The asserted claim to privilege should be judged on its facts by striking a proper balance between freedom of the press and the obligation of all citizens to give relevant testimony with respect to criminal conduct. The balance of these vital constitutional and societal interests on a case-by-case basis accords with the tried and traditional way of adjudicating such questions."); *United States v. Lloyd*, 71 F.3d 1256, 1268-69 (7th Cir. 1995) (quashing subpoena for reporter's testimony not abuse of discretion where substance of proposed testimony was of speculative value at best and offered only to impeach witnesses as to collateral matters); *United States v. Caporale*, 806 F.2d 1487, 1504 (11th Cir. 1986) ("[I]nformation may only be compelled from a reporter claiming privilege if the party requesting the information can show that it is highly relevant, necessary to the proper presentation of the case, and unavailable from other sources.").

[48] *Shoen I*, 5 F.3d at 1294-95.
[49] *Shoen v. Shoen*, 48 F.3d 412, 416 (9th Cir. 1995) ("*Shoen II*").
[50] *Crowe v. County of San Diego*, 242 F. Supp. 2d 740, 750-752 (S.D. Cal. 2003).
[51] *Condit v. National Enquirer, Inc.*, 289 F.Supp. 2d 1175 (E.D. Cal. 2003).
[52] *Wright v. Federal Bureau of Investigation*, 381 F. Supp. 2d 1114, 1116-1118 (C.D. Cal. 2005).

provided. The court of appeals affirmed an order compelling the reporters to testify, and holding them in contempt for refusing to do so. The court recognized a First Amendment privilege applicable at least in civil cases.[53] However, the court stressed that the protection provided by the First Amendment is qualified, and it can be overcome if two requirements are met: (1) The information sought goes to "the heart of the matter"; and (2) the party seeking the information has exhausted "every reasonable alternative source of information."[54] The court found that Lee had met both requirements. The Supreme Court refused to hear the case.[55] In June 2006, the federal government agreed to pay almost $900,000, and five media organizations agreed to pay an additional $700,000, to settle Lee's claims. As a result, the reporters were not required to testify.[56]

A Note on Using the California Shield Law in Federal Cases: The application of state law "privileges" (such as the California shield law) in federal civil and criminal cases is complicated and uncertain. The Ninth Circuit federal court of appeals, whose decisions guide the federal courts in California, has not decided whether the California shield law protects journalists in federal cases. However, while you cannot rely on the protection of the state shield law, keep the shield law in mind and be prepared to argue that it *does* apply, even in a federal case. Federal district court decisions suggest that it may, particularly in civil cases that are in federal court only because the parties are from different states or countries (known as "diversity" cases).[57]

4. Personal Observations of Journalists.

In 1990, a federal trial court refused to quash a subpoena issued to a television news cameraman who witnessed and attempted to film the alleged beating of the plaintiff by police officers at the scene of a fire in the plaintiff's building. The plaintiff sought testimony from the cameraman regarding his personal observations of the incident, including the alleged attempts of firemen at the scene to prevent him from filming. The court rejected the idea that an individual's personal observations could be privileged simply because the individual is a journalist.[58] Moreover, the court said that even if it did recognize a privilege for personal observations of journalists, the balancing required by *Branzburg* and *Farr* would tip in favor of enforcing the subpoena because the testimony would go to the heart of the plaintiff's case (and was not cumulative) and because the rights to be enforced rose to the constitutional level.[59]

---

[53]   *Lee v. Department of Justice*, 413 F.3d 53, 57-59 (D.C. Cir. 2005).
[54]   *Lee v. Department of Justice*, 413 F.3d 53, 59-60 (D.C. Cir. 2005).
[55]   *Drogin v. Wen Ho Lee*, 126 S.Ct. 2351, 165 L.Ed.2d (2006); *Thomas v. Wen Ho Lee*, 126 S.Ct 2373, 165 L.Ed.2d 294 (2006).
[56]   *U.S., Media Settle With Wen Ho Lee: News Organizations Pay To Keep Sources Secret,* Paul Farhi, Washington Post, Saturday, June 3, 2006.
[57]   *See, e.g., Rogers v. Home Shopping Network*, 73 F.Supp.2d 1140, 1142 (C.D. Cal. 1999) (in a diversity case for libel, where discovery of confidential sources was sought from a media defendant, California law held to govern application of privileges, so court applied the test established in *Mitchell v. Superior Court*, and discovery was denied); *Los Angeles Memorial Coliseum Comm. v. National Football League*, 89 F.R.D. 489 (C.D. Cal. 1981) (in a case asserting both federal antitrust claims and state law claims, court considered both federal common law and California shield law and quashed subpoenas to non-party reporters); *Hatfill v. New York Times Co.*, 459 F.Supp.2d 462 (E.D. Va. 2006) (in diversity case for libel, where discovery was sought from media defendant, court applied Virginia state law reporter's privilege but found that qualified privilege was overcome). *But see Lee v. Department of Justice*, 287 F.Supp.2d 15, 17 (D.D.C. 2003), *aff'd* 413 F.2d 53 (D.C. Cir. 2006) (in case asserting claims under federal privacy laws, court held that evidentiary privileges are governed exclusively by federal law and refused to apply local statutory reporter's privilege).
[58]   *Dillon v. City and County of San Francisco*, 748 F. Supp. 722, 726 (N.D. Cal. 1990).
[59]   *Dillon v. City and County of San Francisco*, 748 F. Supp. 722, 727 (N.D. Cal. 1990).

B. WHO CAN INVOKE THE REPORTER'S PRIVILEGE?

In some cases, a court must decide whether an individual is a journalist or its equivalent before applying the test for the federal reporter's privilege.

The Ninth Circuit rejected the argument that a writer engaged in investigative reporting for a book was not entitled to invoke the reporter's privilege because he was not a member of the institutionalized print or broadcast media.[60] The court held that "the critical question for deciding whether a person may invoke the journalist's privilege is whether she is gathering news for dissemination to the public."[61]

The case of blogger and videographer Josh Wolf, discussed earlier, has triggered debate on the question: Who is a journalist for purposes of constitutional or statutory privileges protecting journalists? In the Wolf case itself, the U.S. Justice Department assumed Wolf was a journalist (which triggered an internal agency guideline, said to be complied with in Wolf's case, requiring attorney general approval for serving subpoenas on the press), and the courts shared that assumption.

Also, as noted above, the California Court of Appeal has recognized that bloggers are protected by California's shield law. The shield law applies to any "publisher, editor, reporter, or other person connected with or employed upon a newspaper, magazine, or other periodical publication."[62] The court held that the operator of a news-oriented website that was regularly updated was covered by the state shield law.

C. ENFORCING GAG ORDERS IN FEDERAL COURT.

When information or material is leaked to the media in violation of a protective ("gag") order, the court that issued the order generally has more latitude to compel testimony from journalists to discover the source of the leak than in other situations.

In holding that a reporter who published information from a leaked document was not protected by the First Amendment from incarceration or other punishments for contempt, the Ninth Circuit explained in the *Farr* case mentioned above that:

> [T]he purpose of eliminating collaboration between counsel and the press is to protect the constitutionally guaranteed right of the defendants in criminal cases to due process by means of a fair trial. That constitutional right cannot be so protected if the authority of the court to enforce its orders is diluted. If the newsman's privilege against disclosure of news sources is to serve as a bar to disclosure of the names of those who disobey the court order, then the court is powerless to enforce this method of eliminating encroachment on the due-process right of the defendants.[63]

Gag orders and their enforcement are discussed in more detail in Chapter 6.

---

[60]   *Shoen I*, 5 F.3d at 1293.
[61]   *Shoen I*, 5 F.3d at 1293.
[62]   Cal. Const., article I, section 2(b).
[63]   *Farr v. Pitchess*, 522 F.2d 464, 469 (9th Cir. 1975).

D. FEDERAL REGULATIONS ON SUBPOENAS TO JOURNALISTS.

Justice Department regulations with respect to "the issuance of subpoenas to members of the news media, subpoenas for telephone toll records of the news media, and the interrogation, indictment, or arrest of, members of the news media" state that "the prosecutorial power of the government should not be used in such a way that it impairs a reporter's responsibility to cover as broadly as possible controversial public issues."[64] These regulations are of little use to reporters served with a subpoena, however, because they expressly provide that they "are not intended to create or recognize any legally enforceable right in any person," and courts have declined to use them to give reporters relief from contempt charges.[65]

E. FEDERAL LEGISLATION TO CREATE A REPORTER'S SHIELD LAW.

The high-profile incarcerations of Judith Miller and Josh Wolf (and the threatened incarceration of San Francisco Chronicle reporters Lance Williams and Mark Fainaru-Wada and Time magazine reporter Matthew Cooper) have prompted renewed public debate on whether Congress should take up the Supreme Court's invitation in *Branzburg* to create a statutory reporter's shield. A bill introduced in 2005, but not acted upon, would have prohibited government entities from compelling the news media to disclose the source of news or information or any unpublished news or information procured in the course of gathering news, absent clear and convincing evidence that (1) disclosure is critical and necessary to the resolution of a significant legal issue, (2) the news or information could not be obtained by alternative means; and (3) there is an overriding public interest in disclosure.[66] Bills introduced in 2007 contained similar provisions, but they also excluded bloggers and other nontraditional professional journalists from coverage.

PART IV:
PROTECTION FROM SEARCH WARRANTS

In addition to seeking to compel testimony or source material from journalists, the government can attempt to obtain information from the media by executing a search warrant at the office of the newspaper, radio station, television station, or other news entity, or at the home of a journalist. Although the constitutional protection against such searches is limited, fairly substantial protections against the search and seizure of newsgathering materials exist under California and federal statutes.

A. LIMITED CONSTITUTIONAL PROTECTION.

The U.S. Supreme Court ruled in *Zurcher v. Stanford Daily* that neither the Fourth nor First Amendment prevents the issuance of a warrant to search a newspaper office for evidence relevant to the commission of a crime, even when the journalists working on the premises are not suspects

---

[64]   Code of Federal Regulations, Tilte 28, section 50.10 (28 C.F.R. § 50.10).

[65]   Code of Federal Regulations, Tilte 28, section 50.10(n) (28 C.F.R. 50.10(n)); *see also, e.g., In re Lewis*, 384 F. Supp. 133, 137 (C.D. Cal. 1974); *In re Special Proceedings*, 373 F.3d 37 (1st Cir. 2004); *New York Times Co. v. Gonzales*, 382 F. Supp. 2d 457, 484 (S.D.N.Y. 2005).

[66]   S. 369, 109th Congress (2005).

in the case.[67] The court did recognize and approved the rule that courts must apply the warrant requirements of probable cause, specificity and overall reasonableness with "particular exactitude when First Amendment interests would be endangered by the search."[68]

In practice, the "particular exactitude" standard has been of limited help to reporters in situations where police have used a search warrant. In a recent Virginia case, the federal courts examined a search of a reporter's home office, including the search and seizure of computer equipment belonging to the reporter's employer. The appellate court upheld the search, reasoning that the extra scrutiny prescribed by *Zurcher* does not apply where the items named in the warrant are evidentiary materials and their seizure does not threaten to deprive the public of access to constitutionally protected material.[69]

However, in response to *Zurcher*, both the federal and California governments enacted rules to provide greater protection from search warrants to the news media. Those protections are discussed below.

B. PROTECTIONS FROM SEARCH WARRANTS UNDER CALIFORNIA LAW.

California law prohibits the issuance of search warrants for journalists' notes, outtakes, photographs, tapes and other materials obtained or prepared in gathering, receiving or processing information for communication to the public. The prohibition is embodied in section 1524(g) of the Penal Code, which provides that "no warrant shall issue for any item or items described in Section 1070 of the Evidence Code." (Section 1070 of the Evidence Code is the California shield law, discussed in Part II above.) The scope and effect of Section 1524(g) have not been tested in court. However, the language of the statute is clear.

First, section 1524(g) applies only to journalists (as defined in Evidence Code section 1070). Second, section 1524(g) does not forbid searches of newsrooms and media offices altogether. Rather, it prohibits the search for and seizure of newsgathering *materials* wherever they may be found, including on the premises of news organizations or in journalists' cars, luggage or homes.

A Note on Search Warrants for Journalists' Information: Journalists should be aware that a warrant for protected materials might be issued in error or ignorance of the protections of Section 1524(g). In this situation, the police should be referred to the editorial representative in highest authority on the premises. If possible, contact an attorney whose services may be obtained on short notice. Ask for the opportunity to have the attorney or editor review the contents of the warrant. Pay particular attention to the description of the area to be searched and the materials to be seized, which must be given with specificity, and to the statement of probable cause to believe that such materials are to be found in the place described.

Ask that the attorney or editor be given the opportunity to contact the court to attempt to have the warrant quashed based on the protection of Section 1524(g) or because of other defects on the face of the warrant. Alternatively, contact the local district attorney, who generally has authority over law enforcement activities in the county and may be more familiar with the law. The district attorney may be willing to instruct the police to postpone the execution of the warrant. All this should be accomplished as quickly as possible. As a practical matter, however, officers dispatched to execute a search warrant are not likely to postpone their activity while journalists attempt to have the subpoena quashed. If the officers insist on executing the warrant, it is

---

[67] *Zurcher v. Stanford Daily*, 436 U.S. 547 (1978).
[68] *Zurcher v. Stanford Daily*, 436 U.S. 547, 565 (1978).
[69] *Arkansas Chronicle v. Murphy*, 183 Fed. Appx. 300, 305-06, 34 Media L. Rep. 1837, 1842 (4th Cir. 2006).

important not to interfere with their actions. Interfering with police execution of a warrant can result in criminal liability.

Search warrants issued under California law may also be subject to the federal Privacy Protection Act of 1980, discussed below.

C. PROTECTIONS UNDER FEDERAL STATUTE.

Following *Zurcher*, the federal government enacted the Privacy Protection Act of 1980, a more complicated response than its California counterpart.[70] This act provides protection from searches by all government officials – federal, state and local – for all "work product" and "documentary" materials. It applies to materials held by news representatives, authors, scholars, researchers and anyone who has collected the material "with a purpose to disseminate to the public a newspaper, book, broadcast, or other similar form of communication" in or affecting interstate or foreign commerce.[71] Thus, it may be broader in its application than the California statute discussed above.

The protection provided by the Privacy Protection Act differs somewhat depending on whether the material is classified as "work product" (*i.e.*, the journalist's own thoughts and words recorded for the purpose of communication to the public) or "documentary" (*i.e.*, material gathered by the journalist while researching and writing the story, but not necessarily originally created for that purpose, including film negatives and prints, audio and videotapes, and documents).

1. Work Product Materials.

With respect to work product, the act prohibits search and seizure by government officials unless: (1) There is reason to believe that immediate seizure is necessary to prevent death or serious bodily injury; or (2) probable cause exists to believe that the person in possession of the material has committed or is committing a criminal offense related to the materials. This second exception does not apply, and no search or seizure will be permitted, if the offense at issue consists of the receipt, possession or communication of information unless that information is classified or concerns national defense or the underlying offense is related to child pornography or the sexual exploitation of children.

2. Documentary Materials.

In the case of documentary materials, government searches and seizures are limited in the same way as are searches for work product, but there are two additional exceptions. Documentary materials can also be seized if: (1) There is reason to believe that giving notice pursuant to a subpoena for production of the documents would result in the destruction, alteration or concealment of the materials; or (2) if the materials would not have been produced in accordance with a court order directing compliance with a subpoena, and either all appellate remedies have been exhausted or there is reason to believe that delay in an investigation or trial would threaten the interests of justice. If this fourth exception applies, the person who possesses the materials must be given an opportunity to submit an affidavit in opposition to the seizure.

---

[70] United States Code, Title 42, section 2000aa (42 U.S.C. § 2000aa).

[71] The "in or affecting interstate or foreign commerce" language is necessary to provide the federal government with the authority to regulate such searches and seizures, as they would otherwise be subject only to state law. This "commerce" requirement will be satisfied by virtually any form of dissemination to the public.

Materials that constitute contraband or fruits of a crime, or items designed, intended or used as the means of committing a crime, are not protected from search or seizure by the act.

CHAPTER 10

Access to Judicial Records

IN THIS CHAPTER

The public has a presumptive right of access to criminal and civil court records. That right of access may be limited by court order, in unusual circumstances. This chapter discusses what types of records are commonly found in court files, the circumstances in which access to information contained in the files may be limited, what procedures the court must use before it can limit access to information and how long a limitation on access may last.

PART I:
GENERAL RULES OF ACCESS

The public has the same presumptive right of access to most court records in criminal or civil cases as it does to attend the court proceedings.[1] Court records include, but are not limited to, complaints filed by a district attorney, state attorney general or U.S. attorney in criminal prosecutions, motions filed by either the prosecution or defendant in criminal cases, civil pleadings, official transcripts of judicial proceedings, and evidentiary materials admitted at trial.

California courts have held that the presumptive access right encompasses any record "that accurately and officially reflects the work of the court, such as orders and judgments, its scheduling and administration of cases, and its assignment of judicial officers and administrators."[2] Like court proceedings, the presumptive right of access to records can be defeated when an overriding interest justifies restricted access. There are also statutory limitations on the public's right to access certain records including, but not limited to, probation reports and reports of the results of certain mental examinations. The most important of these exceptions will be discussed in greater detail below.

A. BASIC OF RIGHT OF ACCESS.

Unlike records obtained from other public agencies such as cities or school districts, the public's right to access judicial records is not derived from the California Public Records Act or the federal Freedom of Information Act. The public has qualified rights under both the First Amendment and article I, section 2(a) of California's constitution to access court records. A California appellate court has observed "there can be no doubt that court records are public records, available to the public in general, including news reporters, unless a specific exception makes specific records nonpublic."[3] Even in the absence of constitutional considerations, both California and federal common law make judicial records generally accessible unless a statute provides otherwise or a court orders the record sealed.

---

[1]   U.S. Const. Amend. 1; Cal. Const., art. I, § 2(a).
[2]   *Copley Press v. Superior Court*, 6 Cal. App. 4th 106, 114-115 (1992).
[3]   *Estate of Hearst*, 67 Cal. App. 3d 777 (1977).

B. PROCEDURE FOR ACCESS TO COURT RECORDS.

If seeking records in a criminal or civil litigation file, the traditional method is to go to the courthouse where the lawsuit is pending, provide the clerk with the case number and request to see the file. Increasingly, however, federal and state courts are making at least some court records available via the Internet. In California, the federal courts make records available online in most cases, through a service called PACER (http://pacer.psc.uscourts.gov).[4] The availability of records of state court proceedings varies from county to county, but most urban county superior courts make at least a "register of actions" (*i.e.*, a docket, or list of events that have occurred and documents that have been filed) available online. Some also make court records in civil cases available online. All of the California courts of appeal make some information available online: dockets, court schedules, court minutes and opinions issued by the court. For a list of the Internet websites of the superior courts for each county in California, go to http://www.courtinfo.ca.gov/courts/trial/courtlist.htm. For links to the Internet websites of each of the California courts of appeal, go to http://www.courtinfo.ca.gov/courts/courtsofappeal. Different courts provide different ways to search for and find records, but the most typical and predictable way to find information is with a case number.

If you do not know the case number but know the name of at least one of the parties in a civil case or of the defendant in a criminal prosecution, the court should maintain a listing of recent cases filed by the name of the parties in alphabetical order. The court's website may also allow you to search for cases using the name of one of the parties.

The public is generally entitled to read everything in the file that has not been sealed. Sealed records normally are kept in a special envelope designating that anyone without a court order is prohibited from reading their contents. Violation of that order can result in criminal penalties.

If the document you are looking for is not in the file, and you believe it has been sealed, you must ask the judge for an order granting you access (assuming the parties are unwilling or unable, because of an earlier court order, to provide you with the desired materials). Where a court record is subject to a presumptive constitutional right of access, it may not be sealed unless the court has entered, on the record, a detailed finding of facts justifying the sealing order.[5] Moreover, the public and media must be afforded an opportunity to be heard on the question of their exclusion before a sealing order is issued.[6]

California has adopted guidelines governing when a court record may be sealed. California Rule of Court 2.550 states that court records in both civil and criminal cases may be sealed only when a court finds (1) an overriding interest that overcomes the right of public access to the record, (2) that the overriding interest supports sealing the record, (3) that a substantial probability exists that the overriding interest will be prejudiced if the record is not sealed, (4) the proposed sealing is narrowly tailored and (5) no less-restrictive means exist to achieve the overriding interest.[7]

Examples of interests that might be found to justify sealing in a particular case include a criminal defendant's right to a fair trial, protection of minor victims of sex crimes, privacy interests of prospective jurors, protection of witnesses from extreme embarrassment or intimidation, protection of trade secrets, protection of privileged information, safeguarding

---

[4]   PACER charges for access to court records. Currently, the charge is $.08/page.

[5]   *Press Enterprise Co. v. Superior Court of California* (*Press Enterprise I*), 464 U.S. 501 (1984); *NBC Subsidiary (KNBC-TV), Inc. v. Superior Court,* 20 Cal. 4th 1178 (1999); Cal. Rule of Court 2.550 (formerly Cal. Rule of Court 243.1).

[6]   *Globe Newspaper Co. v. Superior Court*, 457 U.S. 596 (1982); Cal. Rule of Court 2.551(h)(2) (formerly Cal. Rule of Court 243.2).

[7]   Cal. Rule of Court 2.550(d).

national security, ensuring anonymity of juvenile offenders, ensuring fair administration of justice, and preservation of confidential investigative information. In all circumstances, however, only those specific documents, or, if practical, portions of documents, that relate directly to the overriding interest should be sealed. All other portions of the record should be part of the public file.[8]

PART II:
RECORDS OF CRIMINAL PROCEEDINGS

In the 1980s, the U.S. Supreme Court ruled that the First Amendment right of access to criminal trial and pretrial proceedings extends to transcripts of those proceedings as well.[9] Numerous lower courts have since held that the public has a presumptive First Amendment right to inspect and copy most records in the court files of criminal cases.[10] The California Supreme Court has also ruled that there is a constitutional right of access to most records in criminal and civil court cases.[11] This right of access is now reflected in the California Rules of Court.[12]

Because access to judicial records is a constitutional right, access can be limited only by demonstrating that a more compelling interest would be directly threatened by disclosure of the information, no less restrictive alternatives to closure are available, and a substantial probability exists that a sealing order would be effective in preventing harm.[13] Even where a court record is not subject to a constitutional right of access, it may be possible to access the record under an applicable statute, court rule or, as noted above, the common law.

A. RECORDS SUBJECT TO FIRST AMENDMENT RIGHT OF ACCESS.

Courts have adopted a two-part test to assess whether a court record is subject to the qualified First Amendment right of access. First, the courts will examine whether the records pertain to proceedings that historically have been open to the public. For example, a United States court of appeals ruled that because the acceptance or denial of plea agreements historically has occurred in public, that factor supports application of the First Amendment right of access to such documents and related records.[14] Second, courts will consider the functional benefits derived from public access to the records. These benefits include public oversight of the judicial system, judges and

---

8   Cal. Rule of Court 2.550(e)(1)(B).
9   *Press Enterprise Co. v. Superior Court of California* (*Press Enterprise II*): 478 U.S. 1 (1986) (transcripts of voir dire proceedings).
10 *See, e.g., Associated Press v. United States District Court*, 705 F. 2d 1143 (1983) (pretrial motions); *Globe Newspaper Co. v. Pokaski* (1st Cir. 1989) 868 F.2d 497, 502; *In re New York Times Co.* (2d Cir. 1987) 828 F.2d 110, 114, *cert. denied,* 485 U.S. 977 (1988) (documents filed in connection with pretrial suppression hearings); *U.S. v. Smith* (3d Cir. 1985) 776 F.2d 1104, 1111 (bill of particular)]; *Applications of National Broadcasting Co.* (6th Cir. 1987) 828 F.2d 340, 345 (motion to disqualify judge in criminal case); *United States v. Peters* (7th Cir. 1985) 754 F.2d 753, 763 (trial exhibits); *In re Search Warrant for Secretarial Area Outside Office of Gunn* (8th Cir. 1988) 855 F.2d 569, 573 (search warrants); *Washington Post v. Robinson* (D.C. Cir. 1991) 935 F.2d 282, 289 (motions to seal plea agreements and dockets).
11 *NBC Subsidiary (KNBC-TV), Inc. v. Superior Court,* 20 Cal. 4th 1178 (1999).
12 Cal. Rules of Court 2.550 and 2.551 (formerly Cal. Rule of Court 243.1 and 243.2).
13 Cal. Rules of Court 2.550 and 2.551; *Associated Press v. United States District Court*, 705 F. 2d 1143 (1983).
14 *The Oregonian Publishing Co. v. U.S.*, 920 F.2d 1462 (9th Cir. 1990).

prosecutors;[15] education of the public "to ensure that the constitutionally protected 'discussion of governmental affairs' is an informed one"[16] and assurance of the appearance of fairness.[17]

In light of these considerations, courts have applied the First Amendment access right to transcripts of voir dire proceedings;[18] preliminary hearings;[19] suppression hearings;[20] plea agreements;[21] transcripts of sidebar or chamber conferences;[22] criminal discovery documents filed with the court or introduced as evidence; pretrial motion papers;[23] documents filed in pretrial release proceedings;[24] voir dire questionnaires;[25] and post-trial documents,[26] including proffer letters offered in connection with a defendant's motion to reduce his sentence.[27]

B. ACCESS TO EVIDENCE IN CRIMINAL CASES.

When a witness testifies in a criminal trial, the testimony is evidence – information that the judge or jury will use in determining the outcome of the case. Unless a proceeding meets the strict requirements that allow a hearing to be closed to the public, the public has a right to attend and hear testimony of the witnesses. It also has a right to the court transcript of that testimony or proceeding.

Other types of evidence that may be introduced into court and play an important role in the outcome of the case may be tangible items, such as photographs, a written contract, a handwritten note or even a murder weapon. Since these tangible items also help to determine the outcome of the case, courts have recognized a right of public access to these items as well. The strength of the right to access evidence may vary depending on whether it has been "introduced" in the proceeding.

1. Limiting Access When Evidence Is Introduced.

Where evidence is introduced at a hearing, courts may limit the public's access if release would likely jeopardize a criminal defendant's Sixth Amendment right to a fair trial. This may occur if the evidence is introduced at a preliminary hearing or other pre-trial proceeding, when the defendant is still awaiting trial. Criminal defendants often assert, for example, that allowing the public and the press to attend hearings regarding evidence that may be suppressed (not heard at trial) will prevent the defendant from obtaining a fair trial. However, the public disclosure of evidence during pre-trial proceedings rarely causes such harm.[28]

---

[15]   *Press Enterprise II*, 478 U.S. 1.
[16]   *Globe Newspaper Co. v. Superior Court*, 457 U.S. 596 (1982).
[17]   *Press Enterprise II*, 478 U.S. 1.
[18]   *Press Enterprise I*, 464 U.S. 501.
[19]   *Press Enterprise II,* 478 U.S. 1.
[20]   *United States v. Brooklier*, 685 F.2d 1162 (9th Cir. 1982).
[21]   *The Oregonian Publishing Co .v. U.S. District Court*, 920 F.2d 1462 (1990).
[22]   *United States v. Smith*; 787 F.2d 111 (3d Cir. 1986).
[23]   *In re New York Times Co.*, 828 F.2d 110 (2d Cir. 1987).
[24]   *Seattle Times Co. v. United States District Court*, 845 F.2d 1513 (9th Cir. 1988).
[25]   *Lesher Communications, Inc. v.Contra Costa Superior Court*, 224 Cal.App.3d 774 (1990).
[26]   *CBS, Inc. v. U.S. District Court*, 729 F.2d 1174 (9th Cir. 1984).
[27]   *In re McClatchy Newspapers*, 288 F.3d 369 (9th Cir. 2002)
[28]   *See, e.g., Nebraska Press Ass'n v. Stuart*, 427 U.S. 539, 565 (1976) ("[P]retrial publicity, even if pervasive and concentrated, cannot be regarded as leading automatically and in every kind of criminal case to an unfair trial."); *People v. Jennings*, 53 Cal. 3d 334, 362 (1991) ("[t]he fact that a case received enormous publicity does not by itself establish error nor does conceded 'massive' publicity automatically translate into prejudice"); *People v. Mendosa*, 137 Cal. App. 3d 888, 895 (1982) ("there is no presumption that an accused suffers prejudice from unfriendly news stories").

2. Materials That Do Not Become Evidence in the Case.

If a piece of evidence is neither introduced in court nor plays a part in determining the outcome of a proceeding (such as through a motion), the public may have no right to access it. As with civil cases, attorneys on both sides usually discover or prepare more information than can be introduced as evidence in court. The California court rule that makes most court records public does not apply to discovery materials not used at trial or submitted to the courts in connection with substantive motions.[29] Even if some of that material is highly newsworthy, many courts have refused to recognize either a common law or First Amendment right of access to the material.[30]

3. Audiotaped and Videotaped Evidence.

In a 1986 decision, a United States court of appeals ruled that there exists a "strong presumption" in favor of the public's and media's right to copy videotapes introduced into evidence in a criminal trial.[31] California appellate courts agree.[32]

C. ACCESS TO GRAND JURY TRANSCRIPTS AND MATERIALS.

1. Access After Indictment.

Under California law, there are two ways a criminal defendant can be ordered to stand trial. The first is following a charge filed by the local district attorney. If the district attorney files a charge (which is a judicial record open to public inspection), a preliminary hearing is held, during which a judge decides if enough evidence exists to order the defendant to stand trial. The second is by an indictment handed down by a grand jury following the grand jury's review of evidence presented by the district attorney in secret proceedings.

If the grand jury votes to indict a defendant, California Penal Code section 938.1 requires that a copy of the transcript of the grand jury proceedings be delivered to the defendant and that the court clerk file the original. Ten days after the defendant or his or her attorney has received a copy of the transcript, Penal Code section 938.1 provides that the filed transcript is open to public inspection unless the court orders all or part of the transcript sealed. Section 938.1 also gives judges authority to seal all or part of a grand jury transcript until completion of the trial, upon a finding "that there is a reasonable likelihood that making all or any part of the transcript public may prejudice a defendant's right to a fair and impartial trial."

A California court has found sealing to be improper where "there is no basis for concluding that publicity of the contents of the entire grand jury transcript would be so extensive and widespread that it threatens to prejudice the entire jury pool so that twelve unbiased jurors could not be found." [33] The court also found that the trial court had failed in its duty to consider "reasonable alternatives" to sealing the grand jury transcript, such as a change of venue or careful voir dire examination. Consideration of such alternatives is constitutionally required, the court reasoned, because once an indictment has been returned, the First Amendment right of access to judicial records applies to the grand jury transcript.[34]

---

29   California Rule of Court 2.550(a)(2).
30   *See, e.g., Anderson v. Cryovac, Inc.*, 805 F.2d 1, 13 (1st Cir. 1986).
31   *Valley Broadcasting v. U.S. District Court*, 798 F.2d 1289 (9th Cir. 1986).
32   *KNSD Channels 7/39 v. Superior Court*, 63 Cal. App. 4th 1200 (1998).
33   *Press Enterprise v. Superior Court (Press-Enterprise III)*, 22 Cal. App. 4th 498, 504 (1994).
34   *Press Enterprise III*, 22 Cal. App. 4th at 505 n. 5.

When cases are particularly sensational, or involve serious charges or sensitive matters such as minor victims, courts may be more likely to order grand jury transcripts and other court records sealed. For example, a trial court sealed the grand jury transcript, indictment, search warrant affidavits and other court records of the case in which Michael Jackson was indicted on charges including child molestation. A higher court approved the sealing of all of the documents with the exception of parts of the indictment, which it held could be released to the public and media so long as the names of unindicted co-conspirators were redacted.[35]

2. Access If No Indictment.

The California Supreme Court has held that if a grand jury has failed to return an indictment the trial judge has no discretion to release the grand jury transcript under any circumstances.[36]

3. Access to Civil "Watchdog" Grand Jury Materials.

In California, a grand jury can perform other functions in addition to weighing criminal charges and determining whether indictments should be returned. It also serves as the public's "watchdog" by annually investigating and reporting upon the affairs of local government. Penal Code section 929 provides that, with the approval of the presiding or supervising judge, "a grand jury may make available to the public part or all of the evidentiary material, findings, and other information relied upon by or presented to a grand jury for its final report in any civil grand jury investigation." The statute prohibits the release of information that would identify any person who provided information to the grand jury. It also allows judges to require the redaction or masking of any part of the released information, including but not limited to the identity of witnesses or defamatory material.

4. Federal Grand Juries.

Federal prosecutors also use grand juries to obtain felony indictments. There is no statute establishing a right of public access to transcripts of federal grand jury proceedings. The Ninth Circuit Court of Appeals has recognized that federal grand jury proceedings will generally be kept secret. However, this rule is not absolute, and secrecy may be sacrificed at times to serve important countervailing interests. The United States Supreme Court has said that "after the grand jury's functions are ended, disclosure is wholly proper where the ends of justice require it."[37] Thus, information from federal grand jury proceedings may be subject to disclosure if the person seeking the information can show "a particularized and compelling need."[38]

D. ACCESS TO JUROR RECORDS.

A California court of appeal has ruled that master jury lists containing the names of those qualified for jury duty are open to public inspection, but the questionnaires filled out by

---

[35]   *People v. Jackson*, 128 Cal. App. 4th 1009 (2005).

[36]   *Daily Journal Corp. v. Superior Court*, 20 Cal. 4th 1117 (1999).

[37]   *United States v. Socony-Vacuum Oil Co.*, 310 U.S. 150, 234 (1940).

[38]   *U.S. Industries, Inc. v. U.S. District Court*, 345 F.2d 18, 20-21 (9th Cir. 1965); Federal Rule of Civil Procedure 6(e)(2)(B) (listing persons who may not disclose matter occurring before a grand jury, but allowing courts to provide otherwise). *See also United States v. Procter and Gamble Co.*, 356 U.S. 677, 682-683 (1958); *Appeal of Anthony S. Troia*, 580 F.2d 281, 286 (8th Cir. 1978); *U.S. v. Armco Steel Corp.*, 458 F. Supp. 784 (D. Mo. 1978).

prospective jurors to show whether they are qualified to serve are not.[39] California courts have ruled, however, that a more stringent test applies to attempts to seal voir dire questionnaires *after* an individual juror is summoned to the jury box. Such questionnaires are subject to the presumptive constitutional access right and cannot be sealed without the strong showing necessary to overcome that right.[40]

Section 237 of California's Code of Civil Procedure generally requires that the names of those summoned to serve as jurors be made publicly available, absent a compelling countervailing interest. The statute provides, however, that upon the recording of the verdict in a criminal case, "the court's record of personal juror identifying information of trial jurors ... consisting of names, addresses, and telephone numbers, shall be sealed until further order of the court."

A California court of appeal has also upheld a court policy in Los Angeles requiring criminal jurors to be identified only by number after they are seated. In doing so, the court emphasized that the jurors were identified by name on a case information sheet made available to the parties, and noted that nothing "indicates that interested members of the public or news media were precluded from ascertaining jurors' names during the trial."[41]

PART III:
CIVIL CASE RECORDS

Although the U.S. Supreme Court has not expressly extended the constitutional right of access to records of civil cases, it has implied that it does apply.[42] In addition, lower courts have held that it does.[43] The federal court of appeals for the Ninth Circuit, which governs federal district courts in California, has not yet decided the issue, but it has recognized a "common law" right of access to judicial records.[44] The California Supreme Court has ruled that there is a right of access to most records in civil court proceedings that is based on the First Amendment and California law.[45] Moreover, California courts have recognized a qualified common law right of access to all

---

[39]   *Pantos v. City and County of San Francisco*, 151 Cal. App. 3d 258 (1984).

[40]   *Lesher Communications, Inc. v.Contra Costa Superior Court*, 224 Cal. App. 3d 774 (1990)

[41]   *People v. Goodwin*, 59 Cal. App. 4th 1084 (1997).

[42]   In *Richmond Newspapers, Inc. v. Virginia*, 448 U.S. 555 (1980), where the court first clearly recognized a First Amendment right of access to court proceedings, six of the eight justices indicated that the right applies to civil cases as well as criminal ones. *See Richmond Newspapers, Inc.*, 448 U.S. at 580 n. 17 (Burger, C.J.) (plurality opinion) ("Whether the public has a right to attend trials of civil cases is a question not raised by this case, but we note that historically both civil and criminal trials have been presumptively open."); *id.* at 596 (Brennan, J., concurring in the judgment) (referring to the value of open proceedings in civil cases); *id.* at 599 (Stewart, J., concurring in the judgment) ("[T]he First and Fourteenth Amendments clearly give the press and the public a right of access to trials themselves, civil as well as criminal.").

[43]   A majority of the circuits that have squarely faced this issue have recognized that the First Amendment right of access applies to records filed in civil proceedings. *See, e.g., Westmoreland v. Columbia Broadcasting System, Inc.*, 752 F.2d 16, 23 (2d Cir. 1984), *cert. denied, Cable News Network, Inc. v. U.S. District Court*, 472 U.S. 1017 (1985); *Publicker Industries, Inc. v. Cohen*, 733 F.2d 1059, 1067-71 (3d Cir. 1984); *Rushford v. New Yorker Magazine, Inc.*, 846 F.2d 249, 253 (4th Cir. 1988); *Brown & Williamson Tobacco Corp. v. Federal Trade Comm'n*, 710 F.2d 1165, 1179 (6th Cir. 1983), *cert. denied*, 465 U.S. 1100 (1984); *In re Continental Illinois Securities Litigation*, 732 F.2d 1302, 1308 (7th Cir. 1983); *Newman v. Graddick*, 696 F.2d 796, 800-801 (11th Cir. 1983). Only one circuit has taken a contrary view. *See In re Reporters Comm. for Freedom of Press*, 773 F.2d 1325 (D.C. Cir. 1985).

[44]   *San Jose Mercury News, Inc. v. U.S. Dist. Court*, 187 F.3d 1096, 1103 (9th Cir. 1999).

[45]   *NBC Subsidiary (KNBC-TV), Inc. v. Superior Court*, 20 Cal. 4th 1178 (1999).

records filed with the court in civil proceedings.[46] The right of access to records in civil court cases is also imposed by the California Rules of Court.[47]

As in the case of criminal proceedings, decisions recognizing a right of access to civil records generally are based on the historic openness of civil proceedings and the interest of the public in monitoring and being informed about the judicial system. Therefore, complaints, answers, motions to dismiss and other documents filed with a court are treated as presumptively public.

Applying the First Amendment right of access to civil cases, federal courts have held that to limit access to court records the party seeking to prevent access must show that the denial serves an important governmental interest and that there is no less restrictive way to serve that governmental interest.[48]

California state courts, like their federal counterparts, have recognized a broad common law access right to records of civil judicial proceedings. This right can be defeated only upon a showing that revelation would "tend to undermine individual security, personal liberty, or private property, or ... injure the public good."[49] In 1999, California's Supreme Court held that the First Amendment mandates public access to records filed in civil proceedings unless the records were sealed by the court under the guidelines discussed in Part I (B) of this chapter.[50]

A. DISCOVERY MATERIAL IN CIVIL CASES.

Discovery is a process by which litigants are allowed to obtain information from each other about their cases. In both the federal and California courts, litigants and witnesses can be compelled to submit to depositions (oral questioning), interrogatories (written questioning), and inspections of documents, tangible items and places. A litigant normally can discover any evidence believed to be relevant to his or her case and any matter likely to lead to discovery of relevant evidence.

1. Limited Right of Access to Discovery Materials Not Filed in the Action.

Under the federal and California rules, parties are allowed to discover information that may never be introduced at trial. Public access to discovery documents not filed with or considered by the court is limited.[51] Some courts have recognized a presumption of access unless otherwise ordered by the court. For example, a United States court of appeals has ruled that "[a] statutory presumption of openness for discovery materials, even those not used at trial, derives from the Federal Rules of Civil Procedure."[52]

Recently, a California newspaper was able to obtain transcripts of depositions from a lawsuit by California State University employees against the university and others. The court reasoned that the deposition transcripts were otherwise generally available to the public under California Code of Civil Procedure Section 2025.570, and that the California Public Records Act Section 6254(b), which shields documents pertaining to pending legislation to which a public agency is a party, did not apply. Because the deposition transcripts contained no confidential or privileged

---

[46]   *Copley Press v. Superior Court*, 6 Cal. App. 4th 106 (1992); *Estate of Hearst*, 67 Cal. App. 3d 777 (1977).
[47]   Cal. Rules of Court 2.550, 2.551.
[48]   *See, e.g., Rushford v. New Yorker Magazine, Inc.*, 846 F.2d 249, 253 (4th Cir. 1988); *Publicker Industries, Inc. v. Cohen*, 733 F.2d 1059, 1070 (3d Cir. 1984).
[49]   *Estate of Hearst*, 67 Cal. App. 3d 777 (1977).
[50]   *NBC Subsidiary (KNBC-TV), Inc. v. Superior Court*, 20 Cal. 4th 1178 (1999).
[51]   *FTC v. Standard Financial Management Corp.*, 830 F.2d 404 (1st Cir. 1987).
[52]   *Tavoulareas v. Washington Post Co.*, 759 F.2d 90 (1985).

matters, the paper was able to obtain them with only the personal information of the employees redacted.[53]

2. Qualified Right of Access to Discovery Filed and Relied Upon by Court.

Under California law, however, once a litigation document has been formally filed with or received by the court, constitutional and common law presumptions of access apply.[54] Federal law is less clear. However, some federal courts have also indicated that "the filing of a document gives rise to a presumptive right of access."[55]

3. Courts May Issue Protective Orders Upon Showing of "Good Cause."

Courts generally are afforded discretion to issue protective orders requiring that information obtained in discovery not be disclosed to the public or media absent a showing of at least "good cause" and cannot be based on mere speculation of possible harm.[56] Good cause is established when a party shows that disclosure will result in a clearly defined, specific and serious injury, and the party seeking to prevent disclosure has the burden of showing that there is good cause.[57]

While courts used to routinely delegate to the litigation parties the power to undertake discovery in secret by signing broad confidentiality orders that permit any party to designate discovery materials as confidential, subject to the other party's right to challenge the designation, appellate courts increasingly have criticized such orders as an abdication of the judiciary's responsibility to regulate access to court papers. As a United States court of appeals explained, "[t]he District Court cannot abdicate its responsibility to oversee the discovery process and to determine whether filings should be made available to the public. It certainly should not turn over this function to the parties, as it did here, allowing them to modify the terms of a court order without even seeking the consent of the court."[58]

The First Amendment, however, does not necessarily support a litigant's right to disseminate information obtained in discovery. The U.S. Supreme Court has ruled that it is not a violation of a defendant's First Amendment rights to limit use of information obtained from an opposing party through discovery. "A litigant has no First Amendment right of access to information made available only for purposes of trying his suit."[59] The protection for information that is not evidence was justified, the Supreme Court ruled, because parties can use the discovery process to obtain information from their opponents that is irrelevant and, therefore, inadmissible in the trial and also potentially damaging and embarrassing for their opponents if publicized.[60]

This protection may not extend to all pre-trial information that is not ultimately entered into evidence. For example, in class action lawsuits, courts sometimes conduct auctions to determine which plaintiffs' attorneys will be designated as the lead attorneys in a given lawsuit. A U.S. court of appeals has held that bids for lead counsel in class action lawsuits are judicial records subject to

---

[53] *Board of Trustees of the California State University v. Superior Court of San Diego County*, 132 Cal. App. 4th 889 (2005).

[54] *Copley Press v. Superior Court*, 6 Cal. App. 4th 106 (1992).

[55] *Leucadia, Inc. v. Applied Extrusion Technologies, Inc.*, 998 F.2d 157, 161-62 (3d Cir. 1993). *See also Mokhiber v. Davis*, 537 A.2d 1100, 1112 (D.C. 1988).

[56] *See, e.g., Pansy v. Borough of Stroudsburg*, 23 F.3d 772 (3d Cir. 1994); *Shingara v. Skiles*, 420 F.3d 301 (3d Cir. 2005).

[57] *See, e.g., Pansy v. Borough of Stroudsburg*, 23 F.3d 772, 786-787 (3d Cir. 1994); *Shingara v. Skiles*, 420 F.3d 301, 306 (3d Cir. 2005).

[58] *Proctor & Gamble Co. v. Bankers Trust Co.*, 78 F.3d 219 (1995).

[59] *Seattle Times v. Rhinehart*, 467 U.S. 20, 32 (1984).

[60] *Seattle Times v. Rhinehart*, 467 U.S. 20 (1984).

the public right of access and that such auctions should be open to the public.[61] Another federal district court held that a report attached to a pretrial motion for the appointment of a bankruptcy trustee was a judicial record to which the public and media could assert a right of access, even though it never became part of the trial record and was originally submitted under seal.[62]

4. Access to Discovery After Trial.

After a case is over, it may be too late to obtain access to discovery materials. A United States court of appeals ruled that "absent allegations of fraud or other extraordinary circumstances, trial exhibits that were restored to their owner after a case had been completely terminated and that were properly subject to destruction by the clerk ... are no longer judicial records within the 'supervisory power' of the district court," and thus "neither the First Amendment nor the common law right of access empowers the district court to require that litigants return such exhibits to the court for the purposes of copy and inspection by third parties." Exhibits formally admitted into evidence without objection and included in the trial record, however, become subject to public access, even if they were covered by a protective order before their admission.[63]

B. SETTLEMENT RECORDS.

1. Agreements Between Private Litigants.

Most cases are settled before trial. The way a case is settled can have an important effect on the rights of the public to find out the terms of the settlement.

Some disputes are settled prior to the filing of a lawsuit. A typical example is a personal injury claim resulting from an auto accident. An injured party usually will hire an attorney, who will negotiate with the responsible driver's insurance company. The injured party's attorney and the insurance company will often reach an agreement on an acceptable settlement before a lawsuit is filed. When the injured party receives the agreed payment, he or she will sign a release of further claims arising out of the accident. In this scenario, there is no lawsuit, no court involvement and, therefore, no right for the public to access the terms of the settlement. The only exception to this is when one of the parties involved is a government agency, in which case the settlement can be obtained under the California Public Records Act (see Chapter 2).

A second typical scenario is where the injured party and the insurance company are unable to come to an early settlement and the injured party files a lawsuit in state court. Long before the case ever reaches trial or the parties commence the discovery process, attorneys for both sides agree to a settlement. The standard procedure is for the plaintiff immediately to inform the court that a settlement has been reached and that there will be no further prosecution of the case. A formal document is then filed with the court dismissing the lawsuit. However, the terms of the agreement need not be and rarely are filed with the court. Once again, the public generally has no right to access the terms of the settlement.

In some cases, however, the parties will want the court to participate in the settlement process. When that happens, the parties may forfeit their rights to keep the terms of the settlement private, *i.e.*, the public may have a right to access the settlement agreement. Often, this occurs when one side or the other is concerned that the opposing party will not fully perform the terms of the agreement. In a "court-supervised" settlement agreement, the terms of the settlement generally

---

[61]   *In re Cendant Corp.*, 260 F.3d 183 (3d Cir. 2001).

[62]   *In re Peregrine Systems, Inc.*, 311 B.R. 679 (D. Del. 2004).

[63]   *Littlejohn v. BIC Corp.*, 851 F.2d 673 (3d Cir. 1988).

will be agreed to in open court and included in the official court record of the case. Under these circumstances, courts have held that the public is entitled to inform itself of the terms of the agreement by reviewing the case file.[64] An otherwise private settlement also may become part of the judicial record and thus subject to a presumptive right of access when the parties request assistance from the court to enforce the terms of the agreement.[65]

It is fairly common for parties to specify in the settlement agreement that its terms not be disclosed to the public. In this case, the judge who approves the secret settlement typically may order the agreement – and perhaps the transcript of the court proceeding regarding the settlement – to be sealed. The public is thus barred from learning the terms of the agreement. When such confidentiality orders have been challenged by third parties, however, courts generally have ruled that once a settlement agreement has been submitted to and filed with the court, and the court has been called upon either to interpret or to enforce the settlement, the agreement becomes subject to a right of access and cannot be sealed absent at least a showing of "good cause."

A U.S. court of appeals ruled that "[h]aving undertaken to utilize the judicial process to interpret the settlement and enforce it, the parties are no longer entitled to invoke the confidentiality ordinarily accorded settlement agreements. Once a settlement is filed in the district court, it becomes a judicial record, and subject to the access accorded such records."[66]

Certain California state laws restrict the enforcement of confidentiality requirements in settlement agreements in situations such as elder abuse cases or civil cases based on sex offenses.[67] A number of California counties have instituted local rules of court restricting secret settlement agreements in certain types of cases. Local rules of court, available from the clerk's office, will provide any rules affecting access to settlements in a particular California county.

2. Settlement Agreements to Which One Party Is a Governmental Entity.

When one of the parties to a lawsuit is a state or local agency, settlement documents generally are subject to public access pursuant to the California Public Records Act.[68] If a state court is involved in approving or enforcing the settlement, the public generally has a right of access to the settlement agreement pursuant to the constitutional and common law rights of access.[69] If the case is brought and settled in federal court, there exists a similarly strong presumption of access,[70] arguably fortified by the First Amendment.[71]

Courts are not subject to the California Public Records Act. However, a recent case sought information about a settlement in a case in which a court was sued by one of its employees. The parties seeking access to the settlement asserted that the information had to be disclosed under the new civil right of access created by Proposition 59, California Constitution Article I Section 3 (b). After the court's request to have this case rejected at the outset was denied, the court made the settlement available.

---

64   *SEC v. Van Waeyenberghe*, 990 F.2d 845 (5th Cir. 1993).
65   *Bank of America National Trust & Savings Ass'n v. Hotel Rittenhouse Associates*, 800 F.2d 339 (1986).
66   *Bank of America National Trust & Savings Ass'n*, 800 F.2d 339 (3d Cir.).
67   Code of Civil Procedure sections 2031.1 and 2031.2 (elder abuse); Code of Civil Procedure section 1002 (civil action the factual foundation for which is an act that may be prosecuted as a felony sex offense).
68   *Register Division of Freedom Newspapers v. County of Orange*, 158 Cal.App.3d 893 (1984). Note that the Brown Act also requires local government agencies to report on any final settlement agreement, in an open meeting. *See* Government Code section 54957.1.
69   *Copley Press, Inc. v. Superior Court*, 63 Cal. App. 4th 367 (1998).
70   *Pansy v. Borough of Stroudsburg*, 23 F.3d 772 (3d Cir. 1994).
71   *Society of Professional Journalists v. Briggs*, 675 F.Supp. 1308 (D. Utah 1987).

PART IV:
STATUTORY CONFIDENTIALITY

Access to certain types of documents is limited by state or federal statutes. Even if such a statute applies, however, it cannot infringe upon the access right guaranteed by the First Amendment. The following are among the most significant statutory provisions affecting access to judicial records that journalists are likely to encounter:

A. JUVENILE COURT DOCUMENTS.

Access to court records relating to a juvenile court case is usually restricted to the public officers who have some official connection with the case. This rule is reflected in Welfare and Institutions Code section 828, which regulates access to law enforcement records connected with the detention of a juvenile, and section 827, which restricts access to juvenile court records.

However, Section 827 grants the juvenile court discretion to authorize disclosure of juvenile records to the media upon the filing of a petition requesting such disclosure.[72] When disclosure is sought, the juvenile court must conduct a proceeding in the judge's chambers to determine what, if any, material may be disclosed to the media. The court is required to balance the interests of all relevant parties, including the juvenile, other parties to the proceeding, the media and public to determine whether good cause exists to disclose all or part of the contents of a sealed juvenile record. Petitioners must demonstrate a reasonable likelihood that the record in question will disclose information or evidence of substantial relevance to a pending investigation, and disclosure is permitted only insofar as is necessary.[73] Thus, media organizations should be as specific and detailed as possible when arguing for disclosure.

When the records pertain to a juvenile who is deceased, the law favors disclosure of the records. However, information in records relating to deceased children may still be withheld if substantial evidence shows the information is detrimental to the safety, protection, or physical or mental well-being of a living child.[74]

The authority of a juvenile court to order disclosure of the records of deceased juveniles extends beyond records of formal jurisdictional proceedings such as court cases, dependency (ward of the state) or delinquency proceedings. A juvenile court may order disclosure of other agencies' records encompassing informal contact with or monitoring of deceased juveniles.[75] Thus, it may be possible to gain access to other public records concerning deceased juveniles by petitioning a juvenile court.

Another statutory provision allows limited public access to certain documents in cases that involve the allegation of serious felony offenses. Welfare and Institutions Code section 676 states that proceedings of juveniles charged with certain violent crimes shall, subject to certain exceptions, be open and public. (For more detailed discussion of Section 676, see Chapter 5). When a petition (the document stating criminal charges against a juvenile) alleging any of the offenses listed in Section 676 is sustained, the public may inspect the charging petition, minutes of the proceeding, and orders of adjudication and disposition of the court.[76] However, a probation

---

[72]   *In re Keisha T.*, 38 Cal. App. 4th 220 (1995).
[73]   California Rule of Court 1423(b).
[74]   *Pack v. Kings County Department of Human Services*, 89 Cal.App.4th 821 (2001). *See also* Welfare and Institutions Code § 827(a)(2); California Rule of Court 1423(f).
[75]   *In re Elijah S.*, 125 Cal. App. 4th 1532 (2005).
[76]   Welfare & Institutions Code section 676(d).

officer or any party may petition the court to prohibit disclosure, and the court shall do so "if it appears that the harm to the minor, victims, witnesses, or public from the public disclosure outweighs the benefit of public knowledge."

B. SEARCH AND ARREST WARRANT DOCUMENTS.

The U.S. Constitution, as reflected in state and federal statutes, requires law enforcement officers to obtain a warrant before conducting certain searches. (The question of when a warrant is required is beyond the scope of this book.) A search warrant specifies the property to be searched and the items that may be seized. A law enforcement officer seeking a warrant must prepare a sworn affidavit for the court listing the facts that justify a warrant. A judge or magistrate will then review the affidavit to determine if there is sufficient evidence to issue the warrant. In general, a search warrant will expire if it is not executed within 10 days after it is issued.

Law enforcement officers use warrants with the hope of seizing evidence. In many cases, it would frustrate that objective if members of the public, including the suspect, were able to review the warrant or supporting affidavit before law enforcement had an opportunity to execute the warrant. As a result, California Penal Code section 1534 precludes public access to documents and records of the court relating to a warrant until it has been "executed" and "returned" to the court, or until the 10-day period for execution has elapsed. Once the warrant has been executed, the documents are treated as "judicial records." This means that public access can only be denied if the constitutional and common law requirements for sealing judicial records set forth earlier in this chapter are met. The documents that should be in the file and available for public inspection include the affidavit indicating what was expected to be found and where, and the return, which inventories what was actually found and seized. The statute does not give members of the public and media the right to inspect the items seized pursuant to the warrant.[77]

The public has no statutory right to access records relating to a warrant that was not executed. The rationale once again is that police do not want to tip off suspects that they are being investigated.

Warrants are also generally required in order to arrest people who have not committed crimes in the presence of law enforcement officers. (Again, a full discussion of arrest warrants is beyond the scope of this publication.) Documents relating to arrest warrants, which commonly incorporate investigative reports as a basis for the officer's affidavit, are presumptively a matter of public record under the common law. They are not covered by Penal Code section 1534.

A federal court of appeals has ruled that, in contrast to California law, federal law grants members of the public and media no right of access to materials relating to search warrants issued by federal courts while a pre-indictment investigation is under way. The court ruled that the public benefits arising from public access to search warrant materials are outweighed by the risk to law enforcement operations in an ongoing investigation and potential harm to the privacy interests of those mentioned in the materials.[78]

However, in a recent case the Ninth Circuit Court of Appeals allowed a newspaper publisher to access previously sealed materials including a search warrant, its supporting affidavit and an indictment *after* the criminal defendant had pled guilty, reasoning that it was no longer necessary to protect the ongoing investigation or the defendant's right to a fair trial, and that the defendant's and others' reputational and privacy interests were outweighed by the public's right of access.[79] While this case was unpublished, meaning no court is legally required to follow its decision, the

---

[77]   *Oziel v. Superior Court*, 223 Cal. App. 3d 1284 (1990).

[78]   *Times Mirror Co. v. United States*, 873 F.2d 1210 (9th Cir. 1989).

[79]   *U.S. v. Kott*, 135 Fed. Appx. 69, 2005 WL 1400288, 33 Media L. Rep. 1954 (9th Cir. 2005).

court's reasoning was sound and may prove useful in future efforts to gain access to such materials.

C. PROBATION OFFICERS' REPORTS.

Probation reports are filed with the court in criminal cases. The judge considers them in sentencing criminals who have been convicted (either after a trial or based on a plea agreement). They typically contain information on the person's criminal history (if any), personal background, extenuating or aggravating circumstances, and other information.[80]

1. Mandatory Disclosure.

Under Penal Code Section 1203.05, probation reports are required to be made available for public inspection in two circumstances: (1) When someone is convicted of a crime, the report must be made available for a period of 60 days from the date judgment is entered or probation is granted; and (2) when someone is first charged with a crime, any report relating to a prior conviction must be made available from the date the person is charged until 60 days after the date of sentencing or the grant of probation.[81]

2. Discretionary Disclosure.

Even though the period for mandatory disclosure has passed, a member of the general public or media can petition the relevant court for access to any report. When a petition is filed, the individual who is the subject of the report will be given notice of it and the opportunity to argue against inspection/disclosure at a private hearing before the court. If the individual does not seek a hearing, the court should release the entire report, with no redactions.[82]

If the subject of the report objects to the release of any information in the report, the court must weigh the subject's privacy interests against the potential benefit to the public from the release of the report and redact any personal information accordingly. The court should not redact any information that is not "personal" in nature. Details of a defendant's family background; his/her medical and psychological condition; financial status; military record; and history of substance abuse may be personal information that could be redacted at a defendant's request.[83]

The federal court system is much more conservative in granting public access to probation reports. Although Rule 32(c) of the Federal Rules of Criminal Procedure does not absolutely prohibit disclosure of probation reports to non parties, the courts' predominant interpretation has been to limit circulation of these materials to those who are able to show that the balance of interests favors disclosure. The press or the public may be able to meet this requirement in certain cases.[84]

B. PRE-SENTENCING DIAGNOSTIC REPORTS.

California Penal Code section 1203.03 provides that when a defendant is convicted of a crime for which he can be sentenced to state prison, the court has the discretion to order the defendant

---

[80]   California Rule of Court 4.411.5 describes the categories of information that are supposed to be included in probation reports, which are referred to as "presentence reports."

[81]   Penal Code section 1203.05(a); *People v. Connor*, 115 Cal. App. 4th 669, 691, 696 (2004).

[82]   *People v. Connor*, 115 Cal. App. 4th 669, 696-98 (2004).

[83]   *People v. Connor*, 115 Cal. App. 4th 669, 695 (2004).

[84]   *See, e.g., U. S. v. Schlette*, 842 F.2d 1574, 1578 (9th Cir. 1988).

temporarily committed to a facility for a diagnostic examination to determine if the defendant is in need of any special treatment. Penal Code section 1203.03 also provides that the diagnostic reports prepared by the facility are confidential and may only be disclosed to people not expressly granted access (e.g., the judge and prosecuting attorney) upon permission of the defendant.

C. ADOPTION RECORDS.

Judicial records relating to the adoption of a child are generally confidential, pursuant to Family Code section 9200 and the following sections.

D. VICTIM STATEMENTS.

In 1988, California's Legislature enacted Penal Code section 1191.15, which permits a crime victim or his parent, guardian or next of kin to file with the trial court in a criminal case a "written, audiotaped or videotaped statement expressing his or her views concerning the crime, the person responsible, and the need for restitution." Recorded victim statements, an alternative to the victim's right to appear personally and express his or her views at the time of sentencing, must be considered by the court "prior to imposing judgment and sentence."

The section adds, however, that a written transcript of such statements becomes public only after judgment and sentence, and that the originals of the statements, *e.g.*, the tapes themselves, may not be copied. It is not clear whether the public is given the right to listen to or view these tapes without copying them, although the judge, prosecutor, defense attorney and probation officer are expressly authorized to do so, but no earlier than two days prior to sentencing.

E. INDIGENT DEFENSE FUNDING.

Penal Code section 987.9 provides that in the trial of a capital or second-degree murder case, an indigent defendant may apply to the court for a financial subsidy for his or her defense expenses – covering costs of attorneys, investigators and expert witnesses. The fact that such an application has been made and its contents are confidential.

F. WIRETAP RECORDS.

Use of information obtained by law enforcement authorities from electronic surveillance is governed by Title III of the Federal Omnibus Crime Control and Safe Streets Act of 1968, as amended (18 U.S. Code sections 2510-2520). Although the statute does not specifically address the circumstances under which public disclosure of wiretap material may be permitted, courts have permitted public access to such materials once they have been admitted into evidence in a public judicial proceeding.[85] While courts generally have declined to recognize any absolute rule against disclosure, they typically have given considerable weight to countervailing privacy and fair trial interests that disclosure may compromise.

G. CRIMINAL HISTORY INFORMATION.

Penal Code Section 13300 restricts access to "[l]ocal summary criminal history information," commonly known as "rap sheets," which is defined as "the master record of information compiled by any local criminal justice agency ... pertaining to the identification and criminal history of any

---

[85]   *United States v. Cianfrani*, 573 F.2d 835 (1978).

person, such as name, date of birth, physical description, dates of arrests, arresting agencies and booking numbers, charges, dispositions, and similar data about the person." Members of the media and public may obtain such information only "upon a showing of a compelling need."

A California court of appeal has held that a computer database maintained by a county court containing the names, birthdates and zip codes of criminal defendants, along with certain details of their alleged offenses and prosecution, fell within the scope of section 13300 and therefore was not subject to public inspection. The court dismissed out of hand the plaintiff's citation to case law recognizing a general right of access to court records. None of those decisions were controlling, the court reasoned, "because this case involves a contrary statute and a countervailing public policy."[86]

The California attorney general recently issued an opinion that local district attorneys are prohibited by California law (in particular Penal Code sections 13300-13305) from disclosing parole status or criminal history information about people recently arrested, or any details of their prior offenses.[87]

H. COPIES OF COURT AND DEPOSITION TRANSCRIPTS.

The fees for copies of court transcripts are set by statute. California Government Code section 69954 prohibits anyone who has purchased a transcript from providing or selling a copy or copies to any other party or person, except pursuant to court order or rule, or for internal use. Rather, additional copies must be purchased from the court reporter. Whether enforcement of this provision against the media is consistent with the First Amendment is open to question.

I. ELECTRONIC COURT RECORDS.

California Government Code section 68150 provides that trial court records may be preserved in electronic form. The statute states that such records "shall be made reasonably accessible to all members of the public for viewing and duplication as would the paper records," and that "[r]easonable provision shall be made for duplicating the records at cost." The Judicial Council of California has adopted a new standard providing guidance on access to electronic records. The standard gives each county the discretion to adopt its own policy regarding electronic access to court records and strongly encourages that electronic records should be made available one case at a time.

The extent to which the qualified access rights apply to so-called "enhanced" electronic services, which make information about the courts more readily available to the public in electronic form, typically for a fee and sometimes on a for-profit basis, has not yet been extensively explored by the courts. However, a United States district court has ruled that an automated civil case management system established by the Los Angeles courts "is not the type of court record to which [media] have a First Amendment right of access."[88] However, the Superior Court of Santa Clara County settled a case seeking access to an electronic database of docket information (the name of the case, the parties and the events that had occurred in the case), agreeing to make that information available to a newspaper in electronic form for most cases.[89]

---

[86] *Westbrook v. County of Los Angeles*, 27 Cal.App.4th 157 (1994).

[87] 89 Ops. Cal. Atty. Gen. 204, Opinion No. 06-203 (September 20, 2006).

[88] *Los Angeles Times v. County of Los Angeles*, 956 F.Supp. 1530 (C.D. Cal. 1996).

[89] *San Jose Mercury News v. Superior Court of California*, County of Santa Clara, Case No. C 01-20999 (RMW) (N.D. Cal. 2002).

PART V:
RECORDS OF COURT ADMINISTRATION

As explained earlier in this chapter, court records generally are not governed by the California Public Records Act (one limited exception is in Government Code Section 6261, relating to court expenditures), but rather are subject to common law and constitutional rules of access. Records of court administration are "court records" in the sense that they reflect the administration of the judicial system, although perhaps not the details of any particular judicial proceeding. It remains to be seen how the new state constitutional right of access to "the writings of public officials and agencies" will be applied to the court system and court administrative records.[90]

A California court of appeal has explained that the qualified common law and constitutional rights of access apply to all "documentation which accurately and officially reflects the work of the court," specifically including scheduling and administration of cases, assignment of judicial officers and administrators, and the master calendar. The court also ruled, however, that preliminary or draft documents, such as judges' personal notes made during trial, court reporters' original notes, and other kinds of preliminary writings and "rough records" that "may contain tentative or erroneous information or conclusions" are not subject to public inspection. Applying this distinction, the court ruled that because the superior court clerks' "initial or 'rough' minutes" reflect ministerial action by the clerk, are presumably accurate and are "the one repository of easy access which provides a continuous chronology of each court's daily activities," they are subject to the qualified rights of access.[91]

---

[90]   *See* California Constitution Article I Section 3(b)(1).
[91]   *Copley Press v. Superior Court*, 6 Cal. App. 4th 106, 114-115 (1992).

CHAPTER 11

Access to Public and Private Areas and to Government Officials

IN THIS CHAPTER

Courts have recognized that certain places, known as public forums, have been traditionally accessible for speech activities. They also recognize that a high burden must be met before conduct protected by the First Amendment may be restricted. Journalists have special rights to be in certain places and under certain circumstances when access to the public may be restricted. Journalists do not enjoy greater rights to access private property than the general public.

PART I:
INTRODUCTION

The courts have recognized that certain places – such as parks and sidewalks – have traditionally been used for conduct protected by the First Amendment. Such places are called "public forums," and a high standard must be met before conduct protected by the First Amendment can be restricted in these areas.[1] Other areas, not traditionally open to the public for speech- or petition-related activities, are called "nonpublic forums." Restrictions on conduct in these areas need only be reasonable, and they are generally upheld.[2] Finally, there is a third category of areas, called "limited public forums" or "limited purpose public forums." These are areas that have not traditionally been made open to the public but have become public forums for at least some purposes because the government body that regulates a particular area has made it available for use by the public, at least at certain times or for certain purposes. A high standard must be met to regulate conduct in limited purpose public forums if that conduct fits within the time or purpose for which the place has been made open.[3] The First Amendment provides some degree of protection for gathering information.[4] If an area is a public forum or a limited public forum, a greater burden must be met before conduct protected by the First Amendment can be prohibited or limited in that area. If a reporter or a member of the public is trying to gather information in a public forum, attempts by the government to limit or prohibit information-gathering may be improper.

Under the First Amendment, the California Public Records Act, the Ralph M. Brown Act and most other state and federal laws, members of the media generally do not enjoy any greater rights than members of the public. Media representatives usually do not favor special rights for the media. When members of the media are granted special rights, someone – often a government agency – must determine whether a particular person is entitled to exercise those special rights. The practical result is to give government the power to "accredit" certain news representatives or

---

[1]   *See, e.g., Virginia Pharmacy Board v. Virginia Citizens Consumer Council*, 425 U.S. 748, 771 (1976) (in order to be valid, restrictions on protected activities must be "justified without reference to the content of the regulated speech," must "serve a significant governmental interest" and must "leave open ample alternative channels for communication of the information").

[2]   *See, e.g., Perry Educ. Ass'n v. Perry Local Educators' Ass'n*, 460 U.S. 37, 46 (1983).

[3]   *See, e.g., Perry Educ. Ass'n v. Perry Local Educators' Ass'n*, 460 U.S. 37, 45-46 (1983).

[4]   *See, e.g., Branzburg v. Hayes*, 408 U.S. 665,681 (1972); *Davis v. East Baton Rouge Parish School Board,* 78 F. 3d 920, 926-28 (5th Cir. 1996); *Shoen v. Schoen*, 5 F.3d 1289, 1292-93 (9th Cir. 1993).

organizations. It is dangerous to give the government authority to determine who is a member of the media – and, therefore, entitled to special rights – and who is not.

There are some situations, however, in which members of the media have been given special rights of access or subjected to special restrictions. These special rights and restrictions are explored in this chapter. In addition, state law creates certain rights or restrictions that apply to the public generally, including reporters. This chapter also discusses certain situations in which the rights of access of both the media and the public are the same.

PART II:
ACCESS TO DISASTER SITES, CRIME SCENES AND MILITARY AREAS

A. DISASTER SCENES

Law enforcement officers have the right to restrict the general public from accessing disaster and emergency scenes such as fires and accidents.[5] Unlawful entry by the general public constitutes a misdemeanor.[6] Under the California Penal Code, however, "a duly authorized representative of any news service, newspaper, or radio or television station or network" has a right to be present at the scene of disasters and emergencies.[7] The California attorney general has concluded that this exemption prevents law enforcement officials from keeping the media out of disaster and emergency areas provided individual reporters and photographers can present some evidence (*e.g.*, a media badge) issued by their employer to indicate they are "authorized representatives" of a newspaper or other news organization. The attorney general's opinion specifically rejects the argument that "duly authorized" means only those authorized by law enforcement.[8]

The Penal Code does not necessarily grant an absolute right of access to the scenes of all newsworthy events. For example, a news reporter was arrested while gathering news on public property regarding a jetliner crash in a residential section of a city. The court of appeal held that the Penal Code does not override the traditional right of law enforcement to exclude the media from crime scenes.[9]

In addition, the California Penal Code does not grant a right of access irrespective of other property rights. If the disaster is on private property (*e.g.*, an amusement park, a shopping mall or other private property), or involves the military, reporters entering the area may not be exempt from arrest. (See the discussions on military emergency scenes and private property below). In these situations, while an officer may not be entitled to arrest a reporter for violation of the Penal Code, the officer may be permitted to arrest the reporter under criminal trespass statutes.

---

[5]   California Penal Code section 409.5(a).
[6]   California Penal Code section 409.5(c).
[7]   California Penal Code section 409.5(d).
[8]   67 Ops. Cal Atty. Gen. 535 (1984). (Note that opinions of the California attorney general are considered persuasive but are not binding on courts. *Shapiro v. Board of Directors*, 134 Cal. App. 4th 170, 183 n. 17 (2005).)
[9]   *Leiserson v. City of San Diego*, 184 Cal. App. 3d 41 (1986).

B. CRIME AND TACTICAL OPERATIONS SCENES.

Unlike disaster scenes, the media may have no special legal right of access to crime or tactical operation scenes. A California court has ruled that crime scenes may be closed to all unauthorized people, including the media.[10]

The primary concerns of law enforcement agencies at a crime scene are personal safety and the preservation of evidence. Given the uncertainty in the law, a reporter who attempts to enter a crime scene without the permission of the investigating agency could be arrested and charged with interfering with a police investigation, violating a police order or other crimes. As a practical matter, reporters should be prepared to show that they are actually employed by the media, and they should get permission before entering crime scenes. It is always important to work with law enforcement officials to identify a way that allows observation without creating undue danger or interfering with police operations.

C. MILITARY AREAS.

The media's rights of access to emergency and disaster scenes are substantially curtailed when the military is involved. Restrictions on access to military sites have generally been upheld. For example, a federal court ruled against media access to view caskets of deceased soldiers on military property, holding that the First Amendment does not create any *per se* right of access to government property or activities.[11]

1. Military Accident Scenes and "National Defense Areas."

According to the California attorney general, when military equipment is involved in an accident off federal property (*e.g.*, a military plane crash occurring off base), the original base commander has authority to cordon off the impact zone as a National Defense Area for the duration of the rescue, investigation and recovery of the people and equipment involved.[12] Federal law makes it a misdemeanor to enter the area without authorization.[13]

The California attorney general has also concluded that the California Highway Patrol may, upon request of military authorities, assist in enforcing access restrictions under federal law, and it may make arrests if journalists enter a location designated as a National Defense Area without authorization.[14]

2. Combat Troops.

Department of Defense Directive 5122.5 governs decisions regarding media access to combat troops. Enclosure 3 of this directive provides that open and independent reporting shall be the principal means of coverage of U.S. military operations. Enclosure 3 provides for broad media coverage with a few restrictions, including provisions for limited restrictions on media communications for security purposes, expulsion of members of the media who violate rules, and a general statement that special operations restrictions may limit access in some cases. These

---

[10]   *Leiserson v. City of San Diego*, 184 Cal. App. 3d 41 (1986).
[11]   *JB Pictures, Inc. v. Department of Defense*, 86 F.3d 236 (1996).
[12]   66 Ops. Cal. Atty. Gen. 497 (1983).
[13]   United States Code, title 50, section 797 (50 U.S.C. § 797).
[14]   66 Ops. Cal. Atty. Gen. 497 (1983).

restrictions were challenged in a case in which a publisher brought a claim against the Secretary of Defense and U.S. Department of Defense for delaying a reporter's access to U.S. troops in Afghanistan. A federal court upheld the constitutionality of the directive, holding that there is no constitutional right for the press to travel with the military during combat.[15]

3. Photography.

Federal law makes the unauthorized photography or other "graphical representation" of classified (*i.e.*, "top secret," "secret," "confidential" or "restricted") military property a misdemeanor.[16] Publication, sale or exchange of photographs of defense installations without permission from military authorities is a criminal offense.[17] Federal officers – and, where specifically requested to enforce the law, local law enforcement officers such as the CHP – may seize the camera and film of a photographer suspected of violating either the entry or the photography restrictions.[18]

PART III:
PUBLIC SCHOOL GROUNDS

A. THERE IS NO GENERAL RIGHT OF ACCESS TO PUBLIC SCHOOLS UNDER THE FIRST AMENDMENT.

The courts have generally held that public schools are not public forums. "The public schools do not possess all of the attributes of streets, parks, and other traditional public forums that "time out of mind, have been used for purposes of assembly, communicating thoughts between citizens, and discussing public questions."[19] As a result, a public school will generally be considered a public forum only if it has, by policy or in practice, been made available for "indiscriminate use" by the general public.[20]

California has, by law, opened public schools to public use to some extent.[21] However, the law indicates – and the California courts have generally recognized – that restrictions may be imposed on access to public schools to prevent disruption of regular school operations.[22]

---

[15] *Flynt v. Rumsfeld*, 355 F.3d 697 (D.C. Cir. 2004).

[16] United States Code, Title 18, section 795 (18 U.S.C. § 795).

[17] United States Code, Title 18, section 797 (18 U.S.C. § 797).

[18] *See* 66 Ops. Cal. Atty. Gen. 497 (1983).

[19] *Hazlewood School District v. Kuhlmeier*, 484 U.S. 260, 267 (1988); *Planned Parenthood of Southern Nevada, Inc. v. Clark County School District*, 941 F.2d 817, 822 (9th Cir. 1991).

[20] *Hazlewood School District v. Kuhlmeier*, 484 U.S. 260, 267 (1988).

[21] Under California law "[t]here is a civic center at each and every public school facility and grounds within the state where the citizens ... may engage in supervised recreational activities, and where they may meet and discuss, from time to time, as they may desire, any subjects and questions which in their judgment pertain to the educational, political, economic, artistic, and moral interests of the citizens of the communities in which they reside." Education Code section 38131. However, another part of the act establishing such "civic centers" provides that the control of school facilities is vested in the governing board of the school district, which is to promulgate regulations necessary to ensure that "the use of school facilities or grounds is not inconsistent with the use of the school facilities or grounds for school purposes or interferes with the regular conduct of schoolwork." Education Code section 38133.

[22] A school administration may constitutionally limit access by outsiders, regardless of their message or purpose, in order to prevent disruption. *Reeves v. Rocklin Unified School Dist.*, 109 Cal. App. 4th 652, 654 (2003). The courts have held that the purpose of the California statues regarding the establishment of "civic centers" at public schools is "'to make school buildings centers of free public assembly insofar as such

California law also provides certain protections for the exercise of free speech by public school students,[23] but courts have upheld some restrictions on student speech and conduct that occurs in the public schools.[24] (Student speech and student press rights are discussed in more detail in Chapter 13.)

The public does not have a constitutional right of access to public schools during school hours, unless a particular school or school district has adopted a policy or practice of routinely admitting the public onto school grounds at those times.

B. CALIFORNIA LAW GOVERNING ACCESS TO PUBLIC SCHOOLS.

1. Reporters are not required to register before entering public schools.

Section 627.2 of the California Penal Code requires all "outsiders" to register with the principal (or designated official) before entering the buildings or grounds of a public school. However, the definition of "outsider" expressly excludes reporters and other media representatives.[25] Thus, California law provides that reporters may enter the grounds and buildings of a public school without prior permission.[26]

2. Schools may nonetheless try to impose restrictions on media access.

Contrary to existing statutory law, an opinion from the California attorney general, often cited by school administrators, argues that reasonable restrictions may be placed upon members of the news media when they seek access to school grounds.[27] According to the attorney general's opinion, the Legislature has not authorized unlimited and unrestricted access to school premises by news media representatives or anyone else,[28] and school officials may deny access to members of the news media, as they may deny access to anyone, if their presence would interfere with the peaceful conduct of the activities of the school.[29]

The attorney general's opinion asserts that school administrators may require members of the news media to follow reasonable conditions while they are on school grounds in order to prevent

---

assembly does not encroach upon the educational activities, which constitute the primary purpose of the schools." *Howard Jarvis Taxpayers Ass'n. v. Whittier Union High School Dist.*, 15 Cal. App. 4th 730, 735 (1993), quoting *Ellis v. Board of Education*, 27 Cal. 2d 322, 329 (1945). It has also been held that this limitation permits school officials to prohibit a use that the statute would otherwise permit, if it would disrupt normal school operations. *Payroll Guar. Assn. v. Bd. of Education*, 27 Cal. 2d 197, 202-203 (1945).

23   *See* Education Code sections 48907, 48950.

24   *See, e.g., Lopez v. Tulare Joint Union High School District*, 34 Cal. App. 4th 1302 (1995).

25   *See* Penal Code section 627.1. An outsider is defined in part as "any person other than ... [a] person who comes within the provisions of Section 1070 of the Evidence Code by virtue of his or her current employment or occupation." Cal. Pen. Code § 627.1(a)(7). Section 1070 of the Evidence Code applies to "a publisher, editor, reporter, or other person connected with or employed upon a newspaper, magazine, or other periodical publication, or by a press association or wire service, or any person who has been so connected or employed," and to "a radio or television news reporter or other person connected with or employed by a radio or television station, or any person who has been so connected or employed. ..." Evidence Code section 1070.

26   *In re Rudolfo A.*, 110 Cal. App. 3d 845, 852 (1980) ("The general laws thus fail to prohibit unauthorized entry or presence on school grounds except under particular circumstances ...").

27   79 Cal. Ops. Atty. Gen. 58 (1996).

28   79 Cal. Ops. Atty. Gen. 58 (1996).

29   79 Cal. Ops. Atty. Gen. 58 (1996).

interference with the orderly educational activities of the school.[30] These conditions may restrict the news media representatives in the same manner that access by members of the general public may be limited, *i.e.,* requiring registration, accompaniment by a staff member while on school grounds, and denial of permission to enter classes that are in session.[31]

However, the opinion also concludes that school administrators may not require parental permission before allowing members of the news media to interview students because students have a federal constitutional right to freedom of speech.[32] Under California law, students have the right to exercise freedom of speech and of the press including, but not limited to, the use of bulletin boards, the distribution of printed materials or petitions, the wearing of buttons, badges and other insignia, and the right of expression in official publications, except that expression shall be prohibited which is obscene, libelous or slanderous.[33] Accordingly, school officials may not impose prior restraints upon students except in limited circumstances.[34] Requiring parental permission for a student interview would constitute an impermissible prior restraint.[35]

The validity of the attorney general's opinion is open to question. At least with respect to requiring reporters to register before going on school grounds, it appears to be directly contrary to California law. Moreover, unlike a court decision, it does not establish a controlling rule for how the law is to be applied. However, some school districts have adopted registration requirements for journalists. As of the date of this publication, the courts have not addressed the legality of the press registration requirement.

3. Reporters and members of the public may be required to leave public schools if requested to do so.

California law provides that people who are not pupils, parents or employees of a public school, and who are not required by their employment to be at a public school, must leave the school if requested to do so by the principal or the designee of the principal.[36] A request that someone leave the school can only be made on the basis that "it appears reasonable to the principal, or the designee of the principal to conclude that the continued presence of the person requested to depart would be disruptive of, or would interfere with, classes or other activities of the public school program."[37]

Failing to leave after being requested to do so, pursuant to this standard, is a misdemeanor, punishable pursuant to section 626.8 of the Penal Code.[38] However, a person may not be convicted under this section of the Penal Code unless: (1) the person was present at the school "without lawful business thereon"; (2) the person's presence or acts "interfere with the peaceful conduct of the activities of the school or disrupt the school or its pupils or school activities"; and

---

[30]   79 Cal. Ops. Atty. Gen. 58 (1996).

[31]   79 Cal. Ops. Atty. Gen. 58 (1996).

[32]   79 Cal. Ops. Atty. Gen. 58 (1996).

[33]   Education Code section 48907. Also prohibited is material that so incites students as to create a clear and present danger of the commission of unlawful acts on school premises or the violation of lawful school regulations, or the substantial disruption of the orderly operation of the school. Education Code section 48907. *See also* Education Code section 48950 (school districts shall not make or enforce any rule subjecting any high school pupil to disciplinary sanctions solely on the basis of conduct that is speech or other communication that, when engaged in outside of the campus, is protected from governmental restriction by the First Amendment to the United States Constitution or the California Constitution).

[34]   79 Cal. Ops. Atty. Gen. 58 (1996).

[35]   79 Cal. Ops. Atty. Gen. 58 (1996).

[36]   *See* Education Code section 32211.

[37]   Education Code section 32211.

[38]   *See* Education Code section 32211.

(3) the person remains on or returns to the school grounds within seven days after being asked to leave.[39]

If you are asked to leave, you may appeal to the superintendent of the school district where the school is located. An appeal must be made "not later than the second succeeding school day" following your departure. The superintendent must consider the appeal and render a decision within 24 hours. The superintendent's decision may be appealed to the school board. The appeal must be made by the second succeeding school day, and the school board must decide the appeal at its next scheduled regular public meeting. The decision of the school board is final.[40] Reporters have recourse to the courts if they disagree with the school board's decision.

PART IV:
STATE PRISONS, JAILS AND PAROLE BOARD HEARINGS

A. GENERAL RULES OF ACCESS.

Because of overriding security concerns, authorities have broad discretion to control public access to state prisons and county jails. In general, the media have no special rights to access these facilities.

The U.S. Supreme Court has held that the media does not have a greater right to access jails or prisons than the public at large, concluding that "the Constitution does not require government to accord the media special access to information not shared by members of the public generally."[41] The same principal was applied in a California case involving access to a restricted portion of a county jail.[42]

The right of the public to visit state prisons and county jails is extremely limited. Until 1996, state regulations permitted special access to prisons by members of the media who made a request for face-to-face interviews with particular prisoners. In 1996, the California Department of Corrections, citing the decisions of the United States Supreme Court, passed a regulation that abruptly eliminated this right of access. Presently, journalists may only conduct interviews of inmates: (1) after being placed on an inmate's visitor list or (2) if on a tour of a prison facility. Reporters may not conduct interviews of specifically requested inmates.[43] Further, the head of the institution must preapprove the use of cameras or other recording equipment.

Several bills were passed by the California Legislature to restore the ability of reporters to conduct face-to-face interviews with inmates while using the tools of the trade to take notes. These bills were vetoed by governors Pete Wilson, Gray Davis and Arnold Schwarzenegger.

While many of California's counties have created policies on access to jails modeled after the Department of Corrections' regulation, some counties continue to allow access to jail inmates. If you want access to a particular jail inmate, check the access policy of the county where the inmate is housed.

---

[39] *See* Penal Code section 626.8. Section 32211 of the Education Code prohibits returning to the school within seven days of being asked to leave. Penal Code section 626.8 also prohibits returning within seven days of being asked to leave.

[40] Education Code section 32211(c).

[41] *Pell v. Procunier*, 417 U.S. 817 (1974).

[42] *Houchins v. KQED*, 438 U.S. 1 (1978).

[43] California Code of Regulations, Title 15, Div. 3, Ch. 1, section 3261.5.

B. ACCESS TO EXECUTIONS.

Although the media and the public do not have a constitutional right of access to prisons, the media and public do have a constitutional right to attend judicial proceedings, including trials, jury selection and preliminary hearings. (This right is discussed more fully in Chapter 8). The potential conflict between these two rules came to a head in a 1990 lawsuit over the right of the media to attend and broadcast executions inside a California state prison.

Executions in California were conducted in public until 1858, when they were moved inside county jails. In 1891, executions were moved inside state prisons. Under California Penal Code Section 3605, the warden is required to invite certain official witnesses to an execution, as well as "at least 12 reputable citizens." In 1991, the California Court of Appeal held that: (1) wardens may not exclude all media representatives from witnessing the execution; and (2) media representatives may use paper and pencils to note their observations; but (3) the media has no right to use cameras in the execution witness area.[44]

In 2002, a federal appellate court struck down a regulation restricting media access to lethal injections. At issue was a prison regulation allowing witnesses to view the lethal injection process only after the condemned had already been strapped to the gurney and an intravenous saline solution started. The Ninth Circuit Court of Appeals found the regulation was unconstitutional because it was an exaggerated response to defendants' concerns about the safety of prison personnel.[45]

PART V:
PRIVATE PROPERTY

Members of the media have no greater right to access private property than the general public. There is no general statutory or constitutional privilege to enter private lands or structures without the consent of the lawful possessor simply because the purpose is to gather news. Furthermore, the definition of "private" is not limited to a fixed structure or parcel of privately owned land. For example, the California Supreme Court has held that there is a triable issue of fact as to whether people injured in an automobile accident on a public highway have a reasonable expectation of privacy after they have been placed inside a rescue helicopter at the accident site.[46]

A. TYPES OF TRESPASS.

Trespass is discussed in more detail in Chapter 12 ("Legal Perils in Newsgathering"). However, some of the basic concerns regarding access to private property and the law of trespass are also discussed below.

California Penal Code section 602 imposes misdemeanor criminal liability for trespass under a wide variety of circumstances, including the following: (1) Entering any lands, enclosed or not, for the purpose of injuring any property or interfering with any lawful business or occupation being conducted on the property;[47] (2) driving on land not known to be open to the public without the consent of the owner, agent or lawful possessor;[48] (3) refusing or failing to leave private

---

[44] *KQED v. Vasquez*, 18 Media L. Rep 2323 (1991).

[45] *California First Amendment Coalition v. Woodford*, 299 F.3d 868 (9th Cir. 2002).

[46] *Shulman v. Group W. Productions, Inc.*, 18 Cal. 4th 200 (1998).

[47] Penal Code section 602(k).

[48] Penal Code section 602(n).

property when asked to do so by the owner, agent or lawful possessor, or by a peace officer who the owner, agent or possessor has requested to ask the intruder to leave;[49] or (4) refusing to leave a public building during hours when the building is regularly closed to the public upon being requested to do so by a regularly employed guard, watchman or custodian, if the surrounding circumstances would indicate to a reasonable person that the person has no apparent lawful business to pursue.[50]

If reporters or members of the public refuse to leave private property when requested to do so, several possible sanctions can be imposed. First, they could be held criminally liable. Second, they could be sued in a civil action for trespass. Third, they could be sued in a civil action for invasion of privacy. (See Chapter 12, *Legal Perils in Newsgathering*, for a more detailed discussion.)

Trespass is a "strict liability" offense, which means that a person can be held liable even without knowing that he or she was committing a trespass or intending to do so. No court in California or elsewhere has excused a reporter or a member of the public from trespass charges on First Amendment grounds. Note, however, that the broad prohibition on failing to leave private property when asked is subject to a statutory exception providing that it "shall not apply to persons on the premises who are engaging in activities protected by the California or United States Constitution."[51]

B. BUSINESS ESTABLISHMENTS.

1. Businesses Generally.

In general, retail establishments are no different from other types of private property. A proprietor generally has the right to restrict access to the premises. For example, a television news crew filmed the interior of a restaurant over the objections of the proprietor. This action was held to constitute not only an unprivileged civil trespass, but also a willful violation of the owner's rights justifying substantial punitive damages.[52] A federal court upheld an action for trespass where undercover investigative reporters obtained employment at a supermarket and secretly filmed activities in the store's meat department.[53] The California Supreme Court held that a telepsychic had stated a claim for invasion of privacy, where a reporter had posed as a coworker and secretly recorded conversations in the workplace.[54]

2. Shopping Centers and Other Privately Owned Public Places.

In the groundbreaking 1979 California case *Robins v. Pruneyard Shopping Center*, the California Supreme Court held that the free speech provisions of the California constitution – which are more expansive than those of the federal constitution – protect "reasonably exercised" speech and petitioning activities in privately owned shopping centers.[55] In more recent years, however, California courts have narrowed the reach of *Pruneyard*.

---

[49]   Penal Code section 602(o).
[50]   Penal Code section 602(q).
[51]   Penal Code section 602(o).
[52]   *LeMistral v. CBS*, 61 A.D. 2d 491 (1978).
[53]   *Food Lion, Inc. v. Capital Cities/ABC, Inc.*, 194 F.3d 505 (4th Cir. 1999).
[54]   *Sanders v. American Broadcasting Companies, Inc.*, 20 Cal. 4th 907 (1999).
[55]   23 Cal. 3d 899, 910 (1979). The United States Supreme Court held that construing the California Constitution to allow free speech activity on private property did not violate any federal constitutional rights of the property owners. *Pruneyard Shopping Center v. Robins*, 447 U.S. 74 (1980).

In 1999, a Trader Joe's store in Santa Rosa obtained a preliminary injunction against individuals gathering petition signatures on the property.[56] The court that upheld the injunction said that although a stand-alone store like Trader Joe's has opened itself to the public, it has not invited the public to congregate there or do anything other than shop for food and that it was therefore not the kind of public forum that property owners must yield to free speech activities like petitioning.[57] Subsequent decisions considering petitioning and related free speech rights at stand-alone retail establishments followed this reasoning and allowed the property owners to significantly restrict the speech activities.[58]

In a similar case, the California Supreme Court held that the owner of a private apartment complex could prevent a tenant association from distributing unsolicited newsletters to apartments in the complex because the complex, unlike the shopping center in *Pruneyard*, was not the equivalent of a traditional public forum.[59]

These cases do not specifically address information gathering. Nonetheless, they suggest that the owners of businesses or other places open to the public generally have the ability to restrict information-gathering activities on their premises. However, the closer the place in question is to what the courts call a traditional public forum (that is, a place where people congregate to speak, eat and spend time), the stronger the public's interest in gathering news there and the less likely it is that courts will impose liability for trespass.

C. PRIVATE RESIDENCES.

A California court has ruled that a television news crew was not protected by the First Amendment from a suit for trespass, invasion of privacy, and intentional infliction of emotional distress stemming from its filming of fire department paramedics' response to a Los Angeles home emergency. Although the homeowner was present when the paramedics and television news team arrived and permitted entry into her home, the court dismissed the notion that a journalist can borrow the consent given by a homeowner to police or rescue officials who enter a home to provide assistance: "Newsgatherers cannot immunize their conduct by purporting to act jointly with public officials."[60]

More recently, the U.S. Supreme Court held that homeowners asserted a valid state law claim for trespass against a film crew for entering their ranch and being present during the execution of a search warrant that only authorized law enforcement officers to be on the property. The court reasoned that although the federal officers' initial entry onto the ranch was lawful, the homeowners never consented to the entry of a media-owned microphone that one of the officers wore. The warrant did not authorize the media film crew to accompany the officers and videotape the search for the non-governmental purpose of newsgathering.[61]

---

[56]   *Trader Joe's Company v. Progressive Campaigns, Inc.*, 73 Cal. App. 4th 425 (1999).

[57]   *Id.* at 433.

[58]   *See Costco Companies, Inc. v. Gallant*, 96 Cal. App. 4th 740 (2002); Albertson's, Inc. v. Young, 107 Cal. App. 4th 106 (2003); *see also, e.g., Hamburg v. Wal-Mart Stores, Inc.*, 116 Cal. App. 4th 497 (2004) (reversing grant of summary judgment to store on protesters' claims that they had been falsely arrested by Wal-Mart employees).

[59]   *Golden Gateway Center v. Golden Gateway Tenants Ass'n*, 26 Cal. 4th 1013, 1033 (2001).

[60]   *Miller v. National Broadcasting Company*, 187 Cal. App. 3d 1463 (1986).

[61]   *Hanlon v. Berger*, 526 U.S. 808 (1999).

D. LANDLORDS AND RENTED PREMISES.

As a civil wrong, trespass is a violation of the rights of the lawful possessor of real property – the person actually occupying the land or with immediate rights to occupy it – rather than those of the owner. When an owner has leased or rented commercial or residential property to a tenant, it is the tenant and not the owner whose rights are protected by the law of trespass. Thus, a journalist invited onto the premises by the lawful tenant is not liable in a trespass action by the landlord. This point can be of some significance in reporting or photographically documenting the complaints of a tenant against his landlord. So long as the tenant is in lawful possession of the premises, only the permission of the tenant is necessary for the reporter to enter.

PART VI:
ACCESS TO GOVERNMENT OFFICIALS

A complete discussion of constitutional and statutory protections for and restrictions on the ability of the public to obtain information from government officials, and of government officials to provide information, is beyond the scope of this publication. However, some basic principals applicable to the dissemination of information by public officials are provided below.

First, under California law, government officials have the same protection as members of the public and the press when they disseminate information about subjects of public interest. In general, this means that they will not be subject to liability for disclosing information about matters of public concern unless the party seeking to hold them liable can prove that the information is false.[62] Furthermore, government officials cannot be held liable for disseminating even false information about prominent public figures, unless it is to show that they knew the information was false or disseminated it with reckless disregard of its truth or falsity.[63]

Second, California law also imposes some restrictions on the ability of public officials to disclose information. For example (as discussed in greater detail in Chapter 1), under the Ralph M. Brown Act members of public bodies such as city councils and boards of supervisors may be subject to misdemeanor criminal liability for improperly disclosing information discussed in a closed session held pursuant to the terms of the Brown Act.[64]

Third, the First Amendment may limit the ability of government officials to selectively disclose information. For example, in a recent California case, a federal district court determined that a city's exclusion of one television station from a public ceremony, while permitting another station to cover the same event, violated the excluded station's First Amendment rights.[65] However, a federal appellate court recently upheld a governor's instruction prohibiting public employees from communicating with reporters for a particular newspaper.[66]

---

[62]   *Nizam-Aldine v. City of Oakland,* 47 Cal. App. 4th 364 (1996).

[63]   *Nadel v. Regents of the University of California,* 28 Cal. App. 4th 1251 (1994); *Bradbury v. Superior Court,* 49 Cal. App. 4th 1108 (1996).

[64]   Government Code section 54963.

[65]   *Telemundo v. City of Los Angeles,* 238 F.Supp.2d 1095 (C.D. Cal. 2003).

[66]   *Baltimore Sun Co. v. Ehrlich,* 437 F.3d 410 (4th Cir. 2006).

CHAPTER 12

Legal Perils In Newsgathering

IN THIS CHAPTER

In some circumstances, obtaining information – "newsgathering" – can create legal risks. This chapter addresses concerns that arise from how information is obtained. The primary areas of concern are: (1) Getting and using information that others are supposed to keep confidential; (2) impersonating another person or otherwise using misrepresentations to obtain information; (3) committing trespass – entering property without permission in order to obtain information; (4) intruding into private places or private information; and (5) using technology to obtain or record information without consent. These are concerns primarily for professional journalists, but most of them can affect anyone who is trying to obtain information.

PART I:
INTRODUCTION

Although "illegal conduct by a reporter is not privileged simply because the ultimate purpose is to obtain information to publish. ... the First Amendment protects the ordinary newsgathering techniques of reporters."[1] The line separating "ordinary newsgathering techniques" from illegal conduct, however, is not always clear.

The press has considerable latitude with respect to seeking out and receiving confidential information. However, using actual deception to gather information – particularly by impersonating someone else – can trigger both civil and criminal liability. When gathering information, reporters and others need to be aware of the potential for liability for unreasonably intruding into the privacy of others and trespassing on others' property. Because technology – audio and video recording devices, in particular – enhances the ability to capture information that might be considered private, use of such devices also warrants special consideration.

PART II:
CONFIDENTIAL INFORMATION AND DOCUMENTS

The freedom to gather news includes protection for receiving confidential information, as long as the journalist does not break the law to obtain it. California courts recognize that "the news gathering component of freedom of the press – the right to seek out information – is privileged at least to the extent it involves 'routine ... reporting techniques.' Such techniques, of course, include asking persons questions, including those with confidential or restricted

---

[1] *Nicholson v. McClatchy Newspapers*, 177 Cal. App. 3d 509, 512-13 (1986). *See also Taus v. Loftus*, 40 Cal. 4th 683, 737 (2007) (use of "routine . . . reporting techniques, such as asking questions of people with information (including those with confidential or restricted information) could rarely, if ever, be deemed an actionable intrusion.")

information."[2] They also typically include obtaining and reviewing court records and other public records, attending meetings, and observing what takes place in places to which the public or the press have access.

Generally speaking, reporters are protected from liability for receiving information that was intended to be confidential, even if the source of that information was not supposed to disclose it. For example, the U.S. Supreme Court held that despite a state statute requiring the government to keep the names of sexual offense victims private, it was not unlawful for a newspaper to receive (through an erroneously released police report) and publish the name of a sexual assault victim.[3]

In a key California case, *Nicholson v. McClatchy Newspapers*, a court rejected a claim against a newspaper for reporting the fact that a judicial commission had found the plaintiff unqualified for judicial appointment.[4] The commission's report was supposed to be confidential. The court described the plaintiff's complaint as objecting that "the media defendants sought out the newsworthy information which they subsequently published."[5] Such activity, the court said, is protected by the First Amendment, and state law may not punish it absent justification more compelling than the admittedly important interest in preserving the confidentiality of the commission's report.

Similarly, a reporter who receives copies of leaked documents is generally not liable for receiving them and reporting on any newsworthy contents. For example, a federal court for the District of Columbia rejected the claim that "one who receives information from an intruder, knowing it has been obtained by improper intrusion, is guilty of a tort."[6] The court also found that the reporters were not liable for conversion – a tort that involves the interference with someone's right to control his or her own property – because the reporters received only copies and the documents had no independent economic value as intellectual property or proprietary data.[7] If the reporters had received and refused to return *original* documents, the outcome might have been different. A federal court applying California law found that a television station that had received documents taken from a defense contractor without authorization could be liable for conversion for refusing to return even copies of the documents to the company, which claimed to no longer have its own copies.[8]

However, even receiving originals may not be a violation of criminal law, if the press does not know that the documents were stolen when it receives them. A California newspaper, its owner/editor and a reporter were convicted of receiving stolen property – a document removed from the Office of the Attorney General by a former employee. The California Supreme Court threw out their conviction, but not on First Amendment grounds. Rather, the court found no evidence that the journalists knew the document was stolen, which was an element of the crime.[9]

---

2   *Nicholson v. McClatchy Newspapers*, 177 Cal. App. 3d 509, 519 (1986) (quoting *Smith v. Daily Mail Publishing Co.*, 443 U.S. 97, 103 (1979).

3   *Florida Star v. B.J.F.*, 491 U.S. 524 (1989). The Court did note that "[t]o the extent sensitive information rests in private hands, the government may under some circumstances forbid its nonconsensual acquisition." *Id.* at 534. *See also Bartnicki v. Vopper*, 532 U.S. 514 (2001) (imposition of liability on the media for broadcasting part of a telephone conversation between two union representatives that was illegally recorded by an unknown person violated the First Amendment); *Landmark Communications, Inc. v. Virginia*, 435 U.S. 829 (1978) (unconstitutional for state to punish publication of accurate information about confidential proceedings of a judicial review commission).

4   *Nicholson v. McClatchy Newspapers*, 177 Cal. App. 3d 509, 515-522 (1986).

5   *Nicholson v. McClatchy Newspapers*, 177 Cal. App. 3d 509, 520 (1986).

6   *Pearson v. Dodd*, 410 F.2d 701, 705 (D.C. Cir. 1969).

7   *Pearson v. Dodd*, 410 F.2d 701, 707-708 (D.C. Cir. 1969).

8   *FMC Corp. v. Capital Cities/ABC, Inc.*, 915 F.2d 300 (1990).

9   *People v. Kunkin*, 9 Cal. 3d 245, 255-56 (1973).

More recently, a law firm sued a California newspaper that had obtained and published confidential and privileged documents prepared by the firm on behalf of its client, a provider of electronic voting systems. The law firm claimed that the newspaper was liable for conversion, unfair business practices and misappropriation of trade secrets. Although the law firm obtained an emergency court order requiring the newspaper to return all copies of the documents, the documents were published in print and online on the day the order was issued, which led the law firm to dismiss its action.[10]

PART III:
LEGAL LIMITS ON NEWSGATHERING

Although, as a general matter, reporters and members of the public are free to seek out information that is not readily available, they should take care when their attempts to uncover information involve making misrepresentations to get information, being physically present on private property or looking into private areas of individuals' lives. Civil and criminal liability can result from certain forms of impersonation, trespass and invasion of privacy through intrusion into others' affairs.

A. IMPERSONATION.

Although many newsrooms insist that their reporters identify themselves while gathering the news, there is typically no legal obligation for a person to disclose that he or she is a reporter. However, affirmatively pretending to be someone else may, in some cases, trigger civil or criminal liability.

1. California Laws Criminalize Impersonation.

It is a felony under California law to "falsely personate [] another in either his private or official capacity, and in such assumed character ... [do] any act ... whereby any benefit might accrue to the party personating, or to any other person."[11] Although no reported cases have applied this statute to a journalist, anyone who assumes another person's identity in order to obtain information might be guilty of this crime. Additionally, a series of California statutes prohibits the unauthorized wearing or use of the badge or garb of a fraternal or religious society[12] or the impersonation of a peace officer,[13] fire department officer,[14] public utility employee,[15] or state or local officer or employee.[16]

---

[10]   The newspaper filed a motion to strike the law firm's complaint on the grounds that it was a strategic lawsuit against public participation (SLAPP), in that the law firm's causes of action arose from the activity in furtherance of the newspaper's free speech rights. Although the trial court refused to award the newspaper attorneys' fees due to a prevailing party under the anti-SLAPP statute on the grounds that the law firm's action did not arise from activity in furtherance of the newspaper's free speech rights, the court of appeal reversed that decision and remanded the matter to the trial court to determine whether the newspaper was the prevailing party for anti-SLAPP purposes. *Day v. MediaNews Group*, 2005 Cal. App. Unpub. LEXIS 7876 at ¶. at *8-19, 34 Media L. Rep. 1411 (2005).

[11]   Penal Code section 529.
[12]   Penal Code section 538b.
[13]   Penal Code section 538d.
[14]   Penal Code section 538e.
[15]   Penal Code section 538f.
[16]   Penal Code section 538g.

The California Supreme Court recently suggested that the conduct of a reporter who, in investigating whether a public official has a particular medical condition or is taking a particular medication (information that might otherwise be "newsworthy"), "makes a telephone call to a spouse, adult child, or close friend of the official, pretends to be an emergency room physician or paramedic, and asks the relative or friend to disclose the medical information ostensibly to assist in the treatment of the official" would be "highly offensive" conduct and potentially subject the reporter to a claim for invasion of privacy by intrusion.[17] The Supreme Court expressly distinguished this kind of affirmative misrepresentation from "the more familiar practice of a news reporter or an investigator in shading or withholding information regarding his or her motives when interviewing a potential news source."[18]

2. Impersonation as Basis for Fraud or as Factor in Intrusion Analysis.

A journalist misrepresenting his or her identity to gain entrance to the home of a person in crisis could be liable for damages under theories of fraud or intentional/negligent infliction of emotional distress. A federal court applying California law refused to dismiss such claims against a television crew by a woman who admitted the crew into her home in the aftermath of a domestic violence episode, after members of the crew told her that they were members of a victim assistance program and were filming a segment for the district attorney's office.[19]

Even when impersonation is not in itself actionable, it may still factor into the analysis of whether a journalist has committed the tort of invasion of privacy through intrusion, which is discussed in Section C below. For example, pretending to be an ailing person in order to call on a healer might not by itself constitute an invasion of privacy, but using the deception to gain entry to the healer's home for covert recording and photographing of him would factor into the analysis of the healer's action for intrusion.[20] Similarly, the allegation that a television producer wore the garb of hospital personnel when he obtained consent to the filming of a hospitalized individual might have ultimately factored into the analysis of the patient's privacy claims.[21] In a lawsuit that involved a claim that an investigator misrepresented herself as an associate of a mental health professional to obtain information about an individual, the California Supreme Court held that a jury could find such behavior "highly offensive" and actionable because misrepresentations of this nature "could undermine legitimate professional relationships ... because they would take advantage of the desire and willingness of relatives and friends to provide assistance to professionals who they believe will use any personal information that is revealed to help the subject of the inquiry."[22] In addition, juries may be offended by what they perceive as misrepresentations by reporters and award substantial damages at trial.[23]

---

[17]   *Taus v. Loftus*, 40 Cal. 4th 683, 739 (2007).

[18]   *Taus v. Loftus*, 40 Cal. 4th 683, 740 (2007).

[19]   *Baugh v. CBS, Inc.*, 828 F. Supp. 745 (N.D. Cal. 1993).

[20]   *Dietemann v. Time, Inc.*, 449 F.2d 245 (9th Cir. 1971).

[21]   *Carter v. Superior Court*, 2002 Cal. App. Unpub. LEXIS 5017 * 17. The court in this decision did not reach a substantive analysis of plaintiff's intrusion claim but decided that allegations that the producers "disguised themselves as health care providers and entered into secluded areas in which a reasonable person would have an expectation of privacy" did not relate to acts in furtherance of the producers' free speech rights and were therefore not subject to an anti-SLAPP motion.

[22]   *Taus v. Loftus*, 40 Cal. 4th 683, 740 (2007).

[23]   A jury awarded $5 million in punitive damages against a television production company whose reporters used false resumes to obtain jobs at a grocery store in order to prepare their undercover report on unsanitary conditions at the store. This award was later reduced to $315,000, and the fraud judgment was eventually reversed by an appellate court. *Food Lion v. Capital Cities/ABC, Inc.*, 194 F.3d 305 (4th Cir. 1999).

However, not all impersonation will support a claim for invasion of privacy. Television producers who posed as potential investors to secretly videotape a lunch meeting with business people at an outdoor restaurant where waiters and other individuals could hear the conversation were not liable for invasion of privacy.[24]

3. Pretexting.

The practice of obtaining confidential telephone records by "pretexting" – pretending to be someone authorized to receive the records – was spotlighted in the recent scandal involving technology company Hewlett-Packard's use, through investigators, of pretexting to obtain confidential telephone records of several reporters from online and traditional news organizations ranging from CNET News.com to The New York Times.

California prosecutors charged the former chairwoman of HP and four other individuals with using false or fraudulent pretenses to obtain confidential information from a public utility and other crimes related to HP's alleged spying on the reporters and other individuals, although charges against some were subsequently dropped, and a lenient plea agreement was reached with the others.[25] The statute underlying the criminal action could also apply to any reporter who uses "artifice" to obtain customer records or other data from a California public utility.[26] See also California Penal Code Section 638, which bolsters protection against pretexting by making it a crime to obtain telephone records through fraud or deceit.[27] Bills that would outlaw pretexting have also been submitted in Congress.[28]

B. TRESPASS.

Trespass is the unauthorized entry onto the land of another and can trigger both civil and criminal liability.

The discussion of trespass focuses on private property. In general, the law of trespass does not affect access to public places. The press and the public typically have the right to go onto public property that has traditionally been open to the public, such as streets, sidewalks and parks. Access to public places is discussed in detail in Chapter 11.

1. Civil Trespass.

In California, entering another's property without permission can be grounds for a lawsuit, even if the trespasser believed in good faith that the entry was not wrongful.[29] A news crew

---

[24] *Wilkins v. National Broadcasting Company, Inc.*, 71 Cal. App. 4th 1066, 1078 (1999) ("NBC photographed the two men in a public place and taped their conversations which were about business, not personal matters. There was no intrusion into a private place, conversation or matter.").

[25] Felony Complaint, *People v. Dunn, et al.*, DA No. 061027481 (Santa Clara Super. Ct., Oct. 4, 2006).

[26] *See* Penal Code section 538.5. Penal Code section 538.5 provides that "[e]very person who transmits or causes to be transmitted by means of wire, radio or television communication any words, sounds, writings, signs, signals, or pictures for the purpose of furthering or executing a scheme or artifice to obtain, from a public utility, confidential, privileged, or proprietary information, trade secrets, trade lists, customer records, billing records, customer credit data, or accounting data by means of false or fraudulent pretenses, representations, personations, or promises is guilty of an offense punishable by imprisonment in the state prison, or by imprisonment in the county jail not exceeding one year."

[27] S.B. 202 (Cal. 2006). The legislation adds Section 638 to California's Penal Code.

[28] *See, e.g.,* Consumer Telephone Records Protection Act of 2006, H.R. 4662, 109th Cong. (2006).

[29] *See, e.g., Miller v. National Broadcasting Company,* 187 Cal. App. 3d 1463, 1480-81 (1986).

entering a private home without permission from residents was held to be trespassing even if accompanying police or rescue personnel.[30]

The U.S. Supreme Court held that police violated the Fourth Amendment rights of an arrestee by bringing along a reporter and photographer when they entered a private home to execute an arrest warrant.[31] Similarly, a lower federal court held that a television crew that entered an apartment and filmed secret service agents' search of an apartment for broadcast on a weekly television news magazine was not entitled to qualified immunity in a suit for trespass because the videotape was for the non-governmental purpose of newsgathering.[32] While these cases address the potential liability of law enforcement personnel, they indicate that members of the press or the public could also be subject to liability.

A television producer who attended a private acting workshop undercover after signing an agreement stating that she was attending to practice her acting might have been liable for trespass. Even though she had permission to attend the workshop as an actor, she did not have permission to attend as a reporter, and exceeding the scope of the workshop director's consent may have constituted trespass.[33]

Whether damages for trespass can be based on the effect of making public information obtained through the trespass is not clear.[34] However, even if a trespass does not provide a direct basis for claiming damages resulting from the broadcast or publication of information obtained as a result, it may also give rise to liability for invasion of privacy (which does). Accordingly, journalists should generally be careful to get permission from the owner or lawful tenant before entering a residence or other private area.

2. Criminal Trespass.

A number of state statutory provisions impose criminal liability for trespassing, but some protect newsgathering activities.

a. Refusal to leave others' property. Penal Code section 602(o) makes it a misdemeanor to "[r]efus[e] or fail[] to leave land, real property, or structures belonging to or lawfully occupied by another and not open to the general public, upon being requested to leave by" the owner or a peace officer on the owner's behalf.[35] This provision does not apply, however, to "persons on the premises who are engaging in activities protected by the California or United States

---

30   *Miller v. National Broadcasting Company*, 187 Cal. App. 3d 1463, 1480-81 (1986). *See also, Brunette v. Humane Society of Ventura County*, 40 Fed. Appx. 594, 596, 30 Media L. Rep. 2181 (2002) ("Under California law, the Media is subject to trespass liability, irrespective of whether it caused harm, if it intentionally entered land in possession of another [without consent].")*; Copeland v. Hubbard Broadcasting, Inc.*, 23 Med.L.Rptr. 1441 (Minn. Ct. App. 1995) (Minnesota court held that a homeowner's consent to allow a student to accompany an attending veterinarian for education purposes did not confer an implied privilege on the student to secretly videotape the homeowner and her property for television broadcasting).

31   *Wilson v. Layne*, 526 U.S. 603, 614 (1999); *see also Hanlon v. Berger*, 526 U.S. 808, 809-10 (1999).

32   *Ayeni v. CBS, Inc.*, 848 F.Supp. 362 (E.D.N.Y. 1994).

33   *Turnbull v. American Broadcasting Companies*, 2004 U.S. Dist. LEXIS 24351 at pp. *51-52; 32 Media L. Rep. 2442 (C.D. Cal. 2004)

34   *Compare Miller v. National Broadcasting Company*, 187 Cal. App. 3d 1463, 1481 (1986) (California Court of Appeal indicates that a person sued for trespass could be liable for the direct or indirect consequences of conduct engaged in while trespassing, including the emotional distress caused by the gathering or dissemination of news), and *Medical Laboratory Management Consultants v. ABC, Inc.*, 306 F. 806 (9th Cir. 2002) (Ninth Circuit federal Court of Appeals held that television crew's undercover reporting from a medical laboratory may have been trespass, but lab owner could not claim damages for the broadcast of footage that was secretly obtained during the trespass).

35   Penal Code section 602(o).

Constitution."[36] While there are no cases applying this exemption in the newsgathering context, it would almost certainly immunize a journalist from criminal trespass charges as long as she or he was not engaging in conduct – such as damaging property – that would otherwise be wrongful. Note, however, that there is a separate misdemeanor offense, discussed below, for entering or refusing to leave a residential building.

b. Intentional interference with businesses. Similarly, Penal Code section 602.1 prohibits intentional interference with a public business establishment by obstructing or intimidating those attempting to do business, or their customers, and refusing to leave the premises after being asked to do so. A person must both intentionally interfere *and* refuse to leave to be guilty under Section 602.1. This statute specifically exempts those engaged in activities protected by the California or United States constitutions.

In deciding there was insufficient evidence to show that an attorney and amateur photographer who attended a demonstration at a San Francisco convention center had violated Section 602.1, the Ninth Circuit did not consider whether her activity as a photographer and legal observer exempted her from criminal liability under the statute. Instead, the court found that taking photographs of protesters from eight to 10 feet away from the convention center doors and conversing with convention attendees and protesters did not constitute intentional interference with convention business.[37] The court further found that her refusal to leave when asked by a police officer could not itself be the basis for finding an intent to interfere.[38]

Similarly, a California court that considered whether the manager of a Wal-Mart store had falsely made citizen's arrests of protestors under Section 602.1 did not analyze whether the exemption for activities protected by the California or United States constitutions made a charge under Section 602.1 inapplicable to the protestors.[39]

Note that another statute, Penal Code section 602(k), prohibits entering any "lands" (enclosed or not) for the purpose of injuring property or interfering with the lawful business of the occupant.[40] This statute includes no exception for conduct protected by the constitution.

c. Residences. It is a misdemeanor to enter or remain "in any noncommercial dwelling house, apartment, or other residential place" without the consent of the owner or person in lawful possession of the property.[41] Entering or remaining in such a residential place while a resident is present is guilty of aggravated trespass, punishable by imprisonment in county jail for up to a year and/or a fine of up to $1,000.[42] There is no exemption in this statute for newsgathering or other constitutionally protected activities.

---

[36]   Penal Code section 602(o).

[37]   *Dubner v. City and County of San Francisco*, 266 F.3d 959, 966-67 (9th Cir. 2001) (reversing trial court's dismissal of claim for unlawful arrest).

[38]   *Dubner v. City and County of San Francisco*, 266 F.3d 959, 966-67 (9th Cir. 2001).

[39]   *Hamburg v. Wal-Mart Stores, Inc.*, 116 Cal. App. 4th 497, 510-14 (2004) (holding that Wal-Mart failed to carry its burden of establishing that the citizens' arrests were made for the lawful purpose of enforcing Penal Code section 602.1(a) and not for the purpose of suppressing protected speech).

[40]   Penal Code section 602(k) "Entering any lands, whether unenclosed or enclosed by fence, for the purpose of injuring any property or property rights or with the intention of interfering with, obstructing, or injuring any lawful business or occupation carried on by the owner of the land, the owner's agent or by the person in lawful possession."

[41]   Penal Code section 602.05(a).

[42]   Penal Code section 602.05(b).

d. Public agency buildings after hours. Also potentially relevant to journalists, Penal Code section 602(q) makes "[r]efusing or failing to leave a public building of a public agency during those hours of the day or night when the building is regularly closed to the public upon being requested to do so by a regularly employed guard, watchman, or custodian of the public agency owning or maintaining the building or property, if the surrounding circumstances would indicate to a reasonable person that the person has no apparent lawful business to pursue." There is no specific exemption for constitutional activities built into section 602(q), so a reporter should be prepared to make his or her pursuit of lawful business (*i.e.*, gathering news) evident to guards and custodians during off-hours newsgathering at public agency buildings.

3. Who Can Grant or Deny Permission to Enter?

It is not always clear who can grant or deny permission to enter private property. California courts do not appear to have addressed this issue in a case involving the media. However, decisions from other states provide some guidance.

In a 1975 New Jersey case, a court considered whether a farmer could prevent reporters from entering the farm to report on migrant farmworkers who lived there. The court ordered the return of film that police had seized at the insistence of the farmer and cautioned that "those who provide housing for persons other than their own families ... [are] sailing in waters that have been clearly charted as within the public interest."[43] "Reasonable" exercise of the rights of both press and workers required that journalists visit workers during non-working hours, give reasonable notice to the farmer, confine visitation and interviews to the workers and their areas, and obtain freely given consent from interviewees.[44]

A federal court in Pennsylvania found that a television news crew had not trespassed when it entered and filmed the interior of a rented house with the permission of the tenant. Although the owner of the house had not consented to the entry, the consent of the person in possession of the property was a complete defense to trespass.[45]

4. Shopping Centers and Apartment Complexes.

Access to and newsgathering at large shopping centers and apartment complexes is addressed in more detail in Chapter 11. Generally speaking, the courts have held that the California Constitution provides a right to engage in certain types of activities (petition gathering and protests) at large multi-tenant shopping malls,[46] but not at single-tenant stores,[47] nor at apartment complexes.[48]

---

43   *Freedman v. New Jersey State Police*, 135 N.J. Super. 297, 301 (N.J. Super. Ct. Law Div. 1975).

44   *Freedman v. New Jersey State Police*, 135 N.J. Super. 297, 302 (N.J. Super. Ct. Law Div. 1975).

45   *Lal v. CBS, Inc.*, 726 F.2d 97, 100 (3rd Cir. 1984).

46   *Robins v. Pruneyard Shopping Center*, 23 Cal. 3d 899, 910 (1979). The United States Supreme Court held that construing the California Constitution to allow free speech activity on private property did not violate any federal constitutional rights of the property owners. *Pruneyard Shopping Center v. Robins*, 447 U.S. 74 (1980).

47   *Trader Joe's Company v. Progressive Campaigns, Inc.*, 73 Cal. App. 4th 425 (1999). *See also Costco Companies, Inc. v. Gallant*, 96 Cal. App. 4th 740 (2002); *Albertson's, Inc. v. Young*, 107 Cal. App. 4th 106 (2003); *Hamburg v. Wal-Mart Stores, Inc.*, 116 Cal. App. 4th 497 (2004) (reversing grant of summary judgment to store on protesters' claims that they had been falsely arrested by Wal-Mart employees).

48   *Golden Gateway Center v. Golden Gateway Tenants Ass'n*, 26 Cal. 4th 1013, 1033 (2001).

C. INVASION OF PRIVACY BY INTRUSION.

In addition to trespassing on another's property, reporters can also run afoul of the law by intruding on private places, conversations or sources of information. Civil liability can be imposed in California for penetrating a zone of physical or sensory privacy surrounding an individual or obtaining unwanted access to data about an individual.[49]

A plaintiff claiming invasion of privacy through intrusion must prove (1) he or she had an objectively reasonable expectation of seclusion or solitude in the place, conversation, or source of information at issue; and (2) the intrusion was highly offensive.[50]

1. Expectation of Privacy.

Having a reasonable expectation of privacy is fundamental to a claim of intrusion. The California Supreme Court has explained that the reasonable expectation of privacy element of the intrusion claim "is not met when the plaintiff has merely been observed, or even photographed or recorded, in a public place."[51] The expectation need not, however, be of "*absolute* or *complete* privacy."[52]

Videotaping the scene of an automobile accident, including images of a badly injured victim, was not an intrusion into the victim's privacy because the accident occurred on a public roadway and because the victims could not reasonably have expected that the media would be excluded from the scene or prevented from photographing the scene.[53] The victim's privacy might have been invaded, however, by the recording of conversations between her and rescue personnel captured by a wireless microphone worn by a nurse on the scene.[54] The victim's privacy might also have been invaded by the presence of the cameraman in the rescue helicopter and the recording of conversations between her and a nurse during the helicopter ride to the hospital. The California Supreme Court said that the accident victim had a reasonable expectation of privacy in communications taking place inside a rescue vehicle.[55]

Considering the claims of "telepsychic" company employees based on the secret videotaping of their conversations with an undercover reporter posing as a fellow employee, the California Supreme Court explained that an individual at work might have a reasonable expectation of privacy against intrusion by strangers to the workplace even though the employees' conversations could be overheard by coworkers or employers.[56]

Emphasizing that certain private locations may be off-limits to the media, the federal court of appeals affirmed a judgment for invasion of privacy against reporters who secretly photographed and recorded a visit with an unlicensed "healer" in his living room, which the court described as "a sphere from which he could reasonably expect to exclude eavesdropping newsmen."[57] Attendees of an acting workshop who were videotaped by an undercover reporter with a hidden camera had a reasonable expectation their conversations were not being recorded, because the workshop was not open to the general public but rather limited to a small number of people who auditioned and paid

---

[49]   *Shulman v. Group W Productions, Inc.*, 18 Cal. 4th 200, 232 (1998).
[50]   *Shulman v. Group W Productions, Inc.*, 18 Cal. 4th 200, 232 (1998).
[51]   *Sanders v. American Broadcasting Companies, Inc.*, 20 Cal. 4th 907, 914 (1999).
[52]   *Sanders v. American Broadcasting Companies, Inc.*, 20 Cal. 4th 907, 915 (1999) (emphasis in original).
[53]   *Shulman v. Group W Productions, Inc.*, 18 Cal. 4th 200, 232 (1998).
[54]   *Shulman v. Group W Productions, Inc.*, 18 Cal. 4th 200, 233 (1998).
[55]   *Shulman v. Group W Productions, Inc.*, 18 Cal. 4th 200, 232-233 (1998).
[56]   *Sanders v. American Broadcasting Companies, Inc.*, 20 Cal. 4th 907, 915-16 (1999).
[57]   *Dietemann v. Time, Inc.*, 449 F.2d 245, 249 (9th Cir. 1971).

a fee, and because some of the recorded conversations took place in relatively secluded places within the workshop – in the corners of rooms, against walls and in a bathroom.[58] Intentionally recording a telephone conversation in which a police officer informs parents that their son has died of a drug overdose, without the consent of the parents, may qualify as intrusion.[59]

In contrast, as noted above, it was not intrusion for television producers posing as potential investors to secretly videotape a lunch meeting with businesspeople at an outdoor restaurant because waiters and other individuals could hear the conversation.[60]

Nor was a reporter's finding and downloading photographs of Navy SEALs with Iraqi prisoners an intrusion because, among other things, the wife of the Navy SEAL who had posted the pictures could not reasonably have expected the posting of photos online to be private.[61] Similarly, a court rejected the intrusion claim of an individual who was photographed at a large "circuit party" against the gay-oriented magazine that published the photographs. The party was open to anyone who bought a ticket and was attended by at least 1,000 people, and the plaintiff was dancing on an elevated platform when he was photographed, so he could not establish that he had a reasonable expectation of privacy at the party.[62]

2. Offensiveness.

In determining whether intrusion is sufficiently offensive to be actionable, courts look at all the circumstances, including the motives or justification of the intruder.[63] The California Supreme Court has said that motivation or justification is particularly relevant when the intrusion is by the media in the pursuit of news material because:

> "Although ... the First Amendment does not immunize the press
> from liability for torts or crimes committed in an effort to gather
> news, the constitutional protection of the press does reflect the
> strong societal interest in effective and complete reporting of events,
> an interest that may – as a matter of tort law – justify an intrusion
> that would otherwise be considered offensive."[64]

In other words, the social value of newsgathering can lessen the offensiveness of intrusion into privacy. Nevertheless, courts have found reporting to constitute intrusion on a number of occasions – especially where hidden microphones and cameras were involved. The California Supreme Court has noted that "[t]he conduct of journalism does not depend, as a general matter, on the use of secret devices to record private conversations," and it has concluded that it would be reasonable for jurors to decide that placing a microphone on rescue personnel and filming the interior of a rescue vehicle in order to best convey the "feel" of the rescue scene was not justified by the social interest in gathering news and that it was sufficiently offensive to support a claim for intrusion.[65]

---

[58] *Turnbull v. American Broadcasting Companies*, 2004 U.S. Dist. LEXIS 24351 * 36-46; 32 Media L. Rep. 2442 (C.D. Cal. 2004).

[59] *Marich v. MGM/UA Telecommunications, Inc.*, 113 Cal. App. 4th 415, 420-21 (2003).

[60] *Wilkins v. National Broadcasting Company, Inc.*, 71 Cal. App. 4th 1066, 1078 (1999) ("NBC photographed the two men in a public place and taped their conversations which were about business, not personal matters. There was no intrusion into a private place, conversation or matter.").

[61] *Four Navy Seals v. Associated Press*, 413 F.Supp.2d 1136, 1146-47 (S.D. Cal. 2005).

[62] *Prince v. Out Publishing Inc.*, 2002 WL 7999 at pp. *7-8 (Cal. Ct. App. 2002).

[63] *Shulman v. Group W Productions*, 18 Cal. 4th 200, 236 (1998).

[64] *Shulman v. Group W Productions*, 18 Cal. 4th 200, 236 (1998) (internal citations omitted).

[65] *Shulman v. Group W Productions*, 18 Cal. 4th 200, 238 (1998).

A television camera crew entering a heart attack victim's home with paramedics but without permission from the residents could be regarded as "highly offensive" for purposes of intrusion.[66] Similarly, reporter and photographer's entry onto the property of a cat breeder at the invitation of and accompanying Humane Society officers may have been an illegal trespass and therefore would be "sufficiently serious and offensive" to state a claim for invasion of privacy.[67]

In contrast, a reporter who found and downloaded photographs of Navy SEALs with Iraqi prisoners had not intruded offensively into the privacy of the individual who had posted the pictures (the wife of one of the SEALs) because "[c]onducting an internet search and downloading photos from a photo storage and sharing website ... do not rise to the level of exceptional prying into another's private affairs as required for the offensiveness element of intrusion upon seclusion."[68] Noting that "[e]ven if a journalist's conduct is offensive, the motive to gather news can negate the offensiveness element," the court held that the importance of reporting on Iraqi prisoner abuse would have made the locating and downloading of the photographs not offensive for intrusion purposes, even if it otherwise would have been.[69]

PART IV:
SPECIAL CONSIDERATIONS FOR ELECTRONIC NEWSGATHERING

As technology becomes increasingly important in the newsgathering process, reporters should be familiar with the statutes that govern its use. In particular, caution is warranted whenever capturing images or sounds from an individual – especially if the subject is not aware of the recording.

A. OBTAINING, MAKING AND USING AUDIO AND VIDEO RECORDINGS.

As a general matter, any person has the right to capture still or moving images of anything he or she can see from a lawfully occupied vantage point. For example, videotaping a public official as he walked from his car parked in a driveway to his home was not wrongful because, among other things, the individual was in full public view the entire time he was videotaped.[70] If a person trespasses or uses visual or auditory enhancing equipment to obtain images or sound recordings of people engaged in personal or familial activities, however, he or she might be liable under California's anti-paparazzi statute, discussed below. California also has specific laws prohibiting the recording of confidential communications without the consent of all parties involved.

1. The Anti-Paparazzi Statute

California's "anti-paparazzi" statute, enacted in 1998 in a reaction to the reports of photographers' involvement in Princess Diana's death, imposes civil liability for invasively capturing sound or images of people "engaging in a personal or familial activity."[71] The elements of "physical invasion of privacy," as defined by this statute, are:

---

[66]   *Miller v. National Broadcasting Company*, 187 Cal. App. 3d 1463, 1484 (1986).

[67]   *Brunette v. Humane Society of Ventura County*, 40 Fed. Appx. 594, 597, 30 Media L. Rep. 2181 (2002).

[68]   *Four Navy Seals v. Associated Press*, 413 F.Supp.2d 1136, 1147 (S.D. Cal. 2005).

[69]   *Four Navy Seals v. Associated Press*, 413 F.Supp.2d 1136, 1147 (S.D. Cal. 2005).

[70]   *Aisenson v. American Broadcasting Company, Inc.*, 220 Cal. App. 3d 146, 162-63 (1990).

[71]   Civil Code section 1708.8.

a. knowingly entering onto the land of another person without permission or otherwise committing a trespass;

b. in order to physically invade the privacy of the plaintiff with the intent to capture any type of visual image, sound recording or other physical impression;

c. of the plaintiff engaging in a personal or familial activity;

d. with the physical invasion occurring in a manner that is offensive to a reasonable person.[72]

The statute also provides for liability for "constructive invasion of privacy" even when no physical trespass has occurred if visual or auditory enhancing equipment was used to capture images or sound that otherwise could only have been captured by trespassing.[73]

Committing assault with the intent to capture any type of visual image, sound recording or other physical impression also falls within the scope of the statute.[74] Assault, which is defined in California as "an unlawful attempt, coupled with the present ability, to commit a violent injury on the person of another,"[75] could include aggressive driving by paparazzi, as exemplified in incidents involving Princess Diana, Lindsay Lohan and Arnold Schwarzenegger, who signed the assault provision of California's anti-paparazzi statute into law in 2005.

Liability under the anti-paparazzi statute can include up to three times the amount of damages caused by the incident, punitive damages and disgorgement of any money obtained from selling the images or recordings captured in the incident.[76] The sale, publication or broadcast of images or recordings captured is not a violation of the anti-paparazzi law, however.[77] A person can be found liable under the statute even if he or she never actually captured or sold an image or recording.[78]

The relatively young anti-paparazzi statute has been applied in a number of cases, several of which involve the media:

A television producer who attended a private acting workshop undercover and secretly videotaped other workshop participants might have been liable under the anti-paparazzi statute because: (1) She did not have permission to attend as a reporter and may therefore have trespassed; (2) recorded personal conversations without permission; and (3) did so in a manner that was offensive to a reasonable person.[79]

An individual who was videotaped in a hospital while he and a friend were being treated for adverse reactions to a recreational drug brought a claim based on the anti-paparazzi statute. Although the plaintiff gave his written consent to the use of his image for a television program, he claimed that he did so based on representations by the videographer – who was dressed in "hospital apparel" – that the video would be used to train hospital personnel.[80] The videotape was broadcast as part of a television program.[81]

---

72   Civil Code section 1708.8(a).
73   Civil Code section 1708.8(b).
74   Civil Code section 1708.8(c).
75   Penal Code section 240.
76   Civil Code section 1708.8(d).
77   Civil Code section 1708.8(f).
78   Civil Code section 1708.8(j).
79   *Turnbull v. American Broadcasting Companies*, 2004 U.S. Dist. LEXIS 24351 * 52-54; 32 Media L. Rep. 2442 (C.D. Cal. 2004).
80   *Carter v. Superior Court*, 2002 WL 27229 at pp. *1, 5-6 (Cal. Ct. App. 2002).
81   The opinion in *Carter* relates to the media's motion to strike the plaintiff's complaint under California's anti-SLAPP (strategic lawsuit against public participation) statute. The court held that the acts on which the anti-paparazzi claim were based – the videotaping of the plaintiff in his hospital room by videographers disguised

2. Recording Confidential Communications Without Consent of All Parties: Penal Code Section 632

Intentionally recording a "confidential communication," in person or over the telephone, without the consent of all parties involved is a crime under California law, punishable by a fine of up to $2,500 and one year's imprisonment, regardless of whether the recording is actually used or disclosed.[82] A violator can also be sued in a civil action. [83]

In the newsgathering context, violations typically occur when recording a telephone conversation without the permission of the source, or surreptitiously recording a face-to-face conversation (either by an unseen microphone or hidden camera). The fact that a source is voluntarily speaking with someone who has identified him or herself as a reporter does not mean that there is no violation. The act of recording without consent is a crime – whether the recording is later broadcast or not – so long as one party to the conversation has a reasonable expectation that the conversation is not being recorded and will not be overheard by other people.

Applying this law in a recent case, the California Court of Appeal held that a television crew could be liable under Section 632 for recording the phone call by police to the parents of a man who had just died of a drug overdose, informing them of their son's death.[84]

a. What is a confidential communication? By its own terms Section 632 applies only to recording "confidential" communications. The statute defines "confidential communication" to include "any communication carried on in circumstances as may reasonably indicate that any party to the communication desires it to be confined to the parties thereto." For many years, there was uncertainty as to whether this meant that the parties to a conversation must reasonably expect that its contents will not be later divulged to others, or whether they must only reasonably expect that their conversation is not being overheard or recorded. The California Supreme Court finally resolved the debate, adopting the latter test. The court held that a person whose conversation is recorded without his or her consent need only establish an objectively reasonable expectation that the conversations were not being recorded.[85] The court noted that this definition – which does not take into account the nature or contents of the conversation – provides broader protection of privacy rights.[86]

As noted above, whether a communication is confidential under the statute is based on an objective standard – what a reasonable person in the parties' position would expect – and *not* on the subjective assumptions of the parties. In other words, even if a party to a conversation

---

as medical personnel – were not acts in furtherance of the media's right of free speech and therefore did not consider whether the plaintiff was likely to prevail on the claim. *Carter v. Superior Court*, 2002 WL 27229 at p. *6 (Cal. Ct. App. 2002).

[82] Penal Code section 632.

[83] Penal Code section 632.7.

[84] *Marich v. QRZ Media, Inc.*, 86 Cal. Rptr. 2d 406(1999), ordered depublished by the California Supreme Court, 1999 Cal. LEXIS 7291. In the trial on the parents' lawsuit based on the recording, the jury deadlocked over whether the soundman at the scene had intended to record the parents' end of the telephone call and later found for the defendants. *Marich v. MGM/UA Telecommunications, Inc.*, 113 Cal. App. 4th 415, 420-21 (2003). The court of appeal reversed, holding that the trial court should have instructed the jury that intent could have been found if the soundman knew to a substantial certainty that he was recording the conversation. *Id.* at 429-30.

[85] *Flanagan v. Flanagan*, 27 Cal. 4th 766, 774-775 (2003).

[86] *Flanagan v. Flanagan*, 27 Cal. 4th 766, 775 (2003).

sincerely thought it was or was not confidential, that subjective belief is not relevant if the belief was not reasonable under the circumstances.[87]

Not every undisclosed recording of a conversation violates Section 632. A conversation between reporters posing as potential investors that took place in a public restaurant, and that did not include any information claimed to be "secrets" was not a "confidential" communication.[88]

b. Expectation of privacy. An undercover reporter who posed as a "telepsychic" and secretly recorded conversations with fellow telepsychics at their office was sued by them based, in part, on Section 632. The jury rejected this claim, finding that the recorded conversations took place in circumstances – *i.e.*, in workplace cubicles with other employees in the vicinity – in which the parties to the communication might reasonably have expected that their conversation would be overheard. The California Supreme Court later held that this finding with respect to Section 632 did not, however, preclude a successful claim that the reporter invaded the privacy of her fellow employees by intrusion.[89] (See the discussion of invasion of privacy through intrusion in Subsection D, above.)

Similarly, after an undercover reporter secretly recorded conversations in an acting workshop for a segment on a television news show, several of those recorded sued – in part – under Section 632.[90] Noting that the workshops were small (10 to 20 people) and private, the court found that whether or not those recorded had a reasonable expectation of privacy was a question that had to be resolved by a trial.

c. Damages for violations of Section 632. A person injured by a violation of Section 632 can bring an action against the person who committed the violation for the greater of $5,000 or three times the amount of any actual damages sustained.[91] A person damaged by the broadcast of recordings made in violation of Section 632 is limited to damages resulting from the act of recording itself and is not entitled to damages resulting from the dissemination of the recordings.

A doctor whose medical career ended after a local television news broadcast characterized him as having improperly prescribed drugs sued the station whose reporters had secretly recorded his examinations of them. He sued only under Section 632 and did not allege that he had been defamed or that his privacy had been invaded. Although both a trial and appellate court found that the doctor had presented a prima facie case that the reporters had violated Section 632 and that he was entitled to statutory damages, the appellate court cautioned that these damages could not include the injuries he claimed to have suffered as a result of the news broadcast. Rather, he was restricted to either the $5,000 provided for in Section 637.2 or three times the amount of actual damages *caused by the recording itself*. While legal fees incurred in trying to recover recordings made in violation of Section 632 qualify as actual damages caused by the recordings, any injuries caused by the dissemination of the recordings – such as damage to reputation – do not.[92]

---

[87]   *Wilkins v. National Broadcasting Company, Inc.*, 71 Cal. App. 4th 1066, 1080 (1999), quoting *O'Laskey v. Sortino*, 224 Cal. App. 3d 241, 248 (1990).

[88]   *Wilkins v. National Broadcasting Company, Inc.*, 71 Cal. App. 4th 1066, 1080 (1999).

[89]   *Sanders v. American Broadcasting Companies, Inc.*, 20 Cal. 4th 907, 913 (1999).

[90]   *Turnbull v. American Broadcasting Companies, Inc.*, 2004 U.S. Dist. LEXIS 24351 at *24-34, 32 Med. L. Rptr. 2442 (C.D. Cal. 2004).

[91]   Penal Code section 637.2.

[92]   *Lieberman v. KCOP Television, Inc.*, 110 Cal. App. 4th 156, 167 (2003). The *Lieberman* court denied the television station's motion to strike as a strategic lawsuit against public participation (SLAPP) because it found that the doctor was likely to prevail on his claim under Section 632. In doing so, the court declined to create an affirmative defense to Section 632 based on the secret recording's having been made in the course of gathering news. *Id.* at 169-170.

d. Images vs. sound. A school superintendent who installed a camera in a school principal's office to determine whether someone was reading confidential documents in the office did not violate Section 632 because the camera did not record sound and "the taking of pictures of two or more people carrying on a confidential conversation does not constitute the recording of a confidential communication under the statute."[93] Using a camera or other viewing aid to look into the interior of an area in which the occupant has a reasonable expectation of privacy with the intent to invade that privacy, however, is a misdemeanor in California.[94]

e. Public gatherings excluded. Section 632 specifically excludes communications "made in a public gathering or in any legislative, judicial, executive or administrative proceeding open to the public" from the definition of "confidential communication."[95] For example, no permission would be needed to record a speech given by a mayoral candidate at a public forum or to record city council proceedings. Recording of court proceedings would not violate Section 632, but it does require permission. Rules for recording meetings of public agencies are discussed in Chapter 1, and rules for recording judicial proceedings are discussed in Chapter 8.

3. Recording Interviews

Reporters should not assume that by identifying themselves as reporters gathering information for a story they have destroyed any reasonable expectation an interviewee could have that the conversation is confidential. The best way to protect yourself against liability for recording an interview or other conversation is to get express consent for the interview on tape, or at least record your statement telling those involved that you are recording the conversation.

If you are not a reporter, there is little if any possibility that another person will have a reasonable expectation that you are recording a conversation unless you tell them. You should always disclose the fact that you are recording, and ideally you should get consent. Again, the best practice is to record the discussion about recording.

4. Calls Within California vs. Calls Between California and Another State

Laws governing when telephone calls and other conversations may lawfully be recorded vary by state. In many states, only one party's consent is required. In other states, all parties' consent is required, even if the circumstances do not support a reasonable expectation of privacy.

The California Supreme Court recently considered whether a Georgia company was liable under California law for recording its telephone calls with customers in California without those customers' consent.[96] Such recording does not violate Georgia law. The court held that California law should apply and that the plaintiffs should be able to sue for injunctive relief based on Penal Code Section 632. The court dismissed the claims for damages, however, determining that Georgia's interest in protecting its companies from unexpected liability for past actions demanded that California law not apply to the award of damages in the case.

---

[93] *People v. Drennan*, 84 Cal. App. 4th 1349, 1359 (2000).
[94] Penal Code section 647(k), (1).
[95] Penal Code section 632(c).
[96] *Kearney v. Salomon Smith Barney, Inc.*, 39 Cal. 4th 95 (2006).

5. Federal Law: One-Party Consent Rule

Federal laws on recording conversations are generally more liberal than California law. However, *California residents should remember that they can be prosecuted under state law even if the recording does not constitute a crime under the federal rules.*

Under federal law a person who is a party to a conversation – either over the telephone or face to face – may record it as long as the purpose of the recording is not to commit a criminal or tortious act.[97] In another suit stemming from the same undercover telepsychic reporting incident discussed above, employees who were secretly recorded sued under the Federal Wiretapping Act. The federal courts rejected the claim because the reporter who recorded the conversations was always a party to the conversations. Moreover, even if making the recordings was a tortious invasion of the employees' privacy under California law, there was no showing that they were made with an illegal or tortious purpose.[98]

In some circumstances, however, a reporter could potentially be held liable for using an illegally recorded conversation, if he or she knew or should have known that the recording was made with the purpose of committing a criminal or tortious act. In the early 1990s an individual in Michigan secretly recorded telephone conversations with his ex-wife – a local judge – and later attempted to blackmail her with them. A reporter who received and reported on the recordings was held not to have violated the Federal Wiretapping Act because there was no showing that he knew that the recordings were made for the purpose of blackmail, even if he knew they were later used in a blackmail attempt.[99]

Even where a recording was made in violation of the Federal Wiretapping Act, however, the First Amendment may protect disclosure of that information. During contentious collective-bargaining negotiations between a teacher's union and local school board, an unknown person illegally recorded a telephone conversation between two union representatives, and the recording was passed along to the media. The individuals whose conversation was recorded sued the radio commentator who played the recording on his public affairs talk show. The U.S. Supreme Court held that the provisions of the Act that imposed liability for the media's disclosure of the recording violated the First Amendment.[100] Under the terms of the Act, a person who intentionally discloses the contents of an electronic communication when he or she knows or has reason to know that the information was illegally intercepted violates the Act. As applied to the specific situation – the disclosure by the press of a newsworthy communication bearing directly on an issue of public importance – the Act deterred more speech than was necessary to protect the private interests at stake and therefore violated the First Amendment.

---

[97]   United States Code, Title 18, section 2511(2) (18 U.S.C. § 2511(2)(d)). Section 2511 and the following sections, enacted as part of part of Title III of the Omnibus Crime Control and Safe Street Acts, is often known as the Federal Wiretapping Act.

[98]   *Sussman v. American Broadcasting Companies, Inc.*, 186 F.3d 1200, 1202-03 (9th Cir. 1999); *see also Deteresa v. American Broadcasting Companies, Inc.*, 121 F.3d 460, 466-67 (9th Cir. 1997) (reporter who secretly recorded individual at her home did not violate 18 U.S.C. section 2511 because he was a party to the conversation recorded and recording was not made for criminal or tortious purpose).

[99]   *Ferrara v. Detroit Free Press*, 1998 U.S. Dist. LEXIS 8635, 26 Media L. Rep. 2355 (E.D. Mich. 1998).

[100]   *Bartnicki v. Vopper*, 532 U.S. 514 (2001). Notwithstanding the Bartnicki decision, a congressman who received a recording of a telephone call that he should have known was made illegally violated the Federal Wiretap Act (18 U.S.C. § 2511(c)). *Boehner v. McDermott*, 441 F.3d 1010, 1016-17(D.D.C. 2006). The court explained that the difference between the circumstances in *Bartnicki* and *Boehner* "is the difference between someone who discovers a bag containing a diamond ring on the sidewalk and someone who accepts the same bag from a thief, knowing the ring inside to have been stolen." *Id.* at 1017.

6. Intercepting Cell and Cordless Phone Calls

California has a separate statute making the malicious interception or receipt of cell and cordless phone calls punishable by a fine ($2,500 for first-time offenders) and/or imprisonment.[101]

7. Wiretaps

Wiretaps and other unauthorized connections to a telephone line are illegal under California law regardless of whether or not the conversation is confidential.[102]

B. USING POLICE AND EMERGENCY SCANNERS.

Members of the public have monitored emergency calls since the 1930s, when police began broadcasting them over local AM radio stations. As discussed below, state and federal statutes provide liability for monitoring and acting on such communications in certain situations. As a practical matter, journalists must generally concern themselves with avoiding serious interference with public safety operations. In pursuing breaking stories identified by scanners, reporters and photographers on the scene should keep the lowest profile possible, especially if the incident is criminal and if they arrive before law enforcement officers are conspicuously present. Avoid conduct that could be construed to have alerted criminals to impending police action, blocked official access to the scene or endangered officers.

Interference with police activities at a crime scene could subject reporters to liability, as it did the journalists covering the Branch Davidian raid in Waco, Texas.[103]

1. California Law

It is a misdemeanor in California to intercept a public safety radio service communication regarding criminal activity and to divulge the existence or contents of the communication to a person suspected of committing the criminal offense with the intent that the suspect avoid arrest, trial, conviction or punishment.[104] The requirement that the person divulging the communication intend the suspect to avoid police action makes it unlikely that the statute would be applicable to a reporter covering a story identified through a police scanner.

2. Federal Law

The Federal Communications Act says that no one who receives an intercepted radio communication can "divulge or publish the existence, contents, substance, purport, effect, or meaning of such communication (or any part thereof) or use such communication (or any information therein contained) for his own benefit or for the benefit of another not entitled thereto." The Act does not apply, however, to "the receiving, divulging, publishing, or utilizing the contents of any radio communication which is transmitted by any station for the use of the general public [or] which relates to ships, aircraft, vehicles, or persons in distress."[105] Although

---

[101]   Penal Code sections 632.5 (cell phones) and 632.6 (cordless phones).
[102]   Penal Code section 631.
[103]   *See Risenhoover v. England*, 936 F.Supp. 392 (W.D. Tex. 1996).
[104]   Penal Code section 636.5.
[105]   United States Code, Title 47, section 606(a) (47 U.S.C. § 605(a)).

there has been little enforcement of this statute against the media, in 1962 the federal government sued an individual for intercepting police shortwave radio broadcasts and divulging newsworthy portions of the communications to a local radio station.[106]

Special care should be used not to pick up telephone calls through emergency scanners. A Florida couple who used a police scanner to intercept a cellular telephone call between Congressman Newt Gingrich and other members of Republican leadership, and passed a recording of it along to their congressman, were found guilty of and fined $500 for violating the Federal Wiretap Act, which prohibits unauthorized interception of "wire, oral, or electronic communication."[107]

Note, however, that as discussed above, the First Amendment may provide a defense to the disclosure of an intercepted communication by one who did not participate in the original interception.[108]

C. ACCESSING COMPUTERS AND ELECTRONIC DATA.

1. Computer Access: California Law

California law creates civil and criminal liability for knowingly accessing or using computers, computer systems or computer networks without permission, and for knowingly taking or making use of any data from a computer, computer system or computer network without permission.[109] Conviction can result in fines ranging from $400 to $10,000 and imprisonment in state or county jail for up to three years, depending on the seriousness of the intrusion and the damage inflicted.[110]

An unemployed aerospace software engineer was convicted under the California statute after he accessed several computer terminals at a local library and penetrated the public interface to access the operating system and database level – ostensibly out of curiosity and to learn more about the operating system.[111]

2. Computer Access: Federal Law

Accessing without authorization or exceeding the authority to access a facility through which an electronic communication service is provided is a violation of federal law punishable by fine and imprisonment under the Stored Communications Act (SCA).[112] The SCA also provides a basis for civil liability. Reading e-mails obtained from an ISP through an overbroad subpoena was a violation of the SCA.[113] A video game company employee who accessed an electronic bulletin board using a pseudonym and password supplied by an authorized user in order to monitor the

---

[106] *U.S. v. Fuller*, 202 F. Supp. 356 (N.D. Cal. 1962). In 2000, the Sixth Circuit reversed a trial court decision that the interception by a taxi company of a competing company's radio transmissions did not violate Section 605 of the Federal Communications Act (47 U.S.C. § 605). *Cafarelli v. Yancy*, 226 F.3d 492 (6th Cir. 2000).

[107] *United States v. John Martin*, No. 97-115-CR-J-20B (M.D. Fla. 1997); *United States v. Alice Martin*, No. 97-114-CR-J-20C (M.D. Fla. 1997); *see also Boehner v. McDermott*, 441 F.3d 1010, 1013 (D.D.C. 2006). The relevant provision of the Federal Wiretap Act is found in the United States Code, Title 18, section 2511(1)(a) (18 U.S.C. § 2511(1)(a)).

[108] *Bartnicki v. Vopper*, 532 U.S. 514 (2001).

[109] Penal Code section 502(c)(2), (3), (7).

[110] Penal Code section 502(d).

[111] *People v. Lawton*, 48 Cal. App. 4th Supp. 11 (1996).

[112] United States Code, title 18, section 2701 (18 U.S.C. § 2701).

[113] *Theofel v. Farey-Jones*, 341 F.3d 978, 982-85 (9th Cir. 2003).

distribution of pirated video games did not violate the SCA, even though he was not the intended user of the password.[114]

3. GPS Data.

California law prohibits using an electronic tracking device to determine the location or movement of a person without that person's consent. Violation is a misdemeanor.[115]

---

[114]   *Sega Enterprises Ltd. v. MAPHIA*, 948 F. Supp. 923, 930 (N.D. Cal. 1996).
[115]   Penal Code section 637.7.

CHAPTER 13

The Student Press and Student Speech

IN THIS CHAPTER

There are varying degrees of protection for student speech established in both federal and state law. California generally provides greater protection for student speech than does the federal law. Whether California school administrators may exercise some restraint on student speech will depend on factors such as the age of the student, whether the speech occurs as part of the school's educational program, and whether a publication is produced by high school or college or university students. Student newspapers do not enjoy the same First Amendment rights that are enjoyed by professional journalists. Restrictions on high school students' First Amendment rights have been upheld as constitutional by the United States Supreme Court and are imposed by statute in the California Education Code. Student newspapers at public colleges and universities have far greater protections under California law than high school students. Because private schools are not run by government agencies, their students are not generally protected by the First Amendment from actions by private school officials, although California law provides some protections.

PART I:
CONSTITUTIONAL BACKGROUND

Students do not "shed their constitutional rights to freedom of speech and expression at the schoolhouse gate."[1] However, the First Amendment rights of public school students "'are not automatically coextensive with the rights of adults in other settings'" and must be "applied in light of the special characteristics of the school environment."[2]

Courts examining First Amendment claims about student speech generally characterize the expression as falling within one of the following categories:

1. Vulgar, lewd, obscene and "plainly offensive" speech;
2. School-sponsored or curricular speech; and
3. Non-curricular student speech.

The sections below discuss these categories, beginning with the third, which is also the most general because it applies to all non-curricular student speech that is not vulgar, lewd or obscene.

A. NON-CURRICULAR STUDENT SPEECH

The First Amendment protects student speech that is "non-curricular" and not school-sponsored – in other words, speech that is not part of classroom assignments or school-supervised projects or activities. Student speech that is not school-sponsored or curricular, and not vulgar,

---

[1]   *Tinker v. Des Moines School District,* 393 U.S. 503, 506 (1969) ("*Tinker*").
[2]   *Hazelwood School District v. Kulhmeier,* 484 U.S. 260, 266 (1988).

lewd or obscene, is governed by *Tinker v. Des Moines School District*, the 1969 Supreme Court decision that established the principle that students retain First Amendment rights in school.[3]

Tinker involved a group of high school students who were suspended for wearing black armbands to school in protest of the Vietnam War. Punishing the students for their expression violated their First Amendment rights: "Clearly, the prohibition of expression of one particular opinion, at least without evidence that it is necessary to avoid material and substantial interference with schoolwork or discipline, is not constitutionally permissible."[4]

The Supreme Court recognized that school officials generally had broad authority to prescribe and control conduct in the schools but said this authority did not extend to administrative censorship of public school students' non-disruptive expression. Although students' First Amendment rights had to be "applied in light of the special characteristics of the school environment," students could not be "confined to the expression of those sentiments that are officially approved."[5] Instead, students may exercise their right to freedom of expression unless the "conduct by the student, in class or out of it, which for any reason – whether it stems from time, place, or type of behavior – materially disrupts classwork or involves substantial disorder or invasion of the rights of others. ..."

The *Tinker* test does not require that non-curricular student speech be political in nature to qualify for First Amendment protection. In 2006, the Ninth Circuit rejected a lower court's holding that a petition by high school students for the removal of their basketball coach was not protected by the First Amendment because it was not political and did not touch on a matter of public concern. In that case, members of the high school team submitted a petition complaining of their coach's behavior and asking that he be replaced. They later refused to board the team bus to an away game in order to demonstrate their commitment to their position. After being suspended from the team, the boys sued the school, claiming that the suspension was retaliation for their expression and violated the First Amendment. The Ninth Circuit recognized that the students' petition was pure speech and that the school could have punished them for it only if it could show that it reasonably anticipated substantial disruption of school activities as a result of the petition.[6] In contrast, the court found that the students' refusal to board the team bus was not protected by the First Amendment because even if it was expressive conduct, it did substantially disrupt the school-sponsored basketball game.[7] The court remanded the case for a determination of whether the students were suspended from the team only for refusing to board the bus (which would not violate the First Amendment) or also for petitioning against their coach (which *would* violate the First Amendment).[8]

In recent years, courts have considered *Tinker* in light of the prospect of extreme student violence. A federal Court of Appeals held that school officials had not violated a high school student's First Amendment rights when it expelled him on an emergency basis after he showed a teacher a poem he wrote describing the murder of classmates.[9] The decision was rendered, as the court acknowledged, in the post-Columbine era, with awareness of the possibility of wide-scale student-on-student violence. In approving the school's actions, the court stressed that the school based its decision on indicators of possible violence aside from the poem, that it cooperated with the student in offering psychological evaluations, and that it lifted the suspension as soon as those evaluations indicated that the student was not a threat to other students. In the court's view, the

---

[3]   *Tinker*, 393 U.S. 503.
[4]   *Tinker*, 393 U.S. at 511.
[5]   *Tinker*, 393 U.S. at 506, 511.
[6]   *Pinard v. Clatskanie School Dist. 6J*, 467 F.3d 755, 764 (9th Cir. 2006).
[7]   *Pinard v. Clatskanie School Dist. 6J*, 467 F.3d 755, 769-770 (9th Cir. 2006).
[8]   *Pinard v. Clatskanie School Dist. 6J*, 467 F.3d 755, 770-771 (9th Cir. 2006).
[9]   *Lavine v. Blaine School District*, 257 F.3d 981 (9th Cir. 2001).

evidence showed the school was not disciplining the student for his speech but rather was trying to protect its students from violence.[10]

In a similar case, a California Court of Appeal held that administrators of a 4-H program had not violated First Amendment rights of students by suspending them pending investigation of a video they made depicting alienated students murdering classmates with machetes.[11] The court found the case indistinguishable from *Lavine* and therefore affirmed the award of attorneys' fees to defendants based on the plaintiffs' continued litigation of the claims after they had been shown to be groundless.[12]

Further limiting student speech rights, the U.S. Supreme Court recently ruled that another student's First Amendment rights were not violated when a school administrator tore up a banner reading "Bong Hits 4 Jesus" that the student displayed at a public Winter Olympics Torch Relay event across the street from the school. When the case came to the Ninth Circuit Court of Appeals, the court framed the question as "whether a school may, in the absence of concern about disruption of educational activities, punish and censor non-disruptive, off-campus speech by students during school-authorized activities because the speech promotes a social message contrary to the one favored by the school," and it concluded that "[t]he answer under controlling, long-established precedent is plainly 'No.'"[13]

The majority concluded the principal did not violate the First Amendment by confiscating the drug banner and suspending the student responsible for it. The opinion first concluded that Joseph Frederick's "Bong Hits" banner was displayed during a school-sanctioned event, making it a "school speech" case. Writing for the majority, Chief Justice Roberts said that although the message was "cryptic," it was undeniably a "reference to illegal drugs" and the principal reasonably concluded that it "advocated the use of illegal drugs." The majority emphasized the government's "important – indeed, perhaps compelling interest" in fighting drugs. The majority concluded the First Amendment, "does not require schools to tolerate at school events student expression that contributes to those dangers."[14]

Justices Alito and Kennedy wrote a concurring opinion attempting to limit the majority's ruling, agreeing with the majority only so long as "(a) it goes no further than to hold that a public school may restrict speech that a reasonable observer would interpret as advocating illegal drug use and (b) it provides no support for any restriction of speech that can plausibly be interpreted as commenting on any political or social issue, including speech on issues such as "the wisdom of the war on drugs or of legalizing marijuana for medicinal use."[15]

Finally, in a controversial 2006 decision, *Harper v. Poway Unified School District*, the Ninth Circuit held that school administrators could constitutionally forbid a student from wearing a T-shirt bearing the statement "HOMOSEXUALITY IS SHAMEFUL 'Romans 1:27'" on the grounds that such speech impinged upon the rights of other students, in violation, the court said, of *Tinker*.[16] Noting that courts considering student speech issues had attempted to "strike a balance between the free speech rights of students and the special need to maintain a safe, secure and

---

10   *Lavine v. Blaine School District*, 257 F.3d 981, 991 (9th Cir. 2001). The court did, however, affirm the lower court's order prohibiting the school from placing or maintaining any negative documentation regarding the incident in the student's file. *Id.* at 992.

11   *Robbins v. Regents of the University of California*, 127 Cal. App. 4th 653 (2005).

12   *Robbins v. Regents of the University of California*, 127 Cal. App. 4th 653, 665 (2005).

13   *Frederick v. Morse*, 439 F.3d 1114, 1118 (9th Cir. 2006), *cert. granted*, 75 U.S.L.W. 3094 (Dec. 1, 2006) (No. 06-278) ("*Frederick*").

14   *Frederick v. Morse*, 127 S. Ct. 2618 (2007).

15   *Frederick v. Morse*, 127 S. Ct. 2618 (2007) (Kennedy, J., Alito, J., concurring).

16   *Harper v. Poway Unified School District*, 445 F.3d 1166 (9th Cir. 2006), *cert. granted and judgment vacated*, 127 S.Ct. 1484, 75 USLW 3248, 75 USLW 3469, 75 USLW 3472 (Mar 05, 2007) ("*Harper*").

effective learning environment," the court concluded that "[p]ublic school students who may be injured by verbal assaults on the basis of a core identifying characteristic such as race, religion, or sexual orientation, have a right to be free from such attacks while on school campuses."[17] The court considered evidence that anti-gay sentiment at school contributed to underachievement, truancy and dropout among gay and lesbian students and decided that the school "had a valid and lawful basis for restricting [the student's] wearing of his T-shirt on the ground that his conduct was injurious to gay and lesbian students and interfered with their right to learn."[18]

In a vigorous dissent, Judge Kozinski disagreed. Invading the rights of others, he said, could not include anything other than invading "traditional rights, such as those against assault, defamation, invasion of privacy, extortion and blackmail, whose interplay with the First Amendment is well established," and, in particular, did not include "an affirmative right not to be offended."[19] Instead, he argued, the school's action constituted impermissible viewpoint discrimination – particularly because the student wore the T-shirt following a "Day of Silence" held by the school's Gay-Straight Alliance to encourage tolerance. By permitting the "Day of Silence" while forbidding students who "oppose the Day of Silence and the point of view it represents," the dissent argued, the school has unfairly gagged one side of a political debate.[20]

The court of appeals' decision was subsequently vacated by the United States Supreme Court, on procedural grounds.[21] Therefore, the boundaries of school officials' ability to restrict speech in the name of protecting students from discrimination or stigma remain unclear.

B. SCHOOL-SPONSORED OR CURRICULAR SPEECH

In the leading case on school-sponsored or curricular student speech, *Hazelwood School District v. Kuhlmeier*, the U.S. Supreme Court held that school-sponsored student publications do not enjoy the same First Amendment protections as professional publications.[22] The court ruled that a public high school did not violate the First Amendment rights of its student editors when school officials refused to publish two pages of the student newspaper.

The *Hazelwood* case was sparked by the principal's decision to delete two pages from the six-page edition that included an article describing students' experiences with pregnancy and an article about the children of divorced parents. School officials said they were concerned about exposing younger students to discussions of adolescent sexual activity and about the privacy interests of the families discussed in the article dealing with divorce. The principal said the pages were deleted because there was no time to edit the stores before the newspaper's publication deadline.

The court upheld the principal's action, resting its decision on its belief that the student newspaper involved was not a "public forum" and was, therefore, not entitled to the full protection of the First Amendment. Under a longstanding test articulated by the Supreme Court, government agencies are prohibited from regulating the content of speech expressed in a public forum in the absence of a showing that the regulation is needed to further a "compelling government interest."

In this case, the court said the student newspaper was intended to be a vehicle of learning for the students as part of the school's curriculum and did not serve as a "public forum" in the same way as general community publications. Because the newspaper was viewed as part of the curriculum, the court reasoned that the school was entitled to regulate its content in any reasonable

---

[17]   *Harper*, 445 F.3d at 1176-1178.

[18]   *Harper*, 445 F.3d at 1197-1198.

[19]   *Harper*, 445 F.3d at 1198 (Kozinski, J., dissenting).

[20]   *Harper*, 445 F.3d at 1198 (Kozinski, J., dissenting).

[21]   127 S.Ct. 1484, 75 USLW 3248, 75 USLW 3469, 75 USLW 3472 (Mar 05, 2007).

[22]   *Hazelwood School District v. Kuhlmeier*, 484 U.S. 260 (1988) ("*Hazlewood*").

manner. This conclusion is based on the belief that the school – rather than the students – is the publisher of the newspaper and therefore retains ultimate control over its contents:

> Educators are entitled to exercise greater control ... to assure that participants learn whatever lessons the activity is designed to teach, that readers or listeners are not exposed to material that may be inappropriate for their level of maturity, and that the views of the individual speaker are not erroneously attributed to the school. Hence, a school may in its capacity as publisher of a school newspaper or producer of a school play "disassociate itself," ... not only from speech that would "substantially interfere with [its] work ... or impinge upon the rights of other students," ... but also from speech that is, for example, ungrammatical, poorly written, inadequately researched, biased or prejudiced, vulgar or profane, or unsuitable for immature audiences.[23]

The First Amendment rights of students will only be violated, the court said, when the decision of the school to censor content "has no valid educational purpose."[24]

Although the *Hazelwood* decision appears to give public school officials broad discretion to regulate the content of student publications, that discretion is predicated on the court's finding that the newspaper involved was not a public forum. If the court had found it to be a public forum, the court presumably would have been compelled to apply a more exacting standard to determine the constitutionality of the school's actions.

"Public forum," as used by the courts, applies to means of communication using public channels such as parks, streets and bulletin boards, which the government has allowed citizens to use freely for expressive purposes. In *Hazelwood*, the court said that "school facilities may be deemed to be public forums only if school authorities have 'by policy or by practice' opened those facilities 'for indiscriminate use by the general public' ... or by some segment of the public, such as student organizations."[25] Because the student newspaper in question was part of the school's journalism curriculum and was not intended or allowed to be used as a public forum, school officials could constitutionally impose "reasonable restrictions on the speech of students, teachers, and other members of the school community."[26]

In contrast, a student publication found to be a public forum could not be censored under the lenient "reasonable restrictions" standard enunciated in *Hazelwood*. Applying the court's logic, where school officials – by official policy or action – leave student publications open to "indiscriminate use," the school would lose much of its ability to regulate its content. Key factors in determining whether a student publication is a public forum would include whether story assignments are made by student editors or by faculty; whether faculty members are given the opportunity to review articles before their publication; whether students earn credits for participation; and the nature of the audience for which the publication is intended. Thus, it is more likely that a newspaper published by a public university's students who are solely responsible for

---

23 *Hazelwood*, 484 U.S. at 271 (internal citations omitted).

24 *Hazelwood*, 484 U.S. at 273.

25 *Hazelwood*, 484 U.S. at 267. Public high schools in California, in contrast to the typical college campus, are not public forums. *Reeves v. Rocklin Unified School District*, 109 Cal. App. 4th 652, 663 (2003). High school administrators therefore may constitutionally limit access by outsiders wishing to speak to students on campus, regardless of their message, as long as the decision is reasonable in order to limit disruption. *Id.* at 665. *Cf O'Toole v. Superior Court*, 140 Cal. App. 4th 488, 503 (2006) (a permit requirement for outsider speech on a college campus was presumed unconstitutional, based on tradition of universities as "center[s] for free intellectual debate").

26 *Hazelwood*, 484 U.S. at 267.

its day-to-day publication would be considered a public forum than a high school newspaper that is part of the curriculum of a journalism course. At the urging of journalism students, several public college and universities have issued declarations specifically stating that the school newspaper is a public forum.

The Ninth Circuit applied *Hazelwood* in a college setting in 2002, deciding that the First Amendment does not require university professors to assign a passing grade to a graduate student's thesis if the acknowledgements section failed to conform to established academic and professional standards. In that case, the student inserted a "Disacknowledgements" section into his thesis after it had been approved, in which the student "offer[ed] special *F[---] You's* to the following degenerates for being an ever-present hindrance during [his] graduate career."[27] The court observed that "[a]n academic thesis co-signed by a committee of professors is not a public forum, limited or otherwise." Concluding that "educators can, consistent with the First Amendment, restrict student speech provided that the limitation is reasonably related to a legitimate pedagogical purpose," the court said that the school was not obligated to accept work based on a student's bypassing the approval process and preparing an assignment that did not comply with stated approval.[28]

C. VULGAR, LEWD AND OBSCENE SPEECH

Finally, schools have considerable latitude in prohibiting speech that is "vulgar and lewd." The U.S. Supreme Court in *Bethel School District No. 403 v. Fraser* concluded that it was "perfectly appropriate" for high school administrators to suspend a student whose school assembly speech was premised on a sexual metaphor.[29] Noting that the speech triggered audience reactions ranging from raucous sexual gestures to embarrassed bewilderment, the court concluded that "[t]he First Amendment does not prevent the school officials from determining that to permit [such] a vulgar and lewd speech ... would undermine the school's basic educational mission."[30]

However, determining whether any particular expression is "vulgar and lewd" is not necessarily a clear-cut issue. In his concurring opinion in *Fraser*, Justice Brennan noted that he found it difficult to believe that the speech the court called "obscene," "vulgar," "lewd" and "offensively lewd" was the same speech that he had read. He nevertheless agreed that it was appropriate for the school officials to suspend the speaker in light of their discretion to "teach high school students how to conduct civil and effective public discourse, and to prevent disruption of school educational activities."[31]

PART II:
CALIFORNIA LAWS REGARDING STUDENT PRESS AND SPEECH

While the states may not limit the rights of their citizens as guaranteed in the United States Constitution, state and local governments may grant their citizens *greater* rights. The federal constitution merely sets minimum standards with which state and local governments must comply. The California Legislature has enacted a series of laws protecting freedom of speech and freedom of

---

[27]   *Brown v. Li*, 308 F.3d 939, 943 (9th Cir. 2002).

[28]   *Brown v. Li*, 308 F.3d 939, 952 (9th Cir. 2002). The court also noted that the student's thesis committee members "had an affirmative First Amendment right not to approve [the student's] thesis." *Id.*

[29]   *Bethel School District No. 403 v. Fraser*, 478 U.S. 675 (1986).

[30]   *Bethel School District No. 403 v. Fraser*, 478 U.S. 675, 685 (1986).

[31]   *Bethel School District No. 403 v. Fraser*, 478 U.S. 675, 687-90 (1986) (Brennan, J., concurring).

the student press at California high schools, colleges and universities. The protections afforded by California law vary depending on level (secondary vs. colleges and universities) and whether the schools are public or private. They also vary depending on the type of speech involved.

A. STUDENT PRESS AND SPEECH ON PUBLIC HIGH SCHOOL CAMPUSES.

1. Protection for Student Journalism at Public Schools

In California, Education Code section 48907 protects the rights of student journalists. It grants all public school students "the right to exercise freedom of speech and of the press," including the use of bulletin boards, the distribution of printed materials or petitions, the wearing of buttons, badges and other insignia, and the right of expression in official publications. Section 48907 requires each public school district to adopt a "written publications code," but it allows school officials to restrict or punish expression only if it is "obscene, libelous, or slanderous" or "material that so incites students as to create a clear and present danger of the commission of unlawful acts on school premises or in violation of the orderly operation of the school." Section 48907 apparently applies to public schools at all levels below college or university. However, it does not apply to private schools.

The statute specifically gives students the right to produce the news, while the school officials are responsible for overseeing the students' work:

> Student editors of official school publications shall be responsible for assigning and
> editing the news, editorial and feature content of their publications subject to the
> limitations of this section. However, it shall be the responsibility of a journalism
> adviser or advisers of student publications within each school to supervise the
> production of the student staff, to maintain professional standards of English and
> journalism and to maintain the provisions of this section.

2. Schools May Censor Certain Material, But Must Justify the Censorship

The "professional standards of English and journalism" provision in section 48907 may be used to prevent students' use of profanity or obscene expressions. In *Lopez v. Tulare Joint Union High School District*,[32] students challenged the school district's authority to censor the profanity contained in a video they had written and produced in connection with a film class. The court upheld the censorship under section 48907, finding that the intent of the California Legislature was to prohibit profanity in official school publications.[33]

If school officials determine that certain content violates the prohibitions in section 48907, they have the right to prohibit its publication. However, school officials have the burden of showing "without undue delay" that censorship is justified and should establish a swift procedure for administrative review of restrictions on student publications.[34] A student need not exhaust administrative remedies before pursuing a freedom of speech or civil rights claim in court.[35]

---

[32]   *Lopez v. Tulare Joint Union High School District*, 34 Cal. App. 4th 1302 (1995) ("*Lopez*").
[33]   *Lopez*, 34 Cal. App. 4th at 1347.
[34]   *See Leeb v. DeLong*, 98 Cal. App. 3d 47 (1988).
[35]   *Lovell v. Poway Unified School District*, 90 F.3d 367 (9th Cir. 1996).

3. Only "Official Publications" Can Be Censored

The free speech rights established by section 48907 apply not just to official publications, but also to other forms of expression, as long as they are not "obscene, libelous, or slanderous."[36]

Section 48907 does not permit the outright prohibition of speech, except for certain categories of speech contained in official school publications. The court in *Lopez* said that "the power of prior restraint is found only in section 48907 and only as to official school publications."[37] (The same section defines "official school publications" as "material produced by students in the journalism, yearbook, or writing classes and distributed to the student body either free or for a fee.")

However, while other forms of speech apparently may not be censored in advance, section 48907 also says that it does not "prohibit or prevent any governing board of a school district from adopting otherwise valid rules and regulations relating to oral communication by students upon the premises of each school."[38]

In *Lopez* the court did not actually decide the issue of whether a student film or video was an "official publication," but it did say that there was no "policy reason for distinguishing between student expression in school-sponsored activities solely on the basis of the medium by which the expression is conveyed."[39] Thus, although by its express terms the statute seems to cover only written materials, it may also apply to other media, such as videos and websites.

4. Disciplinary Action

In 1992, the California Legislature enacted Education Code Section 48950, protecting the rights of public high school students who engage in constitutionally protected speech or other communication. The intent of the Legislature was "that a student shall have the same right to exercise his or her right to free speech on campus as he or she enjoys when off campus."[40] Section 48950 provides that school districts are prohibited from making or enforcing "any rule subjecting any high school pupil to disciplinary sanctions solely on the basis of conduct that is speech or other communication" that, if engaged in off campus, is protected from government restriction by the First Amendment or by Article I, Section 2(a) of the California Constitution.[41]

Freedom of speech rights, however, are subject to reasonable time, place and manner regulations.[42] In addition, Section 48950 specifically provides that it cannot be construed as limiting or modifying the provisions of Section 48907.[43] Censorship of student speech probably does not constitute "disciplinary action." Instead, the statute seems aimed at traditional disciplinary measures such as suspension or expulsion.

---

[36]   Education Code section 48907.

[37]   *Lopez*, 34 Cal. App. 4th at 1322). Emphasizing this point, the court also said: "[W]e disagree with the conclusion that school authorities may censor (i.e., exercise prior restraint over) student expression which is not prepared for an official school publication." *Id.*, at 1320.

[38]   The extent of permissible regulation of student speech under this provision is not clear. One court of appeal held that an earlier version of section 48907 allowed a school district to adopt regulations prohibiting a student religious group from distributing handbills on campus or advertising in the school yearbook. *Perumal v. Saddleback Valley Unified School Dist.*, 198 Cal. App. 3d 64 (1988). However, that decision was later overruled. *Van Schoick v. Saddleback Valley Unified School Dist.*, 87 Cal. App. 4th 522, 528 n. 7 (2001).

[39]   *Lopez*, 34 Cal. App. 4th at 1320 n.4.

[40]   Section 4 of Stats. 1992, c. 1363 (S.B.1115).

[41]   Education Code section 48950(a).

[42]   Education Code section 48950(f).

[43]   Education Code section 48950(e).

While Sections 48907 and 48950 protect student journalists, high school administrators throughout the state have recently retaliated for the publication of stories that have embarrassed or offended the administration. Because Sections 48907 and 48950 do not protect journalism advisers, a number of high school administrators have threatened advisers with discipline or removed them from their role as adviser, replacing them with teachers with little or no journalism background. Some journalism programs have been shut down entirely. While these are extreme examples, they have been occurring more frequently in the last few years and are evidence of a troubling trend.

B. STUDENT PRESS AND SPEECH AT PUBLIC COLLEGES AND UNIVERSITIES.

California law also protects student press and speech activities at public community colleges, state universities and University of California campuses. These statutes do not regulate private colleges or universities.

Like Education Code section 48950, Education Code section 66301 prohibits administrators from making or enforcing "any rule subjecting any student to disciplinary sanction solely on the basis of conduct that is speech or other communication" that would be protected if engaged in off campus.[44] It applies to the University of California, California State Universities and all community college districts.

Education Code section 76120 is similar to (but not as expansive as) section 48907. It provides for the adoption of regulations governing student expression on community college campuses, but also provides that those regulations "shall not prohibit the right of students to exercise free expression including, but not limited to, the use of bulletin boards, the distribution of printed materials or petitions, and the wearing of buttons, badges, or other insignia." However, it is also subject to several exceptions, allowing speech to be prohibited if it is "libelous or slanderous according to current legal standards," or "so incites students as to create a clear and present danger of the commission of unlawful acts on community college premises, or the violation of lawful community college regulations, or the substantial disruption of the orderly operation of the community college."

In 2006, CNPA sponsored legislation, AB 2581, that amended section 66301. The impetus for the legislation was a federal court of appeals decision, *Hosty v. Carter*,[45] which held that a college administrator could require student editors of a state university's newspaper to submit articles for prior review by the administrator before the newspaper would be sent to the printer for publication. As noted in CNPA's analysis of the legislation, prior to the *Hosty* decision, it was assumed that student publications published in California at the college and university level enjoyed the same First Amendment protections as professional publications. The general counsel of the California State University system sent a memo to the president of each state university indicating that, as a result of the decision, they had greater power to restrict student publications. The purpose of the 2006 amendments is to "prohibit[] censorship of student newspapers at a California college, university, or community college by prohibiting UC, CSU, or CCC officials from exercising prior restraint of student speech or the student press."[46] As a result, censorship of student publications at California colleges and universities is prohibited, unless the speech at issue constitutes "hate violence" as defined by California law, and the regulations prohibiting such speech are consistent with the First Amendment and the California Constitution.[47]

---

[44]   Education Code section 66301(a).
[45]   *Hosty v. Carter*, 412 F.3d 731 (7th Cir. 2005).
[46]   A.B. 2581, Assembly Floor Analysis, May 10, 2006, at p. 2.
[47]   Education Code 66301(e) (effective January 1, 2007).

PART III:
UNDERGROUND STUDENT NEWSPAPERS AND OTHER MATERIALS

As the Supreme Court explained in *Tinker*, the act of walking onto a public school campus does not deprive students of their First Amendment rights.[48] And, as explained in Part One of this chapter, the *Hazelwood* decision is predicated on a determination that a school-sponsored publication or activity is not a "public forum," but rather a part of the educational curriculum.[49] Thus, a student publication that is prepared without the school's sponsorship or involvement is entitled to greater protection than school-sponsored publications.

The U.S. Supreme Court's decision in *Tinker* was cited by a decision of the California Supreme Court in which students were given the right to distribute underground newspapers on public school campuses, *Bright v. Los Angeles Unified School District*.[50] The local school district in *Bright* had a rule that required students to submit materials sought to be distributed on campus, including underground newspapers, to a school official for approval *before* distribution. The principal in this case prohibited the student from distributing her underground newspaper out of concern that the paper contained libelous material. The student sued.[51] The school argued that they were authorized under Education Code Section 10611 (since superseded by Section 48907) to prohibit the publication of materials other than official school publications.[52] The Supreme Court disagreed, saying that schools have no authority to prohibit the distribution of unofficial materials on campus.[53] School authorities therefore have no right to prescreen such materials before distribution.

In another example, in the case *Burch v. Barker*, a high school district in Washington State adopted a policy requiring its students to submit to school officials for approval all student-written material before the material could be distributed on school premises or at official school functions.[54] Following adoption of the policy, students were punished for distributing an underground newspaper at a school-sponsored senior class barbecue on school grounds without submitting the material for pre-distribution review.[55]

The federal court of appeals ruled that the Washington policy was unconstitutional. Once distribution has begun, school authorities wishing to prevent further distribution are required to show, pursuant to the standard in *Tinker*, that the prohibition is necessary to prevent a "substantial interference" with school activities.[56] The *Burch* court also said that school officials have no authority to prohibit the sale of publications on campus. This does not mean that the school is unable to discipline a student for distributing an underground newspaper in class during a test. In that case, the student could be disciplined for his or her disruptive activity. The same student could not be disciplined, however, for distributing the newspaper during lunch unless the school was able to make the showing required in *Tinker*.

---

[48]   *Tinker*, 393 U.S. at 506.
[49]   *See above*, Part I, Section 2.
[50]   *Bright v. Los Angeles Unified School District*, 18 Cal. 3d 450 (1976) ("*Bright*").
[51]   *Bright*, 18 Cal. 3d at 453-55.
[52]   *Bright*, 18 Cal. 3d at 459.
[53]   *Bright*, 18 Cal. 3d at 466-67.
[54]   *Burch v. Barker*, 861 F.2d 1149 (9th Cir. 1988) ("*Burch*").
[55]   *Burch*, 861 F.2d at 1150-51.
[56]   *Burch*, 861 F.2d at 1153-54.

PART IV:
REGULATION OF STUDENT SPEECH BY PRIVATE SCHOOLS

The U.S. Constitution generally protects people only from government action. Moreover, free speech is given the most protection when it takes place in a "public forum." Private schools are not part of the government. In general, therefore, unless a private school creates a public forum (for example, by allowing and perhaps even supporting the creation of a school newspaper over which students exercise complete control and which includes material submitted by people outside the school), First Amendment rules that restrict public schools from punishing certain actions do not apply to private schools.

Since 1992, however, California law has extended the equivalent of some First Amendment rights to students at private secondary schools. Under Sections 48950 of the California Education Code, schools cannot punish public *or private* high school students for actions that would be protected by the First Amendment if engaged in off campus.[57] Exempted from the law are schools controlled by a religious organization, to the extent that application of the statute would be inconsistent with the religious tenets of the organization.[58]

In 1993, California enacted a similar law prohibiting private colleges from subjecting a student to disciplinary action for engaging in expression that would be protected by the First Amendment or the California Constitution's free expression provision if it occurred off campus. It also prohibits any prior restraint of student speech.[59] Section 94367 does not apply to any private postsecondary educational institution that is controlled by a religious organization, to the extent that the application of the law would not be consistent with the religious tenets of the organization.[60]

However, Section 48950 – unlike Section 94367 – applies only to "disciplinary sanctions."[61] It does not expressly prohibit censorship. With regard to censorship of publications, the relevant statutory provision, Education Code Section 48907, applies only to students of "public" schools, and thus it does not afford student journalists at private schools any protection.[62]

PART V:
THEFT OF STUDENT NEWSPAPERS

In the past few years, freely distributed newspapers have been stolen in large numbers based on an unpopular viewpoint expressed in an article, column, editorial or advertisement. College publications have been disproportionately affected by this type of content or viewpoint discrimination. Whether the offenders were students or administrators, it was not uncommon for entire press runs to be removed from newsracks and deposited in a remote dumpster. When the newspaper staff urged local police agencies to halt the thefts, officials responded that they were powerless to prosecute the thefts because the newspapers were complimentary, had no fair market value and therefore could not be "stolen."

In 2006, California enacted a new law to specifically address the growing problem. California Penal Code Section 490.7 prohibits a person from taking more than 25 copies of the current issue of a free or complimentary newspaper if done with the intent to: recycle for cash or other payment; sell or

---

[57]   Education Code section 48950(a); Education Code section 66301.
[58]   Education Code section 48950(e).
[59]   Education Code section 94367.
[60]   Education Code section 94367(c).
[61]   Education Code section 48950(a).
[62]   Education Code section 48907 (referencing "students of the public schools").

barter the newspapers; deprive others of the ability to read or enjoy the newspaper; or harm a business competitor. A first violation is an infraction. A second or subsequent violation is either an infraction or a misdemeanor.

Student journalists who find that a large number of their newsracks are empty soon after they have been filled with the latest issue can go immediately to local law enforcement officials, who now have the tool to pursue the thieves.

APPENDIX A

The Brown Act
California Government Code Sections 54950-54963

54950. Legislative finding and declarations. In enacting this chapter, the Legislature finds and declares that the public commissions, boards and councils and the other public agencies in this State exist to aid in the conduct of the people's business. It is the intent of the law that their actions be taken openly and that their deliberations be conducted openly. The people of this State do not yield their sovereignty to the agencies which serve them. The people, in delegating authority, do not give their public servants the right to decide what is good for the people to know and what is not good for them to know. The people insist on remaining informed so that they may retain control over the instruments they have created.

54950.5. Short Title. This chapter shall be known as the Ralph M. Brown Act.

54951. Local agency – definition. As used in this chapter, "local agency" means a county, city, whether general law or chartered, city and county, town, school district, municipal corporation, district, political subdivision, or any board, commission or agency thereof, or other local public agency.

54952. Legislative body – definition. As used in this chapter, "legislative body" means:
(a) The governing body of a local agency or any other local body created by state or federal statute.
(b) A commission, committee, board, or other body of a local agency, whether permanent or temporary, decision making or advisory, created by charter, ordinance, resolution, or formal action of a legislative body. However, advisory committees, composed solely of the members of the legislative body that are less than a quorum of the legislative body are not legislative bodies, except that standing committees of a legislative body, irrespective of their composition, which have a continuing subject matter jurisdiction, or a meeting schedule fixed by charter, ordinance, resolution, or formal action of a legislative body are legislative bodies for purposes of this chapter.
(c) (1) A board, commission, committee, or other multimember body that governs a private corporation, limited liability company, or other entity that either:
(A) Is created by the elected legislative body in order to exercise authority that may lawfully be delegated by the elected governing body to a private corporation, limited liability company, or other entity.
(B) Receives funds from a local agency and the membership of whose governing body includes a member of the legislative body of the local agency appointed to that governing body as a full voting member by the legislative body of the local agency.
(2) Notwithstanding subparagraph (B) of paragraph (1), no board, commission, committee, or other multimember body that governs a private corporation, limited liability company, or other entity that receives funds from a local agency and, as of February 9, 1996, has a member of the legislative body of the local agency as a full voting member of the governing body of that private corporation, limited liability company, or other entity shall be relieved from the public meeting requirements of this chapter by virtue of a change in status of the full voting member to a nonvoting member.

(d) The lessee of any hospital the whole or part of which is first leased pursuant to subdivision (p) of Section 32121 of the Health and Safety Code after January 1, 1994, where the lessee exercises any material authority of a legislative body of a local agency delegated to it by that legislative body whether the lessee is organized and operated by the local agency or by a delegated authority.

54952.1. Application to elected but unsworn officials. Any person elected to serve as a member of a legislative body who has not yet assumed the duties of office shall conform his or her conduct to the requirements of this chapter and shall be treated for purposes of enforcement of this chapter as if he or she has already assumed office.

54952.2. Meeting – definition. (a) As used in this chapter, "meeting" includes any congregation of a majority of the members of a legislative body at the same time and place to hear, discuss, or deliberate upon any item that is within the subject matter jurisdiction of the legislative body or the local agency to which it pertains.

(b) Except as authorized pursuant to Section 54953, any use of direct communication, personal intermediaries, or technological devices that is employed by a majority of the members of the legislative body to develop a collective concurrence as to action to be taken on an item by the members of the legislative body is prohibited.

(c) Nothing in this section shall impose the requirements of this chapter upon any of the following:

(1) Individual contacts or conversations between a member of a legislative body and any other person.

(2) The attendance of a majority of the members of a legislative body at a conference or similar gathering open to the public that involves a discussion of issues of general interest to the public or to public agencies of the type represented by the legislative body, provided that a majority of the members do not discuss among themselves, other than as part of the scheduled program, business of a specified nature that is within the subject matter jurisdiction of the local agency. Nothing in this paragraph is intended to allow members of the public free admission to a conference or similar gathering at which the organizers have required other participants or registrants to pay fees or charges as a condition of attendance.

(3) The attendance of a majority of the members of a legislative body at an open and publicized meeting organized to address a topic of local community concern by a person or organization other than the local agency, provided that a majority of the members do not discuss among themselves, other than as part of the scheduled program, business of a specific nature that is within the subject matter jurisdiction of the legislative body of the local agency.

(4) The attendance of a majority of the members of a legislative body at an open and noticed meeting of another body of the local agency, or at an open and noticed meeting of a legislative body of another local agency, provided that a majority of the members do not discuss among themselves, other than as part of the scheduled meeting, business of a specific nature that is within the subject matter jurisdiction of the legislative body of the local agency.

(5) The attendance of a majority of the members of a legislative body at a purely social or ceremonial occasion, provided that a majority of the members do not discuss among themselves business of a specific nature that is within the subject matter jurisdiction of the legislative body of the local agency.

(6) The attendance of a majority of the members of a legislative body at an open and noticed meeting of a standing committee of that body, provided that the members of the legislative body who are not members of the standing committee attend only as observers.

54952.6. Action taken – definition. As used in this chapter, "action taken" means a collective decision made by a majority of the members of a legislative body, a collective commitment or promise by a majority of the members of a legislative body to make a positive or a negative decision, or an actual vote by a majority of the members of a legislative body when sitting as a body or entity, upon a motion, proposal, resolution, order or ordinance.

54952.7. Copies of chapter to members. A legislative body of a local agency may require that a copy of this chapter be given to each member of the legislative body and any person elected to serve as a member of the legislative body who has not assumed the duties of office. An elected legislative body of a local agency may require that a copy of this chapter be given to each member of each legislative body all or a majority of whose members are appointed by or under the authority of the elected legislative body.

54953. Open and public meetings. (a) All meetings of the legislative body of a local agency shall be open and public, and all persons shall be permitted to attend any meeting of the legislative body of a local agency, except as otherwise provided in this chapter.

54953. Open and public meetings; teleconferencing. (b) (1) Notwithstanding any other provision of law, the legislative body of a local agency may use teleconferencing for the benefit of the public and the legislative body of a local agency in connection with any meeting or proceeding authorized by law. The teleconferenced meeting or proceeding shall comply with all requirements of this chapter and all otherwise applicable provisions of law relating to a specific type of meeting or proceeding.

(2) Teleconferencing, as authorized by this section, may be used for all purposes in connection with any meeting within the subject matter jurisdiction of the legislative body. All votes taken during a teleconferenced meeting shall be by rollcall.

(3) If the legislative body of a local agency elects to use teleconferencing, it shall post agendas at all teleconference locations and conduct teleconference meetings in a manner that protects the statutory and constitutional rights of the parties or the public appearing before the legislative body of a local agency. Each teleconference location shall be identified in the notice and agenda of the meeting or proceeding, and each teleconference location shall be accessible to the public. During the teleconference, at least a quorum of the members of the legislative body shall participate from locations within the boundaries of the territory over which the local agency exercises jurisdiction, except as provided in subdivision (d). The agenda shall provide an opportunity for members of the public to address the legislative body directly pursuant to Section 54954.3 at each teleconference location.

(4) For the purposes of this section, "teleconference" means a meeting of a legislative body, the members of which are in different locations, connected by electronic means, through either audio or video, or both. Nothing in this section shall prohibit a local agency from providing the public with additional teleconference locations.

(c) No legislative body shall take action by secret ballot, whether preliminary or final.

(d) (1) Notwithstanding the provisions relating to a quorum in paragraph (3) of subdivision (b), when a health authority conducts a teleconference meeting, members who are outside the jurisdiction of the authority may be counted toward the establishment of a quorum when participating in the teleconference if at least 50 percent of the number of members that would establish a quorum are present within the boundaries of the territory over which the authority exercises jurisdiction, and the health authority provides a teleconference number, and associated access codes, if any, that allows any person to call in to participate in the meeting and that number and access codes are identified in the notice and agenda of the meeting.

(2) Nothing in this subdivision shall be construed as discouraging health authority members from regularly meeting at a common physical site within the jurisdiction of the authority or from using teleconference locations within or near the jurisdiction of the authority. A teleconference meeting for which a quorum is established pursuant to this subdivision shall be subject to all other requirements of this section.

(3) For purposes of this subdivision, a health authority means any entity created pursuant to Sections 14018.7, 14087.31, 14087.35, 14087.36, 14087.38, and 14087.9605 of the Welfare and Institutions Code, any joint powers authority created pursuant to Article 1 (commencing with Section 6500) of Chapter 5 of Division 7 for the purpose of contracting pursuant to Section 14087.3 of the Welfare and Institutions Code, and any advisory committee to a county sponsored health plan licensed pursuant to Chapter 2.2 (commencing with Section 1340) of Division 2 of the Health and Safety Code if the advisory committee has 12 or more members.

(4) This subdivision shall remain in effect only until January 1, 2009.

54953.1. Grand jury testimony. The provisions of this chapter shall not be construed to prohibit the members of the legislative body of a local agency from giving testimony in private before a grand jury, either as individuals or as a body.

54953.2. Compliance with Americans with Disabilities Act. All meetings of a legislative body of a local agency that are open and public shall meet the protections and prohibitions contained in Section 202 of the Americans with Disabilities Act of 1990 (42 U.S.C. Sec. 12132), and the federal rules and regulations adopted in implementation thereof.

54953.3. Conditions to attendance. A member of the public shall not be required, as a condition to attendance at a meeting of a legislative body of a local agency, to register his or her name, to provide other information, to complete a questionnaire, or otherwise to fulfill any condition precedent to his or her attendance. If an attendance list, register, questionnaire, or other similar document is posted at or near the entrance to the room where the meeting is to be held, or is circulated to the persons present during the meeting, it shall state clearly that the signing, registering, or completion of the document is voluntary, and that all persons may attend the meeting regardless of whether a person signs, registers, or completes the document.

54953.5. Recordings of meetings. (a) Any person attending an open and public meeting of a legislative body of a local agency shall have the right to record the proceedings with an audio or video tape recorder or a still or motion picture camera in the absence of a reasonable finding by the legislative body of the local agency that the recording cannot continue without noise, illumination, or obstruction of view that constitutes, or would constitute, a persistent disruption of the proceedings.

(b) Any tape or film record of an open and public meeting made for whatever purpose by or at the direction of the local agency shall be subject to inspection pursuant to the California Public Records Act (Chapter 3.5 (commencing with Section 6250) of Division 7 of Title 1), but, notwithstanding Section 34090, may be erased or destroyed 30 days after the taping or recording. Any inspection of a video or tape recording shall be provided without charge on a video or tape player made available by the local agency.

54953.6. Broadcast of meetings. No legislative body of a local agency shall prohibit or otherwise restrict the broadcast of its open and public meetings in the absence of a reasonable finding that the broadcast cannot be accomplished without noise, illumination, or obstruction of view that would constitute a persistent disruption of the proceedings.

54953.7. Adoption of requirements for greater access. Notwithstanding any other provision of law, legislative bodies of local agencies may impose requirements upon themselves which allow greater access to their meetings than prescribed by the minimal standards set forth in this chapter. In addition thereto, an elected legislative body of a local agency may impose such requirements on those appointed legislative bodies of the local agency of which all or a majority of the members are appointed by or under the authority of the elected legislative body.

54954. Time and place of regular meetings; special meetings, emergencies. (a) Each legislative body of a local agency, except for advisory committees or standing committees, shall provide, by ordinance, resolution, bylaws, or by whatever other rule is required for the conduct of business by that body, the time and place for holding regular meetings. Meetings of advisory committees or standing committees, for which an agenda is posted at least 72 hours in advance of the meeting pursuant to subdivision (a) of Section 54954.2, shall be considered for purposes of this chapter as regular meetings of the legislative body.

(b) Regular and special meetings of the legislative body shall be held within the boundaries of the territory over which the local agency exercises jurisdiction, except to do any of the following:

(1) Comply with state or federal law or court order, or attend a judicial or administrative proceeding to which the local agency is a party.

(2) Inspect real or personal property which cannot be conveniently brought within the boundaries of the territory over which the local agency exercises jurisdiction provided that the topic of the meeting is limited to items directly related to the real or personal property.

(3) Participate in meetings or discussions of multiagency significance that are outside the boundaries of a local agency's jurisdiction. However, any meeting or discussion held pursuant to this subdivision shall take place within the jurisdiction of one of the participating local agencies and be noticed by all participating agencies as provided for in this chapter.

(4) Meet in the closest meeting facility if the local agency has no meeting facility within the boundaries of the territory over which the local agency exercises jurisdiction, or at the principal office of the local agency if that office is located outside the territory over which the agency exercises jurisdiction.

(5) Meet outside their immediate jurisdiction with elected or appointed officials of the United States or the State of California when a local meeting would be impractical, solely to discuss a legislative or regulatory issue affecting the local agency and over which the federal or state officials have jurisdiction.

(6) Meet outside their immediate jurisdiction if the meeting takes place in or nearby a facility owned by the agency, provided that the topic of the meeting is limited to items directly related to the facility.

(7) Visit the office of the local agency's legal counsel for a closed session on pending litigation held pursuant to Section 54956.9, when to do so would reduce legal fees or costs.

(c) Meetings of the governing board of a school district shall be held within the district, except under the circumstances enumerated in subdivision (b), or to do any of the following:

(1) Attend a conference on nonadversarial collective bargaining techniques.

(2) Interview members of the public residing in another district with reference to the trustees' potential employment of an applicant for the position of the superintendent of the district.

(3) Interview a potential employee from another district.

(d) Meetings of a joint powers authority shall occur within the territory of at least one of its member agencies, or as provided in subdivision (b). However, a joint powers authority which has members throughout the state may meet at any facility in the state which complies with the requirements of Section 54961.

(e) If, by reason of fire, flood, earthquake, or other emergency, it shall be unsafe to meet in the place designated, the meetings shall be held for the duration of the emergency at the place designated by the presiding officer of the legislative body or his or her designee in a notice to the local media that have requested notice pursuant to Section 54956, by the most rapid means of communication available at the time.

54954.1. Mailed notices to person filing written requests; fees. Any person may request that a copy of the agenda, or a copy of all the documents constituting the agenda packet, of any meeting of a legislative body be mailed to that person. If requested, the agenda and documents in the agenda packet shall be made available in appropriate alternative formats to persons with a disability, as required by Section 202 of the Americans with Disabilities Act of 1990 (42 U.S.C. Sec. 12132), and the federal rules and regulations adopted in implementation thereof. Upon receipt of the written request, the legislative body or its designee shall cause the requested materials to be mailed at the time the agenda is posted pursuant to Section 54954.2 and 54956 or upon distribution to all, or a majority of all, of the members of a legislative body, whichever occurs first. Any request for mailed copies of agendas or agenda packets shall be valid for the calendar year in which it is filed, and must be renewed following January 1 of each year. The legislative body may establish a fee for mailing the agenda or agenda packet, which fee shall not exceed the cost of providing the service. Failure of the requesting person to receive the agenda or agenda packet pursuant to this section shall not constitute grounds for invalidation of the actions of the legislative body taken at the meeting for which the agenda or agenda packet was not received.

54954.2. Agenda posting; action on other matters. (a) (1) At least 72 hours before a regular meeting, the legislative body of the local agency, or its designee, shall post an agenda containing a brief general description of each item of business to be transacted or discussed at the meeting, including items to be discussed in closed session. A brief general description of an item generally need not exceed 20 words. The agenda shall specify the time and location of the regular meeting and shall be posted in a location that is freely accessible to members of the public. If requested, the agenda shall be made available in appropriate alternative formats to persons with a disability, as required by Section 202 of the Americans with Disabilities Act of 1990 (42 U.S.C. Sec. 12132), and the federal rules and regulations adopted in implementation thereof. The agenda shall include information regarding how, to whom, and when a request for disability related modification or accommodation, including auxiliary aids or services, may be made by a person with a disability who requires a modification or accommodation in order to participate in the public meeting.

(2) No action or discussion shall be undertaken on any item not appearing on the posted agenda, except that members of a legislative body or its staff may briefly respond to statements made or questions posed by persons exercising their public testimony rights under Section 54954.3. In addition, on their own initiative or in response
to questions posed by the public, a member of a legislative body or its staff may ask a question for clarification, make a brief announcement, or make a brief report on his or her own activities. Furthermore, a member of a legislative body, or the body itself, subject to rules or procedures of the legislative body, may provide a reference to staff or other resources for factual information, request staff to report back to the body at a subsequent meeting concerning any matter, or take action to direct staff to place a matter of business on a future agenda.

(b) Notwithstanding subdivision (a), the legislative body may take action on items of business not appearing on the posted agenda under any of the conditions stated below. Prior to discussing any item pursuant to this subdivision, the legislative body shall publicly identify the item.

(1) Upon a determination by a majority vote of the legislative body that an emergency situation exists, as defined in Section 54956.5.

(2) Upon a determination by a two-thirds vote of the members of the legislative body present at the meeting, or, if less than two-thirds of the members are present, a unanimous vote of those members present, that there is a need to take immediate action and that the need for action came to the attention of the local agency subsequent to the agenda being posted as specified in subdivision (a).

(3) The item was posted pursuant to subdivision (a) for a prior meeting of the legislative body occurring not more than five calendar days prior to the date action is taken on the item, and at the prior meeting the item was continued to the meeting at which action is being taken.

(c) This section is necessary to implement and reasonably within the scope of paragraph (1) of subdivision (b) of Section 3 of Article I of the California Constitution.

54954.3. Opportunity for public to address legislative body; adoption of regulations. (a) Every agenda for regular meetings shall provide an opportunity for members of the public to directly address the legislative body on any item of interest to the public, before or during the legislative body's consideration of the item, that is within the subject matter jurisdiction of the legislative body, provided that no action shall be taken on any item not appearing on the agenda unless the action is otherwise authorized by subdivision (b) of Section 54954.2. However, the agenda need not provide an opportunity for members of the public to address the legislative body on any item that has already been considered by a committee, composed exclusively of members of the legislative body, at a public meeting wherein all interested members of the public were afforded the opportunity to address the committee on the item, before or during the committee's consideration of the item, unless the item has been substantially changed since the committee heard the item, as determined by the legislative body. Every notice for a special meeting shall provide an opportunity for members of the public to directly address the legislative body concerning any item that has been described in the notice for the meeting before or during consideration of that item.

(b) The legislative body of a local agency may adopt reasonable regulations to ensure that the intent of subdivision (a) is carried out, including, but not limited to, regulations limiting the total amount of time allocated for public testimony on particular issues and for each individual speaker.

(c) The legislative body of a local agency shall not prohibit public criticism of the policies, procedures, programs, or services of the agency, or of the acts or omissions of the legislative body. Nothing in this subdivision shall confer any privilege or protection for expression beyond that otherwise provided by law.

54954.4. Reimbursements to local agencies for costs. (a) The Legislature hereby finds and declares that Section 12 of Chapter 641 of the Statutes of 1986, authorizing reimbursement to local agencies and school districts for costs mandated by the state pursuant to that act, shall be interpreted strictly. The intent of the Legislature is to provide reimbursement for only those costs which are clearly and unequivocally incurred as the direct and necessary result of compliance with Chapter 641 of the Statutes of 1986.

(b) In this regard, the Legislature directs all state employees and officials involved in reviewing or authorizing claims for reimbursement, or otherwise participating in the reimbursement process, to rigorously review each claim and authorize only those claims, or parts thereof, which represent costs which are clearly and unequivocally incurred as the direct and necessary result of compliance with Chapter 641 of the Statutes of 1986 and for which complete documentation exists. For purposes of Section 54954.2, costs eligible for reimbursement shall only include the actual cost to post a single agenda for any one meeting.

(c) The Legislature hereby finds and declares that complete, faithful, and uninterrupted compliance with the Ralph M. Brown Act (Chapter 9 (commencing with Section 54950) of Part 1 of Division 2 of Title 5 of the Government Code) is a matter of overriding public importance. Unless specifically stated, no future Budget Act, or related budget enactments, shall, in any manner, be interpreted to suspend, eliminate, or otherwise modify the legal obligation and duty of local agencies to fully comply with Chapter 641 of the Statutes of 1986 in a complete, faithful, and uninterrupted manner.

54954.5. Closed session agenda descriptions. For purposes of describing closed session items pursuant to Section 54954.2, the agenda may describe closed sessions as provided below. No legislative body or elected official shall be in violation of Section 54954.2 or 54956 if the closed session items were described in substantial compliance with this section. Substantial compliance is satisfied by including the information provided below, irrespective of its format.

(a) With respect to a closed session held pursuant to Section 54956.7:

LICENSE/PERMIT DETERMINATION
Applicant(s): (Specify number of applicants)
(b) With respect to every item of business to be discussed in closed session pursuant to Section 54956.8:

CONFERENCE WITH REAL PROPERTY NEGOTIATORS
Property: (Specify street address, or if no street address, the parcel number or other unique reference, of the real property under negotiation)
Agency negotiator: (Specify names of negotiators attending the closed session) (If circumstances necessitate the absence of a specified negotiator, an agent or designee may participate in place of the absent negotiator so long as the name of the agent or designee is announced at an open session held prior to the closed session.)
Negotiating parties: (Specify name of party (not agent))
Under negotiation: (Specify whether instruction to negotiator will concern price, terms of payment, or both)

(c) With respect to every item of business to be discussed in closed session pursuant to Section 54956.9:

CONFERENCE WITH LEGAL COUNSEL – EXISTING LITIGATION
(Subdivision (a) of Section 54956.9)
Name of case: (Specify by reference to claimant's name, names of parties, case or claim numbers) Or
Case name unspecified: (Specify whether disclosure would jeopardize service of process or existing settlement negotiations)

CONFERENCE WITH LEGAL COUNSEL – ANTICIPATED LITIGATION
Significant exposure to litigation pursuant to subdivision (b) of Section 54956.9: (Specify number of potential cases)
(In addition to the information noticed above, the agency may be required to provide additional information on the agenda or in an oral statement prior to the closed session pursuant to subparagraphs (B) to (E), inclusive, of paragraph (3) of subdivision (b) of Section 54956.9.)

Initiation of litigation pursuant to subdivision (c) of Section 54956.9: (Specify number of potential cases)

(d) With respect to every item of business to be discussed in closed session pursuant to Section 54956.95:

LIABILITY CLAIMS
Claimant: (Specify name unless unspecified pursuant to Section 54961)
Agency claimed against: (Specify name)

(e) With respect to every item of business to be discussed in closed session pursuant to Section 54957:

THREAT TO PUBLIC SERVICES OR FACILITIES
Consultation with: (Specify name of law enforcement agency and title of officer, or name of applicable agency representative and title)

PUBLIC EMPLOYEE APPOINTMENT
Title: (Specify description of position to be filled)

PUBLIC EMPLOYMENT
Title: (Specify description of position to be filled)

PUBLIC EMPLOYEE PERFORMANCE EVALUATION
Title: (Specify position title of employee being reviewed)

PUBLIC EMPLOYEE DISCIPLINE/DISMISSAL/RELEASE
(No additional information is required in connection with a closed session to consider discipline, dismissal, or release of a public employee. Discipline includes potential reduction of compensation.)

(f) With respect to every item of business to be discussed in closed session pursuant to Section 54957.6:

CONFERENCE WITH LABOR NEGOTIATORS
Agency designated representatives: (Specify names of designated representatives attending the closed session) (If circumstances necessitate the absence of a specified designated representative, an agent or designee may participate in place of the absent representative so long as the name of the agent or designee is announced at an open session held prior to the closed session.)
Employee organization: (Specify name of organization representing employee or employees in question) Or
Unrepresented employee: (Specify position title of unrepresented employee who is the subject of the negotiations)

(g) With respect to closed sessions called pursuant to Section 54957.8:

CASE REVIEW/PLANNING
(No additional information is required in connection with a closed session to consider case review or planning.)

(h) With respect to every item of business to be discussed in closed session pursuant to Sections 1461, 32106, and 32155 of the Health and Safety Code or Sections 37606 and 37624.3 of the Government Code:

REPORT INVOLVING TRADE SECRET
Discussion will concern: (Specify whether discussion will concern proposed new service, program, or facility)
Estimated date of public disclosure: (Specify month and year)

HEARINGS
Subject matter: (Specify whether testimony/deliberation will concern staff privileges, report of medical audit committee, or report of quality assurance committee)

(i) With respect to every item of business to be discussed in closed session pursuant to Section 54956.86:

CHARGE OR COMPLAINT INVOLVING INFORMATION PROTECTED BY FEDERAL LAW
(No additional information is required in connection with a closed session to discuss a charge or complaint pursuant to Section 54956.86.)

(j) With respect to every item of business to be discussed in closed session pursuant to Section 54956.96:

CONFERENCE INVOLVING A JOINT POWERS AGENCY (Specify by name)
Discussion will concern: (Specify closed session description used by the joint powers agency)
Name of local agency representative on joint powers agency board: (Specify name)
(Additional information listing the names of agencies or titles of representatives attending the closed session as consultants or other representatives.)

(k) With respect to every item of business to be discussed in closed session pursuant to Section 54956.75:

AUDIT BY BUREAU OF STATE AUDITS

54954.6. New or increased taxes or assessments, hearings; notice. (a) (1) Before adopting any new or increased general tax or any new or increased assessment, the legislative body of a local agency shall conduct at least one public meeting at which local officials shall allow public testimony regarding the proposed new or increased general tax or new or increased assessment in addition to the noticed public hearing at which the legislative body proposes to enact or increase the general tax or assessment.

For purposes of this section, the term "new or increased assessment" does not include any of the following:

(A) A fee that does not exceed the reasonable cost of providing the services, facilities, or regulatory activity for which the fee is charged.

(B) A service charge, rate, or charge, unless a special district's principal act requires the service charge, rate, or charge to conform to the requirements of this section.

(C) An ongoing annual assessment if it is imposed at the same or lower amount as any previous year.

(D) An assessment that does not exceed an assessment formula or range of assessments previously specified in the notice given to the public pursuant to subparagraph (G) of paragraph (2) of subdivision (c) and that was previously adopted by the agency or approved by the voters in the area where the assessment is imposed.

(E) Standby or immediate availability charges.

(2) The legislative body shall provide at least 45 days' public notice of the public hearing at which the legislative body proposes to enact or increase the general tax or assessment. The legislative body shall provide notice for the public meeting at the same time and in the same document as the notice for the public hearing, but the meeting shall occur prior to the hearing.

(b) (1) The joint notice of both the public meeting and the public hearing required by subdivision (a) with respect to a proposal for a new or increased general tax shall be accomplished by placing a display advertisement of at least one-eighth page in a newspaper of general circulation for three weeks pursuant to Section 6063 and by a first-class mailing to those interested parties who have filed a written request with the local agency for mailed notice of public meetings or hearings on new or increased general taxes. The public meeting pursuant to subdivision (a) shall take place no earlier than 10 days after the first publication of the joint notice pursuant to this subdivision. The public hearing shall take place no earlier than seven days after the public meeting pursuant to this subdivision. Notwithstanding paragraph (2) of subdivision (a), the joint notice need not include notice of the public meeting after the meeting has taken place. The public hearing pursuant to subdivision (a) shall take place no earlier than 45 days after the first publication of the joint notice pursuant to this subdivision. Any written request for mailed notices shall be effective for one year from the date on which it is filed unless a renewal request is filed. Renewal requests for mailed notices shall be filed on or before April 1 of each year. The legislative body may establish a reasonable annual charge for sending notices based on the estimated cost of providing the service.

(2) The notice required by paragraph (1) of this subdivision shall include, but not be limited to, the following:

(A) The amount or rate of the tax. If the tax is proposed to be increased from any previous year, the joint notice shall separately state both the existing tax rate and the proposed tax rate increase.

(B) The activity to be taxed.

(C) The estimated amount of revenue to be raised by the tax annually.

(D) The method and frequency for collecting the tax.

(E) The dates, times, and locations of the public meeting and hearing described in subdivision (a).

(F) The phone number and address of an individual, office, or organization that interested persons may contact to receive additional information about the tax.

(c) (1) The joint notice of both the public meeting and the public hearing required by subdivision (a) with respect to a proposal for a new or increased assessment on real property shall be accomplished through a mailing, postage prepaid, in the United States mail and shall be deemed given when so deposited. The public meeting pursuant to subdivision (a) shall take place no earlier than 10 days after the joint mailing pursuant to this subdivision. The public hearing shall take place no earlier than seven days after the public meeting pursuant to this subdivision. The envelope or the cover of the mailing shall include the name of the local agency and the return address of the sender. This mailed notice shall be in at least 10-point type and shall be given to all property owners proposed to be subject to the new or increased assessment by a mailing by name to those persons whose names and addresses appear on the last equalized county assessment roll or the State Board of Equalization assessment roll, as the case may be.

(2) The joint notice required by paragraph (1) of this subdivision shall include, but not be limited to, the following:

(A) The estimated amount of the assessment per parcel. If the assessment is proposed to be increased from any previous year, the joint notice shall separately state both the amount of the existing assessment and the proposed assessment increase.

(B) A general description of the purpose or improvements that the assessment will fund.

(C) The address to which property owners may mail a protest against the assessment.

(D) The phone number and address of an individual, office, or organization that interested persons may contact to receive additional information about the assessment.

(E) A statement that a majority protest will cause the assessment to be abandoned if the assessment act used to levy the assessment so provides. Notice shall also state the percentage of protests required to trigger an election, if applicable.

(F) The dates, times, and locations of the public meeting and hearing described in subdivision (a).

(G) A proposed assessment formula or range as described in subparagraph (D) of paragraph (1) of subdivision (a) if applicable and that is noticed pursuant to this section.

(3) Notwithstanding paragraph (1), in the case of an assessment that is proposed exclusively for operation and maintenance expenses imposed throughout the entire local agency, or exclusively for operation and maintenance assessments proposed to be levied on 50,000 parcels or more, notice may be provided pursuant to this subdivision or pursuant to paragraph (1) of subdivision (b) and shall include the estimated amount of the assessment of various types, amounts, or uses of property and the information required by subparagraphs (B) to (G), inclusive, of paragraph (2) of subdivision (c).

(4) Notwithstanding paragraph (1), in the case of an assessment proposed to be levied pursuant to Part 2 (commencing with Section 22500) of Division 2 of the Streets and Highways Code by a regional park district, regional park and open-space district, or regional open-space district formed pursuant to Article 3 (commencing with Section 5500) of Chapter 3 of Division 5 of, or pursuant to Division 26 (commencing with Section 35100) of, the Public Resources Code, notice may be provided pursuant to paragraph (1) of subdivision (b).

(d) The notice requirements imposed by this section shall be construed as additional to, and not to supersede, existing provisions of law, and shall be applied concurrently with the existing provisions so as to not delay or prolong the governmental decision making process.

(e) This section shall not apply to any new or increased general tax or any new or increased assessment that requires an election of either of the following:

(1) The property owners subject to the assessment.

(2) The voters within the local agency imposing the tax or assessment.

(f) Nothing in this section shall prohibit a local agency from holding a consolidated meeting or hearing at which the legislative body discusses multiple tax or assessment proposals.

(g) The local agency may recover the reasonable costs of public meetings, public hearings, and notice required by this section from the proceeds of the tax or assessment. The costs recovered for these purposes, whether recovered pursuant to this subdivision or any other provision of law, shall not exceed the reasonable costs of the public meetings, public hearings, and notice.

(h) Any new or increased assessment that is subject to the notice and hearing provisions of Article XIIIC or XIIID of the California Constitution is not subject to the notice and hearing requirements of this section.

54955. Adjournment; adjourned meetings. The legislative body of a local agency may adjourn any regular, adjourned regular, special or adjourned special meeting to a time and place specified in the order of adjournment. Less than a quorum may so adjourn from time to time. If all members are absent from any regular or adjourned regular meeting the clerk or secretary of the legislative body may declare the meeting adjourned to a stated time and place and he shall cause a written notice of the adjournment to be given in the same manner as provided in Section 54956 for special meetings, unless such notice is waived as provided for special meetings. A copy of the order or notice of adjournment shall be conspicuously posted on or near the door of the place where the regular, adjourned regular, special or adjourned special meeting was held within 24 hours after the time of the adjournment. When a regular or adjourned regular meeting is adjourned as provided in this section, the resulting adjourned regular meeting is a regular meeting for all purposes. When an order of adjournment of any meeting fails to state the hour at which the adjourned meeting is to be held, it shall be held at the hour specified for regular meetings by ordinance, resolution, bylaw, or other rule.

54955.1. Continuance. Any hearing being held, or noticed or ordered to be held, by a legislative body of a local agency at any meeting may by order or notice of continuance be continued or recontinued to any subsequent meeting of the legislative body in the same manner and to the same extent set forth in Section 54955 for the adjournment of meetings; provided, that if the hearing is continued to a time less than 24 hours after the time specified in the order or notice of hearing, a copy of the order or notice of continuance of hearing shall be posted immediately following the meeting at which the order or declaration of continuance was adopted or made.

54956. Special meetings; call; notice. A special meeting may be called at any time by the presiding officer of the legislative body of a local agency, or by a majority of the members of the legislative body, by delivering written notice to each member of the legislative body and to each local newspaper of general circulation and radio or television station requesting notice in writing. The notice shall be delivered personally or by any other means and shall be received at least 24 hours before the time of the meeting as specified in the notice. The call and notice shall specify the time and place of the special meeting and the business to be transacted or discussed. No other business shall be considered at these meetings by the legislative body. The written notice may be dispensed with as to any member who at or prior to the time the meeting convenes files with the clerk or secretary of the legislative body a written waiver of notice. The waiver may be given by telegram. The written notice may also be dispensed with as to any member who is actually present at the meeting at the time it convenes.

The call and notice shall be posted at least 24 hours prior to the special meeting in a location that is freely accessible to members of the public.

54956.5. Emergency meetings; criteria for call. (a) For purposes of this section, "emergency situation" means both of the following:

(1) An emergency, which shall be defined as a work stoppage, crippling activity, or other activity that severely impairs public health, safety, or both, as determined by a majority of the members of the legislative body.

(2) A dire emergency, which shall be defined as a crippling disaster, mass destruction, terrorist act, or threatened terrorist activity that poses peril so immediate and significant that requiring a legislative body to provide one-hour notice before holding an emergency meeting under this section may endanger the public health, safety, or both, as determined by a majority of the members of the legislative body.

(b) (1) Subject to paragraph (2), in the case of an emergency situation involving matters upon which prompt action is necessary due to the disruption or threatened disruption of public facilities, a legislative body may hold an emergency meeting without complying with either the 24-hour notice requirement or the 24-hour posting requirement of Section 54956 or both of the notice and posting requirements.

(2) Each local newspaper of general circulation and radio or television station that has requested notice of special meetings pursuant to Section 54956 shall be notified by the presiding officer of the legislative body, or designee thereof, one hour prior to the emergency meeting, or, in the case of a dire emergency, at or near the time that the presiding officer or designee notifies the members of the legislative body of the emergency meeting. This notice shall be given by telephone, and all telephone numbers provided in the most recent request of a newspaper or station for notification of special meetings shall be exhausted. In the event that telephone services are not functioning, the notice requirements of this section shall be deemed waived, and the legislative body, or designee of the legislative body, shall notify those newspapers, radio stations, or television stations of the fact of the holding of the emergency meeting, the purpose of the meeting, and any action taken at the meeting as soon after the meeting as possible.

(c) During a meeting held pursuant to this section, the legislative body may meet in closed session pursuant to Section 54957 if agreed to by a two-thirds vote of the members of the legislative body present, or, if less than two-thirds of the members are present, by a unanimous vote of the members present.

(d) All special meeting requirements, as prescribed in Section 54956 shall be applicable to a meeting called pursuant to this section, with the exception of the 24-hour notice requirement.

(e) The minutes of a meeting called pursuant to this section, a list of persons who the presiding officer of the legislative body, or designee of the legislative body, notified or attempted to notify, a copy of the rollcall vote, and any actions taken at the meeting shall be posted for a minimum of 10 days in a public place as soon after the meeting as possible.

54956.6. Fees. No fees may be charged by the legislative body of a local agency for carrying out any provision of this chapter, except as specifically authorized by this chapter.

54956.7. Closed sessions; license applications; rehabilitated criminals. Whenever a legislative body of a local agency determines that it is necessary to discuss and determine whether an applicant for a license or license renewal, who has a criminal record, is sufficiently rehabilitated to obtain the license, the legislative body may hold a closed session with the applicant and the applicant's attorney, if any, for the purpose of holding the discussion and making the determination. If the legislative body determines, as a result of the closed session, that the issuance or renewal of the license should be denied, the applicant shall be offered the opportunity to withdraw the application. If the applicant withdraws the application, no record shall be kept of the discussions or decisions made at the closed session and all matters relating to the closed session shall be confidential. If the applicant does not withdraw the application, the legislative body shall take action at the public meeting during which the closed session is held or at its next public meeting denying the application for the license, but all matters relating to the closed session are confidential and shall not be disclosed without the consent of the applicant, except in an action by an applicant who has been denied a license challenging the denial of the license.

54956.75. Closed session to discuss response to final draft audit report. (a) Nothing contained in this chapter shall be construed to prevent the legislative body of a local agency that has received a confidential final draft audit report from the Bureau of State Audits from holding closed sessions to discuss its response to that report.

(b) After the public release of an audit report by the Bureau of State Audits, if a legislative body of a local agency meets to discuss the audit report, it shall do so in an open session unless exempted from that requirement by some other provision of law.

54956.8. Real property transactions; closed sessions with negotiator. Notwithstanding any other provision of this chapter, a legislative body of a local agency may hold a closed session with its negotiator prior to the purchase, sale, exchange, or lease of real property by or for the local agency to grant authority to its negotiator regarding the price and terms of payment for the purchase, sale, exchange, or lease.

However, prior to the closed session, the legislative body of the local agency shall hold an open and public session in which it identifies its negotiators, the real property or real properties which the negotiations may concern, and the person or persons with whom its negotiators may negotiate.

For purposes of this section, negotiators may be members of the legislative body of the local agency.

For purposes of this section, "lease" includes renewal or renegotiation of a lease.

Nothing in this section shall preclude a local agency from holding a closed session for discussions regarding eminent domain proceedings pursuant to Section 54956.9.

54956.81. Closed session to discuss pension fund investments. Notwithstanding any other provision of this chapter, a legislative body of a local agency that invests pension funds may hold a closed session to consider the purchase or sale of particular, specific pension fund investments. All investment transaction decisions made during the closed session shall be made by rollcall vote entered into the minutes of the closed session as provided in subdivision (a) of Section 54957.2.

54956.86. Closed session to hear charge or complaint regarding agency's health services plan. Notwithstanding any other provision of this chapter, a legislative body of a local agency which provides services pursuant to Section 14087.3 of the Welfare and Institutions Code may hold a closed session to hear a charge or complaint from a member enrolled in its health plan if the member does not wish to have his or her name, medical status, or other information that is protected by federal law publicly disclosed. Prior to holding a closed session pursuant to this section, the legislative body shall inform the member, in writing, of his or her right to have the charge or complaint heard in an open session rather than a closed session.

54956.87. Closed session to discuss health care service information (a) Notwithstanding any other provision of this chapter, the records of a health plan that is licensed pursuant to the Knox-Keene Health Care Service Plan Act of 1975 (Chapter 2.2 (commencing with Section 1340) of Division 2 of the Health and Safety Code) and that is governed by a county board of supervisors, whether paper records, records maintained in the management information system, or records in any other form, that relate to provider rate or payment determinations, allocation or distribution methodologies for provider payments, formulas or calculations for these payments, and contract negotiations with providers of health care for alternative rates are exempt from disclosure for a period of three years after the contract is fully executed. The transmission of the records, or the information contained therein in an alternative form, to the board of supervisors shall not constitute a waiver of exemption from disclosure, and the records and information once transmitted to the board of supervisors shall be subject to this same exemption.

(b) Notwithstanding any other provision of law, the governing board of a health plan that is licensed pursuant to the Knox-Keene Health Care Service Plan Act of 1975 (Chapter 2.2 (commencing with Section 1340) of Division 2 of the Health and Safety Code) and that is governed by a county board of supervisors may order that a meeting held solely for the purpose of discussion or taking action on health plan trade secrets, as defined in subdivision (f), shall be held in closed session. The requirements of making a public report of action taken in closed session, and the vote or abstention of every member present, may be limited to a brief general description without the information constituting the trade secret.

(c) Notwithstanding any other provision of law, the governing board of a health plan may meet in closed session to consider and take action on matters pertaining to contracts and contract negotiations by the health plan with providers of health care services concerning all matters related to rates of payment. The governing board may delete the portion or portions containing trade secrets from any documents that were finally approved in the closed session held pursuant to subdivision (b) that are provided to persons who have made the timely or standing request.

(d) Nothing in this section shall be construed as preventing the governing board from meeting in closed session as otherwise provided by law.

(e) The provisions of this section shall not prevent access to any records by the Joint Legislative Audit Committee in the exercise of its powers pursuant to Article 1 (commencing with Section 10500) of Chapter 4 of Part 2 of Division 2 of Title 2. The provisions of this section also shall not prevent access to any records by the Department of Corporations in the exercise of its powers pursuant to Article 1 (commencing with Section 1340) of Chapter 2.2 of Division 2 of the Health and Safety Code.

(f) For purposes of this section, "health plan trade secret" means a trade secret, as defined in subdivision (d) of Section 3426.1 of the Civil Code, that also meets both of the following criteria:

(1) The secrecy of the information is necessary for the health plan to initiate a new service, program, marketing strategy, business plan, or technology, or to add a benefit or product.

(2) Premature disclosure of the trade secret would create a substantial probability of depriving the health plan of a substantial economic benefit or opportunity.

54956.9. Pending/anticipated litigation; closed session with legal counsel; notice. Nothing in this chapter shall be construed to prevent a legislative body of a local agency, based on advice of its legal counsel, from holding a closed session to confer with, or receive advice from, its legal counsel regarding pending litigation when discussion in open session concerning those matters would prejudice the position of the local agency in the litigation.

For purposes of this chapter, all expressions of the lawyer-client privilege other than those provided in this section are hereby abrogated. This section is the exclusive expression of the lawyer-client privilege for purposes of conducting closed-session meetings pursuant to this chapter.

For purposes of this section, "litigation" includes any adjudicatory proceeding, including eminent domain, before a court, administrative body exercising its adjudicatory authority, hearing officer, or arbitrator.

For purposes of this section, litigation shall be considered pending when any of the following circumstances exist:

(a) Litigation, to which the local agency is a party, has been initiated formally.

(b) (1) A point has been reached where, in the opinion of the legislative body of the local agency on the advice of its legal counsel, based on existing facts and circumstances, there is a significant exposure to litigation against the local agency.

(2) Based on existing facts and circumstances, the legislative body of the local agency is meeting only to decide whether a closed session is authorized pursuant to paragraph (1) of this subdivision.

(3) For purposes of paragraphs (1) and (2), "existing facts and circumstances" shall consist only of one of the following:

(A) Facts and circumstances that might result in litigation against the local agency but which the local agency believes are not yet known to a potential plaintiff or plaintiffs, which facts and circumstances need not be disclosed.

(B) Facts and circumstances, including, but not limited to, an accident, disaster, incident, or transactional occurrence that might result in litigation against the agency and that are known to a potential plaintiff or plaintiffs, which facts or circumstances shall be publicly stated on the agenda or announced.

(C) The receipt of a claim pursuant to the Tort Claims Act or some other written communication from a potential plaintiff threatening litigation, which claim or communication shall be available for public inspection pursuant to Section 54957.5.

(D) A statement made by a person in an open and public meeting threatening litigation on a specific matter within the responsibility of the legislative body.

(E) A statement threatening litigation made by a person outside an open and public meeting on a specific matter within the responsibility of the legislative body so long as the official or employee of the local agency receiving knowledge of the threat makes a contemporaneous or other record of the statement prior to the meeting, which record shall be available for public inspection pursuant to Section 54957.5. The records so created need not identify the alleged victim of unlawful or tortious sexual conduct or anyone making the threat on their behalf, or identify a public employee who is the alleged perpetrator of any unlawful or tortuous conduct upon which a threat of litigation is based, unless the identity of the person has been publicly disclosed.

(F) Nothing in this section shall require disclosure of written communications that are privileged and not subject to disclosure pursuant to the California Public Records Act (Chapter 3.5 (commencing with Section 6250) of Division 7 of Title 1).

(c) Based on existing facts and circumstances, the legislative body of the local agency has decided to initiate or is deciding whether to initiate litigation.

Prior to holding a closed session pursuant to this section, the legislative body of the local agency shall state on the agenda or publicly announce the subdivision of this section that authorizes the closed session. If the session is closed pursuant to subdivision (a), the body shall state the title of or otherwise specifically identify the litigation to be discussed, unless the body states that to do so would jeopardize the agency's ability to effectuate service of process upon one or more unserved parties, or that to do so would jeopardize its ability to conclude existing settlement negotiations to its advantage.

A local agency shall be considered to be a "party" or to have a "significant exposure to litigation" if an officer or employee of the local agency is a party or has significant exposure to litigation concerning prior or prospective activities or alleged activities during the course and scope of that office or employment, including litigation in which it is an issue whether an activity is outside the course and scope of the office or employment.

54956.95. Closed session; insurance pooling; tort liability losses; public liability losses; workers compensation liability. (a) Nothing in this chapter shall be construed to prevent a joint powers agency formed pursuant to Article 1 (commencing with Section 6500) of Chapter 5 of Division 7 of Title 1, for purposes of insurance pooling, or a local agency member of the joint powers agency, from holding a closed session to discuss a claim for the payment of tort liability losses, public liability losses, or workers' compensation liability incurred by the joint powers agency or a local agency member of the joint powers agency.

(b) Nothing in this chapter shall be construed to prevent the Local Agency Self-Insurance Authority formed pursuant to Chapter 5.5 (commencing with Section 6599.01) of Division 7 of Title 1, or a local agency member of the authority, from holding a closed session to discuss a claim for the payment of tort liability losses, public liability losses, or workers' compensation liability incurred by the authority or a local agency member of the authority.

(c) Nothing in this section shall be construed to affect Section 54956.9 with respect to any other local agency.

54956.96. Joint powers agency closed session discussions. (a) Nothing in this chapter shall be construed to prevent the legislative body of a joint powers agency formed pursuant to Article 1 (commencing with Section 6500) of Chapter 5 of Division 7 of Title 1, from adopting a policy or a bylaw or including in its joint powers agreement provisions that authorize either or both of the following:

(1) All information received by the legislative body of the local agency member in a closed session related to the information presented to the joint powers agency in closed session shall be confidential. However, a member of the legislative body of a member local agency may disclose information obtained in a closed session that has direct financial or liability implications for that local agency to the following individuals:

(A) Legal counsel of that member local agency for purposes of obtaining advice on whether the matter has direct financial or liability implications for that member local agency.

(B) Other members of the legislative body of the local agency present in a closed session of that member local agency.

(2) Any designated alternate member of the legislative body of the joint powers agency who is also a member of the legislative body of a local agency member and who is attending a properly noticed meeting of the joint powers agency in lieu of a local agency member's regularly appointed member to attend closed sessions of the joint powers agency.

(b) If the legislative body of a joint powers agency adopts a policy or a bylaw or includes provisions in its joint powers agreement pursuant to subdivision (a), then the legislative body of the local agency member, upon the advice of its legal counsel, may conduct a closed session in order to receive, discuss, and take action concerning information obtained in a closed session of the joint powers agency pursuant to paragraph (1) of subdivision (a).

54957. Closed session; threat to public services, personnel matters; exclusion of witnesses; definition of employees; salary discussions. (a) Nothing contained in this chapter shall be construed to prevent the legislative body of a local agency from holding closed sessions with the Attorney General, district attorney, agency counsel, sheriff, or chief of police, or their respective deputies, or a security consultant or a security operations manager, on matters posing a threat to the security of public buildings, a threat to the security of essential public services, including water, drinking water, wastewater treatment, natural gas service, and electric service, or a threat to the public's right of access to public services or public facilities.

(b) (1) Subject to paragraph (2), nothing contained in this chapter shall be construed to prevent the legislative body of a local agency from holding closed sessions during a regular or special meeting to consider the appointment, employment, evaluation of performance, discipline, or dismissal of a public employee or to hear complaints or charges brought against the employee by another person or employee unless the employee requests a public session.

(2) As a condition to holding a closed session on specific complaints or charges brought against an employee by another person or employee, the employee shall be given written notice of his or her right to have the complaints or charges heard in an open session rather than a closed session, which notice shall be delivered to the employee personally or by mail at least 24 hours before the time for holding the session. If notice is not given, any disciplinary or other action taken by the legislative body against the employee based on the specific complaints or charges in the closed session shall be null and void.

(3) The legislative body also may exclude from the public or closed meeting, during the examination of a witness, any or all other witnesses in the matter being investigated by the legislative body.

(4) For the purposes of this subdivision, the term "employee" shall include an officer or an independent contractor who functions as an officer or an employee but shall not include any elected official, member of a legislative body or other independent contractors. Nothing in this subdivision shall limit local officials' ability to hold closed session meetings pursuant to Sections 1461, 32106, and 32155 of the Health and Safety Code or Sections 37606 and 37624.3 of the Government Code. Closed sessions held pursuant to this subdivision shall not include discussion or action on proposed compensation except for a reduction of compensation that results from the imposition of discipline.

54957.1. Public report of action in closed session. (a) The legislative body of any local agency shall publicly report any action taken in closed session and the vote or abstention on that action of every member present, as follows: (1) Approval of an agreement concluding real estate negotiations pursuant to Section 54956.8 shall be reported after the agreement is final, as follows:

(A) If its own approval renders the agreement final, the body shall report that approval and the substance of the agreement in open session at the public meeting during which the closed session is held.

(B) If final approval rests with the other party to the negotiations, the local agency shall disclose the fact of that approval and the substance of the agreement upon inquiry by any person, as soon as the other party or its agent has informed the local agency of its approval.

(2) Approval given to its legal counsel to defend, or seek or refrain from seeking appellate review or relief, or to enter as an amicus curiae in any form of litigation as the result of a consultation under Section 54956.9 shall be reported in open session at the public meeting during which the closed session is held. The report shall identify, if known, the adverse party or parties and the substance of the litigation. In the case of approval given to initiate or intervene in an action, the announcement need not identify the action, the defendants, or other particulars, but shall specify that the direction to initiate or intervene in an action has been given and that the action, the defendants, and the other particulars shall, once formally commenced, be disclosed to any person upon inquiry, unless to do so would jeopardize the agency's ability to effectuate service of process on one or more unserved parties, or that to do so would jeopardize its ability to conclude existing settlement negotiations to its advantage.

(3) Approval given to its legal counsel of a settlement of pending litigation, as defined in Section 54956.9, at any stage prior to or during a judicial or quasi-judicial proceeding shall be reported after the settlement is final, as follows:

(A) If the legislative body accepts a settlement offer signed by the opposing party, the body shall report its acceptance and identify the substance of the agreement in open session at the public meeting during which the closed session is held.

(B) If final approval rests with some other party to the litigation or with the court, then as soon as the settlement becomes final, and upon inquiry by any person, the local agency shall disclose the fact of that approval, and identify the substance of the agreement.

(4) Disposition reached as to claims discussed in closed session pursuant to Section 54956.95 shall be reported as soon as reached in a manner that identifies the name of the claimant, the name of the local agency claimed against, the substance of the claim, and any monetary amount approved for payment and agreed upon by the claimant.

(5) Action taken to appoint, employ, dismiss, accept the resignation of, or otherwise affect the employment status of a public employee in closed session pursuant to Section 54957 shall be reported at the public meeting during which the closed session is held. Any report required by this

paragraph shall identify the title of the position. The general requirement of this paragraph notwithstanding, the report of a dismissal or of the nonrenewal of an employment contract shall be deferred until the first public meeting following the exhaustion of administrative remedies, if any.

(6) Approval of an agreement concluding labor negotiations with represented employees pursuant to Section 54957.6 shall be reported after the agreement is final and has been accepted or ratified by the other party. The report shall identify the item approved and the other party or parties to the negotiation.

(7) Pension fund investment transaction decisions made pursuant to Section 54956.81 shall be disclosed at the first open meeting of the legislative body held after the earlier of the close of the investment transaction or the transfer of pension fund assets for the investment transaction.

(b) Reports that are required to be made pursuant to this section may be made orally or in writing. The legislative body shall provide to any person who has submitted a written request to the legislative body within 24 hours of the posting of the agenda, or to any person who has made a standing request for all documentation as part of a request for notice of meetings pursuant to Section 54954.1 or 54956, if the requester is present at the time the closed session ends, copies of any contracts, settlement agreements, or other documents that were finally approved or adopted in the closed session. If the action taken results in one or more substantive amendments to the related documents requiring retyping, the documents need not be released until the retyping is completed during normal business hours, provided that the presiding officer of the legislative body or his or her designee orally summarizes the substance of the amendments for the benefit of the document requester or any other person present and requesting the information.

(c) The documentation referred to in subdivision (b) shall be available to any person on the next business day following the meeting in which the action referred to is taken or, in the case of substantial amendments, when any necessary retyping is complete.

(d) Nothing in this section shall be construed to require that the legislative body approve actions not otherwise subject to legislative body approval.

(e) No action for injury to a reputational, liberty, or other personal interest may be commenced by or on behalf of any employee or former employee with respect to whom a disclosure is made by a legislative body in an effort to comply with this section.

(f) This section is necessary to implement, and reasonably within the scope of, paragraph (1) of subdivision (b) of Section 3 of Article I of the California Constitution.

54957.2. Minute book record of closed sessions; inspection. (a) The legislative body of a local agency may, by ordinance or resolution, designate a clerk or other officer or employee of the local agency who shall then attend each closed session of the legislative body and keep and enter in a minute book a record of topics discussed and decisions made at the meeting. The minute book made pursuant to this section is not a public record subject to inspection pursuant to the California Public Records Act (Chapter 3.5 (commencing with Section 6250) of Division 7 of Title 1), and shall be kept confidential. The minute book shall be available only to members of the legislative body or, if a violation of this chapter is alleged to have occurred at a closed session, to a court of general jurisdiction wherein the local agency lies. Such minute book may, but need not, consist of a recording of the closed session.

(b) An elected legislative body of a local agency may require that each legislative body all or a majority of whose members are appointed by or under the authority of the elected legislative body keep a minute book as prescribed under subdivision (a).

54957.5. Agendas and other writings distributed for discussion or consideration at meetings; public records; inspection; closed sessions. (a) Notwithstanding Section 6255 or any other provisions of law, agendas of public meetings and any other writings, when distributed to all, or a majority of all, of the members of a legislative body of a local agency by any person in connection with a matter subject to discussion or consideration at a public meeting of the body, are disclosable public records under the California Public Records Act (Chapter 3.5 (commencing with Section 6250) of Division 7 of Title 1), and shall be made available upon request without delay. However, this section shall not include any writing exempt from public disclosure under Section 6253.5, 6254, 6254.7, or 6254.22.

(b) Writings that are public records under subdivision (a) and that are distributed during a public meeting shall be made available for public inspection at the meeting if prepared by the local agency or a member of its legislative body, or after the meeting if prepared by some other person. These writings shall be made available in appropriate alternative formats upon request by a person with a disability, as required by Section 202 of the Americans with Disabilities Act of 1990 (42 U.S.C. Sec. 12132), and the federal rules and regulations adopted in implementation thereof.

(c) Nothing in this chapter shall be construed to prevent the legislative body of a local agency from charging a fee or deposit for a copy of a public record pursuant to Section 6253, except that no surcharge shall be imposed on persons with disabilities in violation of Section 202 of the Americans with Disabilities Act of 1990 (42 U.S.C. Sec. 12132), and the federal rules and regulations adopted in implementation thereof.

(d) This section shall not be construed to limit or delay the public's right to inspect or obtain a copy of any record required to be disclosed under the requirements of the California Public Records Act (Chapter 3.5 (commencing with Section 6250) of Division 7 of Title 1). Nothing in this chapter shall be construed to require a legislative body of a local agency to place any paid advertisement or any other paid notice in any publication.

54957.6. Closed sessions; collective bargaining with employees; salaries, salary schedules or fringe benefits. (a) Notwithstanding any other provision of law, a legislative body of a local agency may hold closed sessions with the local agency's designated representatives regarding the salaries, salary schedules, or compensation paid in the form of fringe benefits of its represented and unrepresented employees, and, for represented employees, any other matter within the statutorily provided scope of representation.

However, prior to the closed session, the legislative body of the local agency shall hold an open and public session in which it identifies its designated representatives.

Closed sessions of a legislative body of a local agency, as permitted in this section, shall be for the purpose of reviewing its position and instructing the local agency's designated representatives.

Closed sessions, as permitted in this section, may take place prior to and during consultations and discussions with representatives of employee organizations and unrepresented employees.

Closed sessions with the local agency's designated representative regarding the salaries, salary schedules, or compensation paid in the form of fringe benefits may include discussion of an agency's available funds and funding priorities, but only insofar as these discussions relate to providing instructions to the local agency's designated representative.

Closed sessions held pursuant to this section shall not include final action on the proposed compensation of one or more unrepresented employees.

For the purposes enumerated in this section, a legislative body of a local agency may also meet with a state conciliator who has intervened in the proceedings.

(b) For the purposes of this section, the term "employee" shall include an officer or an independent contractor who functions as an officer or an employee, but shall not include any elected official, member of a legislative body, or other independent contractors.

54957.7. Closed sessions; disclosure of items to be discussed; notice. (a) Prior to holding any closed session, the legislative body of the local agency shall disclose, in an open meeting, the item or items to be discussed in the closed session. The disclosure may take the form of a reference to the item or items as they are listed by number or letter on the agenda. In the closed session, the legislative body may consider only those matters covered in its statement. Nothing in this section shall require or authorize a disclosure of information prohibited by state or federal law.

(b) After any closed session, the legislative body shall reconvene into open session prior to adjournment and shall make any disclosures required by Section 54957.1 of action taken in the closed session.

(c) The announcements required to be made in open session pursuant to this section may be made at the location announced in the agenda for the closed session, as long as the public is allowed to be present at that location for the purpose of hearing the announcements.

54957.8. Closed session; legislative body of a multijurisdictional drug law enforcement agency. (a) For purposes of this section, "multijurisdictional law enforcement agency" means a joint powers entity formed pursuant to Article 1 (commencing with Section 6500) of Chapter 5 of Division 7 of Title 1 that provides law enforcement services for the parties to the joint powers agreement for the purpose of investigating criminal activity involving drugs; gangs; sex crimes; firearms trafficking or felony possession of a firearm; high technology, computer, or identity theft; human trafficking; or vehicle theft.

(b) Nothing contained in this chapter shall be construed to prevent the legislative body of a multijurisdictional law enforcement agency, or an advisory body of a multijurisdictional law enforcement agency, from holding closed sessions to discuss the case records of any ongoing criminal investigation of the multijurisdictional law enforcement agency or of any party to the joint powers agreement, to hear testimony from persons involved in the investigation, and to discuss courses of action in particular cases.

54957.9. Disorderly conduct during meeting; clearing of room. In the event that any meeting is willfully interrupted by a group or groups of persons so as to render the orderly conduct of such meeting unfeasible and order cannot be restored by the removal of individuals who are willfully interrupting the meeting, the members of the legislative body conducting the meeting may order the meeting room cleared and continue in session. Only matters appearing on the agenda may be considered in such a session. Representatives of the press or other news media, except those participating in the disturbance, shall be allowed to attend any session held pursuant to this section. Nothing in this section shall prohibit the legislative body from establishing a procedure for readmitting an individual or individuals not responsible for willfully disturbing the orderly conduct of the meeting.

54957.10. Closed session to discuss withdrawal of funds in deferred compensation plan. Notwithstanding any other provision of law, a legislative body of a local agency may hold closed sessions to discuss a local agency employee's application for early withdrawal of funds in a deferred compensation plan when the application is based on financial hardship arising from an unforeseeable emergency due to illness, accident, casualty, or other extraordinary event, as specified in the deferred compensation plan.

54958. Application of chapter. The provisions of this chapter shall apply to the legislative body of every local agency notwithstanding the conflicting provisions of any other state law.

54959. Criminal penalty for unlawful meeting. Each member of a legislative body who attends a meeting of that legislative body where action is taken in violation of any provision of this chapter, and where the member intends to deprive the public of information to which the member knows or has reason to know the public is entitled under this chapter, is guilty of a misdemeanor.

54960. Action taken to prevent violations or to determine applicability of chapter. (a) The district attorney or any interested person may commence an action by mandamus, injunction or declaratory relief for the purpose of stopping or preventing violations or threatened violations of this chapter by members of the legislative body of a local agency or to determine the applicability of this chapter to actions or threatened future action of the legislative body, or to determine whether any rule or action by the legislative body to penalize or otherwise discourage the expression of one or more of its members is valid or invalid under the laws of this state or of the United States, or to compel the legislative body to tape record its closed sessions as hereinafter provided.

(b) The court in its discretion may, upon a judgment of a violation of Section 54956.7, 54956.8, 54956.9, 54956.95, 54957, or 54957.6, order the legislative body to tape record its closed sessions and preserve the tape recordings for the period and under the terms of security and confidentiality the court deems appropriate.

(c) (1) Each recording so kept shall be immediately labeled with the date of the closed session recorded and the title of the clerk or other officer who shall be custodian of the recording.

(2) The tapes shall be subject to the following discovery procedures:

(A) In any case in which discovery or disclosure of the tape is sought by either the district attorney or the plaintiff in a civil action pursuant to Section 54959, 54960, or 54960.1 alleging that a violation of this chapter has occurred in a closed session which has been recorded pursuant to this section, the party seeking discovery or disclosure shall file a written notice of motion with the appropriate court with notice to the governmental agency which has custody and control of the tape recording. The notice shall be given pursuant to subdivision (b) of Section 1005 of the Code of Civil Procedure.

(B) The notice shall include, in addition to the items required by Section 1010 of the Code of Civil Procedure, all of the following:

(i) Identification of the proceeding in which discovery or disclosure is sought, the party seeking discovery or disclosure, the date and time of the meeting recorded, and the governmental agency which has custody and control of the recording.

(ii) An affidavit which contains specific facts indicating that a violation of the act occurred in the closed session.

(3) If the court, following a review of the motion, finds that there is good cause to believe that a violation has occurred, the court may review, in camera, the recording of that portion of the closed session alleged to have violated the act.

(4) If, following the in camera review, the court concludes that disclosure of a portion of the recording would be likely to materially assist in the resolution of the litigation alleging violation of this chapter, the court shall, in its discretion, make a certified transcript of the portion of the recording a public exhibit in the proceeding.

(5) Nothing in this section shall permit discovery of communications which are protected by the attorney-client privilege.

54960.1. Unlawful action by legislative body; action for mandamus or injunction; prerequisites. (a) The district attorney or any interested person may commence an action by mandamus or injunction for the purpose of obtaining a judicial determination that an action taken by a legislative body of a local agency in violation of Section 54953, 54954.2, 54954.5, 54954.6,

54956, or 54956.5 is null and void under this section. Nothing in this chapter shall be construed to prevent a legislative body from curing or correcting an action challenged pursuant to this section.

(b) Prior to any action being commenced pursuant to subdivision (a), the district attorney or interested person shall make a demand of the legislative body to cure or correct the action alleged to have been taken in violation of Section 54953, 54954.2, 54954.5, 54954.6, 54956, or 54956.5. The demand shall be in writing and clearly describe the challenged action of the legislative body and nature of the alleged violation.

(c) (1) The written demand shall be made within 90 days from the date the action was taken unless the action was taken in an open session but in violation of Section 54954.2, in which case the written demand shall be made within 30 days from the date the action was taken.

(2) Within 30 days of receipt of the demand, the legislative body shall cure or correct the challenged action and inform the demanding party in writing of its actions to cure or correct or inform the demanding party in writing of its decision not to cure or correct the challenged action.

(3) If the legislative body takes no action within the 30-day period, the inaction shall be deemed a decision not to cure or correct the challenged action, and the 15-day period to commence the action described in subdivision (a) shall commence to run the day after the 30-day period to cure or correct expires.

(4) Within 15 days of receipt of the written notice of the legislative body's decision to cure or correct, or not to cure or correct, or within 15 days of the expiration of the 30-day period to cure or correct, whichever is earlier, the demanding party shall be required to commence the action pursuant to subdivision (a) or thereafter be barred from commencing the action.

(d) An action taken that is alleged to have been taken in violation of Section 54953, 54954.2, 54954.5, 54954.6, 54956, or 54956.5 shall not be determined to be null and void if any of the following conditions exist:

(1) The action taken was in substantial compliance with Sections 54953, 54954.2, 54954.5, 54954.6, 54956, and 54956.5.

(2) The action taken was in connection with the sale or issuance of notes, bonds, or other evidences of indebtedness or any contract, instrument, or agreement thereto.

(3) The action taken gave rise to a contractual obligation, including a contract let by competitive bid other than compensation for services in the form of salary or fees for professional services, upon which a party has, in good faith and without notice of a challenge to the validity of the action, detrimentally relied.

(4) The action taken was in connection with the collection of any tax.

(5) Any person, city, city and county, county, district, or any agency or subdivision of the state alleging noncompliance with subdivision (a) of Section 54954.2, Section 54956, or Section 54956.5, because of any defect, error, irregularity, or omission in the notice given pursuant to those provisions, had actual notice of the item of business at least 72 hours prior to the meeting at which the action was taken, if the meeting was noticed pursuant to Section 54954.2, or 24 hours prior to the meeting at which the action was taken if the meeting was noticed pursuant to Section 54956, or prior to the meeting at which the action was taken if the meeting is held pursuant to Section 54956.5.

(e) During any action seeking a judicial determination pursuant to subdivision (a) if the court determines, pursuant to a showing by the legislative body that an action alleged to have been taken in violation of Section 54953, 54954.2, 54954.5, 54954.6, 54956, or 54956.5 has been cured or corrected by a subsequent action of the legislative body, the action filed pursuant to subdivision (a) shall be dismissed with prejudice.

(f) The fact that a legislative body takes a subsequent action to cure or correct an action taken pursuant to this section shall not be construed or admissible as evidence of a violation of this chapter.

54960.5. Costs and attorney fees. A court may award court costs and reasonable attorney fees to the plaintiff in an action brought pursuant to Section 54960 or 54960.1 where it is found that a legislative body of the local agency has violated this chapter. The costs and fees shall be paid by the local agency and shall not become a personal liability of any public officer or employee of the local agency.

A court may award court costs and reasonable attorney fees to a defendant in any action brought pursuant to Section 54960 or 54960.1 where the defendant has prevailed in a final determination of such action and the court finds that the action was clearly frivolous and totally lacking in merit.

54961. Discriminatory use of facilities prohibited. (a) No legislative body of a local agency shall conduct any meeting in any facility that prohibits the admittance of any person, or persons, on the basis of race, religious creed, color, national origin, ancestry, or sex, or which is inaccessible to disabled persons, or where members of the public may not be present without making a payment or purchase. This section shall apply to every local agency as defined in Section 54951.

(b) No notice, agenda, announcement, or report required under this chapter need identify any victim or alleged victim of tortuous sexual conduct or child abuse unless the identity of the person has been publicly disclosed.

54962. Closed session by legislative body prohibited. Except as expressly authorized by this chapter, or by Sections 1461, 1462, 32106, and 32155 of the Health and Safety Code, or by Sections 37606, 37606.1, and 37624.3 of the Government Code as they apply to hospitals, or by any provision of the Education Code pertaining to school districts and community college districts, no closed session may be held by any legislative body of any local agency.

54963. Nondisclosability of information obtained in closed session; discipline of member (a) A person may not disclose confidential information that has been acquired by being present in a closed session authorized by Section 54956.7, 54956.8, 54956.86, 54956.87, 54956.9, 54957, 54957.6, 54957.8, or 54957.10 to a person not entitled to receive it, unless the legislative body authorizes disclosure of that confidential information.

(b) For purposes of this section, "confidential information" means a communication made in a closed session that is specifically related to the basis for the legislative body of a local agency to meet lawfully in closed session under this chapter.

(c) Violation of this section may be addressed by the use of such remedies as are currently available by law, including, but not limited to:

(1) Injunctive relief to prevent the disclosure of confidential information prohibited by this section.

(2) Disciplinary action against an employee who has willfully disclosed confidential information in violation of this section.

(3) Referral of a member of a legislative body who has willfully disclosed confidential information in violation of this section to the grand jury.

(d) Disciplinary action pursuant to paragraph (2) of subdivision (c) shall require that the employee in question has either received training as to the requirements of this section or otherwise has been given notice of the requirements of this section.

(e) A local agency may not take any action authorized by subdivision (c) against a person, nor shall it be deemed a violation of this section, for doing any of the following:

(1) Making a confidential inquiry or complaint to a district attorney or grand jury concerning a perceived violation of law, including disclosing facts to a district attorney or grand jury that are necessary to establish the illegality of an action taken by a legislative body of a local agency or the potential illegality of an action that has been the subject of deliberation at a closed session if that action were to be taken by a legislative body of a local agency.

(2) Expressing an opinion concerning the propriety or legality of actions taken by a legislative body of a local agency in closed session, including disclosure of the nature and extent of the illegal or potentially illegal action.

(3) Disclosing information acquired by being present in a closed session under this chapter that is not confidential information.

(f) Nothing in this section shall be construed to prohibit disclosures under the whistleblower statutes contained in Section 1102.5 of the Labor Code or Article 4.5 (commencing with Section 53296) of Chapter 2 of this code.

APPENDIX B

The California Public Records Act
California Government Code Sections 6250-6270

6250. Legislative findings and declarations. In enacting this chapter, the Legislature, mindful of the right of individuals to privacy, finds and declares that access to information concerning the conduct of the people's business is a fundamental and necessary right of every person in this state.

6251. Short title. This chapter shall be known and may be cited as the California Public Records Act.

6252. Definitions. As used in this chapter: (a) "Local agency" includes a county; city, whether general law or chartered; city and county; school district; municipal corporation; district; political subdivision; or any board, commission or agency thereof; other local public agency; or entities that are legislative bodies of a local agency pursuant to subdivisions (c) and (d) of Section 54952.

(b) "Member of the public" means any person, except a member, agent, officer, or employee of a federal, state, or local agency acting within the scope of his or her membership, agency, office, or employment.

(c) "Person" includes any natural person, corporation, partnership, limited liability company, firm, or association.

(d) "Public agency" means any state or local agency.

(e) "Public records" includes any writing containing information relating to the conduct of the public's business prepared, owned, used, or retained by any state or local agency regardless of physical form or characteristics. "Public records" in the custody of, or maintained by, the Governor's office means any writing prepared on or after January 6, 1975.

(f) "State agency" means every state office, officer, department, division, bureau, board, and commission or other state body or agency, except those agencies provided for in Article IV (except Section 20 thereof) or Article VI of the California Constitution.

(g) "Writing" means any handwriting, typewriting, printing, photostating, photographing, photocopying, transmitting by electronic mail or facsimile, and every other means of recording upon any tangible thing any form of communication or representation, including letters, words, pictures, sounds, or symbols, or combinations thereof, and any record thereby created, regardless of the manner in which the record has been stored.

6252.5. Access to records by public officials. Notwithstanding the definition of "member of the public" in Section 6252, an elected member or officer of any state or local agency is entitled to access to public records of that agency on the same basis as any other person. Nothing in this section shall limit the ability of elected members or officers to access public records permitted by law in the administration of their duties.

This section does not constitute a change in, but is declaratory of, existing law.

6252.6. Access to information about deaths of foster children. Notwithstanding paragraph (2) of subdivision (a) of Section 827 of the Welfare and Institutions Code, after the death of a foster child who is a minor, the name, date of birth, and date of death of the child shall be subject to disclosure by the county child welfare agency pursuant to this chapter.

6253. Public records open to inspection; time; guidelines; procedure; adoption of procedures for greater access.

(a) Public records are open to inspection at all times during the office hours of the state or local agency and every person has a right to inspect any public record, except as hereafter provided. Any reasonably segregable portion of a record shall be available for inspection by any person requesting the record after deletion of the portions that are exempted by law.

(b) Except with respect to public records exempt from disclosure by express provisions of law, each state or local agency, upon a request for a copy of records that reasonably describes an identifiable record or records, shall make the records promptly available to any person upon payment of fees covering direct costs of duplication, or a statutory fee if applicable. Upon request, an exact copy shall be provided unless impracticable to do so.

(c) Each agency, upon a request for a copy of records, shall, within 10 days from receipt of the request, determine whether the request, in whole or in part, seeks copies of disclosable public records in the possession of the agency and shall promptly notify the person making the request of the determination and the reasons therefor. In unusual circumstances, the time limit prescribed in this section may be extended by written notice by the head of the agency or his or her designee to the person making the request, setting forth the reasons for the extension and the date on which a determination is expected to be dispatched. No notice shall specify a date that would result in an extension for more than 14 days. When the agency dispatches the determination, and if the agency determines that the request seeks disclosable public records, the agency shall state the estimated date and time when the records will be made available. As used in this section, "unusual circumstances" means the following, but only to the extent reasonably necessary to the proper processing of the particular request:

(1) The need to search for and collect the requested records from field facilities or other establishments that are separate from the office processing the request.

(2) The need to search for, collect, and appropriately examine a voluminous amount of separate and distinct records that are demanded in a single request.

(3) The need for consultation, which shall be conducted with all practicable speed, with another agency having substantial interest in the determination of the request or among two or more components of the agency having substantial subject matter interest therein.

(4) The need to compile data, to write programming language or a computer program, or to construct a computer report to extract data.

(d) Nothing in this chapter shall be construed to permit an agency to delay or obstruct the inspection or copying of public records. The notification of denial of any request for records required by Section 6255 shall set forth the names and titles or positions of each person responsible for the denial.

(e) Except as otherwise prohibited by law, a state or local agency may adopt requirements for itself that allow for faster, more efficient, or greater access to records than prescribed by the minimum standards set forth in this chapter.

6253.1. Duty of agency to assist with request for records.

(a) When a member of the public requests to inspect a public record or obtain a copy of a public record, the public agency, in order to assist the member of the public make a focused and effective request that reasonably describes an identifiable record or records, shall do all of the following, to the extent reasonable under the circumstances:

(1) Assist the member of the public to identify records and information that are responsive to the request or to the purpose of the request, if stated.

(2) Describe the information technology and physical location in which the records exist.

(3) Provide suggestions for overcoming any practical basis for denying access to the records or information sought.

(b) The requirements of paragraph (1) of subdivision (a) shall be deemed to have been satisfied if the public agency is unable to identify the requested information after making a reasonable effort to elicit additional clarifying information from the requester that will help identify the record or records.

(c) The requirements of subdivision (a) are in addition to any action required of a public agency by Section 6253.

(d) This section shall not apply to a request for public records if any of the following applies:

(1) The public agency makes available the requested records pursuant to Section 6253.

(2) The public agency determines that the request should be denied and bases that determination solely on an exemption listed in Section 6254.

(3) The public agency makes available an index of its records.

6253.2. Exemption for information regarding in-home support services. (a) Notwithstanding any other provision of this chapter to the contrary, information regarding persons paid by the state to provide in-home supportive services pursuant to Article 7 (commencing with Section 12300) of Chapter 3 of Part 3 of Division 9 of the Welfare and Institutions Code or personal care services pursuant to Section 14132.95 of the Welfare and Institutions Code, shall not be subject to public disclosure pursuant to this chapter, except as provided in subdivision (b).

(b) Copies of names, addresses, and telephone numbers of persons described in subdivision (a) shall be made available, upon request, to an exclusive bargaining agent and to any labor organization seeking representation rights pursuant to subdivision (c) of Section 12301.6 or Section 12302 of the Welfare and Institutions Code or Chapter 10 (commencing with Section 3500) of Division 4 of Title 1. This information shall not be used by the receiving entity for any purpose other than the employee organizing, representation, and assistance activities of the labor organization.

(c) This section shall apply solely to individuals who provide services under the In-Home Supportive Services Program (Article 7 (commencing with Section 12300) of Chapter 3 of Part 3 of Division 9 of the Welfare and Institutions Code) or the Personal Care Services Program pursuant to Section 14132.95 of the Welfare and Institutions Code.

(d) Nothing in this section is intended to alter or shall be interpreted to alter the rights of parties under the
Meyers-Milias-Brown Act (Chapter 10 (commencing with Section 3500) of Division 4) or any other labor relations law.

6253.4. Adoption of regulations governing agency procedures. (a) Every agency may adopt regulations stating the procedures to be followed when making its records available in accordance with this section. The following state and local bodies shall establish written guidelines for accessibility of records. A copy of these guidelines shall be posted in a conspicuous public place at the offices of these bodies, and a copy of the guidelines shall be available upon request free of charge to any person requesting that body's records:

Department of Motor Vehicles
Department of Consumer Affairs
Department of Transportation
Department of Real Estate
Department of Corrections
Department of the Youth Authority
Department of Justice

Department of Insurance
Department of Corporations
Department of Managed Health Care
Secretary of State
State Air Resources Board
Department of Water Resources
Department of Parks and Recreation
San Francisco Bay Conservation and Development Commission
State Board of Equalization
State Department of Health Services
Employment Development Department
State Department of Social Services
State Department of Mental Health
State Department of Developmental Services
State Department of Alcohol and Drug Abuse
Office of Statewide Health Planning and Development
Public Employees' Retirement System
Teachers' Retirement Board
Department of Industrial Relations
Department of General Services
Department of Veterans Affairs
Public Utilities Commission
California Coastal Commission
State Water Resources Control Board
San Francisco Bay Area Rapid Transit District
All regional water quality control boards
Los Angeles County Air Pollution Control District
Bay Area Air Pollution Control District
Golden Gate Bridge, Highway and Transportation District
Department of Toxic Substances Control
Office of Environmental Health Hazard Assessment

(b) Guidelines and regulations adopted pursuant to this section shall be consistent with all other sections of this chapter and shall reflect the intention of the Legislature to make the records accessible to the public. The guidelines and regulations adopted pursuant to this section shall not operate to limit the hours public records are open for inspection as prescribed in Section 6253.

6253.5. Initiative, referendum, recall petitions and petitions for reorganizing school districts or community college districts deemed not public records; examination by proponents. Notwithstanding Sections 6252 and 6253, statewide, county, city, and district initiative, referendum, and recall petitions, petitions circulated pursuant to Section 5091 of the Education Code, petitions for the reorganization of school districts submitted pursuant to Article 1 (commencing with Section 35700) of Chapter 4 of Part 21 of the Education Code, petitions for the reorganization of community college districts submitted pursuant to Part 46 (commencing with Section 74000) of the Education Code and all memoranda prepared by the county elections officials in the examination of the petitions indicating which registered voters have signed particular petitions shall not be deemed to be public records and shall not be open to inspection except by the public officer or public employees who have the duty of receiving, examining or preserving the petitions or who are responsible for the preparation of that memoranda and, if the petition is found to be insufficient, by the proponents of the petition and the representatives of the proponents as may be designated by the proponents in writing in order to determine which signatures were disqualified and the reasons therefor. However, the Attorney General, the Secretary of State, the Fair Political Practices Commission, a district attorney, a school district or a community college district attorney, and a city attorney shall be permitted to examine the material upon approval of the appropriate superior court.

If the proponents of a petition are permitted to examine the petition and memoranda, the examination shall commence not later than 21 days after certification of insufficiency.

(a) As used in this section, "petition" shall mean any petition to which a registered voter has affixed his or her signature.

(b) As used in this section "proponents of the petition" means the following:

(1) For statewide initiative and referendum measures, the person or persons who submit a draft of a petition proposing the measure to the Attorney General with a request that he or she prepare a title and summary of the chief purpose and points of the proposed measure.

(2) For other initiative and referenda on measures, the person or persons who publish a notice of intention to circulate petitions, or, where publication is not required, who file petitions with the elections official.

(3) For recall measures, the person or persons defined in Section 343 of the Elections Code.

(4) For petitions circulated pursuant to Section 5091 of the Education Code, the person or persons having charge of the petition who submit the petition to the county superintendent of schools.

(5) For petitions circulated pursuant to Article 1 (commencing with Section 35700) of Chapter 4 of Part 21 of the Education Code, the person or persons designated as chief petitioners under Section 35701 of the Education Code.

(6) For petitions circulated pursuant to Part 46 (commencing with Section 74000) of the Education Code, the person or persons designated as chief petitioners under Sections 74102, 74133, and 74152 of the Education Code.

6253.6. Bilingual ballot pamphlet requests not public records. (a) Notwithstanding the provisions of Sections 6252 and 6253, information compiled by public officers or public employees revealing the identity of persons who have requested bilingual ballots or ballot pamphlets, made in accordance with any federal or state law, or other data that would reveal the identity of the requester, shall not be deemed to be public records and shall not be provided to any person other than public officers or public employees who are responsible for receiving those requests and processing the same.

(b) Nothing contained in subdivision (a) shall be construed as prohibiting any person who is otherwise authorized by law from examining election materials, including, but not limited to, affidavits of registration, provided that requests for bilingual ballots or ballot pamphlets shall be subject to the restrictions contained in subdivision (a).

6253.8. Required posting of enforcement order. (a) Every final enforcement order issued by an agency listed in subdivision (b) under any provision of law that is administered by an entity listed in subdivision (b), shall be displayed on the entity's Internet website, if the final enforcement order is a public record that is not exempt from disclosure pursuant to this chapter.

(b) This section applies to the California Environmental Protection Agency and to all of the following entities within the agency:

(1) The State Air Resources Board.

(2) The California Integrated Waste Management Board.

(3) The State Water Resources Control Board, and each California regional water quality control board.

(4) The Department of Pesticide Regulation.

(5) The Department of Toxic Substances Control.

(c) (1) Except as provided in paragraph (2), for purposes of this section, an enforcement order is final when the time for judicial review has expired on or after January 1, 2001, or when all means of judicial review have been exhausted on or after January 1, 2001.

(2) In addition to the requirements of paragraph (1), with regard to a final enforcement order issued by the State Water Resources Control Board or a California regional water quality control board, this section shall apply only to a final enforcement order adopted by that board or a regional board at a public meeting.

(d) An order posted pursuant to this section shall be posted for not less than one year.

(e) The California Environmental Protection Agency shall oversee the implementation of this section.

(f) This section shall become operative April 1, 2001.

6253.9. Electronic Records. (a) Unless otherwise prohibited by law, any agency that has information that constitutes an identifiable public record not exempt from disclosure pursuant to this chapter that is in an electronic format shall make that information available in an electronic format when requested by any person and, when applicable, shall comply with the following:

(1) The agency shall make the information available in any electronic format in which it holds the information.

(2) Each agency shall provide a copy of an electronic record in the format requested if the requested format is one that has been used by the agency to create copies for its own use or for provision to other agencies. The cost of duplication shall be limited to the direct cost of producing a copy of a record in an electronic format.

(b) Notwithstanding paragraph (2) of subdivision (a), the requester shall bear the cost of producing a copy of the record, including the cost to construct a record, and the cost of programming and computer services necessary to produce a copy of the record when either of the following applies:

(1) In order to comply with the provisions of subdivision (a), the public agency would be required to produce a copy of an electronic record and the record is one that is produced only at otherwise regularly scheduled intervals.

(2) The request would require data compilation, extraction, or programming to produce the record.

(c) Nothing in this section shall be construed to require the public agency to reconstruct a record in an electronic format if the agency no longer has the record available in an electronic format.

(d) If the request is for information in other than electronic format, and the information also is in electronic format, the agency may inform the requester that the information is available in electronic format.

(e) Nothing in this section shall be construed to permit an agency to make information available only in an electronic format.

(f) Nothing in this section shall be construed to require the public agency to release an electronic record in the electronic form in which it is held by the agency if its release would jeopardize or compromise the security or integrity of the original record or of any proprietary software in which it is maintained.

(g) Nothing in this section shall be construed to permit public access to records held by any agency to which access is otherwise restricted by statute.

6254. Exemption of particular records. Except as provided in Sections 6254.7 and 6254.13, nothing in this chapter shall be construed to require disclosure of records that are any of the following:

(a) Preliminary drafts, notes, or interagency or intra-agency memoranda that are not retained by the public agency in the ordinary course of business, if the public interest in withholding those records clearly outweighs the public interest in disclosure.

(b) Records pertaining to pending litigation to which the public agency is a party, or to claims made pursuant to Division 3.6 (commencing with Section 810), until the pending litigation or claim has been finally adjudicated or otherwise settled.

(c) Personnel, medical, or similar files, the disclosure of which would constitute an unwarranted invasion of personal privacy.

(d) Contained in or related to any of the following:

(1) Applications filed with any state agency responsible for the regulation or supervision of the issuance of securities or of financial institutions, including, but not limited to, banks, savings and loan associations, industrial loan companies, credit unions, and insurance companies.

(2) Examination, operating, or condition reports prepared by, on behalf of, or for the use of, any state agency referred to in paragraph (1).

(3) Preliminary drafts, notes, or interagency or intra-agency communications prepared by, on behalf of, or for the use of, any state agency referred to in paragraph (1).

(4) Information received in confidence by any state agency referred to in paragraph (1).

(e) Geological and geophysical data, plant production data, and similar information relating to utility systems development, or market or crop reports, that are obtained in confidence from any person.

(f) Records of complaints to, or investigations conducted by, or records of intelligence information or security procedures of, the office of the Attorney General and the Department of Justice, and any state or local police agency, or any investigatory or security files compiled by any other state or local police agency, or any investigatory or security files compiled by any other state or local agency for correctional, law enforcement, or licensing purposes. However, state and local law enforcement agencies shall disclose the names and addresses of persons involved in, or witnesses other than confidential informants to, the incident, the description of any property involved, the date, time, and location of the incident, all diagrams, statements of the parties involved in the incident, the statements of all witnesses, other than confidential informants, to the victims of an incident, or an authorized representative thereof, an insurance carrier against which a claim has been or might be made, and any person suffering bodily injury or property damage or loss, as the result of the incident caused by arson, burglary, fire, explosion, larceny, robbery, carjacking, vandalism, vehicle theft, or a crime as defined by subdivision (b) of Section 13951, unless the disclosure would endanger the safety of a witness or other person involved in the investigation, or unless disclosure would endanger the successful completion of the investigation or a related investigation. However, nothing in this division shall require the disclosure of that portion of those investigative files that reflects the analysis or conclusions of the investigating officer.

Customer lists provided to a state or local police agency by an alarm or security company at the request of the agency shall be construed to be records subject to this subdivision.

Notwithstanding any other provision of this subdivision, state and local law enforcement agencies shall make public the following information, except to the extent that disclosure of a particular item of information would endanger the safety of a person involved in an investigation or would endanger the successful completion of the investigation or a related investigation:

(1) The full name and occupation of every individual arrested by the agency, the individual's physical description including date of birth, color of eyes and hair, sex, height and weight, the

time and date of arrest, the time and date of booking, the location of the arrest, the factual circumstances surrounding the arrest, the amount of bail set, the time and manner of release or the location where the individual is currently being held, and all charges the individual is being held upon, including any outstanding warrants from other jurisdictions and parole or probation holds.

(2) Subject to the restrictions imposed by Section 841.5 of the Penal Code, the time, substance, and location of all complaints or requests for assistance received by the agency and the time and nature of the response thereto, including, to the extent the information regarding crimes alleged or committed or any other incident investigated is recorded, the time, date, and location of occurrence, the time and date of the report, the name and age of the victim, the factual circumstances surrounding the crime or incident, and a general description of any injuries, property, or weapons involved. The name of a victim of any crime defined by Section 220, 261, 261.5, 262, 264, 264.1, 273a, 273d, 273.5, 286, 288, 288a, 289, 422.6, 422.7, 422.75, or 646.9 of the Penal Code may be withheld at the victim's request, or at the request of the victim's parent or guardian if the victim is a minor. When a person is the victim of more than one crime, information disclosing that the person is a victim of a crime defined by Section 220, 261, 261.5, 262, 264, 264.1, 273a, 273d, 286, 288, 288a, 289, 422.6, 422.7, 422.75, or 646.9 of the Penal Code may be deleted at the request of the victim, or the victim's parent or guardian if the victim is a minor, in making the report of the crime, or of any crime or incident accompanying the crime, available to the public in compliance with the requirements of this paragraph.

(3) Subject to the restrictions of Section 841.5 of the Penal Code and this subdivision, the current address of every individual arrested by the agency and the current address of the victim of a crime, where the requester declares under penalty of perjury that the request is made for a scholarly, journalistic, political, or governmental purpose, or that the request is made for investigation purposes by a licensed private investigator as described in Chapter 11.3 (commencing with Section 7512) of Division 3 of the Business and Professions Code. However, the address of the victim of any crime defined by Section 220, 261, 261.5, 262, 264, 264.1, 273a, 273d, 273.5, 286, 288, 288a, 289, 422.6, 422.7, 422.75, or 646.9 of the Penal Code shall remain confidential. Address information obtained pursuant to this paragraph may not be used directly or indirectly, or furnished to another, to sell a product or service to any individual or group of individuals, and the requester shall execute a declaration to that effect under penalty of perjury. Nothing in this paragraph shall be construed to prohibit or limit a scholarly, journalistic, political, or government use of address information obtained pursuant to this paragraph.

(g) Test questions, scoring keys, and other examination data used to administer a licensing examination, examination for employment, or academic examination, except as provided for in Chapter 3 (commencing with Section 99150) of Part 65 of the Education Code.

(h) The contents of real estate appraisals or engineering or feasibility estimates and evaluations made for or by the state or local agency relative to the acquisition of property, or to prospective public supply and construction contracts, until all of the property has been acquired or all of the contract agreement obtained. However, the law of eminent domain shall not be affected by this provision.

(i) Information required from any taxpayer in connection with the collection of local taxes that is received in confidence and the disclosure of the information to other persons would result in unfair competitive disadvantage to the person supplying the information.

(j) Library circulation records kept for the purpose of identifying the borrower of items available in libraries, and library and museum materials made or acquired and presented solely for reference or exhibition purposes. The exemption in this subdivision shall not apply to records of fines imposed on the borrowers.

(k) Records, the disclosure of which is exempted or prohibited pursuant to federal or state law, including, but not limited to, provisions of the Evidence Code relating to privilege.

(l) Correspondence of and to the Governor or employees of the Governor's office or in the custody of or maintained by the Governor's Legal Affairs Secretary. However, public records shall not be transferred to the custody of the Governor's Legal Affairs Secretary to evade the disclosure provisions of this chapter.

(m) In the custody of or maintained by the Legislative Counsel, except those records in the public database maintained by the Legislative Counsel that are described in Section 10248.

(n) Statements of personal worth or personal financial data required by a licensing agency and filed by an applicant with the licensing agency to establish his or her personal qualification for the license, certificate, or permit applied for.

(o) Financial data contained in applications for financing under Division 27 (commencing with Section 44500) of the Health and Safety Code, where an authorized officer of the California Pollution Control Financing Authority determines that disclosure of the financial data would be competitively injurious to the applicant and the data is required in order to obtain guarantees from the United States Small Business Administration. The California Pollution Control Financing Authority shall adopt rules for review of individual requests for confidentiality under this section and for making available to the public those portions of an application that are subject to disclosure under this chapter.

(p) Records of state agencies related to activities governed by Chapter 10.3 (commencing with Section 3512), Chapter 10.5 (commencing with Section 3525), and Chapter 12 (commencing with Section 3560) of Division 4 of Title 1, that reveal a state agency's deliberative processes, impressions, evaluations, opinions, recommendations, meeting minutes, research, work products, theories, or strategy, or that provide instruction, advice, or training to employees who do not have full collective bargaining and representation rights under these chapters. Nothing in this subdivision shall be construed to limit the disclosure duties of a state agency with respect to any other records relating to the activities governed by the employee relations acts referred to in this subdivision.

(q) Records of state agencies related to activities governed by Article 2.6 (commencing with Section 14081), Article 2.8 (commencing with Section 14087.5), and Article 2.91 (commencing with Section 14089) of Chapter 7 of Part 3 of Division 9 of the Welfare and Institutions Code, that reveal the special negotiator's deliberative processes, discussions, communications, or any other portion of the negotiations with providers of health care services, impressions, opinions, recommendations, meeting minutes, research, work product, theories, or strategy, or that provide instruction, advice, or training to employees.

Except for the portion of a contract containing the rates of payment, contracts for inpatient services entered into pursuant to these articles, on or after April 1, 1984, shall be open to inspection one year after they are fully executed. If a contract for inpatient services that is entered into prior to April 1, 1984, is amended on or after April 1, 1984, the amendment, except for any portion containing the rates of payment, shall be open to inspection one year after it is fully executed. If the California Medical Assistance Commission enters into contracts with health care providers for other than inpatient hospital services, those contracts shall be open to inspection one year after they are fully executed.

Three years after a contract or amendment is open to inspection under this subdivision, the portion of the contract or amendment containing the rates of payment shall be open to inspection.

Notwithstanding any other provision of law, the entire contract or amendment shall be open to inspection by the Joint Legislative Audit Committee and the Legislative Analyst's Office. The committee and that office shall maintain the confidentiality of the contracts and amendments until the time a contract or amendment is fully open to inspection by the public.

(r) Records of Native American graves, cemeteries, and sacred places and records of Native American places, features, and objects described in Sections 5097.9 and 5097.993 of the Public

Resources Code maintained by, or in the possession of, the Native American Heritage Commission, another state agency, or a local agency.

(s) A final accreditation report of the Joint Commission on Accreditation of Hospitals that has been transmitted to the State Department of Health Services pursuant to subdivision (b) of Section 1282 of the Health and Safety Code.

(t) Records of a local hospital district, formed pursuant to Division 23 (commencing with Section 32000) of the Health and Safety Code, or the records of a municipal hospital, formed pursuant to Article 7 (commencing with Section 37600) or Article 8 (commencing with Section 37650) of Chapter 5 of Division 3 of Title 4 of this code, that relate to any contract with an insurer or nonprofit hospital service plan for inpatient or outpatient services for alternative rates pursuant to Section 10133 or 11512 of the Insurance Code. However, the record shall be open to inspection within one year after the contract is fully executed.

(u) (1) Information contained in applications for licenses to carry firearms issued pursuant to Section 12050 of the Penal Code by the sheriff of a county or the chief or other head of a municipal police department that indicates when or where the applicant is vulnerable to attack or that concerns the applicant's medical or psychological history or that of members of his or her family.

(2) The home address and telephone number of peace officers, judges, court commissioners, and magistrates that are set forth in applications for licenses to carry firearms issued pursuant to Section 12050 of the Penal Code by the sheriff of a county or the chief or other head of a municipal police department.

(3) The home address and telephone number of peace officers, judges, court commissioners, and magistrates that are set forth in licenses to carry firearms issued pursuant to Section 12050 of the Penal Code by the sheriff of a county or the chief or other head of a municipal police department.

(v) (1) Records of the Major Risk Medical Insurance Program related to activities governed by Part 6.3 (commencing with Section 12695) and Part 6.5 (commencing with Section 12700) of Division 2 of the Insurance Code, and that reveal the deliberative processes, discussions, communications, or any other portion of the negotiations with health plans, or the impressions, opinions, recommendations, meeting minutes, research, work product, theories, or strategy of the board or its staff, or records that provide instructions, advice, or training to employees.

(2) (A) Except for the portion of a contract that contains the rates of payment, contracts for health coverage entered into pursuant to Part 6.3 (commencing with Section 12695) or Part 6.5 (commencing with Section 12700) of Division 2 of the Insurance Code, on or after July 1, 1991, shall be open to inspection one year after they have been fully executed.

(B) If a contract for health coverage that is entered into prior to July 1, 1991, is amended on or after July 1, 1991, the amendment, except for any portion containing the rates of payment, shall be open to inspection one year after the amendment has been fully executed.

(3) Three years after a contract or amendment is open to inspection pursuant to this subdivision, the portion of the contract or amendment containing the rates of payment shall be open to inspection.

(4) Notwithstanding any other provision of law, the entire contract or amendments to a contract shall be open to inspection by the Joint Legislative Audit Committee. The committee shall maintain the confidentiality of the contracts and amendments thereto, until the contract or amendments to a contract is open to inspection pursuant to paragraph (3).

(w) (1) Records of the Major Risk Medical Insurance Program related to activities governed by Chapter 14 (commencing with Section 10700) of Part 2 of Division 2 of the Insurance Code, and that reveal the deliberative processes, discussions, communications, or any other portion of the negotiations with health plans, or the impressions, opinions, recommendations, meeting minutes, research, work product, theories, or strategy of the board or its staff, or records that provide instructions, advice, or training to employees.

(2) Except for the portion of a contract that contains the rates of payment, contracts for health coverage entered into pursuant to Chapter 14 (commencing with Section 10700) of Part 2 of Division 2 of the Insurance Code, on or after January 1, 1993, shall be open to inspection one year after they have been fully executed.

(3) Notwithstanding any other provision of law, the entire contract or amendments to a contract shall be open to inspection by the Joint Legislative Audit Committee. The committee shall maintain the confidentiality of the contracts and amendments thereto, until the contract or amendments to a contract is open to inspection pursuant to paragraph (2).

(x) Financial data contained in applications for registration, or registration renewal, as a service contractor filed with the Director of Consumer Affairs pursuant to Chapter 20 (commencing with Section 9800) of Division 3 of the Business and Professions Code, for the purpose of establishing the service contractor's net worth, or financial data regarding the funded accounts held in escrow for service contracts held in force in this state by a service contractor.

(y) (1) Records of the Managed Risk Medical Insurance Board related to activities governed by Part 6.2 (commencing with Section 12693) or Part 6.4 (commencing with Section 12699.50) of Division 2 of the Insurance Code, and that reveal the deliberative processes, discussions, communications, or any other portion of the negotiations with health plans, or the impressions, opinions, recommendations, meeting minutes, research, work product, theories, or strategy of the board or its staff, or records that provide instructions, advice, or training to employees.

(2) (A) Except for the portion of a contract that contains the rates of payment, contracts entered into pursuant to Part 6.2 (commencing with Section 12693) or Part 6.4 (commencing with Section 12699.50) of Division 2 of the Insurance Code, on or after January 1, 1998, shall be open to inspection one year after they have been fully executed.

(B) In the event that a contract entered into pursuant to Part 6.2 (commencing with Section 12693) or Part 6.4 (commencing with Section 12699.50) of Division 2 of the Insurance Code is amended, the amendment shall be open to inspection one year after the amendment has been fully executed.

(3) Three years after a contract or amendment is open to inspection pursuant to this subdivision, the portion of the contract or amendment containing the rates of payment shall be open to inspection.

(4) Notwithstanding any other provision of law, the entire contract or amendments to a contract shall be open to inspection by the Joint Legislative Audit Committee. The committee shall maintain the confidentiality of the contracts and amendments thereto until the contract or amendments to a contract are open to inspection pursuant to paragraph (2) or (3).

(5) The exemption from disclosure provided pursuant to this subdivision for the contracts, deliberative processes, discussions, communications, negotiations with health plans, impressions, opinions, recommendations, meeting minutes, research, work product, theories, or strategy of the board or its staff shall also apply to the contracts, deliberative processes, discussions, communications, negotiations with health plans, impressions, opinions, recommendations, meeting minutes, research, work product, theories, or strategy of applicants pursuant to Part 6.4 (commencing with Section 12699.50) of Division 2 of the Insurance Code.

(z) Records obtained pursuant to paragraph (2) of subdivision (c) of Section 2891.1 of the Public Utilities Code.

(aa) A document prepared by or for a state or local agency that assesses its vulnerability to terrorist attack or other criminal acts intended to disrupt the public agency's operations and that is for distribution or consideration in a closed session.

(bb) Critical infrastructure information, as defined in Section 131(3) of Title 6 of the United States Code, that is voluntarily submitted to the California Office of Homeland Security for use by that office, including the identity of the person who or entity that voluntarily submitted the information. As used in this subdivision, "voluntarily submitted" means submitted in the absence of the office exercising any legal authority to compel access to or submission of critical infrastructure information. This subdivision shall not affect the status of information in the possession of any other state or local governmental agency.

(cc) All information provided to the Secretary of State by a person for the purpose of registration in the Advance Health Care Directive Registry, except that those records shall be released at the request of a health care provider, a public guardian, or the registrant's legal representative.

Nothing in this section prevents any agency from opening its records concerning the administration of the agency to public inspection, unless disclosure is otherwise prohibited by law.

Nothing in this section prevents any health facility from disclosing to a certified bargaining agent relevant financing information pursuant to Section 8 of the National Labor Relations Act (29 U.S.C. Sec. 158).

6254.1. Disclosure of residential mailing address. (a) Except as provided in Section 6254.7, nothing in this chapter requires disclosure of records that are the residence address of any person contained in the records of the Department of Housing and Community Development, if the person has requested confidentiality of that information, in accordance with Section 18081 of the Health and Safety Code.

(b) Nothing in this chapter requires the disclosure of the residence or mailing address of any person in any record of the Department of Motor Vehicles except in accordance with Section 1808.21 of the Vehicle Code.

(c) Nothing in this chapter requires the disclosure of the results of a test undertaken pursuant to Section 12804.8 of the Vehicle Code.

6254.2. Pesticide safety and efficacy information; public disclosure; limitations; procedures. (a) Nothing in this chapter exempts from public disclosure the same categories of pesticide safety and efficacy information that are disclosable under paragraph (1) of subsection (d) of Section 10 of the federal Insecticide, Fungicide, and Rodenticide Act (7 U.S.C. Sec. 136h(d)(1)), if the individual requesting the information is not an officer, employee, or agent specified in subdivision (h) and signs the affirmation specified in subdivision (h).

(b) The Director of Pesticide Regulation, upon his or her initiative, or upon receipt of a request pursuant to this chapter for the release of data submitted and designated as a trade secret by a registrant or applicant, shall determine whether any or all of the data so submitted is a properly designated trade secret. In order to assure that the interested public has an opportunity to obtain and review pesticide safety and efficacy data and to comment prior to the expiration of the public comment period on a proposed pesticide registration, the director shall provide notice to interested persons when an application for registration enters the registration evaluation process.

(c) If the director determines that the data is not a trade secret, the director shall notify the registrant or applicant by certified mail.

(d) The registrant or applicant shall have 30 days after receipt of this notification to provide the director with a complete justification and statement of the grounds on which the trade secret privilege is claimed. This justification and statement shall be submitted by certified mail.

(e) The director shall determine whether the data is protected as a trade secret within 15 days after receipt of the justification and statement or, if no justification and statement is filed, within 45 days of the original notice. The director shall notify the registrant or applicant and any party who has requested the data pursuant to this chapter of that determination by certified mail. If the director determines that the data is not protected as a trade secret, the final notice shall also specify a date, not sooner than 15 days after the date of mailing of the final notice, when the data shall be available to any person requesting information pursuant to subdivision (a).

(f) "Trade secret" means data that is nondisclosable under paragraph (1) of subsection (d) of Section 10 of the federal Insecticide, Fungicide, and Rodenticide Act.

(g) This section shall be operative only so long as, and to the extent that, enforcement of paragraph (1) of subsection (d) of Section 10 of the federal Insecticide, Fungicide, and Rodenticide Act has not been enjoined by federal court order, and shall become inoperative if an unappealable federal court judgment or decision becomes final that holds that paragraph invalid, to the extent of the invalidity.

(h) The director shall not knowingly disclose information submitted to the state by an applicant or registrant pursuant to Article 4 (commencing with Section 12811) of Chapter 2 of Division 7 of the Food and Agricultural Code to any officer, employee, or agent of any business or other entity engaged in the production, sale, or distribution of pesticides in countries other than the United States or in countries in addition to the United States, or to any other person who intends to deliver this information to any foreign or multi-national business or entity, unless the applicant or registrant consents to the disclosure. To implement this subdivision, the director shall require the following affirmation to be signed by the person who requests such information:

AFFIRMATION OF STATUS

This affirmation is required by Section 6254.2 of the Government Code.

I have requested access to information submitted to the Department of Pesticide Regulation (or previously submitted to the Department of Food and Agriculture) by a pesticide applicant or registrant pursuant to the California Food and Agricultural Code. I hereby affirm all of the following statements:

(1) I do not seek access to the information for purposes of delivering it or offering it for sale to any business or other entity, including the business or entity of which I am an officer, employee, or agent engaged in the production, sale, or distribution of pesticides in countries other than the United States or in countries in addition to the United States, or to the officers, employees, or agents of such a business or entity.

(2) I will not purposefully deliver or negligently cause the data to be delivered to a business or entity specified in paragraph (1) or its officers, employees, or agents.

I am aware that I may be subject to criminal penalties under Section 118 of the Penal Code if I make any statement of material facts knowing that the statement is false or if I willfully conceal any material fact.

_____

_____
Name of Requester   Name of Requester's Organization

_____
Signature of Requester   Address of Requester

_____ _____
Date   Request No.   Telephone Number of Requester

_____

Name, Address, and Telephone Number of Requester's Client, if the requester has requested access to the information on behalf of someone other than the requester or the requester's organization listed above.

(i) Notwithstanding any other provision of this section, the director may disclose information submitted by an applicant or registrant to any person in connection with a public proceeding conducted under law or regulation, if the director determines that the information is needed to determine whether a pesticide, or any ingredient of any pesticide, causes unreasonable adverse effects on health or the environment.

(j) The director shall maintain records of the names of persons to whom data is disclosed pursuant to this section and the persons or organizations they represent and shall inform the applicant or registrant of the names and the affiliation of these persons.

(k) Section 118 of the Penal Code applies to any affirmation made pursuant to this section.

(l) Any officer or employee of the state or former officer or employee of the state who, because of this employment or official position, obtains possession of, or has access to, material which is prohibited from disclosure by this section, and who, knowing that disclosure of this material is prohibited by this section, willfully discloses the material in any manner to any person not entitled to receive it, shall, upon conviction, be punished by a fine of not more than ten thousand dollars ($10,000), or by imprisonment in the county jail for not more than one year, or by both fine and imprisonment.

For purposes of this subdivision, any contractor with the state who is furnished information pursuant to this section, or any employee of any contractor, shall be considered an employee of the state.

(m) This section does not prohibit any person from maintaining a civil action for wrongful disclosure of trade secrets.

(n) The director may limit an individual to one request per month pursuant to this section if the director determines that a person has made a frivolous request within the past 12-month period.

6254.3. State and school district employee home address and phone numbers as public records.
(a) The home addresses and home telephone numbers of state employees and employees of a school district or county office of education shall not be deemed to be public records and shall not be open to public inspection, except that disclosure of that information may be made as follows:

(1) To an agent, or a family member of the individual to whom the information pertains.

(2) To an officer or employee of another state agency, school district, or county office of education when necessary for the performance of its official duties.

(3) To an employee organization pursuant to regulations and decisions of the Public Employment Relations Board, except that the home addresses and home telephone numbers of employees performing law enforcement-related functions shall not be disclosed.

(4) To an agent or employee of a health benefit plan providing health services or administering claims for health services to state, school districts, and county office of education employees and their enrolled dependents, for the purpose of providing the health services or administering claims for employees and their enrolled dependents.

(b) Upon written request of any employee, a state agency, school district, or county office of education shall not disclose the employee's home address or home telephone number pursuant to paragraph (3) of subdivision (a) and an agency shall remove the employee's home address and home telephone number from any mailing list maintained by the agency, except if the list is used exclusively by the agency to contact the employee.

6254.4. Voter registration information; confidentiality. (a) The home address, telephone number, e-mail address, precinct number, or other number specified by the Secretary of State for voter registration purposes, and prior registration information shown on the voter registration card for all registered voters, are confidential and shall not be disclosed to any person, except pursuant to Section 2194 of the Elections Code.

(b) For purposes of this section, "home address" means street address only, and does not include an individual's city or post office address.

(c) The California driver's license number, the California identification card number, the social security number, and any other unique identifier used by the State of California for purposes of voter identification shown on a voter registration card of a registered voter, or added to the voter registration records to comply with the requirements of the Help America Vote Act of 2002 (42 U.S.C. Sec. 15301 et seq.), are confidential and shall not be disclosed to any person.

(d) The signature of the voter that is shown on the voter registration card is confidential and shall not be disclosed to any person.

6254.5. Disclosure of public record; waiver of exemption; agency; inapplicability of section; agreement not disclosed by government agency. Notwithstanding any other provisions of the law, whenever a state or local agency discloses a public record which is otherwise exempt from this chapter, to any member of the public, this disclosure shall constitute a waiver of the exemptions specified in Sections 6254, 6254.7, or other similar provisions of law. For purposes of this section, "agency" includes a member, agent, officer, or employee of the agency acting within the scope of his or her membership, agency, office, or employment.

This section, however, shall not apply to disclosures:

(a) Made pursuant to the Information Practices Act (commencing with Section 1798 of the Civil Code) or discovery proceedings.

(b) Made through other legal proceedings or as otherwise required by law.

(c) Within the scope of disclosure of a statute which limits disclosure of specified writings to certain purposes.

(d) Not required by law, and prohibited by formal action of an elected legislative body of the local agency which retains the writings.

(e) Made to any governmental agency which agrees to treat the disclosed material as confidential. Only persons authorized in writing by the person in charge of the agency shall be permitted to obtain the information. Any information obtained by the agency shall only be used for purposes which are consistent with existing law.

(f) Of records relating to a financial institution or an affiliate thereof, if the disclosures are made to the financial institution or affiliate by a state agency responsible for the regulation or supervision of the financial institution or affiliate.

(g) Of records relating to any person that is subject to the jurisdiction of the Department of Corporations, if the disclosures are made to the person that is the subject of the records for the purpose of corrective action by that person, or if a corporation, to an officer, director, or other key personnel of the corporation for the purpose of corrective action, or to any other person to the extent necessary to obtain information from that person for the purpose of an investigation by the Department of Corporations.

(h) Made by the Commissioner of Financial Institutions under Section 1909, 8009, or 18396 of the Financial Code.

(i) Of records relating to any person that is subject to the jurisdiction of the Department of Managed Health Care, if the disclosures are made to the person that is the subject of the records for the purpose of corrective action by that person, or if a corporation, to an officer, director, or other key personnel of the corporation for the purpose of corrective action, or to any other person to the extent necessary to obtain information from that person for the purpose of an investigation by the Department of Managed Health Care.

6254.6. Private industry wage data from federal bureau of labor statistics; identity of employers; confidentiality. Whenever a city and county or a joint powers agency, pursuant to a mandatory statute or charter provision to collect private industry wage data for salary setting purposes, or a contract entered to implement that mandate, is provided this data by the federal Bureau of Labor Statistics on the basis that the identity of private industry employers shall remain confidential, the identity of the employers shall not be open to the public or be admitted as evidence in any action or special proceeding.

6254.7. Air pollution data; public records; notices and orders to building owners; trade secrets; data used to calculate costs of obtaining emission offsets. (a) All information, analyses, plans, or specifications that disclose the nature, extent, quantity, or degree of air contaminants or other pollution which any article, machine, equipment, or other contrivance will produce, which any air pollution control district or air quality management district, or any other state or local agency or district, requires any applicant to provide before the applicant builds, erects, alters, replaces, operates, sells, rents, or uses the article, machine, equipment, or other contrivance, are public records.

(b) All air or other pollution monitoring data, including data compiled from stationary sources, are public records.

(c) All records of notices and orders directed to the owner of any building of violations of housing or building codes, ordinances, statutes, or regulations which constitute violations of standards provided in Section 1941.1 of the Civil Code, and records of subsequent action with respect to those notices and orders, are public records.

(d) Except as otherwise provided in subdivision (e) and Chapter 3 (commencing with Section 99150) of Part 65 of the Education Code, trade secrets are not public records under this section. "Trade secrets," as used in this section, may include, but are not limited to, any formula, plan, pattern, process, tool, mechanism, compound, procedure, production data, or compilation of information which is not patented, which is known only to certain individuals within a commercial concern who are using it to fabricate, produce, or compound an article of trade or a service having commercial value and which gives its user an opportunity to obtain a business advantage over competitors who do not know or use it.

(e) Notwithstanding any other provision of law, all air pollution emission data, including those emission data which constitute trade secrets as defined in subdivision (d), are public records. Data used to calculate emission data are not emission data for the purposes of this subdivision and data which constitute trade secrets and which are used to calculate emission data are not public records.

(f) Data used to calculate the costs of obtaining emissions offsets are not public records. At the time that an air pollution control district or air quality management district issues a permit to construct to an applicant who is required to obtain offsets pursuant to district rules and regulations, data obtained from the applicant consisting of the year the offset transaction occurred, the amount of offsets purchased, by pollutant, and the total cost, by pollutant, of the offsets purchased is a public record. If an application is denied, the data shall not be a public record.

6254.8. Disclosure of employee contract information required. Every employment contract between a state or local agency and any public official or public employee is a public record which is not subject to the provisions of Sections 6254 and 6255.

6254.9. Computer software; status of public record; sale; lease or license authorized; limitations. (a) Computer software developed by a state or local agency is not itself a public record under this chapter. The agency may sell, lease, or license the software for commercial or noncommercial use.

(b) As used in this section, "computer software" includes computer mapping systems, computer programs, and computer graphics systems.

(c) This section shall not be construed to create an implied warranty on the part of the State of California or any local agency for errors, omissions, or other defects in any computer software as provided pursuant to this section.

(d) Nothing in this section is intended to affect the public record status of information merely because it is stored in a computer. Public records stored in a computer shall be disclosed as required by this chapter.

(e) Nothing in this section is intended to limit any copyright protections.

6254.10. Disclosure of archaeological site information not required. Nothing in this chapter requires disclosure of records that relate to archaeological site information and reports maintained by, or in the possession of, the Department of Parks and Recreation, the State Historical Resources Commission, the State Lands Commission, the Native American Heritage Commission, another state agency, or a local agency, including the records that the agency obtains through a consultation process between a California Native American tribe and a state or local agency.

6254.11. Volatile organic compounds or chemical information. Nothing in this chapter requires the disclosure of records that relate to volatile organic compounds or chemical substances information received or compiled by an air pollution control officer pursuant to Section 42303.2 of the Health and Safety Code.

6254.12. Disclosure of securities dealers disciplinary information not required. Any information reported to the North American Securities Administrators Association/National Association of Securities Dealers' Central Registration Depository and compiled as disciplinary records which are made available to the Department of Corporations through a computer system, shall constitute a public record. Notwithstanding any other provision of law, the Department of Corporations may disclose that information and the current license status and the year of issuance of the license of a broker-dealer upon written or oral request pursuant to Section 25247 of the Corporations Code.

6254.13. Disclosure of certain educational testing materials required. Notwithstanding Section 6254, upon the request of any Member of the Legislature or upon request of the Governor or his or her designee, test questions or materials that would be used to administer an examination and are provided by the State Department of Education and administered as part of a statewide testing program of pupils enrolled in the public schools shall be disclosed to the requester. These questions or materials may not include an individual examination that has been administered to a pupil and scored. The requester may not take physical possession of the questions or materials, but may view the questions or materials at a location selected by the department. Upon viewing this information, the requester shall keep the materials that he or she has seen confidential.

6254.14. Disclosure of Department of Corrections' contracts relating to health care services not required. (a) Except as provided in Sections 6254 and 6254.7, nothing in this chapter shall be construed to require disclosure of records of the Department of Corrections that relate to health care services contract negotiations, and that reveal the deliberative processes, discussions, communications, or any other portion of the negotiations, including, but not limited to, records related to those negotiations such as meeting minutes, research, work product, theories, or strategy of the department, or its staff, or members of the California Medical Assistance Commission, or its staff, who act in consultation with, or on behalf of, the department.

Except for the portion of a contract that contains the rates of payment, contracts for health services entered into by the Department of Corrections or the California Medical Assistance Commission on or after July 1, 1993, shall be open to inspection one year after they are fully executed. In the event that a contract for health services that is entered into prior to July 1, 1993, is amended on or after July 1, 1993, the amendment, except for any portion containing rates of payment, shall be open to inspection one year after it is fully executed.

Three years after a contract or amendment is open to inspection under this subdivision, the portion of the contract or amendment containing the rates of payment shall be open to inspection.

Notwithstanding any other provision of law, the entire contract or amendment shall be open to inspection by the Joint Legislative Audit Committee and the Bureau of State Audits. The Joint Legislative Audit Committee and the Bureau of State Audits shall maintain the confidentiality of the contracts and amendments until the contract or amendment is fully open to inspection by the public.

It is the intent of the Legislature that confidentiality of health care provider contracts, and of the contracting process as provided in this subdivision, is intended to protect the competitive nature of the negotiation process, and shall not affect public access to other information relating to the delivery of health care services.

(b) The inspection authority and confidentiality requirements established in subdivisions (q), (v), and (w) of Section 6254 for the Legislative Audit Committee shall also apply to the Bureau of State Audits.

6254.15. Disclosure of certain information provided to state by private company. Nothing in this chapter shall be construed to require the disclosure of records that are any of the following: corporate financial records, corporate proprietary information including trade secrets, and information relating to siting within the state furnished to a government agency by a private company for the purpose of permitting the agency to work with the company in retaining, locating, or expanding a facility within California. Except as provided below, incentives offered by state or local government agencies, if any, shall be disclosed upon communication to the agency or the public of a decision to stay, locate, relocate, or expand, by a company, or upon application by that company to a governmental agency for a general plan amendment, rezone, use permit, building permit, or any other permit, whichever occurs first.

The agency shall delete, prior to disclosure to the public, information that is exempt pursuant to this section from any record describing state or local incentives offered by an agency to a private business to retain, locate, relocate, or expand the business within California.

6254.16. Disclosure of certain municipal utility information. Nothing in this chapter shall be construed to require the disclosure of the name, credit history, utility usage data, home address, or telephone number of utility customers of local agencies, except that disclosure of name, utility usage data, and the home address of utility customers of local agencies shall be made available upon request as follows:

(a) To an agent or authorized family member of the person to whom the information pertains.

(b) To an officer or employee of another governmental agency when necessary for the performance of its official duties.

(c) Upon court order or the request of a law enforcement agency relative to an ongoing investigation.

(d) Upon determination by the local agency that the utility customer who is the subject of the request has used utility services in a manner inconsistent with applicable local utility usage policies.

(e) Upon determination by the local agency that the utility customer who is the subject of the request is an elected or appointed official with authority to determine the utility usage policies of the local agency, provided that the home address of an appointed official shall not be disclosed without his or her consent.

(f) Upon determination by the local agency that the public interest in disclosure of the information clearly outweighs the public interest in nondisclosure.

6254.17. Nondisclosability of victim information. (a) Nothing in this chapter shall be construed to require disclosure of records of the California Victim Compensation and Government Claims Board that relate to a request for assistance under Article 1 (commencing with Section 13950) of Chapter 5 of Part 4 of Division 3 of Title 2.

(b) This section shall not apply to a disclosure of the following information, if no information is disclosed that connects the information to a specific victim, derivative victim, or applicant under Article 1 (commencing with Section 13950) of Chapter 5 of Part 4 of Division 3 of Title 2:

(1) The amount of money paid to a specific provider of services.

(2) Summary data concerning the types of crimes for which assistance is provided.

6254.18. Nondisclosability of reproductive health services facility information. (a) Nothing in this chapter shall be construed to require disclosure of any personal information received, collected, or compiled by a public agency regarding the employees, volunteers, board members, owners, partners, officers, or contractors of a reproductive health services facility who have notified the public agency pursuant to subdivision (d) if the personal information is contained in a document that relates to the facility.

(b) For purposes of this section, the following terms have the following meanings:

(1) "Contractor" means an individual or entity that contracts with a reproductive health services facility for services related to patient care.

(2) "Personal information" means the following information related to an individual that is maintained by a public agency: social security number, physical description, home address, home telephone number, statements of personal worth or personal financial data filed pursuant to subdivision (n) of Section 6254, personal medical history, employment history, electronic mail address, and information that reveals any electronic network location or identity.

(3) "Public agency" means all of the following:

(A) The State Department of Health Services.

(B) The Department of Consumer Affairs.

(C) The Department of Managed Health Care.

(4) "Reproductive health services facility" means the office of a licensed physician and surgeon whose specialty is family practice, obstetrics, or gynecology, or a licensed clinic, where at least 50 percent of the patients of the physician or the clinic are provided with family planning or abortion services.

(c) Any person may institute proceedings for injunctive or declarative relief or writ of mandate in any court of competent jurisdiction to obtain access to employment history information pursuant to Sections 6258 and 6259. If the court finds, based on the facts of a particular case, that the public interest served by disclosure of employment history information clearly outweighs the public interest served by not disclosing the information, the court shall order the officer or person charged with withholding the information to disclose employment history information or show cause why he or she should not do so pursuant to Section 6259.

(d) In order for this section to apply to an individual who is an employee, volunteer, board member, officer, or contractor of a reproductive health services facility, the individual shall notify the public agency to which his or her personal information is being submitted or has been submitted that he or she falls within the application of this section. The reproductive health services facility shall retain a copy of all notifications submitted pursuant to this section. This notification shall be valid if it complies with all of the following:

(1) Is on the official letterhead of the facility.

(2) Is clearly separate from any other language present on the same page and is executed by a signature that serves no other purpose than to execute the notification.

(3) Is signed and dated by both of the following:

(A) The individual whose information is being submitted.

(B) The executive officer or his or her designee of the reproductive health services facility.

(e) The privacy protections for personal information authorized pursuant to this section shall be effective from the time of notification pursuant to subdivision (d) until either one of the following occurs:

(1) Six months after the date of separation from a reproductive health services facility for an individual who has served for not more than one year as an employee, contractor, volunteer, board member, or officer of the reproductive health services facility.

(2) One year after the date of separation from a reproductive health services facility for an individual who has served for more than one year as an employee, contractor, volunteer, board member, or officer of the reproductive health services facility.

(f) Within 90 days of separation of an employee, contractor, volunteer, board member, or officer of the reproductive health services facility who has provided notice to a public agency pursuant to subdivision (c), the facility shall provide notice of the separation to the relevant agency or agencies.

(g) Nothing in this section shall prevent the disclosure by a government agency of data regarding age, race, ethnicity, national origin, or gender of individuals whose personal information is protected pursuant to this section, so long as the data contains no individually identifiable information.

6254.20. Nondisclosability of personal information collected electronically. Nothing in this chapter shall be construed to require the disclosure of records that relate to electronically collected personal information, as defined by Section 11015.5, received, collected, or compiled by a state agency.

6254.21. Posting of public official home address information prohibited. (a) No state or local agency shall post the home address or telephone number of any elected or appointed official on the Internet without first obtaining the written permission of that individual.

(b) No person shall knowingly post the home address or telephone number of any elected or appointed official, or of the official's residing spouse or child on the Internet knowing that person is an elected or appointed official and intending to cause imminent great bodily harm that is likely to occur or threatening to cause imminent great bodily harm to that individual. A violation of this subdivision is a misdemeanor. A violation of this subdivision that leads to the bodily injury of the official, or his or her residing spouse or child, is a misdemeanor or a felony.

(c) (1) No person, business, or association shall publicly post or publicly display on the Internet the home address or telephone number of any elected or appointed official if that official has made a written demand of that person, business, or association to not disclose his or her home address or telephone number. A written demand made under this paragraph by a state constitutional officer, a mayor, or a Member of the Legislature, a city council, or a board of supervisors shall include a statement describing a threat or fear for the safety of that official or of any person residing at the official's home address. A written demand made under this paragraph by an elected official shall be effective for four years, regardless of whether or not the official's term has expired prior to the end of the four-year period. For this purpose, "publicly post" or "publicly display" means to intentionally communicate or otherwise make available to the general public.

(2) An official whose home address or telephone number is made public as a result of a violation of paragraph (1) may bring an action seeking injunctive or declarative relief in any court of competent jurisdiction. If a jury or court finds that a violation has occurred, it may grant injunctive or declarative relief and shall award the official court costs and reasonable attorney's fees.

(d) (1) No person, business, or association shall solicit, sell, or trade on the Internet the home address or telephone number of an elected or appointed official with the intent to cause imminent great bodily harm to the official or to any person residing at the official's home address.

(2) Notwithstanding any other provision of law, an official whose home address or telephone number is solicited, sold, or traded in violation of paragraph (1) may bring an action in any court of competent jurisdiction. If a jury or court finds that a violation has occurred, it shall award damages to that official in an amount up to a maximum of three times the actual damages but in no case less than four thousand dollars ($4,000).

(e) An interactive computer service or access software provider, as defined in Section 230(f) of Title 47 of the United States Code, shall not be liable under this section unless the service or provider intends to abet or cause imminent great bodily harm that is likely to occur or threatens to cause imminent great bodily harm to an elected or appointed official.

(f) For purposes of this section, "elected or appointed official" includes, but is not limited to, all of the following:

(1) State constitutional officers.

(2) Members of the Legislature.

(3) Judges and court commissioners.

(4) District attorneys.

(5) Public defenders.

(6) Members of a city council.

(7) Members of a board of supervisors.

(8) Appointees of the Governor.

(9) Appointees of the Legislature.

(10) Mayors.

(11) City attorneys.

(12) Police chiefs and sheriffs.

(13) A public safety official as defined in Section 6254.24.

(14) State administrative law judges.

(15) Federal judges and federal defenders.

(16) Members of the United States Congress and appointees of the President.

(g) Nothing in this section is intended to preclude punishment instead under Sections 69, 76, or 422 of the Penal Code, or any other provision of law.

6254.22. Nondisclosability of health plan information. Nothing in this chapter or any other provision of law shall require the disclosure of records of a health plan that is licensed pursuant to the Knox-Keene Health Care Service Plan Act of 1975 (Chapter 2.2 (commencing with Section 1340) of Division 2 of the Health and Safety Code) and that is governed by a county board of supervisors, whether paper records, records maintained in the management information system, or records in any other form, that relate to provider rate or payment determinations, allocation or distribution methodologies for provider payments, formulae or calculations for these payments, and contract negotiations with providers of health care for alternative rates for a period of three years after the contract is fully executed. The transmission of the records, or the information contained therein in an alternative form, to the board of supervisors shall not constitute a waiver of exemption from disclosure, and the records and information once transmitted to the board of supervisors shall be subject to this same exemption. The provisions of this section shall not prevent access to any records by the Joint Legislative Audit Committee in the exercise of its powers pursuant to Article 1 (commencing with Section 10500) of Chapter 4 of Part 2 of Division 2 of Title 2. The provisions of this section also shall not prevent access to any records by the Department of Corporations in the exercise of its powers pursuant to Article 1 (commencing with Section 1340) of Chapter 2.2 of Division 2 of the Health and Safety Code.

6254.23. Nondisclosability of risk assessment or railroad infrastructure protection program information Nothing in this chapter or any other provision of law shall require the disclosure of a risk assessment or railroad infrastructure protection program filed with the Public Utilities Commission, the Director of Homeland Security, and the Office of Emergency Services pursuant to Article 7.3 (commencing with Section 7665) of Chapter 1 of Division 4 of the Public Utilities Code.

6254.24. Definition of public safety official. As used in this chapter, "public safety official" means the following:

(a) An active or retired peace officer as defined in Sections 830 and 830.1 of the Penal Code.

(b) An active or retired public officer or other person listed in Sections 1808.2 and 1808.6 of the Vehicle Code.

(c) An "elected or appointed official" as defined in subdivision (f) of Section 6254.21.

(d) An attorney employed by the Department of Justice, the State Public Defender, or a county office of the district attorney or public defender, the United States Attorney, or the Federal Public Defender.

(e) A city attorney and an attorney who represent cities in criminal matters.

(f) A specified employee of the Department of Corrections and Rehabilitation who supervises inmates or is required to have a prisoner in his or her care or custody.

(g) A sworn or nonsworn employee who supervises inmates in a city police department, a county sheriff's office, the Department of the California Highway Patrol, federal, state, or a local detention facility, and a local juvenile hall, camp, ranch, or home, and a probation officer as defined in Section 830.5 of the Penal Code.

(h) A federal prosecutor, a federal criminal investigator, and a National Park Service Ranger working in California.

(i) The surviving spouse or child of a peace officer defined in Section 830 of the Penal Code, if the peace officer died in the line of duty.

(j) State and federal judges and court commissioners.

(k) An employee of the Attorney General, a district attorney, or a public defender who submits verification from the Attorney General, district attorney, or public defender that the employee represents the Attorney General, district attorney, or public defender in matters that routinely place that employee in personal contact with persons under investigation for, charged with, or convicted of, committing criminal acts.

(l) A nonsworn employee of the Department of Justice or a police department or sheriff's office that, in the course of his or her employment, is responsible for collecting, documenting, and preserving physical evidence at crime scenes, testifying in court as an expert witness, and other technical duties, and a nonsworn employee that, in the course of his or her employment, performs a variety of standardized and advanced laboratory procedures in the examination of physical crime evidence, determines their results, and provides expert testimony in court.

6254.25. Legal counsel memorandum subject to limited work product privilege. Nothing in this chapter or any other provision of law shall require the disclosure of a memorandum submitted to a state body or to the legislative body of a local agency by its legal counsel pursuant to subdivision (q) of Section 11126 or Section 54956.9 until the pending litigation has been finally adjudicated or otherwise settled. The memorandum shall be protected by the attorney work-product privilege until the pending litigation has been finally adjudicated or otherwise settled.

6254.26. Nondisclosability of certain alternative investments. (a) Notwithstanding any provision of this chapter or other law, the following records regarding alternative investments in which public investment funds invest shall not be subject to disclosure pursuant to this chapter, unless the information has already been publicly released by the keeper of the information:

(1) Due diligence materials that are proprietary to the public investment fund or the alternative investment vehicle.

(2) Quarterly and annual financial statements of alternative investment vehicles.

(3) Meeting materials of alternative investment vehicles.

(4) Records containing information regarding the portfolio positions in which alternative investment funds invest.

(5) Capital call and distribution notices.

(6) Alternative investment agreements and all related documents.

(b) Notwithstanding subdivision (a), the following information contained in records described in subdivision (a) regarding alternative investments in which public investment funds invest shall be subject to disclosure pursuant to this chapter and shall not be considered a trade secret exempt from disclosure:

(1) The name, address, and vintage year of each alternative investment vehicle.

(2) The dollar amount of the commitment made to each alternative investment vehicle by the public investment fund since inception.

(3) The dollar amount of cash contributions made by the public investment fund to each alternative investment vehicle since inception.

(4) The dollar amount, on a fiscal yearend basis, of cash distributions received by the public investment fund from each alternative investment vehicle.

(5) The dollar amount, on a fiscal yearend basis, of cash distributions received by the public investment fund plus remaining value of partnership assets attributable to the public investment fund's investment in each alternative investment vehicle.

(6) The net internal rate of return of each alternative investment vehicle since inception.

(7) The investment multiple of each alternative investment vehicle since inception.

(8) The dollar amount of the total management fees and costs paid on an annual fiscal yearend basis, by the public investment fund to each alternative investment vehicle.

(9) The dollar amount of cash profit received by public investment funds from each alternative investment vehicle on a fiscal year-end basis.

(c) For purposes of this section, the following definitions shall apply:

(1) "Alternative investment" means an investment in a private equity fund, venture fund, hedge fund, or absolute return fund.

(2) "Alternative investment vehicle" means the limited partnership, limited liability company, or similar legal structure through which the public investment fund invests in portfolio companies.

(3) "Portfolio positions" means individual portfolio investments made by the alternative investment vehicles.

(4) "Public investment fund" means any public pension or retirement system, and any public endowment or foundation.

6255. Catch all exemption; balancing test. (a) The agency shall justify withholding any record by demonstrating that the record in question is exempt under express provisions of this chapter or that on the facts of the particular case the public interest served by not disclosing the record clearly outweighs the public interest served by disclosure of the record.

(b) A response to a written request for inspection or copies of public records that includes a determination that the request is denied, in whole or in part, shall be in writing.

6257.5. Denial of access based on purpose of record request prohibited. This chapter does not allow limitations on access to a public record based upon the purpose for which the record is being requested, if the record is otherwise subject to disclosure.

6258. Proceedings to enforce right to inspect or to receive copy of record. Any person may institute proceedings for injunctive or declarative relief or writ of mandate in any court of competent jurisdiction to enforce his or her right to inspect or to receive a copy of any public record or class of public records under this chapter. The times for responsive pleadings and for hearings in these proceedings shall be set by the judge of the court with the object of securing a decision as to these matters at the earliest possible time.

6259. Order of court; review; contempt; court costs and attorneys fees. (a) Whenever it is made to appear by verified petition to the superior court of the county where the records or some part thereof are situated that certain public records are being improperly withheld from a member of the public, the court shall order the officer or person charged with withholding the records to disclose the public record or show cause why he or she should not do so. The court shall decide the case after examining the record in camera, if permitted by subdivision (b) of Section 915 of the Evidence Code, papers filed by the parties and any oral argument and additional evidence as the court may allow.

(b) If the court finds that the public official's decision to refuse disclosure is not justified under Section 6254 or 6255, he or she shall order the public official to make the record public. If the judge determines that the public official was justified in refusing to make the record public, he or she shall return the item to the public official without disclosing its content with an order supporting the decision refusing disclosure.

(c) In an action filed on or after January 1, 1991, an order of the court, either directing disclosure by a public official or supporting the decision of the public official refusing disclosure, is not a final judgment or order within the meaning of Section 904.1 of the Code of Civil Procedure from which an appeal may be taken, but shall be immediately reviewable by petition to the appellate court for the issuance of an extraordinary writ. Upon entry of any order pursuant to this section, a party shall, in order to obtain review of the order, file a petition within 20 days after service upon him or her of a written notice of entry of the order, or within such further time not exceeding an additional 20 days as the trial court may for good cause allow. If the notice is served by mail, the period within which to file the petition shall be increased by five days. A stay of an order or judgment shall not be granted unless the petitioning party demonstrates it will otherwise sustain irreparable damage and probable success on the merits. Any person who fails to obey the order of the court shall be cited to show cause why he or she is not in contempt of court.

(d) The court shall award court costs and reasonable attorney fees to the plaintiff should the plaintiff prevail in litigation filed pursuant to this section. The costs and fees shall be paid by the public agency of which the public official is a member or employee and shall not become a personal liability of the public official. If the court finds that the plaintiff's case is clearly frivolous, it shall award court costs and reasonable attorney fees to the public agency.

6260. No effect on judicial records. The provisions of this chapter shall not be deemed in any manner to affect the status of judicial records as it existed immediately prior to the effective date of this section, nor to affect the rights of litigants, including parties to administrative proceedings, under the laws of discovery of this state, nor to limit or impair any rights of discovery in a criminal case.

6261. Disclosure of expenditures and disbursements required. Notwithstanding Section 6252, an itemized statement of the total expenditures and disbursement of any agency provided for in Article VI of the California Constitution shall be open for inspection.

6262. Disclosure of arrest record information to district attorneys allowed. The exemption of records of complaints to, or investigations conducted by, any state or local agency for licensing purposes under subdivision (f) of Section 6254 shall not apply when a request for inspection of such records is made by a district attorney.

6263. Disclosure of non-exempt public record to district attorneys required. A state or local agency shall allow an inspection or copying of any public record or class of public records not exempted by this chapter when requested by a district attorney.

6264. Procedure for district attorney to enforce rights under the Act. The district attorney may petition a court of competent jurisdiction to require a state or local agency to allow him to inspect or receive a copy of any public record or class of public records not exempted by this chapter when the agency fails or refuses to allow inspection or copying within 10 working days of a request. The court may require a public agency to permit inspection or copying by the district attorney unless the public interest or good cause in withholding such records clearly outweighs the public interest in disclosure.

6265. Status of public record unaffected by disclosure to district attorney. Disclosure of records to a district attorney under the provisions of this chapter shall effect no change in the status of the records under any other provision of law.

6267. Libraries supported by public funds; registration and circulation records; confidentiality; exceptions. All registration and circulation records of any library which is in whole or in part supported by public funds shall remain confidential and shall not be disclosed to any person, local agency, or state agency except as follows:

(a) By a person acting within the scope of his or her duties within the administration of the library.

(b) By a person authorized, in writing, by the individual to whom the records pertain, to inspect the records.

(c) By order of the appropriate superior court.

As used in this section, the term "registration records" includes any information which a library requires a patron to provide in order to become eligible to borrow books and other materials, and the term "circulation records" includes any information which identifies the patrons borrowing particular books and other material.

This section shall not apply to statistical reports of registration and circulation nor to records of fines collected by the library.

6268. Public records in custody or control of governor leaving office; transfer to state archives; restriction on public access; conditions. Public records, as defined in Section 6252, in the custody or control of the Governor when he or she leaves office, either voluntarily or involuntarily, shall, as soon as is practical, be transferred to the State Archives. Notwithstanding any other provision of law, the Governor, by written instrument, the terms of which shall be made public, may restrict public access to any of the transferred public records, or any other writings he or she may transfer, which have not already been made accessible to the public. With respect to public records, public access, as otherwise provided for by this chapter, shall not be restricted for a period greater than 50 years or the death of the Governor, whichever is later, nor shall there be any restriction whatsoever with respect to enrolled bill files, press releases, speech files, or writings relating to applications for clemency or extradition in cases which have been closed for a period of at least 25 years. Subject to any restrictions permitted by this section, the Secretary of State, as custodian of the State Archives, shall make all such public records and other writings available to the public as otherwise provided for in this chapter.

Except as to enrolled bill files, press releases, speech files, or writings relating to applications for clemency or extradition, this section shall not apply to public records or other writings in the direct custody or control of any Governor who held office between 1974 and 1988 at the time of leaving office, except to the extent that that Governor may voluntarily transfer those records or other writings to the State Archives.

Notwithstanding any other provision of law, the public records and other writings of any Governor who held office between 1974 and 1988 may be transferred to any educational or research institution in California provided that with respect to public records, public access, as otherwise provided for by this chapter, shall not be restricted for a period greater than 50 years or the death of the Governor, whichever is later. No records or writings may be transferred pursuant to this paragraph unless the institution receiving them agrees to maintain, and does maintain, the materials according to commonly accepted archival standards. No public records transferred shall be destroyed by that institution without first receiving the written approval of the Secretary of State, as custodian of the State Archives, who may require that the records be placed in the State Archives rather than being destroyed. An institution receiving those records or writings shall allow the Secretary of State, as custodian of the State Archives, to copy, at state expense, and to make available to the public, any and all public records, and inventories, indices, or finding aids relating to those records, which the institution makes available to the public generally. Copies of those records in the custody of the state Archives shall be given the same legal effect as is given to the originals.

6270. Limitations on selling public records to private entities. (a) Notwithstanding any other provision of law, no state or local agency shall sell, exchange, furnish, or otherwise provide a public record subject to disclosure pursuant to this chapter to a private entity in a manner that prevents a state or local agency from providing the record directly pursuant to this chapter. Nothing in this section requires a state or local agency to use the State Printer to print public records. Nothing in this section prevents the destruction of records pursuant to law.

(b) This section shall not apply to contracts entered into prior to January 1, 1996, between the County of Santa Clara and a private entity for the provision of public records subject to disclosure under this chapter.

Editor's note: An index of records or information that may not be required to be disclosed pursuant to other provisions of California law has been identified in Government Code Sections 6276-6276.48. These code sections as well as an electronic version of the Public Records Act can be easily accessed at the legislative analyst's website, www.leginfo.ca.gov.

APPENDIX C

Sample California Public Records Act Request Letter

Chief Executive
Name of Agency
Subject: Request to Inspect and Copy Public Records

Dear_____:

This letter is to request access to records in the possession of (Name of agency and/or department, division, etc.) for the purpose of inspection and copying pursuant to the California Public Records Act (Government Code Section 6250 et seq.) and Article I, Section 3 of the California Constitution.

The information that I ask to inspect is as follows: (Describe the record as specifically as possible, including if known, the form in which it is recorded – writings, electronic data, maps, photographs, audio or video tapes etc. – and, if known, the designation of the file or register where it is to be found. You need not state any reason for your request, unless the request is for the names and addresses of private individuals held by a state agency, in which case you should specify that your purpose is the gathering of newsworthy facts by a publisher as provided in Sections 1798.3 (j) and 1798.60 of the Civil Code).

This request reasonably describes (an) identifiable record(s) or information to be produced from that record. If you are unable comply with this request because you believe it is not focused or effective, California Government Code Section 6253.1(a) requires you to (1) assist me in identifying the records and information that are responsive to my request or to the purpose of my request; (2) describe the information technology and physical location in which the records exist; and (3) provide me with suggestions for overcoming any practical basis for denying access to the records or information I am seeking.

Pursuant to Government Code Section 6253(b), I ask that you make the record(s) "promptly available," for inspection and copying, based on my payment of "fees covering direct costs of duplication, or statutory fee, if applicable." I believe that no express provisions of law exist that exempt the record(s) from disclosure. As you determine whether this request seeks copies of disclosable public records, be mindful that Article I, Section 3 (b)(2) of the California Constitution requires you to broadly construe a statute, court rule, or other authority if it furthers the right of access to the information I have requested and to narrowly construe a statute, court rule, or other authority if it limits my right of access.

If a portion of the information I have requested is exempt from disclosure by express provisions of law, Government Code Section 6253(a) additionally requires segregation and deletion of that material in order that the remainder of the information may be released. If you determine that an express provision of law exists to exempt from disclosure all or a portion of the material I have requested, Government Code Section 6253(c) requires notification to me of the reasons for the determination not later than 10 days from your receipt of this request.

Government Code Section 6253(d) prohibits the use of the 10-day period, or any provisions of the Public Records Act "to delay access for purposes of inspecting public records."

To expedite compliance, I am sending a copy of this request to the office of your legal adviser.

Thank you for your timely attention to my request.

Sincerely,

S/_____

cc: Name and title of agency's legal adviser

NOTES ON PUBLIC RECORDS ACT REQUEST LETTER: The sample letter is to be used only as an example. It is written in rather formal language and cites the law upon which your request is based. You may wish to send the letter, as written, depending on the need to educate the agency, or if you have already reached a point where your relationship with the agency might be characterized as "adversarial." However, reporters know that it takes more than the assertion of rights under the law to create and maintain relationships that foster access. Depending on your relationship with the agency, you may wish to edit your letter to delete citations of statutes or the courtesy copy to the agency's legal adviser, or to eliminate entirely the educational sections of the letter when it is clear that the agency knows the law.

APPENDIX D

Sample Demand for Cure or Correction; Alleged Violation of Brown Act

(Send registered mail, return receipt requested)

Presiding Officer, Members
Name of Legislative Body
Name of Local Agency

Dear_____:

     This letter is to call your attention to what I believe was a substantial violation of a central provision of the Ralph M. Brown Act and Article I, Section 3 of the California Constitution, which may jeopardize the finality of the action taken by (name of legislative body and local agency).

     The nature of the violation is as follows. In its meeting of (date), the (name of legislative body) took action to (describe the action taken, specifying the proposal and the manner in which it was acted upon, i.e. by either a formal vote, an "approval in concept" or some other expression of a consensus that the body would or would not act in a certain manner in the future).

     The action taken was not in compliance with the Brown Act and Article I, Section 3 of the California Constitution because (specify one or both) it occurred as the culmination of a discussion in closed session of a matter which the Act does not permit to be discussed in closed session (and/or) there was no adequate notice to the public on the posted agenda for the meeting that the matter acted upon would be discussed, and there was no finding of fact by the (name of the legislative body) that urgent action was necessary on a matter unforeseen at the time the agenda was posted.

     In the event it appears to you that the conduct of the (name of the legislative body) specified herein did not amount to the taking of action, I call your attention to Government Code Section 54952.6, which defines "action taken" for purposes of the Act very expansively.

     As you are aware, the Brown Act allows the legal remedy of judicial invalidation of illegally taken action. Pursuant to Government Code Section 54960.1, I demand that the (name of the legislative body) cure or correct the illegally taken action as follows: (specify whatever corrective action you believe necessary to redress the illegality by providing the public with access to the information acquisition, deliberative process and opportunity to comment of which it was deprived. Examples might include the formal and explicit withdrawal from any commitment made, coupled with a disclosure at a subsequent meeting of the reasons why individual members of the legislative body took the positions that they did, with the full opportunity for informed comment by members of the public at the same meeting, notice of which is properly included on the posted agenda. In some cases informed comment might require public access to any and all documents in the possession of the public agency related to the action taken, with copies available to the public on request at the offices of the agency and also at the meeting at which reconsideration of the matter is to occur).

     As provided by Section 54960.1, you have 30 days from the receipt of this demand to either cure or correct the challenged action, or inform me of your decision not to do so. If you fail to cure or correct as demanded, I am entitled to seek judicial invalidation of the action pursuant to Section 54960.1, in which case I would seek the award of court costs and reasonable attorney fees pursuant to Section 54960.5.

Sincerely,
S/_____

cc: Name and title of agency's legal adviser

APPENDIX E

Sample Freedom of Information Request Letter

Agency Head or FOIA Officer
Name of Agency
Subject: FOIA Request

Dear_____:

Pursuant to the Freedom of Information Act (5 U.S.C. 552) I am requesting access to _____ (specifically identify with as much precision as possible, the records you seek). (Be sure to check to see whether the agency has promulgated regulations that may provide better access to information than FOIA. You also may want to consider filing an expedited request pursuant to 5 U.S.C. § 552(a)(6)(E)(i) and the agency's own regulations)

I am a reporter, editor, etc. for (name of newspaper) and am preparing a report for which the requested information is an important element. The information concerns government operations and activities, namely _____, and the records will contribute to my understanding of those operations and activities. My report will thereby significantly contribute to public understanding of the subject because _____.

For these reasons, as provided in 5 U.S.C. § 552(a)(4)(A)(iii), I ask that fees be waived. If fees are not waived, I agree to pay reasonable duplication fees in an amount not to exceed $_____, but I request to be notified before processing incurs expenses in excess of that amount.

If a portion of the information I have requested is exempt from disclosure by express provisions of law, 5 U.S.C. 552(b) additionally requires segregation and deletion of that material in order that the remainder of the information may be released. If you determine that an express provision of law exists to exempt from disclosure all or a portion of the material I have requested, 5 U.S.C. § 552(a)(6)(A)(i) requires notification to me of the reasons for the determination not later than 20 days from your receipt of this request.

Thank you for your prompt attention to this request, and I look forward to a response within the statutory 20-day period.

Sincerely,

S/_____

APPENDIX F

Sample Freedom of Information Act Appeal Letter

(Send within 30 days of denial)

Name of Agency Official Originally Addressed, Title

Name of Agency
Subject: FOIA Appeal

Dear_____:

This is to appeal the denial of my request pursuant to the Freedom of Information Act, 5 U.S.C. 552.

I received a letter on (date) from (name and title) of your agency, denying my request for access to (description of information). Enclosed are copies of the denial and of my request.

I am confident that upon examining these materials you will conclude that the information I am requesting should be disclosed. (If the reasons for the denial invite any obvious rebuttal, you may rebut them in the appeal letter. It is not necessary to do so, however).

I thank you for your prompt attention to this matter, and I look forward to a response within the statutory 20-day period.

Sincerely,

S/_____
Name of Newspaper Address

TABLE OF CASES

216 Sutter Bay Associates v. County of Sutter
    58 Cal. App. 4th 860, 877 (1997) 15
ABC Inc. v. Powell
    47 M.J. 363 (C.A.A.F. 1997) 119
ABC Inc. v. Stewart
    360 F.3d 90 (2d Cir. 2004) 149
ACLU v. Deukmejian
    32 Cal. 3d 440 (1982) 72
Aisenson v. American Broadcasting Company, Inc.
    220 Cal. App. 3d 146 (1990) 221
Albertson's, Inc. v. Young
    107 Cal. App. 4th 106 (2003) 218
American Federation of State, County and Municipal Employees v. Regents of UC
    80 Cal. App. 3d 913 (1978) 66
Anderson v. Cryovac, Inc.
    805 F.2d 1 (1st Cir. 1986) 100, 185
Appeal of Anthony S. Troia
    580 F.2d 281 (8th Cir. 1978) 186
Applications of National Broadcasting Co.
    828 F.2d 340 (6th Cir. 1987) 183
Arkansas Chronicle v. Murphy
    183 Fed. Appx. 300, 34 Media L. Rep. 1837 (4th Cir. 2006) 178
Associated Press v. U.S. District Court
    705 F.2d 1143 (9th Cir. 1983) 138, 183
Ayeni v. CBS, Inc.
    848 F.Supp. 362 (E.D.N.Y. 1994) 216
Baca v. Moreno Valley Unified School Dist.
    936 F. Supp. 719 (C.D.Cal.1996) 8
Bakersfield City School Dist. v. Superior Court
    118 Cal. App. 4th 1041 (2004) 66
Balboa Island Village Inn, Inc. v. Lemen
    156 P.3d 339 (57 Cal.Rptr.3d 320, 2007) 133
Baltimore Sun Co. v. Ehrlich
    437 F.3d 410 (4th Cir. 2006) 153, 209
Bank of America National Trust & Savings Ass'n v. Hotel Rittenhouse Associates
    800 F.2d 339 (3d Cir. 1986) 191
Bantam Books, Inc. v. Sullivan
    372 U.S. 58, 70 (1963) 129
Bartnicki v. Vopper
    532 U.S. 514 (2001) 212, 226, 228
Baugh v. CBS, Inc.
    828 F. Supp. 745 (N.D. Cal. 1993) 213
Bell v. Vista Unified School Dist.
    82 Cal. App. 4th 672 (2000) 5
Belth v. Gillespie
    232 Cal. App. 3d 896 (1991) 79
Bethel School District No. 403 v. Fraser
    478 U.S. 675 (1986) 236
Black Panther Party v. Kehoe
    42 Cal. App. 3d 645 (1974) 61
Board of Trustees of California State University v. Superior Court
    132 Cal. App. 4th 889 (2005) 64, 65
Board of Trustees of the California State University v. Superior Court of San Diego County
    132 Cal. App. 4th 889 (2005) 189

Boehner v. McDermott
    441 F.3d 1010 (D.D.C. 2006) 226, 228
Bollinger v. San Diego Civil Service Commission
    71 Cal. App. 4th 568 (1999) 24
Borreca v. Fasi
    369 F. Supp. 906 (D. Haw. 1974) 100, 105
Bradbury v. Superior Court.
    49 Cal. App. 4th 1108 (1996) 209
Bradshaw v. City of Los Angeles
    221 Cal. App. 3d 908 (1990) 74
Branzburg v. Hayes
    408 U.S. 665 (1972) .... 170, 171, 173, 177, 199, passim
Braun v. City of Taft
    154 Cal. App. 3d 332 (1984) 66
Brian W. v. Superior Court
    20 Cal. 3d 618 (1978) 116
Bright v. Los Angeles Unified School District
    18 Cal. 3d 450 (1976) 239
Brown & Williamson Tobacco Corp. v. Federal Trade Comm'n
    710 F.2d 1165 (6th Cir. 1983) 187
Brown v. Li
    308 F.3d 939 (9th Cir. 2002) 236
Bruce v. Gregory
    65 Cal.2d 666 (1967) 58
Brunette v. Humane Society of Ventura County
    40 Fed. Appx. 594, 30 Media L. Rep. 2181 (2002) 216, 221
BRV, Inc. v. Superior Court (Dunsmuir Joint Union High School Dist.)
    143 Cal. App. 4th 742 (2006) 66, 97
Burch v. Barker
    861 F.2d 1149 (9th Cir. 1988) 240
Burkle v. Burkle
    135 Cal. App. 4th 1045 (2006) 139, 142, 141
Butterworth v. Smith
    494 U.S. 624 (1990) 158
Cable News Network v. U.S. (Deaver)
    824 F.2d 1046 (D.C. Cir. 1987) (per curiam) 148
Cable News Network, Inc. v. U.S. District Court
    472 U.S. 1017 (1985) 187
Cafarelli v. Yancy
    226 F.3d 492 (6th Cir. 2000) 227
California Alliance for Utility Etc. Education v. City of San Diego
    56 Cal. App. 4th 1024, 1029-1031 (1997) 38
California Commission on Peace Officer Standards and Training v. Superior Court
    128 Cal. App. 4th 281 (2005) 96
California First Amendment Coalition v. Superior Court (Wilson)
    67 Cal. App. 4th 159 (1998) 71
California First Amendment Coalition v. Woodford
    299 F.3d 868 (9th Cir. 2002) 206
California First Amendment Coalition, et al. v. San Antonio Water Co.
    Appeal No.E033804, 2005 WL 19449 (Jan. 4. 2005) 96
California State University v. Superior Court
    90 Cal. App. 4th 810 (2001) 56
Carlson v. Paradise Unified School District
    18 Cal. App. 3d 196 (1979) 20, 41
Carter v. Superior Court
    2002 Cal. App. Unpub. LEXIS 5017 .... 214, 222
CBS v. Block
    42 Cal 3d 646 (1986) 72

CBS v. District Court
     729 F. 2d 1174 (1984) 132

CBS, Inc. v. U.S. District Court
     729 F.2d 1174 (9th Cir. 1984) 184

Chaffee v. San Francisco Public Library Commission
     134 Cal. App. 4th 109 (2005) 8

Cheyenne K. v. Superior Court
     208 Cal. App. 3d 331, 336 (1989) 116, 117

Cincinnati Gas & Electric Co. v. General Electric Co.
     854 F.2d 900 (1988) 140

City of Hemet v. Superior Court
     37 Cal. App. 4th 1411, (1995) 63, 74

City of Los Angeles v. Superior Court
     41 Cal. App. 4th 1083 (1996) 64

City of Richmond v. Superior Court
     32 Cal. App. 4th 1430 (1995) 74

City of San Jose v. Superior Court
     74 Cal. App. 4th 1008 (1999) 72

Civil Service Commission v. National Association of Letter Carriers *AFL-CIO*
     75, 413 U.S. 548 (1982) 102

Coalition of Labor, Agriculture & Business v. County of Santa Barbara Bd. Of Supervisors
     129 Cal. App. 4th 205 (2005) 8

Coastal States Gas Corp. v. Department of Energy
     617 F.2d 854, 866 (D.C. Cir. 1980) 92

Cohan v. City of Thousand Oaks
     30 Cal. App. 4th 547 (1994) 22

Commission on Peace Officer Standards and Training v. Superior Court
     Case No. S134072, 2007 WL 2410091 (2007) 74, 96

Common Cause v. Stirling
     119 Cal. App. 3d 658 (1981) 14, 38, 39

Condit v. Dunne
     225 F.R.D. 113 (2004) 141

Condit v. National Enquirer, Inc.
     289 F.Supp. 2d 1175 (E.D. Cal. 2003) 174

Contra Costa Newspapers, Inc. v. Superior Court (Bishop)
     61 Cal. App. 4th 862 (1998) 156

Cooke v. Connolly
     21 Media L. Rptr. 1575 (Cal. Super. Ct. 1993) 165

Coordinated Pretrial Proceedings in Petroleum Products Antitrust Litigation
     680 F.2d 5 (2d Cir. 1982) 173

Copeland v. Hubbard Broadcasting, Inc.
     23 Med.L.Rptr. 1441 (Minn. Ct. App. 1995) 216

Copley Press, Inc. v. Superior Court
     39 Cal. 4th 1272 (2006) .... 67, 74, 81, passim

Copley Press, Inc. v. Superior Court
     228 Cal. App. 3d 774 (1991) 152

Copley Press v. Superior Court
     6 Cal. App. 4th 106 (1992) ....181, 188, 189, 197, passim

Copley Press, Inc. v. Superior Court
     63 Cal. App. 4th 367 (1998) 65, 19

Costco Companies, Inc. v. Gallant
     96 Cal. App. 4th 740 (2002) 208, 218

County of Los Angeles v. Superior Court
     18 Cal. App. 4th 588, 601 (1993) 68

County of Los Angeles v. Superior Court (Axelrad)
     82 Cal. App. 4th 819 (2000) 63

Craig v. Harney
     331 U.S. 367 (1947) 124

Crowe v. County of San Diego
    242 F. Supp. 2d 740 (S.D. Cal. 2003) 174
Daily Journal Corp. v. Superior Court
    20 Cal. 4th 1117 (1999) 157, 186
Davis v. East Baton Rouge Parish School Board
    78 F. 3d 920 (5th Cir. 1996) 199
Day v. MediaNews Group
    2005 Cal. App. Unpub. LEXIS 7876, 34 Media L. Rep. 1411 (2005) 213
Delaney v. Superior Court
    50 Cal. 3d 785 (1990) .... 163, 164, 165, 166, passim
Deteresa v. American Broadcasting Companies, Inc.
    121 F.3d 460 (9th Cir. 1997) 226
Dietemann v. Time, Inc.
    449 F.2d 245 (9th Cir. 1971) 214, 219
Dillon v. City and County of San Francisco
    748 F. Supp. 722 (N.D. Cal. 1990) 175
Drogin v. Wen Ho Lee
    126 S.Ct. 2351, 165 L.Ed.2d (2006) 175
Dubner v. City and County of San Francisco
    266 F.3d 959 (9th Cir. 2001) 217
Duval v. Board of Trustees
    93 Cal. App. 4th 902, 906-907 (2001) 38
DVD Copy Control Assn., Inc. v. Bunner
    31 Cal. 4th 864 (2003) 133
El Vocero de Puerto Rico v. Puerto Rico
    508 U.S. 147 (1993) 111
Ellis v. Board of Education
    27 Cal. 2d 322 (1945) 203
EPA v. Mink
    410 U.S. 73 (1973) 92
Epstein v. Hollywood Entertainment Dist. II Business Improvement Dist.
    87 Cal. App. 4th 862 (2001) 5, 13
Erickson v. Superior Court
    55 Cal.App.4th 755 (1997) 152
Eskaton Monterey Hospital v. Myers
    134 Cal. App. 3d 788 (1982) 66, 73
Estate of Hearst
    67 Cal. App. 3d 777 (1977) 181, 188
Fairley v. Superior Court
    66 Cal. App. 4th 1414 (1998) 63
Farr v. Pitchess
    522 F.2d 464 (9th Cir. 1975) .... 171, 172, 173, 176, passim
Ferrara v. Detroit Free Press
    1998 U.S. Dist. LEXIS 8635, 26 Media L. Rep. 2355 (E.D. Mich. 1998) 226
Filarsky v. Superior Court
    28 Cal. 4th 419 (2002) 79
Fire Fighters Association v. Barry
    742 F. Supp. 1182 (D.D.C. 1990) 103
Fischer v. Los Angeles Unified School Dist.
    70 Cal. App. 4th 87 (1999) 25
Flanagan v. Flanagan
    27 Cal. 4th 766 (2003) 223
Florida Star v. B.J.F.
    491 U.S. 524 (1989) 212
Flynt v. Rumsfeld
    355 F.3d 697 (D.C. Cir. 2004) 202
FMC Corp. v. Capital Cities/ABC, Inc.
    915 F.2d 300 (7th Cir. 1990) 212

Food Lion v. Capital Cities/ABC, Inc.
          194 F.3d 305 (4th Cir. 1999) 207, 214
Fost v. Superior Court
          80 Cal. App. 4th 724 (2000) 166, 167
Four Navy Seals v. Associated Press
          413 F.Supp.2d 1136 (S.D. Cal. 2005) 220, 221
Frazer v. Dixon Unified School Dist.
          18 Cal. App. 4th (1993) .... 10, 14, 15, passim
Frederick v. Morse
          439 F.3d 1114, 1118 (9th Cir. 2006) 232
Freedman v. New Jersey State Police
          135 N.J. Super. 297, 301 (N.J. Super. Ct. Law Div. 1975) 218
Freedom Newspapers, Inc. v. Orange County Employees Retirement System
          6 Cal. 4th 821 (1993) 10
FTC v. Standard Financial Management Corp.
          830 F.2d 404 (1st Cir. 1987) 188
Furtado v. Sierra Community College
          68 Cal. App. 4th 876 (1998) 25
Gannett Co. v. De Pasquale
          443 U.S. 368 (1979) 112, 138
Garcetti v. Ceballos
          126 S. Ct. 1951 (2006) 103
Gentile v. State Bar of Nevada
          501 U.S. 1030 (1991) 125, 128
Gilbert v. National Enquirer, Inc.
          43 Cal. App. 4th 1135 (1996) 130
Gillespie v. San Francisco Pub. Library Commission
          67 Cal. App. 4th 1165 (1998) 24
Globe Newspaper Co. v. Pokaski
          868 F.2d 497 (1st Cir. 1989) 191
Globe Newspaper Co. v. Superior Court
          457 U.S. 596 (1982) .... 112, 120, 182, 183, passim
Golden Gateway Center v. Golden Gateway Tenants Association
          26 Cal. 4th 1013 (2001) 208, 218
Grady v. Blair
          529 F. Supp. 370 (N.D. Ill. 1981) 108
Hamburg v. Wal-Mart Stores, Inc.
          116 Cal. App. 4th 497 (2004) 208, 217, 219
Hanlon v. Berger
          526 U.S. 808 (1999) 208, 216
Harper v. Poway Unified School District
          445 F.3d 1166 (9th Cir. 2006) 232
Hatfill v. New York Times Co.
          459 F.Supp.2d 462 (E.D. Va. 2006) 175
Haynie v. Superior Court
          26 Cal. 4th 1061 (2001) 60, 68
Hazlewood School District v. Kuhlmeier
          484 U.S. 260, 267 (1988) .... 202, 233, passim
Hoffman-Pugh v. Keenan
          338 F.3d 1136 (10th Cir. 2003) 158
Hosty v. Carter
          412 F.3d 731 (7th Cir. 2005) 238
Houchins v. KQED
          438 U.S. 1 (1978) 205
Howard Jarvis Taxpayers Association v. Whittier Union High School Dist.
          15 Cal. App. 4th 730 (1993) 203
Hurvitz v. Hoefflin
          84 Cal. App. 4th 1232 (2000) 125, 129

In re Cendant Corp.
     260 F.3d 183 (3d Cir. 2001) 190
In re Clarance B.
     37 Cal. App. 3d 676 (1974) 117
In re Continental Illinois Securities Litigation
     732 F.2d 1302 (7th Cir. 1984) 137, 187
In re: Coordinated Pretrial Proceedings in Petroleum Products Antitrust Litigation
     680 F.2d 5, 8 (2d Cir. 1982) 173
In re Daedler
     194 Cal. 320 (1924) 117
In re Elijah S.
     125 Cal. App. 4th 1532 (2005) 192
In re Express News Corp.
     695 F.2d 807, 810 (5th Cir. 1982) 156, 157
In re Globe Newspaper
     920 F.2d 88, 94, 98 (1st Cir. 1990) 147, 153
In re Grand Jury Subpoena, Joshua Wolf
     2006 U.S. App. LEXIS 23315 (9th Cir. 2006) 171
In re Grand Jury Subpoena, Judith Miller
     370 U.S. App. D.C. 4 (D.C. Cir. 2005) 171
In re Grand Jury Subpoenas to Mark Fainaru-Wada and Lance Williams
     438 F. Supp. 2d 1111 (N.D. Cal. 2006) 171
In re Howard
     136 Cal. App. 2d 816, 819 (1955) 165
In re Iowa Freedom of Information Council
     724 F.2d 658 (8th Cir. 1983) 140
In Re Keisha T.
     38 Cal. App. 4th 220 (1995) 192
In re Lewis
     384 F. Supp. 133, 137 (C.D. Cal. 1974) 177
In re Marriage of Candiotti
     34 Cal. App. 4th 718 (1995) 130
In re Marriage of Lechowick
     65 Cal. App. 4th 1406 (1998) 139
In re McClatchy Newspapers
     288 F.3d 369 (9th Cir. 2002) 184
In re New York Times Co.
     828 F.2d 11 (2d Cir. 1987) 183, 184
In re Peregrine Systems, Inc.
     311 B.R. 679 (D. Del. 2004) 190
In re Providence Journal
     820 F.2d 1342 (1986) 135
In re Providian Credit Card Cases
     96 Cal. App. 4th 292 (2002) 140
In re Reporters Committee for Freedom of Press
     773 F.2d 1325 (D.C. Cir. 1985) 187
In re Rudolfo A.
     110 Cal. App. 3d 845 (1980) 203
In re Russell
     726 F.2d 1007 (1984) 128
In re Santa Barbara Criminal Grand Jury
     No. 04-00 (Cal. Super. Ct. Mar. 24, 2004) 159
In re Search Warrant for Secretarial Area Outside Office of Gunn
     855 F.2d 569 (8th Cir. 1988) 183
In re South Carolina Press Association
     946 F.2d 1037, 1039 (4th Cir. 1991) 149
In re Special Proceedings
     373 F.3d 37 (1st Cir. 2004) 177

In re Subpoena To Testify Before Grand Jury
    864 F.2d 1559 (11th Cir. 1989) 158

In re the Baltimore Sun
    841 F.2d 74 (4th Cir.1988) 153

International Federation of Professional Engineers v. Superior Court
    Case No. S134253 66

International Longshoreman's and Warehousemen's Union v. Los Angeles Export Terminal Inc.
    69 Cal. App. 4th 287 (1999) 12

Jackson v. Metropolitan Edison Co.
    419 U.S. 345 (1974) 106

JB Pictures, Inc. v. Department of Defense
    86 F.3d 236 (1996) 201

Joiner v. City of Sebastopol
    125 Cal. App. 3d 799 (1981) 10, 11

Journal Pub. Co. v. Mecham
    801 F.2d 1233 (10th Cir. 1986) 126

Kavanaugh v. West Sonoma County Union High School Dist.
    29 Cal. 4th 911 (2003) 10

KCST-TV Channel 39 v. Municipal Court
    201 Cal. App. 3d 143 (1988) 132

Kearney v. Salomon Smith Barney, Inc.
    39 Cal. 4th 95 (2006) 225

KFMB-TV Channel 8 v. Municipal Ct.
    221 Cal. App. 3d 1362 (1990) 145

KGTV Channel 10 v. Superior Court
    26 Cal. App. 4th 1673 (1994) 117, 118, 132

Kleitman v. Superior Court (Wesley)
    74 Cal. App. 4th 324 (1999) 38

KNSD Channels 7/39 v. Superior Court
    63 Cal. App. 4th 1200 (1998) 185

Kotwica v. Tucson
    801 F.2d 1182 (9th 1986) 103

KPNX Broad. Co. v. Arizona Supreme Court
    459 U.S. 1302 (1982) 155

KQED v. Vasquez
    18 Media L. Rep 2323 (1991) 206

Lal v. CBS, Inc.
    726 F.2d 97 (3rd Cir. 1984) 218

Landmark Communications, Inc. v. Virginia
    435 U.S. 829 (1978) 212

Lavine v. Blaine School District
    257 F.3d 981 (9th Cir. 2001) 231, 232

Lee v. Department of Justice
    413 F.3d 53, (D.C. Cir. 2005) 175

Leeb v. DeLong
    198 Cal. App. 3d 47 (1988) 237

Legi-Tech, Inc. v. Keiper
    776 F.2d 728 (2d Cir. 1985) 101

Leiserson v. City of San Diego
    184 Cal. App. 3d 41 (1986) 200, 201

LeMistral v. CBS
    61 A.D. 2d 491 (1978) 207

Lesher Communications, Inc. v. Contra Costa Superior Court
    224 Cal. App. 3d 774 (1990) 150, 184, 187

Leucadia, Inc. v. Applied Extrusion Technologies, Inc.
    998 F.2d 157 (3d Cir. 1993) 189

Leventhal v. Vista Unified School Dist.
    973 F. Supp. 951 (1997) 8

Levine v. District Court
    775 F.2d 1054 (1985) 128
Lewis v. Baxley
    368 F. Supp. 768 (M.D. Ala. 1973) 105
Lieberman v. KCOP Television, Inc.
    110 Cal. App. 4th 156 (2003) 224
Lindelli v. Town of San Anselmo
    111 Cal. App. 4th 1099 (2003) 8
Littlefield v. Superior Court
    Appeal No. A049935 (Cal. Court of Appeal 1991)... 169
Littlejohn v. BIC Corp.
    851 F.2d 673 (3d Cir. 1988) 190
Lopez v. Tulare Joint Union High School District
    34 Cal. App. 4th 1302 (1995) 203, 237
Los Angeles Free Press v. Los Angeles
    9 Cal. App. 3d 448 (1970) 106
Los Angeles Memorial Coliseum Comm. v. National Football League
    89 F.R.D. 489 (C.D. Cal. 1981) 175
Los Angeles Times Communications LLC v. Los Angeles County Bd. of Supervisors
    112 Cal. App. 4th 1313 (2003) 39
Los Angeles Times v. County of Los Angeles
    956 F. Supp. 1530 (C.D. Cal. 1996) 196
Lovell v. Poway Unified School District
    90 F.3d 367 (9th Cir. 1996) 235
Lucas v. Board of Trustees
    (1971) 18 Cal. App. 3d 988 24
Ludtke v. Kuhn
    461 F. Supp. 86 (S.D.N.Y. 1978) 107
M.K.B. v. Warden
    540 U.S. 1213, 124 S. Ct. 1405 (2004) 120
Mapother v. Department of Justice
    3 F.3d 1533 (D.C. Cir. 1993) 92
Marich v. MGM/UA Telecommunications, Inc.
    113 Cal. App. 4th 415 (2003) 220, 223
Marich v. QRZ Media, Inc.
    86 Cal. Rptr. 2d 406 (1999) 223
McKee v. Los Angeles Interagency Metropolitan Police Apprehension Crime Task Force
    134 Cal. App. 4th 354 (2005) 11, 32, 35
McKee v. Orange Unified School District
    110 Cal. App. 4th 1310 (2003) 36
Medical Laboratory Management Consultants v. ABC, Inc.
    306 F.3d 806 (9th Cir. 2002) 216
Michaelis, Montanari & Johnson v. Superior Court
    38 Cal. 4th 1065 (2006) 70, 81
Miller v. National Broadcasting Company
    187 Cal. App. 3d 1463 (1986) 208, 215, 216, 220
Miller v. Superior Court
    21 Cal. 4th 883, 887 (1999) 167
Mintz v. Dept of Motor Vehicles
    9 Media L. Rep. 1301 (9th Cir. 1982) 106
Mitchell v. Superior Court
    37 Cal. 3d 268 (1984) 168, 175
Mokhiber v. Davis
    537 A.2d 1100, 1112 (D.C. 1988) 189
Monarch Healthcare v. Superior Court
    78 Cal. App. 4th 1282 (2000) 169
Moreno v. City of King
    127 Cal. App. 4th 17 (2005) 21

310

Morris Communications Corp. v. PGA Tour, Inc.
        364 F.3d 1288 (11th Cir. 2004) 107
Morrison v. Housing Authority of the City of Los Angeles Bd. of Commissioners
        107 Cal. App. 4th 860 (2003) 23, 24
Muller v. Conlisk
        429 F.2d 901 (7th Cir. 1970) 103
Nadel v. Regents of the University of California
        28 Cal. App. 4th 1251 (1994) 209
National Parks & Conservation Association v. Morton
        498 F.2d 765 (D.C. Cir. 1974) 91
NBA v. Motorola, Inc.
        105 F.3d 841 (2d Cir. 1997) 107
NBC Subsidiary (KNBC-TV), Inc. v. Superior Court
        20 Cal. 4th 1178 (1999) .... 109, 112, 113, 114, 137, passim
Nebraska Press Association v. Stuart
        427 U.S. 539, 427 U.S. 539 (1976) .... 123, 125, 129, 130, passim
New York Times Co. v. Gonzales
        382 F. Supp. 2d 457 (S.D.N.Y. 2005), rev'd, 459 F.3d 160 (2d Cir. 2006) 172, 177
New York Times Co. v. Superior Court
        51 Cal. 3d 453 (1990) .... 166, 168, 170, passim
New York Times Co. v. Superior Court
        52 Cal. App. 4th 97 (1997) 67, 72, 74
New York Times Co. v. United States
        403 U.S. 713 (1971) 130, 134
Newman v. Graddick
        696 F.2d 796 (11th Cir. 1983) 187
Nicholson v. McClatchy Newspapers
        177 Cal. App. 3d 509 (1986) 211, 212
Nizam-Aldine v. City of Oakland
        47 Cal. App. 4th 364 (1996) 209
North County Parents Organization v. Department of Education
        23 Cal. App. 4th 144 (1994) 59
O'Grady v. Superior Court
        139 Cal. App. 4th 1423 (2006) 164
O'Laskey v. Sortino
        224 Cal. App. 3d 241 (1990) 223
Organization for a Better Austin v. Keefe
        402 U.S. 415 (1971) 130
O'Toole v. Superior Court
        140 Cal. App. 4th 488 (2006) 235
Oziel v. Superior Court
        223 Cal. App. 3d 1284 (1990) 193
Pack v. Kings County Department of Human Services
        89 Cal.App. 4th 821 (2001) 192
Pansy v. Borough of Stroudsburg
        23 F.3d 772 (3d Cir. 1994) 189, 191
Pantos v. City and County of San Francisco
        151 Cal. App. 3d 258 (1984) 150, 187
Payroll Guar. Assn. v. Bd. of Education
        27 Cal. 2d 197 (1945) 203
Pearson v. Dodd
        410 F.2d 701 (D.C. Cir. 1969) 212
Pell v. Procunier
        417 U.S. 817 (1974) 205
People v. Connor
        115 Cal. App. 4th 669 (2004) 194
People v. Cummings
        4 Cal. 4th 1233, 1299 (1993) 112, 117

People v. Drennan
    84 Cal. App. 4th 1349, (2000) 225

People v. Dunn, et al
    DA No. 061027481 (Santa Clara Super. Ct., Oct. 4, 2006) 215

People v. Gonzales
    12 Cal. 4th 804 (1996) 135

People v. Goodwin
    59 Cal. App. 4th 1084 (1998) 153, 189

People v. Harris
    10 Cal. App. 4th 672 (1992) 113

People v. Jackson
    128 Cal. App. 4th 1009 (2005) 186

People v. Jennings
    53 Cal. 3d 334 (1991) 131, 184

People v. Kunkin
    9 Cal. 3d 245 (1973) 212

People v. Lawton
    48 Cal. App. 4th Supp. 11 (1996) 228

People v. Mendosa
    137 Cal. App. 3d 888 (1982) 184

People v. Phillips
    56 Cal. App. 4th 1307 (1997) 153

People v. Swanson
    30 Media L. Rptr. 2396 (Cal. Super. Ct. 2000) 165

People v. Vasco
    131 Cal. App. 4th 137 (2005) 167

People v. Von Villas
    10 Cal. App. 4th 201 (1992) 163

People v. Woodward
    4 Cal. 4th 376 (1992) 111

Perry Education Association v. Perry Local Educators' Association
    460 U.S. 37, 46 (1983) 199

Perumal v. Saddleback Valley Unified School Dist.
    198 Cal. App. 3d 64 (1988) 238

Pickering v. Board of Education
    391 U.S. 563 (1968) 102

Pinard v. Clatskanie School Dist. 6J
    467 F.3d 755 (9th Cir. 2006) 232

Planned Parenthood of Southern Nevada, Inc. v. Clark County School District
    941F.2d 817 (9th Cir. 1991) 202

Playboy Enterprises v. Superior Court
    154 Cal. App. 3d 14 (1984) 165

Poway Unified School District v. Superior Court of San Diego County
    62 Cal. App. 4th 1498 (1998) 63, 65

Powers v. City of Richmond
    10 Cal. 4th 85(1995) 79

Press Enterprise Co. v. Superior Court of California (Press Enterprise I)
    464 U.S. 501 (1984) .... 111, 113, 138, 182, passim

Press Enterprise Co. v. Superior Court of California (Press Enterprise II)
    478 U.S. 1 (1986) .... 111, 113, 117, 120, passim

Press Enterprise v. Superior Court (Press-Enterprise III)
    22 Cal. App. 4th 498, (1994) 185

Press Enterprise v. Superior Court (Scott)
    22 Cal. App. 4th 498 (1994) 157

Press Enterprise v. Superior Court
    Case No. RIC444406 97

Prince v. Out Publishing Inc.
    2002 WL 7999 at pp. *7-8 (Cal. Ct. App. 2002) 220

312

Procter & Gamble Co. v. Bankers Trust Co.
  78 F.3d 219 (6th Cir. 1996) 130, 133
Providence Journal Co. v. Newton
  17 Med. L. Rptr. 1033 (1990) 134
Pruneyard Shopping Center v. Robins
  447 U.S. 74 (1980) 207, 218
Public Citizen v. Liggett Group, Inc.
  858 F.2d 775 (1st Cir. 1988) 141
Publicker Industries, Inc. v. Cohen
  733 F.2d 1059 (3d Cir. 1984) 87, 188
Quad-City Community News Service, Inc. v. Hebens
  334 F. Supp. 8 (S.D. Iowa 1971) 100, 105
Quinn v. Aetna Life & Casualty Co.
  482 F.Supp. 22 (1979) 10
Radio & Television News Ass'n v. U.S. District Court
  781 F.2d 1443 (9th Cir. 1986) 126
Rancho Publications v. Superior Court
  68 Cal. App. 4th 1538 (1999) 164
Rankin v. McPherson
  483 U.S. 378, 390 (1987) 103
Reeves v. Rocklin Unified School Dist.
  109 Cal. App. 4th 652 (2003) 203, 235
Regents of the University of California v. Superior Court
  20 Cal. 4th 509 (1999) 44
Register Division of Freedom Newspapers v. County of Orange
  158 Cal. App. 3d 893 (1984) 65, 191
Religious Technology Center v. Netcom On-Line
  923 F.Supp. 1231 (N.D. Cal. 1995) 123
Richmond Newspapers, Inc. v. Commonwealth of Virginia
  448 U.S. 555 (1980) .... 109, 145, 187, passim
Rifkin v. Esquire
  7 Med. L. Rptr. 1231 (1981) 133
Rim of the World Unified School Dist. v. Superior Court
  104 Cal. App. 4th 1393 (2002) 77
Risenhoover v. England
  936 F.Supp. 392 (W.D. Tex. 1996) 227
Rivero v. Superior Court
  54 Cal. App. 4th 1048 (1997) 68
Robbins v. Regents of the University of California
  127 Cal. App. 4th 653 (2005) 232
Roberts v. City of Palmdale
  5 Cal. 4th 363 (1993) 64, 65
Robins v. Pruneyard Shopping Center
  23 Cal. 3d 899 (1979) 207, 218
Rogers v. Home Shopping Network
  73 F.Supp.2d 1140 (C.D. Cal. 1999) 175
Rogers v. Superior Court
  19 Cal. App. 4th 469 (1993) 71
Rowen v. Santa Clara Unified School District
  121 Cal. App. 3d 231 (1981) 23, 25
Rushford v. New Yorker Magazine, Inc.
  846 F.2d 249 (4th Cir. 1988) 187, 188
Sacramento Newspaper Guild v. Sacramento County Bd. of Supervisors
  263 Cal. App. 2d 41 (1968) 5, 14, 17
San Bernardino County Dept. of Public Social Services v. Superior Court
  232 Cal. App. 3d 188 (1991) 114, 118, 119
San Diego Police Officers' Assn. v. City of San Diego Civil Service Com.
  104 Cal. App. 4th 275 (2002) 74

San Diego Union v. City Council
146 Cal. App. 3d 947 (1983) 25, 26, 27, 44
San Gabriel Tribune v. Superior Court
143 Cal. App. 3d 762 (1983) 23, 56
San Jose Mercury News v. Superior Court of California
County of Santa Clara, Case No. C 01-20999 (RMW) (N.D. Cal. 2002) 196
San Jose Mercury News, Inc. v. Criminal Grand Jury of Santa Clara County
122 Cal. App. 4th 410 (2004) 125, 158
San Jose Mercury News, Inc. v. U.S. Dist. Ct.
187 F.3d 1096 (9th Cir. 1999) 138, 187
Sanders v. American Broadcasting Companies, Inc.
20 Cal. 4th 907 (1999) 207, 219, 224
Santa Clara Federation of Teachers v. Governing Board
116 Cal. App. 3d 831 (1981) 24
Seattle Times Co. v. United States District Court
845 F.2d 1513 (9th Cir. 1988) 184
Seattle Times v. Rhinehart
467 U.S. 20 (1984) 189
SEC v. Van Waeyenberghe
990 F.2d 845 (5th Cir. 1993) 193
Sega Enterprises Ltd. v. MAPHIA
948 F. Supp. 923 (N.D. Cal. 1996) 228
Shapiro v. Board of Directors
134 Cal. App. 4th 170 (2005) .... 23, 94, 200, passim
Shapiro v. San Diego City Council
96 Cal. App. 4th 904 (2002) .... 20, 23, 29, 33, 38, passim
Sheppard v. Maxwell
384 U.S. 333 (1966) 125
Sherrill v. Knight
569 F.2d 124 (D.C. Cir. 1977) 105, 106
Shingara v. Skiles
420 F.3d 301 (3d Cir. 2005) 189
Shoen v. Schoen
5 F.3d 1289 (9th Cir. 1993) .... 173, 174, 119, passim
Shoen v. Shoen ("Shoen II")
48 F.3d 412 (9th Cir. 1995) 174
Shulman v. Group W. Productions, Inc.
18 Cal. 4th 200 (1998) 206, 219, 220
Smith v. Daily Mail Publishing Co.
442 U.S. 97 (1979) 118, 126, 214
Society of Professional Journalists v. Briggs
675 F.Supp. 1308 (D. Utah 1987) 191
South Coast Newspapers, Inc. v. Superior Court
85 Cal. App. 4th 866 (2000) 131
Southern California Edison Co. v. Peevey
31 Cal. 4th 781 (2003) 44
Southwestern Newspapers Corp. v. Curtis
584 S.W.2d 362 (Tex. App. 1979) 105
Stadish v. Superior Court
71 Cal. App. 4th 1130 (1999) 140
State of Florida v. Rolling
20 Media L. Rptr. 1127 (1992) 126
Stockton Newspapers, Inc. v. Redevelopment Agency
171 Cal. App. 3d 95 (1985) 9, 13
Sussman v. American Broadcasting Companies, Inc.
186 F.3d 1200 (9th Cir. 1999) 226
Tafoya v. Hastings College
191 Cal. App. 3d 437 (1987) 47

Taus v. Loftus
        40 Cal. 4th 683 (2007) 211, 214
Tavoulareas v. Washington Post Co.
        759 F.2d 90 (1985) 188
Taxpayers for Livable Communities v. City of Malibu
        126 Cal. App. 4th 1123 (2005) 10, 12
Telemundo of Los Angeles v. United States District Court
        283 F. Supp. 2d 1095 (C.D. Cal. 2003) 100
The Oregonian Publishing Co. v. U.S.
        920 F.2d 1462 (9th Cir. 1990) 183, 184
Theofel v. Farey-Jones
        341 F.3d 978, (9th Cir. 2003) 228
Thomas v. Wen Ho Lee
        126 S.Ct 2373, 165 L.Ed.2d 294 (2006) 175
Times Mirror Co. v. Superior Court
        53 Cal. 3d 1325 (1991) 71
Times Mirror Co. v. United States
        873 F.2d 1210 (9th Cir. 1989) 193
Times Picayune Publishing Corp. v. Lee
        15 Med. L. Rep. 1713 (E.D. La. 1988) 100
Tinker v. Des Moines School District
        393 U.S. 503 (1969) .... 230, 231, passim
Trader Joe's Company v. Progressive Campaigns, Inc.
        73 Cal. App. 4th 425 (1999) 208
Trancas Property Owners Assn. v. City of Malibu
        138 Cal. App. 4th 172 (2006) 23, 29
Tribune Newspapers West, Inc. v. Superior Court
        172 Cal. App. 3d 443 (1985) 116
Turnbull v. American Broadcasting Companies
        2004 U.S. Dist. 32 Media L. Rep. 2442 (C.D. Cal. 2004) .... 216, 219, 222, 224, passim
U.S. Industries, Inc. v. U.S. District Court
        345 F.2d 18 (9th Cir. 1965) 186
U.S. v. Anderson
        46 MJ 728 (Army Crim. App. 1997) 119
U.S. v. Armco Steel Corp.
        458 F. Supp. 784 (D. Mo. 1978) 186
U.S. v. Collazo-Aponte
        216 F.3d 163 (1st Cir. 2000) 154
U.S. v. Edmond
        52 F.3d 1080 (D.C. Cir. 1995) 154
U.S. v. Fuller
        202 F. Supp. 356 (N.D. Cal. 1962) 228
U.S. v. King
        140 F.3d 76 (2d Cir. 1998) 149
U.S. v. Kott
        135 Fed. Appx. 69, 2005 WL 1400288, 33 Media L. Rep. 1954 (9th Cir.2005) 193
U.S. v. Marrerro-Ortiz
        160 F.3d 768 (1st Cir. 1998) 154
U.S. v. Noriega
        917 F.2d 1543 (1990) 132
U.S. v. Ross
        33 F.3d 1507 (11th Cir. 1994) 154
U.S. v. Salvatore
        110 F.3d 1131 (5th Cir. 1997) 154
U.S. v. Schlette
        842 F.2d 1574, 1578 (9th Cir. 1988) 194
U.S. v. Scott
        48 M.J. 663 (Army Crim. App. 1998) 119

315

U.S. v. Smith
    776 F.2d 1104 (3d Cir. 1985) 183
U.S. v. Travers
    25 M.J. 61, 62 (CMA 1987) 119
Ukiah Daily Journal v. Superior Court
    165 Cal. App. 3d 788 (1985) 149
Unabom Trial Media Coal. v. District Court
    183 F.3d 949 (9th Cir. 1999) 153
United States v. Alice Martin
    No. 97-114-CR-J-20C (M.D. Fla. 1997) 228
United States v. Antar
    38 F.3d 1348 (3d Cir. 1994) 151
United States v. Bakker
    882 F.2d 850 (1989) 113
United States v. Barnes
    604 F.2d 121 (2d. Cir. 1979) 154
United States v. Branch
    91 F.3d 699 (5th Cir. 1996) 153
United States v. Brooklier
    685 F.2d 1162 (9th Cir. 1982) .... 112, 148, 151, 184, passim
United States v. Brown
    250 F.3d 907 (5th Cir. 2001) 154
United States v. Burke
    700 F.2d 70 (2d Cir. 1983) 172, 173
United States v. Caporale
    806 F.2d 1487 (11th Cir. 1986) 174
United States v. Cianfrani
    573 F.2d 835 (1978) 154
United States v. Criden
    633 F.2d 346 (3d Cir. 1980) 174
United States v. Crockett
    979 F.2d 1204 (7th Cir. 1992) 154
United States v. Cuthbertson
    630 F.2d 139 (3d Cir. 1980) 174
United States v. Darden
    70 F.3d 1507 (8th Cir. 1995) 154
United States v. Edwards
    823 F.2d 111 (5th Cir. 1987) 149
United States v. Gotti
    787 F. Supp. 319 (E.D.N.Y. 1992) 149
United States v. Harrelson ("El Paso Times")
    713 F.2d 1114 (5th Cir. 1983) 156
United States v. John Martin
    No. 97-115-CR-J-20B (M.D. Fla. 1997) 228
United States v. LaRouche Campaign
    841 F.2d 1176 (1st Cir. 1988) 173
United States v. Lloyd
    71 F.3d 1256, 1268-69 (7th Cir. 1995) 174
United States v. Nixon
    418 U.S. 683 (1974) 173
United States v. Paccoine
    949 F.2d 1183 (2d Cir. 1991) 154
United States v. Peters
    754 F.2d 753 (7th Cir. 1985) 185
United States v. Procter and Gamble Co.
    356 U.S. 677 (1958) 186
United States v. Schneider
    68 Fed. Appx. 5 (2003 U.S. App.) 173

United States v. Sherman
        581 F.2d 1358 (9th Cir. 1978) 156
United States v. Smith
        787 F.2d 111 (3d Cir. 1986) 184
United States v. Socony-Vacuum Oil Co.
        310 U.S. 150 (1940) 186
United States v. Talley
        164 F.3d 989 (6th Cir. 1999) 154
United States v. Valenti
        987 F.2d 708 (11th Cir. 1993) 112, 114
United States v. Wilson
        160 F.3d 732 (D.C. Cir. 1998) 154
United States. v. Thornton
        1 F.3d 149 (3d Cir. 1993) 154
United Teachers of Dade v. Stierheim
        213 F. Supp. 2d 1368 (S.D. Fla. 2002) 101, 105
Uribe v. Howie
        19 Cal. App. 3d 194 (1971) 68, 73
Valley Broadcasting v. U.S. District Court
        798 F.2d 1289 (9th Cir. 1986) 185
Van Schoick v. Saddleback Valley Unified School Dist.
        87 Cal. App. 4th (2001) 238
Vance v. Universal Amusement Co., Inc.
        445 U.S. 308 (1980) 129
Vaughn v. Rosen
        523 F.2d 1136 (D.C. Cir. 1975) 93
Versaci v. Superior Court
        127 Cal. App. 4th 805 (2005) 98, 97
Virginia Pharmacy Board v. Virginia Citizens Consumer Council
        425 U.S. 748 (1976) 199
Walker v. City of Birmingham
        388 U.S. 307 (1967) 135
Washington Post v. Robinson
        935 F.2d 282 (D.C. Cir. 1991) 183
Watson v. Cronin
        384 F. Supp. 652 (D. Colo. 1974) 106
Welsh v. City and County of San Francisco
        887 F. Supp. 1293 (N.D. Cal. 1995) 142
Wescott v. County of Yuba
        104 Cal. App. 3d 103 (1980) 69
Westbrook v. County of Los Angeles
        27 Cal.App.4th 157 (1994) 196
Westinghouse Broadcasting Co. v. Dukakis
        409 F. Supp. 895 (D. Mass. 1976) 101
Westmoreland v. Columbia Broadcasting System, Inc.
        752 F.2d 16 (2d Cir. 1984) 187
Wilder v. Superior Court
        66 Cal. App. 4th 77 (1998) 64
Wilkins v. National Broadcasting Company, Inc.
        71 Cal. App. 4th 1066, 1078 (1999) 215, 220, 223, 224
Williams v. Superior Court
        5 Cal. 4th 337 (1993) 68
Wilson v. Layne
        526 U.S. 603 (1999) 217
Wilson v. Superior Court
        51 Cal. App. 4th 1136 (1997) 66, 71
Wolf v. Aberdeen
        758 F. Supp. 551 (D.S.D. 1991) 104

317

Wolfe v. City of Fremont
    144 Cal. App. 4th 533 (2006) 15
Wood v. Georgia
    370 U.S. 375 (1962) 104
Wright v. Federal Bureau of Investigation
    381 F. Supp. 2d 1114 (C.D. Cal. 2005) 174
Youngstown Publishing Co. v. United States District Court
    2005 U.S. Dist. LEXIS 9476 (N.D. Ohio 2005) 101
Zook v. Brown
    865 F.2d 887 (7th 1989) 103
Zurcher v. Stanford Daily
    436 U.S. 547 (1978) 178, 180, 181